Fortuna Bona!

Amicus tuus,

Tom

THE LOEB CLASSICAL LIBRARY

FOUNDED BY JAMES LOEB, LL.D.

EDITED BY

G.P. GOOLD, PH.D.

PREVIOUS EDITORS

ST. AUGUSTINE'S
CONFESSIONS

II

ST. AUGUSTINE'S CONFESSIONS

WITH AN ENGLISH TRANSLATION BY

WILLIAM WATTS

1631

IN TWO VOLUMES

II

CAMBRIDGE, MASSACHUSETTS
HARVARD UNIVERSITY PRESS
LONDON

WILLIAM HEINEMANN LTD
MCMLXXXVIII

American ISBN 0–674–99030–7
British ISBN 0 434 99027 2

Frist printed in 1912
Reprinted in 1919, 1931, 1946, 1951, 1961,
1970, 1979, 1988

Printed in Great Britain by
Richard Clay Ltd, Bungay, Suffolk

PREFACE

In finishing this volume the Editor offers his sincere thanks to the Reverend W. Emery Barnes, D.D., Hulsean Professor of Divinity in the University of Cambridge, for valuable help in making doubtful points clear.

EDITORIAL NOTE (1979)

A select bibliography of modern work on Augustine will be found on pages lxxxiii – lxxxix of volume one of the Loeb edition of *The City of God*. The following, which contain further bibliographical information, require special mention.

Peter Brown, *Augustine of Hippo*, London 1967
Pierre Courcelle, *Recherches sur les Confessions de Saint Augustin*, Paris 1950

BIBLIOGRAPHY

Editio Princeps :

> Collected Works : Amerbach, Basle, 1506 ; re-
> printed Paris, 1515.
> Confessions : Mediolani, 1475.

Latest Critical Edition :

> Confessions : P. Knöll, Teubner, 1909.

Translations (of the Confessions) :

> Sir Tobie Matthew, 1624.
> William Watts, London, 1631.
> E. B. Pusey (with Latin text and notes), Riv-
> ington, 1838, 2 vols.
> C. Bigg, Books I.-IX., Methuen, 1897-1909.

Illustrative Works :

> Opera emendata studio monachorum ordinis
> S. Benedicti. Paris, 1679-1700 ; reprinted
> Gaume, Paris 1836-39 ; with life.
> Schröckh : Kirchengeschichte, vol. xv.
> Neander : Geschichte der Christlichen Religion
> und Kirche, vol. ii.
> Cunningham : St. Austin and his place in the
> History of Christian Thought, London, 1886.
> Gwatkin : The Knowledge of God, 1908, vol. ii.

We now have the edition by P. Knöll, Leipzig,
Teubner, 1920 ; and the edition with French translation by P. de Labriolle (Budé), Paris. Books 1-8,
1925 ; Books 9-13, 1926.

BOOK IX

LIBER NONVS

I

O DOMINE, ego servus tuus, ego servus tuus et filius
ancillae tuae. disrupisti vincula mea; tibi sacri-
ficabo hostiam laudis. laudet te cor meum et lingua
mea, et omnia ossa mea dicant: domine, quis similis
tibi? dicant, et responde mihi et dic animae meae:
salus tua ego sum. quis ego et qualis ego? quid
non mali aut facta mea aut, si non facta, dicta mea
aut, si non dicta, voluntas mea fuit? tu autem,
domine, bonus et misericors, et dextera tua respiciens
profunditatem mortis meae, et a fundo cordis mei
exhauriens abyssum corruptionis. et hoc erat totum
nolle, quod volebam, et velle, quod volebas. sed ubi
erat tam annoso tempore, et de quo imo altoque
secreto evocatum est in momento liberum arbitrium
meum, quo subderem cervicem leni iugo tuo, et
umeros levi sarcinae tuae, Christe Iesu, adiutor meus
et redemptor meus? quam suave mihi subito factum
est carere suavitatibus nugarum, et quas amittere
metus fuerat, iam dimittere gaudium erat. eiciebas
enim eas a me, vera tu et summa suavitas, eiciebas

2

THE NINTH BOOK

I

He praiseth God's Goodness; and acknowledgeth his own wretchedness

O LORD, I am thy servant, I am thy servant, and the son of thy handmaid. Thou hast broken my bonds in sunder; to thee I will offer the sacrifice of praise. Let my heart praise thee and my tongue; yea, let all my bones say, O Lord, who is like unto thee? Let them say, and answer thou me, and say unto my soul, I am thy Salvation. Who am I, and what manner of man? What evil have not either my deeds been, or if not my deeds, yet my words; or if not my words, yet my will? But thou, O Lord, art good and merciful, and thy right hand had respect unto the profoundness of my death, and drew forth of the bottom of my heart that bottomless gulf of corruption: which was, to nill all that thou willedst, and to will all that thou nilledst. But where was that right hand for so long a time, and out of what bottom and secret corner was my free will called forth in a moment, whereby I submitted my neck to thy easy yoke, and my shoulders unto thy light burden, O Jesus Christ, my Helper and my Redeemer? How pleasant was it all on the sudden made unto me, to be without the sweets of those toys! Yea, what I before feared to lose, was now a joy unto me to forgo. For thou didst cast them out from me, even thou that true and chiefest Sweetness: thou didst cast them out, and instead of them camest in

3

et intrabas pro eis omni voluptate dulcior, sed non
carni et sanguini, omni luce clarior, sed omni secreto
interior, omni honore sublimior, sed non sublimibus in
se. iam liber erat animus meus a curis mordacibus
ambiendi et adquirendi et volutandi atque scalpendi
scabiem libidinum; et garriebam tibi, claritati meae
et divitiis et saluti meae, domino deo meo.

II

Et placuit mihi in conspectu tuo non tumultuose
abripere, sed leniter subtrahere ministerium linguae
meae nundinis loquacitatis; ne ulterius pueri, (medi-
tantes non legem tuam, non pacem tuam, sed insanias
mendaces et bella forensia), mercarentur ex ore meo
arma furori suo. et opportune iam paucissimi dies
supererant ad vindemiales ferias; et statui tolerare
illos, ut sollemniter abscederem, et redemptus a te
iam non redirem venalis. consilium ergo nostrum
erat coram te, coram hominibus autem nisi nostris
non erat. et convenerat inter nos, ne passim cui-
quam effunderetur, quamquam tu nobis in convalle
plorationis ascendentibus, et cantantibus canticum
graduum, dederas sagittas acutas, et carbones vasta-
tores, adversus linguam subdolam velut consulendo

thyself, sweeter than all pleasure, though not to flesh CHAP.
and blood : brighter than all light, but more privy I
than all secrets : higher than all honour, but not to
the high in their own conceits. Now became my
soul free from those biting cares of aspiring, and
getting, and weltering in filth, and scratching off
that itch of lust. And I talked more familiarly now
with thee, my Honour, and my Riches, and my
Health, my Lord God.

II

He gives over his Teaching of Rhetoric

AND I resolved in thy sight, though not tumultuously CHAP.
to snatch away, yet fairly to withdraw the service II
of my tongue from those marts of lip-labour : that
young students, (no students in thy Law, nor in thy
peace, but in lying dotages, and law skirmishes,)
should no longer buy at my mouth the engines for
their own madness. And very seasonably fell it
out, that it was but a few days unto the vacation of
the vintage : till when I resolved to endure them,
that I might then take my leave the more solemnly ;
when, being bought off by thee, I purposed to return
no more to be their mercenary. Our purpose therefore was known openly unto thee ; but to men,
other than our own friends, was it not known. And
we had agreed among ourselves not to disclose it
abroad to anybody : although us, now ascending
in the valley of tears, and singing that song of
degrees, hadst thou armed with sharp arrows and
hot burning coals, to destroy such subtle tongues as Ps. cxx. 4
would cross us in our purpose, by seeming to advise

S. AVGVSTINI CONFESSIONVM LIBER IX

contradicentem, et sicut cibum assolet, amando consumentem.

Sagittaveras tu cor nostrum caritate tua, et gestabamus verba tua transfixa visceribus, et exempla servorum tuorum, quos de nigris lucidos et de mortuis vivos feceras, congesta in sinum cogitationis nostrae, urebant et absumebant gravem torporem, ne in ima vergeremus; et accendebant nos valide, ut omnis ex lingua subdola contradictionis flatus inflammare nos acrius posset, non extinguere. verum tamen quia propter nomen tuum, quod ˙sanctificasti per terras, etiam laudatores utique haberet votum et propositum nostrum, iactantiae simile videbatur non opperiri tam proximum feriarum tempus, sed de publica professione atque ante oculos omnium sita ante discedere, ut conversa in factum meum ora cunctorum intuentium, quam vicinum vindemialium diem praevenire voluerim, multa dicerent, quod quasi appetissem magnus videri. et quo mihi erat istuc, ut putaretur et disputaretur de animo meo, et blasphemaretur bonum nostrum?

Quin etiam quod ipsa aestate litterario labori nimio pulmo meus cedere coeperat, et difficulter trahere suspiria, doloribusque pectoris testari se saucium vocemque clariorem productioremve recusare; primo perturbaverat me, quia magisterii illius sarcinam paene iam necessitate ponere cogebat, aut si curari e

us, and make an end of us, pretending to love us,
as men do with their meat.

Thou hadst shot through our hearts with thy
charity, and we carried thy words as it were sticking
in our bowels: and the examples of thy servants,
whom of black, thou hadst made bright, and of
dead, alive, being piled together in the bosom of
our thoughts, did burn and utterly consume that
slothfulness of ours, that we might no more be
plunged into the deeps by it. Yea, they set us on
fire so vehemently, as that all the blasts of the
subtle tongues of gainsaying might inflame us the
more fiercely, but never extinguish us. Nevertheless,
because for the sake of thy Name which thou hast
sanctified throughout the earth, our desire and purpose
would surely find commenders: it would, I feared,
look something like ostentation for me not to expect
the time of vacation now so near, but beforehand to
give over my public profession which every man had
an eye upon; so that the faces of all the beholders
being turned upon my act (that I had wished to go
off before the time of vintage so near approaching),
they would give it out, that I did it purposely, to
appear some great man. And to what end would
it have served me, to have people censure and
dispute upon my purpose, and to have our good to
be evil spoken of?

Furthermore, for that in the summer time my
lungs began to decay with my over much painstaking
in my school, and to breathe with difficulty, and by
the pain in my breast to signify themselves to be
hurt, and to refuse too loud or too long speaking: at first I had been much troubled at the
matter, for that, namely, I was constrained even
upon necessity to lay down that burden of teaching;

CAP.
II
convalescere potuissem, certe intermittere. sed ubi
plena voluntas vacandi, et videndi, quoniam tu es
dominus, oborta mihi est atque firmata—nosti,
deus meus—etiam gaudere coepi, quod haec quoque
suberat non mendax excusatio, quae offensionem
hominum temperaret, qui propter liberos suos me
liberum esse numquam volebant. plenus igitur tali
gaudio, tolerabam illud intervallum temporis, donec
decurreret—nescio utrum vel viginti dies erant—sed
tamen fortiter tolerabantur, quia recesserat cupiditas,
quae mecum solebat ferre grave negotium, et ego
premendus remanseram, nisi patientia succederet.
peccasse me in hoc quisquam servorum tuorum,
fratrum meorum, dixerit, quod iam pleno corde
militia tua, passus me fuerim vel una hora sedere
in cathedra mendacii. at ego non contendo. sed
tu, domine misericordissime, nonne et hoc peccatum,
cum ceteris horrendis et funereis, in aqua sancta
ignovisti et remisisti mihi?

III

CAP.
III
MACERABATUR anxitudine Verecundus de isto nostro
bono, quod propter vincula sua, quibus tenacissime
tenebatur, deseri se nostro consortio videbat. nondum

or if in case I could possibly be cured and grow CHAP.
sound again, at least for a while to forbear it. But II
so soon as this full resolution to give myself leisure,
and to see how that thou art the Lord, first arose, Ps. xlvi. 10
and was afterwards settled in me; God, thou
knowest how I began to rejoice, that I had this
also, no feigned excuse, which might something
take off the offence taken by such parties, who for
their children's good, would by their good wills that
I should never have given over schooling. Full
therefore of such like joy, I held out till that
interim of time were run. I know not well whether
there might be some twenty days of it; yet I
courageously underwent them, because that ambition,
which was wont to bear part of the business, had
now quite left me, and I should have been crushed,
had not patience stept up in its room. Some of thy
servants, my brethren, may say perchance, that I
sinned in this; for that being with full consent of
heart enrolled thy soldier, I suffered myself to sit
one hour in the chair of lying. And for my part
I do not dispute it. But hast not thou, O most
merciful Lord, both pardoned and remitted this,
amongst other most horrible and deadly sins, in the
holy waters of Baptism?

III

Verecundus lends them his Country House

VERECUNDUS became lean again with vexing at CHAP.
himself upon this good hap of ours, for that being III.
detained by the bonds, by which he was most

CAP.
III

Christianus, coniuge fideli, ea tamen ipsa artiore prae
ceteris conpede ab itinere, quod aggressi eramus,
retardabatur; nec Christianum esse alio modo se velle
dicebat quam illo, quo non poterat. benigne tamen
obtulit, ut, quamdiu ibi essemus, in re eius essemus.
retribues illi, domine, in retributione iustorum, quia
iam ipsam sortem retribuisti ei. quamvis enim
absentibus nobis, cum Romae iam essemus, corporali
aegritudine correptus, et in ea Christianus et fidelis
factus, ex hac vita emigravit. ita misertus es non
solum eius sed etiam nostri, ne cogitantes egregiam
erga nos amici humanitatem, nec eum in grege tuo
numerantes, dolore intolerabili cruciaremur. gratias
tibi, deus noster! tui sumus: indicant hortationes et
consolationes tuae. fidelis promissor reddis Vere-
cundo pro rure illo eius Cassiciaco, ubi ab aestu
saeculi requievimus in te, amoenitatem sempiternae
virentis[1] paradisi tui, quoniam dimisisti ei peccata
super terram in monte incaseato, monte tuo, monte
uberi.

Angebatur ergo tunc ipse, Nebridius autem con-
laetabatur. quamvis enim et ipse nondum Christianus
in illam foveam perniciosissimi erroris inciderat, ut
veritatis filii tui carnem phantasma crederet, tamen
inde emergens sic sibi erat, nondum imbutus ullis

---

[1] virtutis, *Knöll; i.e.,* Christ (1 Cor. i. 24).

strongly held, he saw himself likely to lose our CHAP. III
company. Being not yet a Christian, though his
wife were indeed baptised, by her, in fact, as the
clog that hung closer to him than all the rest, was
he chiefly kept from that journey which we now
intended; and a Christian he would not, as he said,
be any other ways made, than by that way, which
he as yet could not. However, most courteously
did he proffer us, that we might make use of his
country house, so long as we meant to stay there.
Thou, O Lord, shalt reward him for it in the resur- Luke xiv. 14
rection of the just, seeing thou hast already ren-
dered to him the lot of the just. For although in Ps. cxxv. 3
our absence, as being then at Rome, he was taken
with a bodily sickness, and he departed this life,
being both made a Christian and baptized. Thus
hadst thou mercy, not upon him only, but upon us
also; lest we remembering ourselves of the humanity
received from our friend, and not allowed to reckon
him in the number of thy flock, should be tortured
with intolerable sorrow for him. Thanks unto thee,
O our God, we are now thine: thy inspirations and
consolations tell us so. Thou, O faithful promiser,
shalt repay Verecundus for his country house of
Cassiciacum, (where from the troubles of the world
we rested ourselves in thee), with pleasantness of
thy Paradise which is ever green: for that thou hast
forgiven him his sins upon earth, in that mountain of
spices, thine own mountain, that fruitful mountain. Cant. viii. 14; in Ps. lxviii. 15

Verecundus therefore was much perplexed, but
Nebridius was as joyful as we. For although whenas
he was not yet a Christian, he had fallen into the the old rendering is *incaseato*, used here for the play on words
same pit of most pernicious error with us, believing
the flesh of thy Son's truth to be fantastical: yet
getting out from thence, he was in this position, not

CAP.
III

ecclesiae tuae sacramentis, sed inquisitor ardentissimus veritatis. quem non multo post conversionem nostram et regenerationem per baptismum tuum› ipsum etiam fidelem Catholicum, castitate perfecta atque continentia tibi servientem in Africa apud suos, cum tota domus eius per eum Christiana facta esset, carne solvisti: et nunc ille vivit in sinu Abraham. quidquid illud est, quod illo significatur sinu, ibi Nebridius meus vivit, dulcis amicus meus, tuus autem adoptivus ex liberto filius : ibi vivit. nam quis alius tali animae locus ? ibi vivit, unde me multa interrogabat homuncionem inexpertum. iam non ponit aurem ad os meum, sed spiritale os ad fontem tuum, et bibit, quantum potest, sapientiam pro aviditate sua, sine fine felix. nec eum sic arbitror inebriari ex ea, ut obliviscatur mei, cum tu, domine, quem potat ille, nostri sis memor. sic ergo eramus, Verecundum consolantes tristem, salva amicitia de tali conversione nostra, et exhortantes ad fidem gradus sui, vitae scilicet coniugalis : Nebridium autem opperientes, quando sequeretur. quod de tam proximo poterat, et erat iam iamque facturus, cum ecce evoluti sunt dies illi tandem. nam longi et multi videbantur, prae amore libertatis otiosae, ad cantandum de medullis omnibus : tibi dixit cor meum, quaesivi vultum tuum ; vultum tuum, domine, requiram.

as yet entered into any Sacraments of thy Church, but
a most zealous searcher out of the truth. Whom, not
long after our conversion and regeneration by thy
Baptism, being also baptized in the Catholic faith,
serving thee in perfect chastity and continence
amongst his own friends in Africa, having first converted his whole family into Christianity, didst thou
take out of the flesh; and now he lives in the bosom
of Abraham. Whatsoever that estate be, which is
signified by that bosom, there lives Nebridius my
sweet friend, thy child adopted and no longer a
freedman: he lives there. For what other place
is there for such a soul? In that place he lives,
concerning which he sometimes demanded of me,
poor unskilful man, so many questions. Now lays
he his ear no longer unto my mouth; but lays his
spiritual mouth unto thy fountain, and drinketh as
much of wisdom as he is able to contain, propor-
tionable to his thirst: now without end happy. Nor
do I yet think that he is so inebriated with it, as
to forget me; seeing thou O Lord, of whom he
drinketh, art still mindful of us. Thus fared it then
with us: sorrowful Verecundus we comforted, re-
serving our friendship entire notwithstanding our
conversion; and exhorting him to continue in the
fidelity of his degree, namely of his married estate.
Nebridius we stayed for, expecting when he would
follow us: which being so near he might well do, and
even now he was about to do it, when behold those days
of interim were at length come to an end. For long
and many they seemed unto me, even for the love I
bare to that easeful liberty: that we might sing unto
thee out of our inmost parts, My heart hath said Ps. xxvii. 8
unto thee, I have sought thy face, thy face Lord will
I seek.

IV

CAP.
IV

ET venit dies, quo etiam actu solverer a professione rhetorica, unde iam cogitatu solutus eram. et factum est: eruisti linguam meam, unde iam erueras cor meum, et benedicebam tibi gaudens, profectus in villam cum meis omnibus. ubi quid egerim in litteris (iam quidem servientibus tibi, sed adhuc superbiae scholam tamquam in pausatione anhelantibus) testantur libri disputati cum praesentibus et cum ipso me solo coram te; quae autem cum absente Nibridio, testantur epistulae. et quando mihi sufficiat tempus conmemorandi omnia magna erga nos beneficia tua, in illo tempore praesertim, ad alia maiora properanti? revocat enim me recordatio mea, et dulce mihi fit, domine, confiteri tibi, quibus internis me stimulis perdomueris; et quemadmodum me conplanaveris, humilitatis montibus et collibus cogitationum mearum, et tortuosa mea direxeris, et aspera lenieris; quoque modo ipsum etiam Alypium, fratrem cordis mei, subegeris nomini unigeniti tui, domini et salvatoris nostri Iesu Christi, quod primo dedignabatur inseri litteris nostris. magis enim eas volebat redolere gymnasiorum cedros, quas iam contrivit dominus,

14

IV

What things he wrote with Nebridius

Now was the day come, wherein I was indeed to be CHAP. discharged of my rhetoric professorship, from which IV in my thoughts I was already discharged. And done it was: thou deliveredst my tongue whence thou hadst before delivered my heart, and I blessed thee for it, rejoicing, I and mine going all to the country house. What there in point of learning I did, (which was now wholly at thy service, though yet breathing the school of pride as though resting after a round) my books may witness, both those Contra Aca-which I disputed with my friends present, and those demicos, which I composed alone with myself, before thee: De Beata Vita, De and what intercourse I had with Nebridius now Ordine absent, my epistles can testify. And when could I have time enough to make rehearsal of all the great benefits which thou at that time bestowedst upon me, especially seeing I am now making haste to tell of greater matters? For my remembrance now calls upon me, and most pleasant it is to me, O Lord, to confess unto thee by what inward prongs thou hast thus tamed me; and how thou hast taken me down, by bringing low those mountains and hills of my high Is. xl. 4 imaginations, and madest my crookedness straight, and my rough ways smooth; and by what means thou also subduedst that brother of my love, Alypius, unto the Name of thy only begotten Son our Lord and Saviour Jesus Christ, which he at first would not vouchsafe to have put into our writings. For, rather would he have had them savour of the lofty cedars of the schools, which the Lord had now broken Ps. xxix. 5

quam salubres herbas ecclesiasticas adversas serpentibus.

Quas tibi, deus meus, voces dedi, cum legerem
psalmos David, cantica fidelia, sonos pietatis exclu-
dentes turgidum spiritum, rudis in germano amore
tuo, catechumenus in villa cum catechumeno Alypio
feriatus, matre adhaerente nobis, muliebri habitu,
virili fide, anili securitate, materna caritate, Christiana'
pietate! quas tibi voces dabam in psalmis illis, et
quomodo in te inflammabar ex eis, et accendebar eos
recitare, si possem, toto orbi terrarum, adversum
typhum generis humani! et tamen toto orbe cantantur, et non est qui se abscondat a calore tuo. quam
vehementi et acri dolore indignabar Manichaeis, et
miserabar eos rursus, quod illa sacramenta, illa medicamenta nescirent, et insani essent adversus anti-
dotum, quo sani esse potuissent! vellem, ut alicubi
iuxta essent tunc, et me nesciente, quod ibi essent,
intuerentur faciem meam et audirent voces meas,
quando legi quartum psalmum in illo tunc otio, quid
de me fecerit ille psalmus: (Cum invocarem te, ex-
audisti me, deus iustitiae meae; in tribulatione dila_
tasti mihi: Miserere mei, domine, et exaudi oratio-
nem meam): audirent ignorante me, utrum audirent,
16

down; than of those wholesome herbs of thy Church, CHAP.
which are so powerful against serpents.   IV

What cries I sent up unto thee, my God, whenas
I read the Psalms of David; those faithful songs,
those sounds of devotion, quite excluding the swelling
spirit of ostentation: when namely, I was but rude
in thy true love, as being but a Catechumen as yet
in the country house, keeping holiday, together with
Alypius, a Catechumen also; and with my mother
likewise inseparably sticking unto us, in a woman's
habit verily, but with a masculine faith, void of
worldly care as a woman in her years should be, yet
employing a matronly charity and a Christian piety.
What cries made I unto thee in those Psalms! Oh,
how was I inflamed towards thee by them! Yea, I
was on fire to have resounded them, had I been
able, in all the world, against the pride of mankind:
though verily they be already sung all over the world,
nor can any hide themselves from thy heat. With Ps. xix. 6
what vehement and bitter sorrow was I angered at
the Manichees! Whom yet again I pitied, for that
they knew nothing of those Sacraments, those medi-
caments; and for that they were so mad at that
antidote, which had been able to recover them. I
heartily wished they had been somewhere or other
near me (I not knowing that they did then hear me,
or were then so near me) that they might have beheld
my face, and heard my words, whenas I read the
fourth Psalm in that time of my leisure, and how that
Psalm wrought upon me:—When I called upon thee, Ps. iv.
thou heardest me, O God of my righteousness, thou
hast enlarged me in my distress: Have mercy upon
me, O Lord, and hear my prayer:—that they might
hear, I say, what I uttered at the reading of these
words, I not knowing whether they heard me or no,

17

ne me propter se illa dicere putarent, quae inter
haec verba dixerim, quia et re vera nec ea dicerem
nec sic ea dicerem, si me ab eis audiri viderique sen-
tirem: nec, si dicerem, sic acciperent, quomodo mecum
et mihi coram te de familiari affectu animi mei.

Inhorrui timendo, ibidemque inferbui sperando et
exultando in tua misericordia, pater. et haec omnia
exibant per oculos et vocem meam, cum conversus
ad nos spiritus tuus bonus ait nobis: Filii hominum,
quousque graves corde? Vt quid diligitis vanitatem
et quaeritis mendacium? dilexeram enim vanitatem
et quaesieram mendacium. et tu, domine, iam magni-
ficaveras sanctum tuum, suscitans eum a mortuis et
collocans ad dexteram tuam, unde mitteret ex alto
promissionem suam, paracletum, spiritum veritatis.
et miserat eum iam, sed ego nesciebam. miserat
eum, quia iam magnificatus erat resurgens a mortuis
et ascendens in caelum. ante autem spiritus nondum
erat datus, quia Iesus nondum erat clarificatus. et
clamat prophetia: Quousque graves corde? Vt quid
diligitis vanitatem et quaeritis mendacium? Et scitote,
quoniam dominus magnificavit sanctum suum. clamat
quousque, clamat scitote, et ego tamdiu nesciens
vanitatem dilexi et mendacium quaesivi, et ideo
audivi et contremui, quoniam talibus dicitur, qualem
me fuisse reminiscebar. in phantasmatis enim, quae
pro veritate tenueram, vanitas erat et mendacium.

18

lest they should think I spake it purposely on their account; because in good truth, neither would I have spoken the same things, nor in the same manner, had I perceived them to have both heard and seen me. But had I so spoken, yet would not they so have understood, how I spake with myself, and to myself before thee, out of the natural feelings of my soul.

I quaked for fear, and boiled again with hope and with rejoicing in thy mercy, O Father. And all these expressions of myself passed forth by mine eyes and voice; at what time as thy good Spirit turning himself towards us, said, O ye sons of men, how long will ye be dull of heart? Why do ye love vanity, and seek after leasing? For I myself had sometimes loved vanity, and sought after leasing; and thou, O Lord, hadst already magnified thy holy one, Ps. iv. 3 raising him from the dead, and placing him at thy right hand, whence from on high he should send his promise, the Comforter, the Spirit of Truth. And he had sent him already, but I knew it not. He had already sent him; because he was now exalted by rising from the dead, and ascended up into heaven. For till then, the Holy Ghost was not given, because Jesus was not yet glorified. And the Prophet cries out, How long, O ye slow of heart? Why do ye love vanity and seek after leasing? Know this, that the Lord hath magnified his Holy One. He cries out, How long; he cries out, Know this: and I so long ignorant, have loved vanity and sought after leasing, and therefore I heard and trembled, because it was spoken unto such, as I remembered myself to have been. For verily in those fantastical fictions which I once held for truths, was there both vanity and leasing. And I roared out many things earnestly

et insonui multa graviter et fortiter in dolore recordationis meae. quae utinam audissent qui adhuc usque diligunt vanitatem et quaerunt mendacium: forte conturbarentur et evomuissent illud, et exaudires eos, cum clamarent ad te: quoniam vera morte carnis mortuus est pro nobis, qui te interpellat pro nobis.

Legebam: Irascimini et nolite peccare. et quomodo movebar, deus meus, qui iam didiceram irasci mihi de praeteritis, ut de cetero non peccarem: et merito irasci, quia non alia natura gentis tenebrarum de me peccabat, sicut dicunt qui sibi non irascuntur, et thesaurizant sibi iram in die irae et revelationis iusti iudicii tui! nec iam bona mea foris erant, nec oculis carneis in isto sole quaerebantur. volentes enim gaudere forinsecus facile vanescunt, et effunduntur in ea, quae videntur et temporalia sunt, et imagines eorum famelica cogitatione lambiunt. et o si fatigentur inedia et dicant: Quis ostendet nobis bona? et dicamus, et audiant: Signatum est in nobis lumen vultus tui, domine. non enim lumen nos sumus, quod inluminat omnem hominem, sed inluminamur a te, ut, qui fuimus aliquando tenebrae, simus lux in te. o si viderent internum aeternum, quod ego quia gustaveram, frendebam, quoniam non eis poteram

and forcibly, whilst I grieved at what I now remembered. All which I wish they had heard, who yet love vanity and seek after leasing. They would perchance have been troubled, and have vomited up their poison, and so thou mightest have heard them, when they cried unto thee. For he died a true death in the flesh for us, who now makes intercession unto thee for us.

CHAP.
IV

I further read : Be angry, and sin not. And how I was moved, O my God, I who had then learned to be angry at myself for things passed, that I might not sin in time to come ! yea, to be justly angry ; for that it was not any other nature of the kingdom of darkness, which sinned by me : as the Manichees affirm it to be, who are not angry at themselves ; and who treasure up wrath against the day of wrath, and of the revelation of the just judgment of God. Nor was my good any longer without me, nor to be caught with the eyes of flesh under the sun : seeing they that take joy in anything without themselves, do easily become vain, and spill themselves upon those things which are seen and are but temporal ; yea, and with their hunger-starved thoughts lick their very shadows. And oh that they were once wearied out with their hunger, and come to say : Who will show us any good ? Let us say so, and let them hear : The light of thy countenance is sealed upon us. For we ourselves are not that light which enlighteneth every man that cometh into the world ; but we are enlightened by thee : as who having been sometime darkness, may now be light in thee. Oh that they might once see that internal Eternal Light ; which for that myself had once tasted, I gnashed my teeth at them, because I was not able to make them see it : no not though they should bring me their

Ps. iv. 4
Eph. iv. 26

Rom. ii. 5

Ps. iv. 6

John i. 9

Eph. v. 8

21

CAP.
IV
ostendere, si afferrent ad me cor in oculis suis foris a
te et dicerent: Quis ostendit nobis bona? ibi enim,
ubi mihi iratus eram, intus in cubili, ubi conpunctus
eram, ubi sacrificaveram, mactans vetustatem meam,
et inchoata meditatione renovationis meae, sperans in
te, ibi mihi dulcescere coeperas et dederas laetitiam
in corde meo. et exclamabam, legens haec foris et
agnoscens intus, nec volebam multiplicari terrenis
bonis, et devorans tempora et devoratus temporibus,
cum haberem in aeterna simplicitate aliud frumentum
et vinum et oleum.

Et clamabam in consequenti versu clamore alto
cordis mei: O in pace! O in id ipsum! O quid dixit:
obdormiam et somnum capiam? quoniam quis re-
sistet nobis, cum fiet sermo, qui scriptus est: Absorpta
est mors in victoria? et tu es id ipsum valde, qui
non mutaris, et in te requies obliviscens laborum
omnium, quoniam nullus alius tecum, nec ad alia
adipiscenda, quae non sunt quod tu, sed tu, domine,
singulariter in spe constituisti me. legebam et arde-
bam, nec inveniebam, quid facerem surdis mortuis,
ex quibus fueram, pestis, latrator amarus et caecus
adversus litteras, de melle caeli melleas, et de lumine
tuo luminosas, et super inimicis scripturae huius
tabescebam.

Quando recordabor omnia dierum illorum feriato-
rum? sed nec oblitus sum, nec silebo, flagelli tui

heart in their eyes, (which are ever roving from thee) CHAP.
and should say : Who will show us any good?   But   IV
there, where I was angry with myself in my chamber,
where I was inwardly pricked, where I had offered
my sacrifice, slaying my old man, and beginning the
purpose of my newness of life, putting my hope in
thee : there didst thou begin to grow sweet unto me,
and to put gladness in my heart.   And I cried out as Ps. iv. 7
I read this outwardly, recognising them inwardly.
Nor would I be any more increased with worldly
goods; wasting away my time, and being wasted by
these temporal things; whereas I had in thy eternal
simplicity other corn and wine and oil.

And with a loud cry of my heart called I out in
the next verse, Oh in peace, Oh for that Self-same !
Oh what said he : I will lay me down and sleep : for
who shall hinder us, whenas that saying shall be
brought to pass which is written, Death is swallowed 1 Cor. xv.
up in victory ?   And thou surpassingly art that Self-   54
same, thou who art not changed, and in thee is that
rest which forgets all troubles ; since there is no
other besides thee : no, nor hast thou appointed me
to seek after those many other things, which are not
the same that thou art : but thou, Lord, after a
special manner hast made me dwell in hope.   These
things I read, and burnt again ; nor could I tell what
to do to those deaf and dead, of whom myself was
sometimes a pestilent member, a snarling and a blind
bawler against thy Scriptures, all behonied over with
the honey of heaven, and all lightsome with thine
own light : yea, I consumed away with zeal at the
enemies of these Scriptures.

When shall I call to mind everything that I did,
in those days of my retirement ?   Nor have I yet
forgotten, neither will I pass in silence, the smarting

CAP.
IV
asperitatem, et misericordiae tuae mirabilem celeritatem. dolore dentium tunc excruciabas me, et cum in tantum ingravesceret, ut non valerem loqui, ascendit in cor meum admonere omnes meos, qui aderant, ut deprecarentur te pro me, deum salutis omnimodae. et scripsi hoc in cera et dedi, ut eis legeretur. mox ut genua simplici affectu fiximus, fugit dolor ille. sed quis dolor ? aut quomodo fugit ? expavi, fateor, domine meus et deus meus : nihil enim tale ab ineunte aetate expertus fueram. et insinuati sunt mihi in profundo nutus tui, et gaudens in fide laudavi nomen tuum ; et ea fides me securum esse non sinebat de praeteritis peccatis meis, quae mihi per baptismum tuum remissa nondum erant.

V

CAP.
V
Renuntiavi peractis vindemialibus, ut scholasticis suis Mediolanenses venditorem verborum alium providerent, quod et tibi ego servire delegissem, et illi professioni prae difficultate spirandi ac dolore pectoris non sufficerem. et insinuavi per litteras antistiti tuo, viro sancto Ambrosio, pristinos errores meos et praesens votum meum, ut moneret, quid

of thy scourge, and the wonderful swiftness of thy CHAP. mercy. Thou didst in those days torment me with IV the toothache; which when it had grown so fierce upon me, that I was not able to speak, it came into my heart to desire my friends present to pray for me unto thee, the God of all manner of health. And this I wrote in wax, and gave it to them to read. Immediately, so soon as with an humble devotion we had bowed our knees, that pain went away. But what pain? Or how went it away? I was much afraid, O my Lord, my God; seeing from mine infancy I had never felt the like. And thou gavest me a secret item by this, how powerful thy beck was; for which I much rejoicing in faith, gave praise unto thy name. And that faith suffered me not to be secure in the remembrance of my fore passed sins, which hitherto were not forgiven me by thy baptism.

V

Ambrose directs him what Books to read

AT the end of the vintage, I gave the citizens of CHAP. Milan warning to provide their scholars of another V master to sell words to them; for that I had made choice to serve thee; and for that by reason of my difficulty of breathing, and the pain in my breast, I was not able to go on in the professorship. And by letters I signified to that Prelate of thine, the holy man Ambrose, my former errors and present resolution, desiring him to advise me what part of thy

CAP.
V
mihi potissimum de libris tuis legendum esset, quo
percipiendae tantae gratiae paratior aptiorque fierem.
at ille iussit Esaiam prophetam, credo, quod prae
ceteris evangelii vocationisque gentium sit prae-
nuntiator apertior. verum tamen ego primam huius
lectionem non intellegens, totumque talem arbitrans,
distuli repetendum exercitatior in dominico eloquio.

VI

CAP.
VI
INDE ubi tempus advenit, quo me nomen dare
oporteret, relicto rure Mediolanium remeavimus.
placuit et Alypio renasci in te mecum, iam induto
humilitate sacramentis tuis congrua, et fortissimo
dominatori corporis, usque ad Italicum solum glaciale
nudo pede obterendum insolito ausu. adiunximus
etiam nobis puerum Adeodatum, ex me natum
carnaliter de peccato meo. tu bene feceras eum.
annorum erat ferme quindecim, et ingenio praevenie-
bat multos graves et doctos viros. munera tua tibi
confiteor, domine deus meus, creator omnium, et
multum potens formare nostra deformia : nam ego
in illo puero praeter delictum non habebam. quod
enim et nutriebatur a nobis in disciplina tua, tu
inspiraveras nobis, nullus alius : munera tua tibi

Scriptures were best for my reading, to make me CHAP.
V readier and fitter for the receiving of so great a grace. He recommended Esaias the Prophet to me: for this reason, I believe, for that he is a more clear foreshewer of the Gospel, and of the calling of the Gentiles, than are the rest of the Prophets. But I, not understanding the first part of him, and imagining all the rest to be like that, laid it by, intending to fall to it again, when I were better practised in our Lord's manner of speech.

VI

He is Baptized at Milan

WHEN the time was come wherein I was to give in CHAP.
VI my name, we removed out of the country into Milan. Alypius also was for company resolved to be born again in thee, as having by this put on such humility as is fitting for thy Sacraments; and being become so valiant a tamer of his own body, as even to wear the frosty earth of Italy with bare feet, an unusual undertaking. We took also with us the boy Adeodatus, carnally begotten by me in fornication. Thy part of him was well made up: for being now but almost fifteen years of age, he for wit excelled many a grave and learned man. I confess unto thee thine own gifts, O Lord my God, Creator of all, who art abundantly able to reform all our defects: for I had no part in this boy but the sin: for that we brought him up in thy fear, 'twas thou, and none else that inspired us. I confess thine own gifts unto thee. There is a book of ours extant

CAP. confiteor. est liber noster, qui inscribitur "de
VI Magistro": ipse ibi mecum loquitur. tu scis illius
esse sensa omnia, quae inseruntur ibi ex persona
conlocutoris mei, cum esset in annis sedecim. multa
eius alia mirabiliora expertus sum. horrori mihi
erat illud ingenium : et quis praeter te talium
miraculorum opifex? cito de terra abstulisti vitam
eius, et securior eum recordor, non timens quicquam
pueritiae nec adulescentiae nec omnino homini illi.
sociavimus eum coaevum nobis in gratia tua,
educandum in disciplina tua: et baptizati sumus, et
fugit a nobis sollicitudo vitae praeteritae. nec satia-
bar in illis diebus dulcitudine mirabili considerare
altitudinem consilii tui super salute generis humani.
quantum flevi in hymnis et canticis tuis, suave sonantis
ecclesiae tuae vocibus conmotus acriter ! voces illae
influebant auribus meis, et eliquabatur veritas in cor
meum, et exaestuabat inde affectus pietatis, et curre-
bant lacrimae, et bene mihi erat cum eis.

VII

CAP. Non longe coeperat Mediolanensis ecclesia genus
VII hoc consolationis et exhortationis celebrare, magno
studio fratrum concinentium vocibus et cordibus.

called of The Master: a dialogue it is betwixt him CHAP.
and me. Thou knowest that all these conceits are VI
his own, which go there under the name of him
that discourses with me, when he was sixteen years
old. I had trial of many more admirable abilities
of his. His great wit struck a kind of awe into me.
And who but thyself can be the work-master of such
wonders? Soon didst thou take his life from off the
earth; and without anxiety do I now remember him,
for that I fear nothing committed either in his childhood or youth, nor anything at all in him. Him
we took along with us, as old as ourselves in grace, to be
brought up according to thy discipline; and baptized
we were together: and then all anguish of mind
for our former ill-led life vanished away. Nor could
I be satisfied in those days, while with admirable
sweetness I considered upon the deepness of thy
counsels concerning the salvation of mankind. How
abundantly did I weep to hear those hymns and
canticles of thine, being touched to the very quick
by the voices of thy sweet church song! Those
voices flowed into mine ears, and thy truth pleasingly
distilled into my heart, which caused the affections
of my devotion to overflow, and my tears to run over,
and happy did I find myself therein.

VII

A Persecution in the Church miraculously diverted

NOT long before had the Church of Milan begun to CHAP.
celebrate this kind of consolation and exhortation, VII
and that with the great delight of the brethren,
singing together both with voice and hearts. For

CAP. nimirum annus erat aut non multo amplius, cum
VII Iustina, Valentiniani regis pueri mater, hominem
tuum Ambrosium persequeretur haeresis suae causa,
qua fuerat seducta ab Arrianis. excubabat pia plebs
in ecclesia, mori parata cum episcopo suo, servo tuo.
ibi mater mea, ancilla tua, sollicitudinis et vigilia-
rum primas tenens, orationibus vivebat. nos adhuc
frigidi a calore spiritus tui, excitabamur tamen civitate adtonita atque turbata. tunc hymni et psalmi
ut canerentur secundum morem orientalium partium,
ne populus maeroris taedio contabesceret, institutum
est: ex illo in hodiernum retentum multis iam ac
paene omnibus gregibus tuis et per cetera orbis
imitantibus.

Tunc memorato antistiti tuo per visum aperuisti,
quo loco laterent martyrum corpora Protasi et Ger-
vasi, quae per tot annos incorrupta in thesauro
secreti tui reconderas, unde opportune promeres ad
coercendam rabiem femineam, sed regiam. cum
enim prolata et effossa digno cum honore transfer-
rentur ad Ambrosianam basilicam, non solum quos
inmundi vexabant spiritus, confessis eisdem daemon-
ibus, sanabantur, verum etiam quidam plures annos
caecus civis civitatique notissimus, cum populi tumul-
tuante laetitia causam quaesisset atque audisset,
exsiluit, eoque se ut duceret suum ducem rogavit.
quo perductus inpetravit admitti, ut sudario tangeret
30

about a year it was, or not much above, that Justina,
mother to the boy Emperor Valentinian, persecuted
thy servant Ambrose, in favour of her heresy, to which
she was seduced by the Arians: the devout people
watched day and night in the Church, ready to die
with their Bishop, thy servant. There my mother,
thy handmaid, bearing a chief part of those troubles
and watchings, even lived by prayer: yea, we also,
still unwarmed by the heat of thy spirit, were yet
stirred up by the example of the amazed and dis-
quieted city. At this time was it here first instituted after the manner of the Eastern Churches,
that hymns and psalms should be sung, lest the
people should wax faint through the tediousness of
sorrow: which custom being retained from that day
to this, is still imitated by divers, yea, almost by
all thy congregations throughout other parts of the
world.

At that time didst thou by a vision discover unto
thy forenamed Bishop, the place where the bodies
of Gervasius and Protasius the martyrs did lie hid;
which thou hadst in the treasury of thy secret preserved uncorrupted so many years, from whence thou
mightest thus seasonably bring them to light, to
repress the fury of this woman the Empress. For
whenas they were once discovered and digged up,
and with due honours translated to Ambrose's
Church; not only they who were vexed with unclean spirits (the devils confessing themselves to be
so) were cured; but a certain man also having been
blind many years, (a citizen well known to that
city) asking and hearing the reason of the people's
confused joy; sprang forth, desiring his guide to
lead him thither. And being come to that place,
requested the favour, that with his handkerchief he

31

CAP.
VII
feretrum pretiosae in conspectu tuo mortis sanctorum tuorum. quod ubi fecit atque admovit oculis, confestim aperti sunt. inde fama discurrens, inde laudes tuae ferventes, lucentes, inde illius inimicae animus etsi ad credendi sanitatem non applicatus, a persequendi tamen furore conpressus est. gratias tibi, deus meus! unde et quo duxisti recordationem meam, ut haec etiam confiterer tibi, quae magna oblitus praeterieram? et tamen tunc, cum ita fragraret odor unguentorum tuorum, non currebamus post te; ideo plus flebam inter cantica hymnorum tuorum, olim suspirans tibi et tandem respirans, quantum patet aura in domo faenea.

VIII

CAP.
VIII
Qui habitare facis unanimes in domo, consociasti nobis et Euodium iuvenem ex nostro municipio. qui cum Agens in Rebus militaret, prior nobis ad te conversus est et baptizatus, et relicta militia saeculari accinctus in tua. simul eramus, simul habitaturi placito sancto. quaerebamus, quisnam locus nos utilius haberet servientes tibi: pariter remeabamus

might touch the bier of thy saints, whose death is CHAP.
precious in thy sight. Which when he had done, VII
and put unto his eyes, they were forthwith opened. Ps. cxvi. 5
Hereupon was the fame spread; hereupon thy praises
glowed and shone; hereupon was the mind of that
enemy, though not brought to be healed by believing,
yet restrained from her fury of persecuting. Thanks
be to thee, O my God; whence, and whither hast
thou thus led my remembrance that I should also
confess these great things unto thee, which I had
forgotten and passed over? And yet even then,
whenas the odours of thy ointments were so fragrant, Cant. i. 2, 3
did we not run after thee: and for this reason did I
more abundantly weep at the singing of thy hymns,
as having once sighed after thee, and now at last
breathing in thee, as far as there can be freedom
of air in this house of grass.

VIII

The Conversion of Euodius. A Discourse
of his Mother

THOU that makest men of one mind to dwell in one CHAP.
house, didst bring Euodius, a young man of our own VIII
town, also to consort himself with us. Who being an
Agent for Public Affairs, was converted unto thee
and baptized before us; and having quit his secular
warfare, girded himself to thine. We kept company
with one another, intending still to dwell together in
our devout purpose. We sought out now for some
place where we might more conveniently serve thee
in, we removed thereupon back again into Africa:

CAP.
VIII
in Africam. et cum apud Ostia Tiberina essemus, mater defuncta est. multa praetereo, quia multum festino. accipe confessiones meas et gratiarum actiones, deus meus, de rebus innumerabilibus etiam in silentio. sed non praeteribo quidquid mihi anima parturit de illa famula tua, quae me parturivit, et carne, ut in hanc temporalem, et corde, ut in aeternam lucem nascerer. non eius, sed tua dicam dona in eam. neque enim se ipsa fecerat aut educaverat se ipsam : tu creasti eam, nec pater nec mater sciebat, qualis ex eis fieret. et erudivit eam in timore tuo virga Christi tui, regimen unici tui in domo fideli, bono membro ecclesiae tuae. nec tantam erga suam disciplinam diligentiam matris praedicabat, quantam famulae cuiusdam decrepitae, quae patrem eius infantem portaverat, sicut dorso grandiuscularum puellarum parvuli portari solent. cuius rei gratia, et propter senectam ac mores optimos, in domo Christiana satis a dominis honorabatur. unde etiam curam dominicarum filiarum conmissam diligentur gerebat, et erat in eis coercendis, cum opus esset, sancta severitate vehemens, atque in docendis sobria prudentia. nam eas praeter illas horas, quibus ad mensam parentum moderatissime alebantur, etiamsi exardescerent siti, nec aquam bibere sinebat, praecavens consuetudinem malam et

whitherward being on our way as far as Ostia, my
mother departed this life. Many things do I overpass,
because I make haste. Receive my confessions and
thanksgivings, O my God, for innumerable things
which I am silent in. But omit I will not whatsoever
my soul can bring forth concerning that handmaid of
thine, which brought forth me : both in her flesh, that
I might be born to this temporal light, and in her
heart too, that I might be born again to the eternal
light. Not her gifts will I mention, but thine in
her. For neither did she give birth nor education
unto herself : thou createdst her, nor did her father
and mother know what kind of creature was to
proceed out of their loins. And it was the sceptre
of thy Christ, the discipline of thine only Son, that
educated her in thy fear, in a faithful household,
which was a good member of thy Church. Yet was
she wont not so much to commend the diligence of
her mother in her education, as the care of a certain
decrepit servant of hers, who had also carried her
father being a child, as little ones use to be carried
at the backs of bigger maid servants. For which
reason, and because she was well in years, and of
excellent conversation, was she in that Christian
family very well respected by her master and
mistress : having thereupon the charge of her mistress's daughters committed unto her, which she
with much diligence performed, being sharp to hold
them in, when so required, with a holy severity, and
using a grave manner of discretion in teaching of
them. For except at those hours wherein they were
most temperately fed at their parents' table, would
she not suffer them, were they never so thirsty, to
drink so much as a draught of water : preventing
thereby a naughty custom, and giving them this

CAP.
VIII
addens verbum sanum : " modo aquam bibitis, quia in potestate vinum non habetis ; cum autem ad maritos veneritis, factae dominae apothecarum et cellariorum, aqua sordebit, sed mos potandi praevalebit." hac ratione praecipiendi et auctoritate imperandi frenabat aviditatem tenerioris aetatis, et ipsam puellarum sitim formabat ad honestum modum, ut iam non liberet quod non deceret.

Et subrepserat tamen, sicut mihi filio famula tua narrabat, subrepserat ei vinulentia. nam cum de more puella sobria iuberetur a parentibus de cupa vinum depromere, submisso poculo, qua desuper patet, priusquam in lagunculam funderet merum, primoribus labris sorbebat exiguum, quia non poterat amplius sensu recusante. non enim ulla temulenta cupidine faciebat hoc, sed quibusdam superfluentibus aetatis excessibus, qui ludicris motibus ebulliunt, et in puerilibus annis maiorum pondere premi solent. itaque ad illud modicum cotidianum cotidiana modica addendo— quoniam qui modica spernit, paulatim decidit —in eam consuetudinem lapsa erat, ut prope iam plenos mero caliculos inhianter hauriret. ubi tunc sagax anus et vehemens illa prohibitio ? numquid valebat aliquid adversus latentem morbum, nisi tua medicina, domine, vigilaret super nos ? absente patre et matre et nutritoribus, tu praesens, qui creasti, qui vocas, qui etiam per praepositos homines boni

wholesome item withal: Go to, now ye drink water CHAP.
because ye are not suffered to have wine; but when VIII
once you come to be married, and be made mistresses
of butteries and cellars, you will scorn water then,
but the custom of drinking will prevail upon you.
By this way of tutoring, and the authority she had in
awing of them, did she moderate the longing of their
tender ages, yea and brought the girls' thirst to so
honest a moderation, as that now they cared not for
what was not comely.

But there stole for all this, (as thy handmaid told
me her son,) there stole upon her a lickerish inclination toward wine. For when, as the manner was,
she, being thought to be a sober maiden, was bidden
by her parents sometimes to draw wine out of the
hogshead, she holding the pot under the tap, would
at the mouth of it, before she poured the wine into
the flagon, wet her lips as it were with a little sip of
it: for much would not her taste suffer her to take
in. For she did not this out of any drunken desire,
but upon such overflowing excesses as youth is subject
unto, who boil over with gamesomeness: which in
youthful spirits is wont to be kept under by the
gravity of their elders. And thus unto that daily little
every day adding a little more, (for whoever con- Ecclus.
temneth small things, falls by little and little) fell xix. 1
she at last to get such a custom, that she would
greedily take off her cups brimful almost of wine.
Where was then that watchful old woman, with all
her earnest countermanding? Was anything of force
enough to prevail against a secret disease, if thy
physic, O Lord, did not watch over us? Her father,
mother, and governors not being by, thyself wert at
hand, who createdst, who callest us, who also by
means of these people that are set over us, workest

aliquid agis ad animarum salutem.   quid tunc egisti,
deus meus?   unde curasti?   unde sanasti?   nonne
protulisti durum et acutum ex altera anima convicium,
tamquam medicinale ferrum ex occultis provisionibus
tuis, et uno ictu putredinem illam praecidisti?   ancilla
enim, cum qua solebat accedere ad cupam, litigans
cum domina minore, ut fit, sola cum sola, obiecit hoc
crimen amarissima insultatione, vocans meribibulam.
quo illa stimulo percussa respexit foeditatem suam,
confestimque damnavit atque exuit.   sicut amici
adulantes pervertunt, sic inimici litigantes plerumque corrigunt.   nec tu quod per eos agis, sed quod
ipsi voluerunt, retribuis eis.   illa enim irata exagi-
tare appetivit minorem dominam, non sanare, et
ideo clanculo, aut quia ita eas invenerat locus et
tempus litis, aut ne forte et ipsa periclitaretur, quod
tam sero prodidisset.   at tu, domine, rector caelitum
et terrenorum, ad usus tuos contorquens profunda
torrentis, fluxum saeculorum ordinate turbulentum,
etiam de alterius animae insania sanasti alteram, ne
quisquam, cum hoc advertit, potentiae suae tribuat,
si verbo eius alius corrigatur, quem vult corrigi.

something towards the salvation of our souls. What CHAP. didst thou, at that time, O my God? How didst VIII thou cure her? Which way didst thou heal her? Didst thou not out of another soul bring forth a hard and a sharp check, as it were a surgeon's knife out of thy secret store; and with one blow quite cut off that putrefied custom of hers? For a maid which she used to go withal into the cellar, falling to words, as it happened, hand to hand with her little mistress, hit her in the teeth in a most bitter insulting manner, calling her wine-bibber: with which taunt she being struck to the quick, reflected upon the foulness of her fault, yea, and instantly condemned it to herself, leaving it quite. Even as friends by flattering make us worse, so enemies oftentimes by reproaching, make us better. Yet dost not thou render unto them according to that which by them thou doest, but according to that which themselves intended. For she being in a choler had a desire rather to vex her young mistress than to amend her; and therefore did she it thus privately; either for that the opportuuity of the time and place of their brabble found them thus alone, or else for fear herself should have had anger, for discovering it no sooner. But thou, O Lord, the Governor both of heavenly and earthly things, who convertest to thine own purposes the very depths of the running streams, and disposest of the wild flood of all ages; didst by the fury of one soul, thus cure the ill custom of another; and that lest any man, when he observes this, should attribute it unto his own power, if another man chance to be reformed by a word of his, whom he meant to have reformed.

IX

CAP.
IX
EDUCATA itaque pudice ac sobrie, potiusque a te subdita parentibus quam a parentibus tibi, ubi plenis
annis nubilis facta est, tradita viro servivit veluti
domino, et sategit eum lucrari tibi, loquens te illi
moribus suis, quibus eam pulchram faciebas et reve-
renter amabilem atque mirabilem viro, ita autem
toleravit cubilis iniurias, ut nullam de hac re cum
marito haberet umquam simultatem. expectabat
enim misericordiam tuam super eum, ut in te credens
castificaretur. erat vero ille praeterea sicut benevo-
lentia praecipuus, ita ira fervidus. sed noverat haec
non resistere irato viro, non tantum facto, sed ne
verbo quidem. iam vero refractum et quietum cum
opportunum viderat, rationem facti sui reddebat, si
forte ille inconsideratius commotus fuerat. denique
cum matronae multae, quarum viri mansuetiores
erant, plagarum vestigia etiam dehonestata facie
gererent, inter amica conloquia illae arguebant mari-
torum vitam, haec earum linguam, veluti per iocum
graviter admonens, ex quo illas tabulas, quae matri-
moniales vocantur, recitari audissent, tamquam in-
strumenta, quibus ancillae factae essent, deputare

IX

His Mother Monica's carriage towards her Husband.
A description of a rare Wife

BEING thus modestly and soberly brought up, and
made subject by thee to her parents rather than by
her parents unto thee; so soon as she proved mar-
riageable, was she bestowed upon a husband, whom
she was as serviceable unto, as to her Lord: endeavouring thereby to win him unto thee, preaching
thee unto him by her character; by which thou
madest her to appear beautiful, and reverently ami-
able, yea and admirable unto her husband. For she
so discreetly endured his wronging of her bed, that
she never had any jealous quarrel with her husband
for that matter. Because she still expected thy
mercy upon him, that believing in thee, he might
turn chaster. And he was besides this, as of a passing good nature, also very hot and choleric: but she
knew well enough that a husband in choler is not to
be contradicted; not in deed only, but not so much
as in word. But as soon as he was grown calm and
quieter, when she saw her opportunity, would she
render him an account of her actions; if so be he
had been offended upon too slight an occasion. In a
word, whenas many matrons, who had much milder
husbands, carried the marks of the blows even in
their disfigured faces, they would in their gossipings
tell many a tale of their husbands' manner of living,
she as it were in jest, gravely advised their too free
tongues, that from the time they first heard those
tables which they called matrimonial to be first read
unto them, they should account of them as deeds,

41

debuisse ; proinde memores conditionis superbire adversus dominos non oportere. cumque mirarentur illae, scientes quam ferocem coniugem sustineret, numquam fuisse auditum aut aliquo indicio claruisse, quod Patricius ceciderit uxorem, aut quod a se invicem vel unum diem domestica lite dissenserint, et causam familiariter quaererent, docebat illa institutum suum, quod supra memoravi. quae observabant, expertae gratulabantur; quae non observabant, subiectae vexabantur.

Socrum etiam suam, primo susurris malarum ancillarum adversus se irritatam, sic vicit obsequiis, perseverans tolerantia et mansuetudine, ut illa ultro filio suo medias linguas famularum proderet, quibus inter se et nurum pax domestica turbabatur, expeteretque vindictam. itaque posteaquam ille, et matri obtemperans et curans familiae disciplinam et concordiae suorum consulens, proditas ad prodentis arbitrium verberibus coercuit, promisit illa talia de se praemia sperare debere, quaecumque de sua nuru sibi, quo placeret, mali aliquid loqueretur, nullaque iam audente memorabili inter se benevolentiae suavitate vixerunt.

Hoc quoque illi bono mancipio tuo, in cuius utero

whereby themselves were made servants; and that therefore being always mindful of their own condition, they ought not to pride up themselves against their masters. And whenas they admired (knowing what a choleric husband she endured) for that it had never been heard, nor by any token perceived, that Patricius had once beaten his wife, or that there had been any one household difference between them for so much as one day; and whenas they familiarly asked the reason of it, she taught them her rule which I have before mentioned. Those wives that observed it, finding the good, gave her thanks for it; those that did not, were kept under and afflicted.

Her mother-in-law also, being at first incensed at her by the whisperings of naughty servants; she so far overcame by observance, persevering so long in patience and meekness, that she of her own accord discovered unto her son the tales that the maid servants had carried between them, whereby the peace of the house had been disturbed, betwixt her and her daughter-in-law, requiring him to give them correction for it. When he therefore, both out of obedience to his mother, and out of a care to the well ordering of his family, and to provide withal for the concord of his people, had with stripes corrected the servants thus discovered, according to the pleasure of her that had discovered it, herself also added this promise, that every one should look for the like reward at her hands, whosoever, to pick a thank by it, should speak any ill of her daughter-in-law: which none being so hardy afterwards as to do, they lived ever after with a most memorable sweetness of mutual courtesies.

This great gift thou bestowedst also, O God my

S. AVGVSTINI CONFESSIONVM LIBER IX

me creasti, deus meus, misericordia mea, munus
grande donaveras, quod inter dissidentes atque dis-
cordes quaslibet animas, ubi poterat, tam se prae-
bebat pacificam, ut cum ab utraque multa de invicem
audiret amarissima, (qualia solet eructuare turgens
atque indigesta discordia, quando praesenti amicae
de absente inimica per acida conloquia cruditas ex-
halatur odiorum,) nihil tamen alteri de altera proderet, nisi quod ad eas reconciliandas valeret.
parvum hoc bonum mihi videretur, nisi turbas innumerabiles tristis experirer, nescio qua horrenda pesti-
lentia peccatorum latissime pervagante, non solum
iratorum inimicorum iratis inimicis dicta prodere,
sed etiam quae non dicta sunt addere: cum contra
homini humano parum esse debeat inimicitias hominum nec excitare nec augere male loquendo, nisi eas
etiam extinguere bene loquendo studuerit. qualis
illa erat docente te magistro intimo in schola
pectoris.

Denique etiam virum suum iam in extrema vita
temporali eius lucrata est tibi; nec in eo iam fideli
planxit, quod in nondum fideli toleraverat.   erat
etiam serva servorum tuorum. quisquis eorum noverat eam, multum in ea laudabat, et honorabat et
diligebat te, quia sentiebat praesentiam tuam in
corde eius sanctae conversationis fructibus testibus.

44

Mercy, upon that good handmaid of thine, out of whose womb thou broughtest me; namely, that she ever did, where she was able, carry herself so peacefully between any parties that were at difference and discord, as that after she had on both sides heard many a bitter word, (such as swelling and indigested choler uses to break forth into, whenas unto a present friend, the undigested heart-burning is with biting tittle-tattle breathed up at an absent enemy) she never for all that, would discover more of the one party unto the other than might further their reconcilement. This virtue might seem a small one unto me, if to my grief I had not had experience of innumerable companies, (I know not by what horrible infection of sin spreading far and near,) who used not only to discover the speeches of enemies angered on both sides to one another, but to add withal some things that were never spoken: whereas on the contrary, it ought to be not enough in a humane man, to forbear merely to procure or increase ill will amongst people by ill speaking, unless he study withal how to quench it by making the best of everything. And such a one was she, thyself being her most intimate master, teaching her in the school of her breast.

Finally, her own husband, now towards the latter end of his life, did she gain unto thee; having now no more cause to complain of those things in him when he was once converted, which she had formerly borne withal, before he was converted. Yea, she was also the servant of thy servants; and whosoever of them knew her, did both commend much in her, and honoured and loved thee: for that he perceived thyself to be within the heart of her holy conversation, the fruits of it being witnesses.

fuerat enim unius viri uxor, mutuam vicem parentibus reddiderat, domum suam pie tractaverat, in
operibus bonis testimonium habebat. nutrierat filios
totiens eos parturiens, quotiens abs te deviare cerne-
bat. postremo nobis, domine, omnibus, quia ex
munere tuo sinis loqui servis tuis, qui ante dormi-
tionem eius in te iam consociati vivebamus percepta
gratia baptismi tui, ita curam gessit, quasi omnes
genuisset, ita servivit, quasi ab omnibus genita
fuisset.

X

CAP. IMPENDENTE autem die, quo ex hac vita erat exitura
X —quem diem tu noveras ignorantibus nobis—pro-
venerat, ut credo, procurante te occultis tuis modis,
ut ego et ipsa soli staremus incumbentes ad quandam
fenestram, unde hortus intra domum, quae nos
habebat, prospectabatur, illic apud Ostia Tiberina, ubi
remoti a turbis post longi itineris laborem instaura-
bamus nos navigationi. conloquebamur ergo soli
valde dulciter; et praeterita obliviscentes in ea quae
ante sunt extenti, quaerebamus inter nos apud
praesentem veritatem, quod tu es, qualis futura esset
vita aeterna sanctorum, quam nec oculus vidit nec

For she had been the wife of one man : she had CHAP.
repaid the duty she ought unto her parents; she IX
had governed her house very religiously ; for good 1 Tim. v. 9
works she had a good report; she had brought up
her children, so often travailing in birth of them Gal. iv. 19
again, as she saw them swerving from thee.

Lastly, of all of us thy servants, O Lord, (since
for this favour received thou sufferest us to speak,
us, who before her sleeping in thee already lived in
society together, having received the grace of thy
Baptism) did she so take care of, as if she had been
the mother to us all : and was withal so serviceable,
as if she had been the daughter to us all.

X

*Of a Conference he had with his Mother about
the Kingdom of Heaven*

THE day now approaching that she was to depart CHAP.
this life, (which day thou well knewest, though we X.
were not aware of it) it fell out, thyself, as I believe,
by thine own secret ways so casting it, that she and I
should stand alone leaning in a certain window, which
looked into the garden within the house where we
now lay, at Ostia by Tiber ; where being sequestered
from company after the wearisomeness of a long
journey, we were recruiting ourselves for a sea voyage.
There conferred we hand to hand very sweetly ; and
forgetting those things which are behind, we reached Phil. iii. 13
forth unto those things which are before : we did
betwixt ourselves seek at that Present Truth (which
thou art) in what manner the eternal life of the
saints was to be, which eye hath not seen, nor ear 1 Cor. ii. 9

47

CAP.
X
auris audivit nec in cor hominis ascendit. sed inhiabamus ore cordis in superna fluenta fontis tui, fontis vitae, qui est apud te; ut inde pro captu nostro aspersi, quoquo modo rem tantam cogitaremus.

Cumque ad eum finem sermo perduceretur, ut carnalium sensuum delectatio quantalibet, in quantalibet luce corporea, prae illius vitae iucunditate non conparatione, sed ne conmemoratione quidem digna videretur, erigentes nos ardentiore affectu in id ipsum, perambulavimus gradatim cuncta corporalia, et ipsum caelum, unde sol et luna et stellae lucent super terram. et adhuc ascendebamus, interius cogitando et loquendo et mirando opera tua, et venimus in mentes nostras et transcendimus eas, ut attingeremus regionem ubertatis indeficientis, unde pascis Israel in aeternum veritate pabulo, et ibi vita sapientia est, per quam fiunt omnia ista, et quae fuerunt et quae futura sunt. et ipsa non fit, sed sic est, ut fuit, et sic erit semper: quin potius fuisse et futurum esse non est in ea, sed esse solum, quoniam aeterna est: nam fuisse et futurum esse non est aeternum. et dum loquimur et inhiamus illi, attingimus eam modice toto ictu cordis; et suspiravimus, et reliquimus ibi religatas primitias spiritus, et remeavimus ad strepitum oris nostri, ubi verbum et incipitur et

heard, nor hath it entered into the heart of man.
But yet we panted with the mouth of our heart after
those upper streams of thy fountain, the fountain of
life; that being besprinkled with it according to our
capacity, we might in some sort meditate upon so
high a mystery.

And when our discourse was once come unto that
point, that the highest pleasure of the carnal senses,
and that in the brightest beam of material light,
was, in respect of the sweetness of that life, not only
not worthy of comparison, but not so much as of
mention; we cheering up ourselves with a more
burning affection towards that Self-same, did by
degrees course over all these corporeals, even the
heaven itself, from whence both sun, and moon, and
stars do shine upon this earth. Yea, we soared higher
yet, by inward musing, and discoursing upon thee,
and by admiring of thy works; and last of all, we
came to our own souls, which we presently went
beyond, so that we advanced as high as that region
of never-wasting plenty, whence thou feedest Israel
for ever with the food of truth, and where life is
that wisdom by which all these things are made,
both which have been, and which are to come.
And this wisdom is not made; but it is at this
present, as it hath ever been, and so shall it ever be:
nay rather the terms to have been, and to be hereafter, are not at all in it, but to be now, for that it
is eternal: for to have been, and to be about to be,
is not eternal. And while we were thus discoursing
and panting after it, we arrived to a little touch
of it with the whole effort of our heart; and we
sighed, and even there we left behind us the first
fruits of our spirits enchained unto it; returning
from these thoughts to vocal expressions of our

S. AVGVSTINI CONFESSIONVM LIBER IX

finitur.   et quid simile verbo tuo, domino nostro, in
se permanenti sine vetustate atque innovanti omnia ?

Dicebamus ergo : " si cui sileat tumultus carnis,
sileant phantasiae terrae et aquarum et aeris, sileant
et poli et ipsa sibi anima sileat, et transeat se non
se cogitando, sileant somnia et imaginariae revela-
tiones, omnis lingua et omne signum et quidquid
transeundo fit si cui sileat omnino—quoniam si quis
audiat, dicunt haec omnia : Non ipsa nos fecimus,
sed fecit nos qui manet in aeternum :—his dictis
si iam taceant, quoniam erexerunt aurem in eum, qui
fecit ea, et loquatur ipse solus non per ea, sed per
se ipsum, ut audiamus verbum eius, non per linguam
carnis neque per vocem angeli nec per sonitum nubis
nec per aenigma similitudinis, sed ipsum, quem in
his amamus, ipsum sine his audiamus, sicut nunc
extendimus nos et rapida cogitatione attingimus aeternam sapientiam super omnia manentem, si continuetur
hoc et subtrahantur aliae visiones longe inparis generis, et haec una rapiat et absorbeat et recondat in
interiora gaudia spectatorem suum, ut talis sit sempiterna vita, quale fuit hoc momentum intellegentiae,
cui suspiravimus, nonne hoc est : Intra in gaudium
domini tui ?   et istud quando ?   an cum omnes re-
surgimus, sed non omnes inmutabimur ? "

mouth, where a word has both beginning and ending. CHAP.
How unlike unto thy Word, our Lord, who remains X
in himself for ever without becoming aged, and yet
renewing all things?

We said therefore: If to any man the tumults of
flesh be silenced, if fancies of the earth, and waters,
and air be silenced also: if the poles of heaven be
silent also: if the very soul be silent to herself, and
by not thinking upon self surmount self: if all
dreams and imaginary revelations be silenced, every
tongue, and every sign, if whatsoever is transient be
silent to any one—since if any man could hearken
unto them, all these say unto him, We created not
ourselves, but he that remains to all eternity: if then,
having uttered this, they also be then silent, (as
having raised our ear unto him that made them) and
if he speak alone; not by them but by himself, that
we may hear his own word; not pronounced by any
tongue of flesh, nor by the voice of the angels, nor
by the sound of thunder, nor in the dark riddle of a
resemblance; but that we may hear him whom we
love in these creatures, himself without these (like
as we two now strained up ourselves unto it, and in
swift thought arrived unto a touch of that eternal
Wisdom, which is over all) :—could this exaltation
of spirit have ever continued, and all other visions of
a far other kind been quite taken away, and that this
one exaltation should ravish us, and swallow us up,
and so wrap up their beholder among these more
inward joys, as that his life might be for ever like to
this very moment of understanding which we now
sighed after: were not this as much as Enter into Matt. xxv.
thy Master's joy? But when shall that be? Shall 21
it be when we shall all rise again, though all shall 1 Cor. xv.
not be changed?

CAP.
X

Dicebam talia, etsi non isto modo et his verbis, tamen, domine, tu scis, quod illo die, cum talia loqueremur et mundus iste nobis inter verba vilesceret cum omnibus delectationibus suis, tunc ait illa: "fili, quantum ad me adtinet, nulla re iam delector in hac vita. quid hic faciam adhuc et cur hic sim, nescio, iam consumpta spe huius saeculi. unum erat, propter quod in hac vita aliquantum inmorari cupiebam, ut te Christianum catholicum viderem, priusquam morerer. cumulatius hoc mihi deus praestitit, ut te etiam contemta felicitate terrena servum eius videam. quid hic facio?"

XI

CAP.
XI

Ad haec ei quid responderim, non satis recolo, cum interea vix intra quinque dies aut non multo amplius decubuit febribus. et cum aegrotaret, quodam die defectum animae passa est et paululum subtracta a praesentibus. nos concurrimus, sed cito reddita est sensui, et aspexit astantes me et fratrem meum et ait nobis quasi quaerenti similis: "ubi eram?" deinde nos intuens maerore attonitos: "ponitis hic" inquit "matrem vestram." ego silebam et fletum frenabam.

Such discourse we then had, and though not pre- CHAP
cisely after this manner, and in these selfsame   X
words; yet, Lord thou knowest, that in that day
when we thus talked of these things, that this world
with all its delights grew contemptible to us, even
as we were speaking of it. Then said my mother:
Son, for mine own part I have delight in nothing in
this life. What I should here do any longer, and to
what end I am here, I know not, now that my hopes
in this world are vanished. There was indeed one
thing for which I sometimes desired to be a little while
reprieved in this life; namely, that I might see thee
to become a Christian Catholic before I died. My
God hath done this for me more abundantly; for
that I now see thee withal having contemned all
earthly happiness, to be made his servant: what
then do I here any longer?

XI

Of the Extasy and Death of his Mother

WHAT answer I then made her unto these things, I CHAP.
do not now remember: but in the mean time (scarce XI
five days after, or not much more,) she fell into a
fever; and in that sickness one day she fell into a
swoon, being for a while taken from visible things.
We ran to her, but she quickly came to herself again;
and looking wistly upon me and my brother standing
by her, said unto us in manner of a question, Where
was I? And fixing her eyes upon us, all with grief
amazed; Here, saith she, you bury your mother.
I held my peace and refrained weeping: but my

53

CAP.
XI
frater autem meus quiddam locutus est, quo eam non in peregre, sed in patria defungi tamquam felicius optaret. quo audito illa vultu anxio, reverberans eum oculis, quod talia saperet, atque inde me intuens : " vide " ait " quid dicit." et mox ambobus : " ponite " inquit " hoc corpus ubicumque : nihil vos eius cura conturbet ; tantum illud vos rogo, ut ad domini altare memineritis mei, ubiubi fueritis." cumque hanc sententiam verbis quibus poterat explicasset, conticuit et ingravescente morbo exercebatur.

Ego vero cogitans dona tua, deus invisibilis, quae immittis in corda fidelium tuorum, et proveniunt inde fruges admirabiles, gaudebam et gratias tibi agebam, recolens, quod noveram, quanta cura semper aestuasset de sepulchro, quod sibi providerat et praeparaverat iuxta corpus viri sui. quia enim valde concorditer vixerant, id etiam volebat, ut est animus humanus minus capax divinorum, adiungi ad illam felicitatem et conmemorari ab hominibus, concessum sibi esse post transmarinam peregrinationem, ut coniuncta terra amborum coniugum terra tegeretur. quando autem ista inanitas plenitudine bonitatis tuae coeperat in eius corde non esse, nesciebam ; et laetabar admirans, quod sic mihi apparuisset, quamquam et in

54

brother spake something to her, insinuating his
desire to have her die, not in a strange place, but in
her own country, as being the happier. At hearing
of which, she with an anxious countenance, check-
ing him with her eye, for that he had not yet lost
the relish of these earthly thoughts: and then looking upon me: Behold, quoth she, what he saith.
And soon after to us both: Lay, saith she, this body
anywhere, let not the care for that disquiet you:
this only I request, that you would remember me at
the Lord's Altar wherever you be. And when she
had delivered this her opinion in words as well as
she could, she held her peace, being in agony by her
sickness growing more strong upon her.

But I considering with myself thy gifts, O thou
my invisible God, which thou instillest into the
hearts of thy faithful ones, from whence such
admirable fruits do spring forth, did greatly rejoice
and give thanks unto thee, calling now to mind, what
I before knew, with how much carefulness, namely,
concerning her place of burial she had always troubled
herself; which she had appointed and prepared by
the body of her husband. For because they two
had lived so lovingly together, her earnest desire
had still been (as human nature is hardly capable of
divine considerations) to make this addition unto
that happiness, and to have it talked of by the
people; that God had granted unto her, after a long
pilgrimage beyond the seas, to have now at last in her
own native country, the earthly part of both man and
wife covered with the same earth. But when this
empty conceit began, by the fulness of thy goodness,
to be thrust out of her heart, I knew not: but I
rejoiced with much admiration, that I now so plainly
saw it to have done so: though indeed in that

CAP. illo sermone nostro ad fenestram, cum dixit : "iam
XI quid hic facio ?" non apparuit desiderare in patria
mori. audivi etiam postea, quod iam, cum Ostiis
essemus, cum quibusdam amicis meis materna fiducia
conloquebatur quodam die, de contemtu vitae huius
et bono mortis, ubi ipse non aderam, illisque stupen-
tibus virtutem feminae—quoniam tu dederas ei—
quaerentibusque, utrum non formidaret tam longe a
sua civitate corpus relinquere : "nihil" inquit "longe
est deo, neque timendum est, ne ille non agnoscat in
fine saeculi, unde me resuscitet." ergo die nono
aegritudinis suae, quinquagensimo et sexto anno
aetatis suae, tricensimo et tertio aetatis meae, anima
illa religiosa et pia corpore soluta est.

XII

CAP Premebam oculos eius ; et confluebat in praecordia mea
XII maestitudo ingens et transfluebat in lacrimas ; ibidemque oculi mei violento animi imperio resorbebant
fontem suum usque ad siccitatem, et in tali luctamine
valde male mihi erat. tum vero, ubi efflavit extremum, puer Adeodatus exclamavit in planctu, atque
ab omnibus nobis coercitus tacuit. hoc modo etiam
meum quiddam puerile, quod labebatur in fletus
iuvenali voce, voce cordis, coercebatur et tacebat

speech which we had in the window, whenas she CHAP.
said, What do I here any longer? she made show of XI
no desire of dying in her own country. I heard
afterwards also, that in the time we were at Ostia,
how with a matronly confidence she discoursed with
certain of my friends when I was absent, about the
contempt of this life, and of the benefit of death:
they being much astonished at the courage of the
woman, since thou gavest it to her, demanding
of her, whether she were not afraid to leave her
body so far from her own city? Unto which she
replied; Nothing is far from God; nor is it to be
feared lest he should not know at the end of the
world, the place whence he is to raise me up. In
the ninth day therefore of her sickness, and the six
and fiftieth year of her age, and the three and
thirtieth of mine, was that religious and holy soul
released from the body.

XII

He laments his Mother's Death

I CLOSED her eyes: and there flowed withal an un- CHAP.
speakable sorrow into my heart, which overflowed XII
into tears: mine eyes at the same time by the violent
command of my mind, pumped their well dry, and
woe was me in that same agony. Then as soon as she
had breathed her last, the boy Adeodatus brake out
into a loud lamentation; till being pressed by us all,
he held his peace. In like manner also something
childish of mine own, which slipped from me in
tears, restrained by the man's voice, the voice of my
heart, was at last silenced. For fitting we did not

neque enim decere arbitrabamur funus illud questibus lacrimosis gemitibusque celebrare, quia his plerumque solet deplorari quaedam miseria morientium aut quasi omnimoda extinctio. at illa nec misere moriebatur nec omnino moriebatur. hoc et documentis morum eius et fide non ficta rationibusque certis tenebamus.

Quid ergo, quod intus mihi graviter dolebat, nisi ex consuetudine simul vivendi dulcissima et carissima repente dirrupta vulnus recens? gratulabar quidem testimonio eius, quod in ea ipsa ultima aegritudine obsequiis meis interblandiens appellabat me pium; et conmemorabat grandi dilectionis affectu, numquam se audisse ex ore meo iaculatum in se durum aut contumeliosum sonum. sed tamen quid tale, deus meus, qui fecisti nos, quid conparabile habebat honor a me delatus illi et servitus ab illa mihi? quoniam itaque deserebar tam magno eius solacio, sauciabatur anima et quasi dilaniabatur vita, quae una facta erat ex mea et illius.

Cohibito ergo a fletu illo puero, psalterium arripuit Euodius et cantare coepit psalmum. cui respondebamus omnis domus: Misericordiam et iudicium cantabo tibi, domine. audito autem, quid ageretur, convenerunt multi fratres ac religiosae feminae, et de more illis, quorum officium erat, funus curantibus, ego in parte, ubi decenter poteram, cum eis, qui me non

58

think it to solemnize that funeral with lamentations, CHAP.
tears, and howlings; for that this is the fashion XII
whereby those that die miserably, or be utterly
perished as it were, use to be lamented : whereas
she neither died in any miserable condition, nor
indeed died she utterly. For thus much were we
assured of by sure reasons, the witness of her good
conversation and her faith unfeigned.

What might that be therefore which did thus
grievously pain me within, but a wound newly taken,
by having that most sweet and dear custom of living
with her thus suddenly broken off ? I much rejoiced
to receive that testimony from her, whereby in the
latter end of her sickness, mingling her endearments
with my acts of respectful dutifulness, she called me
a dutiful child : mentioning with great affection of
love, how that she never heard any harsh word or
reproachful term to come out of my mouth against
her. But for all this, O my God, that madest us
both, what comparison is there betwixt that honour
that I performed to her, and that slavery of hers
to me ? Because therefore I was left thus desti-
tute of so great a comfort, was my very soul
wounded ; yea, and my life torn in pieces as it
were : which had been made one out of hers and
mine together.

That boy now being stilled from weeping, Euodius
took up the Psalter, and began to sing (the whole
house answering him) the Psalm : I will sing of Ps. ci.
mercy and judgment unto thee O Lord. But when
it was once heard what we were a doing, there came
together very many brethren and religious women :
and whilst they whose office it was, were, as the
manner is, taking order for the burial ; myself in
a part of the house where most properly I could,

59

CAP.
XII

deserendum esse censebant, quod erat tempori congruum disputabam; eoque fomento veritatis mitiga-
bam cruciatum, tibi notum, illis ignorantibus et intente
audientibus et sine sensu doloris me esse arbitrantibus.
at ego in auribus tuis, ubi eorum nullus audiebat,
increpabam mollitiam affectus mei, et constringebam
fluxum maeroris, cedebatque mihi paululum: rur-
susque impetu suo ferebatur, non usque ad eruptionem
lacrimarum nec usque ad vultus mutationem, sed ego
sciebam, quid corde premerem. et quia mihi vehementer displicebat tantum in me posse haec humana,
quae ordine debito et sorte conditionis nostrae acci-
dere necesse est, alio dolore dolebam dolorem meum
et duplici tristitia macerabar.

Cum ecce corpus elatum est, imus, redimus, sine
lacrimis. nam neque in eis precibus, quas tibi fudi-
mus, cum offerretur pro ea sacrificium pretii nostri,
iam iuxta sepulchrum posito cadavere, priusquam de-
poneretur, sicut illic fieri solet, nec in eis ergo precibus flevi: sed toto die graviter in occulto maestus
eram, et mente turbata rogabam te, ut poteram, quo
sanares dolorem meum, nec faciebas, credo, conmen-
dans memoriae meae vel hoc uno documento omnis
consuetudinis vinculum etiam adversus mentem, quae
iam non fallaci verbo pascitur. visum etiam mihi est,

together with those who thought it not fit to leave
me, discoursed upon something which I thought
fittest for the time : by the applying of which
plaster of truth, did I assuage that inward torment,
known only unto thyself; though not by them perceived, who very attentively listing unto me, conceived me to be without all sense of sorrow. But in thy
ears, where none of them overheard me, did I blame
the weakness of my passion, and refrain my flood of
grieving : which giving way a little unto me, did for
all that break forth with his wonted violence upon
me, though not so far as to burst out into tears, nor
to any great change of countenance, yet knew I
well enough what I kept down in my heart. And
for that it very much offended me that these
human respects had such power over me, (which
must in their due order, and out of the vitality
of our natural condition, of necessity come to pass)
I grieved for mine own grief with a new grieving, being by this means afflicted with a double
sorrow.

And behold, whenas the corpse was carried to the
burial, we both went and returned without tears.
For neither in those prayers which we poured forth
unto thee, whenas the Sacrifice of our Redemption
was offered up unto thee for her, the corpse standing
by the grave side, before it was put into the ground
(as the manner there is) did I so much as shed a
tear all the prayer time : yet all that day was I most
sad in secret, and with a troubled mind did I beg of
thee, so well as I could, that thou wouldest mitigate
my sorrow, which for all that thou didst not: impress-
ing, I believe, upon my memory by this one experi-
ment, how strong is the bond of all custom, even upon
that soul which now feeds upon no deceiving word. It

S. AVGVSTINI CONFESSIONVM LIBER IX

ut irem lavatum, quod audieram inde balneis nomen
inditum, quia Graeci βαλανεῖον dixerint, quod anxie-
tatem pellat ex animo.   ecce et hoc confiteor misericordiae tuae, pater orphanorum, quoniam lavi et talis
eram, qualis priusquam lavissem. neque enim exudavit
de corde meo maeroris amaritudo. deinde dormivi, et
vigilavi, et non parva ex parte mitigatum inveni dolorem meum, atque ut eram in lecto meo solus, recordatus sum veridicos versus Ambrosii tui : tu es enim,

> deus, creator omnium
> polique rector vestiens
> diem decoro lumine,
> noctem sopora gratia,
>   artus solutos ut quies
> reddat laboris usui
> mentesque fessas allevet
> luctuque solvat anxios.

Atque inde paulatim reducebam in pristinum sensum ancillam tuam, conversationemque eius piam in
te et sancte in nos blandam atque morigeram, qua
subito destitutus sum, et libuit flere in conspectu
tuo de illa et pro illa, de me et pro me. et dimisi
lacrimas, quas continebam, ut effluerent quantum vellent, substernens eas cordi meo : et requievit in eis,
quoniam ibi erant aures tuae, non cuiusquam hominis superbe interpretantis ploratum meum. et nunc,

62

would, I thought, do me some good to go and bathe
myself; and that because I had heard the bath to take his name from the Greeks calling it βαλανεῖον, for that it drives sadness out of the mind. And this I also confess unto thy mercy, O Father of the fatherless; because that after I had bathed, I was the same man I was before, and that the bitterness of my sorrow could not be sweat out of my heart. I fell to sleep upon it; and upon my waking I found my grief to be not a little abated. Whereupon lying in my bed alone, there came to my mind those true verses of thy Ambrose. For, thou art

As though from βάλλω and ἀνία

> God that all things dost create,
> Who knowst the heavens to moderate,
> And cloth'st the day with beauteous light,
> With benefit of sleep, the night.
>
> Which may our weakened sinews make
> Able new pains to undertake,
> And all our tired minds well ease
> And our distempered griefs appease.

And then again by little and little I recalled my former thoughts of thy handmaid, her devout and holy conversation towards thee, her pleasing and most observant behaviour towards us, of which too suddenly I was now deprived: it gave me some content to weep in thy sight; both concerning her, and for her; concerning myself, and for myself. And I gave way to these tears which I before restrained, to overflow as much as they desired, laying them for a pillow under my heart; and it rested upon them: for there were thy ears, and not the ears of man, who would have scornfully interpreted this my

CAP.
XII
domine, confiteor tibi in litteris. legat qui volet et in-
terpretetur, ut volet, et si peccatum invenerit, flevisse
me matrem exigua parte horae, matrem oculis meis
interim mortuam, quae me multos annos fleverat, ut
oculis tuis viverem, non inrideat, sed potius, si est
grandi caritate, pro peccatis meis fleat ipse ad te,
patrem omnium fratrum Christi tui.

XIII

CAP.
XIII
Ego autem iam sanato corde ab illo vulnere, in quo
postea redargui carnales affectus, fundo tibi, deus
noster, pro illa famula tua longe aliud lacrimarum
genus, quod manat de concusso spiritu, consideratione
periculorum omnis animae, quae in Adam moritur.
quamquam illa in Christo vivificata, etiam nondum
a carne resoluta, sic vixerit, ut laudetur nomen tuum
in fide moribusque eius, non tamen audeo dicere, ex
quo eam per baptismum regenerasti, nullum verbum
exisse ab ore eius contra praeceptum tuum. et dictum est a veritate, filio tuo : Si quis dixerit fratri suo :
fatue, reus erit gehennae ignis ; et vae etiam lauda-
bili vitae hominum, si remota misericordia discutias
eam ! quia omnino non exquiris delicta vehementer,
fiducialiter speramus aliquem apud te locum. quis-

weeping. But now in writing I confess it unto thee, CHAP.
O Lord, read it, who will; and interpret it, how he XII
will: and if he finds me to have offended in bewailing my mother so small a portion of an hour (that
mother, I say, now dead and departed from mine
eyes, who had so many years wept for me, that I
might live in thine eyes,) let him not deride me;
but if he be a man of any great charity, let him
rather weep for my sins unto thee, the Father of all
the brethren of thy Christ.

XIII

He prayeth for his dead Mother

BUT my heart now cured of that wound, (in which CHAP.
afterwards I blamed a carnal kind of affection) I XIII
pour out unto thee, O our God, in behalf of that
handmaid of thine, a far different kind of tears; such
as flow from a broken spirit, out of a serious consideration of the danger of every soul that dieth in
Adam. And notwithstanding she for her part being
quickened in Christ, even before her dissolution from
the flesh, had so lived that there is cause to praise
thy name, both for her faith and conversation; yet
dare I not say for all this, that from the time of thy
regenerating her by Baptism, there issued not from
her mouth any one word or other against thy commandment. Thy Son, who is truth, hath pronounced
it: Whosoever shall say unto his brother, Thou fool, Matt. v. 22
shall be in danger of hell fire: and woe it is even
unto the most commendable life of men, if laying
aside thy mercy, thou shouldst rigorously examine it.
But because thou too narrowly enquirest not after Ps. cxxx. 3

CAP.
XIII

quis autem tibi enumerat vera merita sua, quid tibi enumerat nisi munera tua? o si cognoscant se homines homines, et qui gloriatur, in domino glorietur!

Ego itaque, laus mea et vita mea, deus cordis mei, sepositis paulisper bonis eius actibus, pro quibus tibi gaudens gratias ago, nunc pro peccatis matris meae deprecor te; exaudi me per medicinam vulnerum nostrorum, quae pependit in ligno, et sedens ad dexteram tuam te interpellat pro nobis. scio misericorditer operatam, et ex corde dimisisse debita debitoribus suis: dimitte et tu illi debita sua, si qua etiam contraxit per tot annos post aquam salutis, dimitte, domine, dimitte, obsecro, ne intres cum ea in iudicium. superexultet misericordia iudicio, quoniam eloquia tua vera sunt et promisisti misericordiam misericordibus. quod ut essent, tu dedisti eis, qui misereberis, cui misertus eris, et misericordiam praestabis, cui misericors fueris.

Et, credo, iam feceris quod te rogo, sed voluntaria oris mei adproba, domine. namque illa imminente die resolutionis suae, non cogitavit suum corpus sumptuose contegi aut condi aromatis, aut monumentum electum concupivit aut curavit sepulchrum patrium: non ista mandavit nobis, sed tantummodo memoriam

sins, we assuredly hope to find some place of pardon CHAP. with thee. But whosoever stands to reckon up his XIII own merits unto thee, what reckons he up unto thee but thine own gifts? O that men would know themselves to be but men; and that he that glorieth 2 Cor. x. 17 would glory in the Lord.

I therefore, O my Praise and my Life, thou God of my heart, laying aside for a while her good deeds, for which with rejoicing I give thanks unto thee, do now beseech thee for the sins of my mother. Hearken unto me by him, I entreat thee, that is the true medicine of our wounds, who hung upon the tree, and now sitting at thy right hand maketh inter- Rom. viii. cession for us. I know that she hath dealt merci- 34 fully, and that she hath from her very heart forgiven those that trespassed against her: do thou also forgive her trespasses; whatever she hath drawn upon herself in so many years, since her cleansing by the water of Baptism, forgive her Lord, forgive her, I beseech thee; enter not into judgment with her: let thy mercy be exalted above thy justice, and that because thy words are true, and thou hast Matt. v. 7 promised mercy unto the merciful; which that people might be, was thy gift to them, who wilt have Rom. ix. 18 mercy on whom thou wilt have mercy, and wilt shew deeds of mercy unto whom thou hast been mercifully inclined.

And I now believe that thou hast already done what I request of thee; but take in good part, O Lord, these voluntary petitions of my mouth. For she, the day of her dissolution being at hand, took no thought to have her body sumptuously wound up, or embalmed with spices; nor was she ambitious of any choice monument, or cared to be buried in her own country. These things she gave us no command

CAP sui ad altare tuum fieri desideravit, cui nullius diei
XIII
praetermissione servierat, unde sciret dispensari vic-
timam sanctam, qua deletum est chirographum, quod
erat contrarium nobis, qua triumphatus est hostis
computans delicta nostra, et quaerens, quod obiciat,
et nihil inveniens in illo, in quo vincimus. quis ei
refundet innocentem sanguinem ? quis ei restituet
pretium, quo nos emit, ut nos auferat ei ? ad cuius
pretii nostri sacramentum ligavit ancilla tua animam
suam vinculo fidei. nemo a protectione tua dir-
rumpat eam. non se interponat nec vi nec insidiis leo
et draco : neque enim respondebit illa nihil se debere,
ne convincatur et obtineatur ab accusatore callido,
sed respondebit dimissa debita sua ab eo, cui nemo
reddet, quod pro nobis non debens reddidit.

Sit ergo in pace cum viro, ante quem nulli et post
quem nulli nupta est, cui servivit fructum tibi afferens
cum tolerantia, ut eum quoque lucraretur tibi. et
inspira, domine meus, deus meus, inspira servis tuis,
fratribus meis, filiis tuis, dominis meis, quibus et
corde et voce et litteris servio, ut quotquot hoc lege-
rint, meminerint ad altare tuum Monnicae, famulae
tuae, cum Patricio, quondam eius coniuge, per quorum carnem introduxisti me in hanc vitam, quemadmodum nescio. meminerint cum affectu pio parentum

for; but desired only to have her name commemo- CHAP. XIII
rated at thy Altar, which she had served without
intermission of one day; from whence she knew that
holy Sacrifice to be dispensed, by which that hand-
writing that was against us, is blotted out; through Col. ii. 14
which Sacrifice the enemy was triumphed over; he,
who summing up our offences, and seeking for something to lay to our charge, found nothing in him, in John xiv.
whom we are conquerors. Who shall restore unto 30
him his innocent blood? Who shall repay him the
price with which he bought us, and so be able
to take us out of his hands? Unto the Sacrament
of which price of our Redemption this handmaid of
thine had bound her own soul by the bond of faith.
Let none pluck her away from thy protection: let
neither the lion nor the dragon interpose himself by
force or fraud. For she will not answer that she
owes nothing, lest she be disproved and gotten the
better of by that crafty accuser: but she will answer,
now that her sins are forgiven her by him, unto
whom none is able to repay that price which he who
owed nothing laid down for us.

Let her rest therefore in peace together with her
husband, before, or after whom, she had never any
other: whom she obeyed, through patience bringing
forth fruit unto thee, that she might bring him also
unto thee. And inspire, O Lord my God, inspire
thy servants, my brethren thy sons, my masters,
whom with voice, and heart, and pen I serve, that so
many of them as shall read these Confessions, may at
thy Altar remember Monnica thy handmaid, together
with Patricius her sometimes husband, by whose
bodies thou broughtest me into this life, though how
I know not. May they with devout affection be
mindful of these parents of mine in this transitory

S. AVGVSTINI CONFESSIONVM LIBER IX

meorum in hac luce transitoria, et fratrum meorum
sub te patre in matre catholica, et civium meorum
in aeterna Hierusalem, cui suspirat peregrinatio populi tui ab exitu usque ad reditum,
ut quod a me illa poposcit extremum
uberius ei praestetur in multo-
rum orationibus per confessiones quam per ora-
tiones meas.

life, and of my brethren that are under thee our
Father in our Catholic mother: and of those
who are to be my fellow citizens in that eternal
Jerusalem, which thy people here in their pilgrimage so sigh after even from their birth
unto their return thither: that so what
my mother in her last words desired
of me, may be fulfilled for her in
the prayers of many, more
plentifully through my
Confessions than
through my
prayers.

BOOK X

LIBER DECIMVS.

I

CAP.
I Cognoscam te, cognitor meus, cognoscam, sicut et cognitus sum. virtus animae meae, intra in eam et coapta tibi, ut habeas et possideas sine macula et ruga. haec est mea spes, ideo loquor et in ea spe gaudeo, quando sanum gaudeo. cetera vero vitae huius tanto minus flenda, quanto magis fletur, et tanto magis flenda, quanto minus fletur in eis. ecce enim veritatem dilexisti, quoniam qui facit eam, venit ad lucem. volo eam facere in corde meo coram te in confessione, in stilo autem meo coram multis testibus.

II

CAP.
II Et tibi quidem, domine, cuius oculis nuda est abyssus humanae conscientiae, quid occultum esset in me, etiamsi nollem confiteri tibi? te enim mihi absconderem, non me tibi. nunc autem quod gemitus meus testis est displicere me mihi, tu refulges et places et amaris et desideraris, ut erubescam de me et abiciam

74

THE TENTH BOOK

I

The Confessions of the Heart

LET me know thee, O Lord, who knowest me : let me know thee as I am known of thee. O thou the Virtue of my soul, make thy entrance into it, and so fit it for thyself, that thou mayest have and hold it without spot or wrinkle. This is my hope, and therefore do I now rejoice, when I rejoice healthfully. As for other things of this life, they deserve so much the less to be lamented, by how much the more we do lament them : and again, so much the more to be lamented, by how much the less we do lament them. For behold, thou hast loved truth, and he that doth it, cometh to the light. This will I do before thee in the confession of my heart; and in my writings before many witnesses.

II

Secret Things are known unto God

AND from thee, O Lord, unto whose eyes the bottom of man's conscience is laid bare, what could be hidden in me though I would not confess it ? For so should I hide thee from me, not myself from thee. But now, for that my groaning is witness for me that I am displeased with myself, thou shinest out unto me, and art pleasing to me, yea, longed for and beloved of me : so that I am ashamed of myself, yea, and I

CAP.
II

me atque eligam te, et nec tibi nec mihi placeam nisi
de te. tibi ergo, domine, manifestus sum, quicumque sim. et quo fructu tibi confitear, dixi. neque
id ago verbis carnis et vocibus, sed verbis animae et
clamore cogitationis, quem novit auris tua. cum enim
malus sum, nihil est aliud confiteri tibi quam displicere mihi; cum vero pius, nihil est aliud confiteri
tibi quam hoc non tribuere mihi : quoniam tu, domine,
benedicis iustum, sed prius eum iustificas impium.
confessio itaque mea, deus meus, in conspectu tuo
tibi tacite fit et non tacite. tacet enim strepitu,
clamat affectu. neque enim dico recti aliquid hominibus, quod non a me tu prius audieris, aut etiam tu
aliquid tale audis a me, quod non mihi tu prius
dixeris.

III

CAP.
III

Quid mihi ergo est cum hominibus, ut audiant confessiones meas, quasi ipsi sanaturi sint omnes languores meos? curiosum genus ad cognoscendam
vitam alienam, desidiosum ad corrigendam suam.
quid a me quaerunt audire qui sim, qui nolunt a te
audire qui sint? et unde sciunt, cum a me ipso de
me ipso audiunt, an verum dicam, quandoquidem

renounce mine own self and make choice of thee; CHAP.
and never please thee or myself, but of thee. Unto II
thee therefore, O Lord, I am laid open, whatever I
am; and with what fruit I confess unto thee, I
have before spoken. Nor do I it with words and
speeches of the body, but with the words of my
soul, and the cry of my thoughts, which thy ear
understandeth. For when I am wicked, then to
confess unto thee is no other thing but to displease
myself: but when I am well given, to confess unto
thee is no other thing but not to attribute this goodness unto myself: because it is thou, O Lord, that
blessest the just, but first thou justifiest him being
wicked. My confession therefore, O my God, in
thy sight is made unto thee silently: and yet not
silently; for in respect of noise it is silent, but yet it
cries aloud in respect of my affection. For neither
do I utter anything that is right unto men, which
thyself hath not before heard from me: nor dost
thou hear any such thing from me, which thyself
hast not first said unto me.

III

The Confession of our ill deeds, what it helps us

WHAT therefore have I to do with men, that they CHAP.
should hear my confessions, as if they would cure III
all my infirmities? A curious people to pry into
another man's life, but slothful enough to amend
their own. Why do they desire to hear from me
what I am, who will not hear from thee what themselves are? And how know they whenas they hear
myself confessing of myself, whether I say true or
no; seeing none knows what is in man, but the 1 Cor. ii. 11

nemo scit hominum, quid agatur in homine, nisi
spiritus hominis, qui in ipso est? si autem a te
audiant de se ipsis, non poterunt dicere: "mentitur
dominus." quid est enim a te audire de se nisi
cognoscere se? quis porro cognoscit et dicit:
"falsum est," nisi ipse mentiatur? sed quia caritas
omnia credit, (inter eos utique, quos conexos sibimet
unum facit,) ego quoque, domine, etiam sic tibi confiteor, ut audiant homines, quibus demonstrare non
possum, an vera confitear; sed credunt mihi, quorum
mihi aures caritas aperit.

Verum tamen tu, medice meus intime, quo fructu
ista faciam, eliqua mihi. nam confessiones praeteritorum malorum meorum, (quae remisisti et texisti,
ut beares me in te, mutans animam meam fide et
sacramento tuo,) cum leguntur et audiuntur, excitant
cor, ne dormiat in desperatione et dicat: "non
possum," sed evigilet in amore misericordiae tuae et
dulcedine gratiae tuae, qua potens est omnis infirmus,
qui sibi per ipsam fit conscius infirmitatis suae. et
delectat bonos audire praeterita mala eorum, qui iam
carent eis, nec ideo delectat, quia mala sunt, sed quia
fuerunt et non sunt. quo itaque fructu, domine meus,
cui cotidie confitetur conscientia mea, spe misericordiae tuae securior quam innocentia sua, quo fructu,
quaeso, etiam hominibus coram te confiteor per has
litteras, adhuc quis ego sim, non quis fuerim? nam

spirit of man which is in himself? But if they hear
from thee anything concerning themselves, they
cannot say, The Lord lieth. For what else is it from
thee to hear of themselves, but to know themselves?
And who is he that knowing himself, can say, It
is false, unless himself lies? But because charity
believeth all things; (that is to say, amongst those
whom by knitting unto itself it maketh one) I therefore, O Lord, do also confess unto thee, as that
men may hear: to whom though I be not able to
demonstrate whether I confess truly; yet give they
credit unto me, whose ears charity hath set open
unto me.

But do thou, O my most private Physician, make
apparent unto me what fruit I may reap by doing it.
For the confessions of my past sins (which thou hast
forgiven and covered, that thou mightest make me
happy in thee, in changing my life by thy faith and
sacrament) whenas they read and hear, they stir up
the heart that it may not sleep in despair, and say:
I cannot; but that it may keep wakeful in the love of
thy mercy, and the sweetness of thy grace: by which
every weak person is made strong, who is by it made
conscious to himself of his own infirmity. As for those
that are good, they take delight to hear of their past
errors, (those I mean that are now freed from them;)
yet are they not therefore delighted because they
are errors; but for that for that they having so been,
are not so now. Then with what fruit, O Lord my
God, to whom my conscience (more secure upon
the hope of thy mercy, than in her own innocency)
maketh her daily confession, with what fruit, I
beseech thee, do I by this book before thee also
confess unto men, what at this time I now am, not
what I have been? For, as for that fruit, I have

CAP.
III
illum fructum vidi et conmemoravi. sed quis adhuc sim, ecce in ipso tempore confessionum mearum, et multi hoc nosse cupiunt, qui me noverunt, et non me noverunt, qui ex me vel de me aliquid audierunt, sed auris eorum non est ad cor meum, ubi ego sum quicumque sum. volunt ergo audire confitente me, quid ipse intus sim, quo nec oculum nec aurem nec mentem possunt intendere; credituri tamen volunt, numquid cognituri? dicit enim eis caritas, qua boni sunt, non mentiri me de me confitentem, et ipsa in eis credit mihi.

IV

CAP.
IV
SED quo fructu id volunt? an congratulari mihi cupiunt, cum audierint, quantum ad te accedam munere tuo, et orare pro me, cum audierint, quantum retarder pondere meo? indicabo me talibus. non enim parvus est fructus, domine deus meus, ut a multis tibi gratiae agantur de nobis et a multis rogeris pro nobis. amet in me fraternus animus quod amandum doces, et doleat in me quod dolendum doces. animus ille hoc faciat fraternus, non extraneus, non filiorum alienorum, quorum os locutum est vanitatem, et dextera eorum dextera iniquitatis, sed fraternus ille, qui cum approbat me, gaudet de me,

both seen and spoken of it: but as for what I now am, behold, yea in the very time of the making of these Confessions, divers people desire to know, both they that personally know me, and those also that do not, they that have heard anything either from me or of me: but their ear is not at my heart, wherever or whatever I am. They are desirous therefore to hear me confess what I am within; whither neither their eye, nor ear, nor understanding is able to dive; they desire it, as ready to believe me, but will they know me? For that charity, by which they are made good, says unto them, that I would never belie myself in my Confessions. And 'tis that charity in them which gives credit to me.

IV

Of the great Fruit of Confession

BUT for what fruit would they hear this? Do they desire to congratulate with me, whenas they shall hear how near (by thy grace) I am now come unto thee? And to pray for me, when they shall once hear how much I am cast behind by mine own heaviness? To such will I discover myself: for it is no mean fruit, O Lord my God, that by many 2 Cor. i. 11 thanks should be given unto thee on our behalf, and thou be entreated for us by many. Let the brotherly mind love that in me, which thou teachest is to be loved: and lament in me, what thou teachest is to be lamented. Let the brotherly mind, not that of strangers, not that of the strange children, whose Ps. cxliv. 11 mouth talketh vanity, and their right hand is a right hand of iniquity; but that brotherly mind which when it approveth of me, doth also rejoice for me; and when

cum autem improbat me, contristatur pro me, quia sive approbet sive improbet me, diligit me. indicabo me talibus: respirent in bonis meis, suspirent in malis meis. bona mea instituta tua sunt et dona tua, mala mea delicta mea sunt et iudicia tua. respirent in illis et suspirent in his, et hymnus et fletus ascendant in conspectum tuum de fraternis cordibus, turibulis tuis. tu autem, domine, delectatus odore sancti templi tui, miserere mei secundum magnam misericordiam tuam, propter nomen tuum, et nequaquam deserens coepta tua consumma imperfecta mea.

Hic est fructus confessionum mearum, non qualis fuerim, sed qualis sim, ut hoc confitear non tantum coram te secreta exultatione cum tremore, et secreto maerore cum spe, sed etiam in auribus credentium filiorum hominum, sociorum gaudii mei et consortium mortalitatis meae, civium meorum et mecum peregrinorum, praecedentium et consequentium et comitum viae meae. hi sunt servi tui, fratres mei, quos filios tuos esse voluisti, dominos meos, quibus iussisti ut serviam, si volo tecum de te vivere. et hoc mihi verbum tuum parum erat si loquendo praeciperet, nisi et faciendo praeiret. et ego id ago factis et dictis, id ago sub alis tuis, nimis cum ingenti periculo, nisi quia sub alis tuis tibi subdita est anima mea et infirmitas mea tibi nota est. parvulus sum, sed vivit semper pater meus et idoneus est mihi tutor meus ;

it disapproveth is sorry for me: because whether it CHAP.
approveth or disapproveth, it loveth me. To such will   IV
I discover myself: let them breathe freely at my good
deeds, and sigh for my ill. My good deeds are thine
appointments and thy gifts: my evil ones are my own
faults, and thy judgments. Let them breathe freely
at the one, sigh at the other; and let now both
thanksgiving and bewailing ascend up into thy sight,
out of the hearts of my brethren, which are thy
censers. And when thou, O Lord, art once delighted
with the incense of thy holy Temple, have mercy Ps. li. 1
upon me according to thy great mercy, for thine own
name's sake: and no ways giving over what thou hast
begun in me, finish up what in me is imperfect.

This is the fruit of my Confessions, not of what
I have been, but of what I am: namely, to confess this not before thee only, in a secret rejoicing
mixed with trembling, and in a secret sorrowfulness
allayed with hope: but in the ears also of the believing sons of men, sharers of my joy, and partners in
mortality with me; my fellow citizens, and fellow
pilgrims: both those that are gone before, and those
that are to follow after me, and those too that accom-
pany me along in this life. These are thy servants,
my brethren; those whom thou hast willed to be thy
sons; my masters whom thou hast commanded me to
serve, if I would live with thee and of thee. But this
thy saying were little, did it give the command only
by speaking, and not go before me in performing.
This therefore I now do both in deed and word:
this I do under thy wings; and that with too
much danger, were not my soul sheltered under thy
wings, and my infirmity known unto thee. I am but
a little one; but my Father liveth for ever, and my
Protector is sufficient for me. For 'tis the very same he

CAP.
IV
idem ipse est enim, qui genuit me et tuetur me, et tu ipse es omnia bona mea, tu omnipotens, qui mecum es et priusquam tecum sim. indicabo ergo talibus, qualibus iubes ut serviam, non quis fuerim, sed quis iam sim et quis adhuc sim; sed neque me ipsum diiudico. sic itaque audiar.

V

CAP.
V
Tu enim, domine, diiudicas me, quia etsi nemo scit hominum, quae sunt hominis, nisi spiritus hominis, qui in ipso est, tamen est aliquid hominis, quod nec ipse scit spiritus hominis, qui in ipso est, tu autem, domine, scis eius omnia, qui fecisti eum. ego vero quamvis prae tuo conspectu me despiciam, et aestimem me terram et cinerem, tamen aliquid de te scio, quod de me nescio. et certe videmus nunc per speculum in aenigmate, nondum facie ad faciem; et ideo, quamdiu peregrinor abs te, mihi sum praesentior quam tibi; et tamen te novi nullo modo posse violari; ego vero quibus temptationibus resistere valeam quibusve non valeam, nescio. et spes est, quia fidelis es, qui nos non sinis temptari supra quam possumus ferre, sed facis cum temptatione etiam exitum, ut possimus sustinere. confitear ergo quid de me sciam, confitear et quid de me nesciam, quoniam et quod de

that begat me, and that defends me : and thou thyself CHAP.
art all my goods ; even thou, O Omnipotent, who art IV
present with me, and that before I am come unto
thee. To such therefore, will I discover myself,
whom thou commandest me to serve : not discovering what I have been, but what I now am, and what
I am yet. But I do not judge myself. Thus there- 1 Cor. iv. 3
fore let me be heard.

V

That Man knoweth not himself thoroughly : and
knows not God but in a glass darkly

For thou, O Lord, dost judge me : because, that CHAP.
although no man knows the things of a man, but the V
spirit of man which is in him; yet is there some 1 Cor. ii. 11
thing of man, that the very spirit of man that is in
him, knoweth not. But thou knowest all of him,
who hast made him. As for me, though in thy sight
I despise myself, accounting myself but dust and
ashes; yet know I something of thee, which I know
not of myself. For surely, now we see through a 1 Cor. xiii.
glass darkly, not face to face as yet : so long there- 12
fore as I be absent from thee, I am nearer unto my- 2 Cor. v. 6
self than unto thee; and yet know I thee not possible
to be any ways violated : whereas for myself, I neither See above,
know what temptations I am able to resist, or what Bk. VII. ii.
I am not. But there is hope, because thou art faithful, who wilt not suffer us to be tempted above that 1 Cor. x. 13
we are able : but wilt with the temptation also make
a way to escape, that we may be able to bear it. I
will confess therefore; what I know by myself will I
confess, yea, and what I know not. And that because

CAP.
V
me scio, te mihi lucente scio, et quod de me nescio, tamdiu nescio, donec fiant tenebrae meae sicut meridies in vultu tuo.

VI

CAP.
VI
Non dubia, sed certa conscientia, domine, amo te. percussisti cor meum verbo tuo, et amavi te. sed et caelum et terra et omnia, quae in eis sunt, ecce undique mihi dicunt, ut te amem, nec cessant dicere omnibus, ut sint inexcusabiles. altius autem tu misereberis, cui misertus eris, et misericordiam praestabis, cui misericors fueris: alioquin caelum et terra surdis locuntur laudes tuas. quid autem amo, cum te amo? non speciem corporis nec decus temporis, non candorem lucis ecce istum amicum oculis, non dulces melodias cantilenarum omnimodarum, non florum et ungentorum et aromatum suaveolentiam, non manna et mella, non membra acceptabilia carnis amplexibus: non haec amo, cum amo deum meum. et tamen amo quandam lucem et quandam vocem et quendam odorem et quendam cibum et quendam amplexum, cum amo deum meum, lucem, vocem, odorem, cibum, amplexum interioris hominis mei, ubi fulget animae meae,

what I do know of myself, by thy showing it me, I
come to know it : and what I know not of myself, I
am so long ignorant of, until my darkness be made
as the noon day in thy countenance.

VI

What God is, and how known

NOT out of a doubtful, but with a certain conscience
do I love thee, O Lord : thou hast stricken my heart
with thy word, and thereupon I loved thee. Yea,
also the heaven, and the earth, and all that is in
them, behold they bid me on every side that I should
love thee ; nor cease they to say so to all, to make them
inexcusable. But more profoundly wilt thou have
mercy on whom thou wilt have mercy, and wilt have
compassion upon whom thou wilt have compassion :
for else do the heaven and the earth speak forth thy
praises unto the deaf. What now do I love, whenas
I love thee ? Not the beauty of any corporal thing ;
not the order of times, not the brightness of the
light which we do behold, so gladsome to our eyes :
not the pleasant melodies of songs of all kinds ;
nor the fragrant smell of flowers, and ointment, and
spices : not manna and honey ; nor any fair limbs
that are so acceptable to fleshly embracements. I
love none of these things whenas I love my God :
and yet I love a certain kind of light, and a kind of
voice, and a kind of fragrance, and a kind of meat,
and a kind of embracement, whenas I love my God ;
who is both the light and the voice, and the sweet
smell, and the meat, and the embracement of my
inner man : where that light shineth into my soul,

CAP. VI quod non capit locus, et ubi sonat, quod non rapit tempus, et ubi olet, quod non spargit flatus, et ubi sapit, quod non minuit edacitas, et ubi haeret, quod non divellit satietas. hoc est quod amo, cum deum meum amo.

Et quid est hoc? interrogavi terram, et dixit: "non sum"; et quaecumque in eadem sunt, idem confessa sunt. interrogavi mare et abyssos et reptilia animarum vivarum, et responderunt: "non sumus deus tuus; quaere super nos." interrogavi auras flabiles, et inquit universus aer cum incolis suis: "fallitur Anaximenes; non sum deus." interrogavi caelum, solem, lunam, stellas: "neque nos sumus deus, quem quaeris," inquiunt. et dixi omnibus, quae circumstant fores carnis meae: "dicite mihi de deo meo, quod vos non estis, dicite mihi de illo aliquid." et exclamaverunt voce magna: "ipse fecit nos." interrogatio mea intentio mea, et responsio eorum species eorum. et direxi me ad me et dixi mihi: "tu quis es?" et respondi: "homo." et ecce corpus et anima in me mihi praesto sunt, unum exterius et alterum interius. quid horum est, unde quaerere debui deum meum, quem iam quaesiveram per corpus a terra usque ad caelum, quousque potui mittere nuntios radios oculorum meorum? sed melius quod interius. ei quippe renuntiabant omnes nuntii corporales praesidenti et iudicanti de responsionibus caeli et terrae et omnium, quae in eis sunt, dicentium: "non sumus deus" et: "ipse fecit nos."

which no place can receive; that voice soundeth, CHAP.
VI which time deprives me not of; and that fragrancy smelleth, which no wind scatters; and that meat tasteth, which eating devours not; and that embracement clingeth to me, which satiety divorceth not. This it is which I love, whenas I love my God.

And what is this? I asked the earth, and that answered me: I am not it; and whatsoever are in it made the same confession. I asked the sea and the deeps, and the creeping things, and they answered me: We are not thy God, seek above us. I asked the fleeting winds, and the whole air with his inhabitants answered me, That Anaximenes was A. held that deceived; I am not God. I asked the heavens, the the air was sun and moon and stars: Nor, say they, are we the ment God whom thou seekest. And I replied unto all these, which stand so round about these doors of my flesh: Answer me concerning my God, since that you are not he, answer me something of him. And they cried out with a loud voice: He made us. My questioning with them was my thought; and their answer was their beauty. And I turned myself unto myself, and said to myself: Who art thou? And I answered: A man; for behold here is a soul and a body in me; one without, and the other within. By which of these two ought I to have sought my God, whom by my body I had enquired after from earth to heaven, even so far as I was able to send those beams of mine eyes in ambassage? But the better part is the inner part; unto which all these my bodily messengers gave up their intelligence, as being the president and judge of all the several answers of heaven and earth, and of all things that are therein, who said, We are not God, and He made us. These things did my inner man know by the

CAP. homo interior cognovit haec per exterioris ministe-
VI rium; ego interior cognovi haec, ego, ego animus
per sensum corporis mei. interrogavi mundi molem
de deo meo, et respondit mihi: " ñon ego sum, sed
ipse me fecit."

Nonne omnibus, quibus integer sensus est, apparet
haec species? cur non omnibus eadem loquitur?
animalia pusilla et magna vident eam, sed interrogare
nequeunt. non enim praeposita est in eis nuntiantibus
sensibus iudex ratio. homines autem possunt interrogare, ut invisibilia dei per ea, quae facta sunt,
intellecta conspiciant, sed amore subduntur eis et
subditi iudicare non possunt. nec respondent ista
interrogantibus nisi iudicantibus, nec vocem suam
mutant, id est speciem suam, si alius tantum videat,
alius autem videns interroget, ut aliter illi appareat,
aliter huic, sed eodem modo utrique apparens illi
muta est, huic loquitur: immo vero omnibus loquitur,
sed illi intellegunt, qui eius vocem acceptam foris
intus cum veritate conferunt. veritas enim dicit
mihi: "non est deus tuus caelum et terra neque omne
corpus." hoc dicit eorum natura. vident: moles est
minor in parte quam in toto. iam tu melior es, tibi
dico, anima, quoniam tu vegetas molem corporis tui
praebens ei vitam, quod nullum corpus praestat
corpori. deus autem tuus etiam tibi vitae vita est.

ministry of the outer man. And I the inner man
knew all this; I, I the soul, by means of the senses
of the body. I asked the whole frame of the world
concerning my God, and that answered me : I am
not he, but he made me.

Doth not this corporeal figure evidently appear to
all those that have their perfect senses? Why then
speaks it not the same things to all? The creatures
both great and small do see this corporeal figure well
enough, but they are not able to ask any questions of it : because reason is not president over
their senses to judge on what they report. But
men are well able to ask, that so they may clearly
see the invisible things of God, which are under- Rom. i. 20
stood by the things that are made. But by inor-
dinate love of them, they make themselves subjects
unto them : and subjects are not fit to judge. Nor
will the creatures answer to such as ask of them,
unless the askers be able to judge : nor so much as
alter their voice, (that is their outward appearance) if
so be one man only sees, another seeing it asks, so as
to appear one way to this man, and another way to
that man : but appearing the same way unto both,
it is dumb to this man, speaks unto that. Nay,
verily, it speaks unto all; but they only understand it
who compare that voice received from without by the
senses, with the truth which is within. For truth says
unto me: Neither heaven, nor earth, nor any other
body is thy God. This their very nature says. They
behold : there is less bulk in the part of a thing,
than in the whole. Now unto thee I speak, O my
soul. Thou art my better part ; for thou quickenest
this bulk of my body, by giving life unto it, which no
body can give unto a body : but thy God is the life of
thy life unto thee.

VII

CAP.
VII
Quid ergo amo, cum deum amo? quis est ille super
caput animae meae? per ipsam animam meam ascen-
dam ad illum. transibo vim meam, qua haereo
corpori et vitaliter compagem eius repleo. non ea
vi reperio deum meum: nam reperiret et equus et
mulus, quibus non est intellectus, et est eadem vis,
qua vivunt etiam eorum corpora. est alia vis, non
solum qua vivifico sed etiam qua sensifico carnem
meam, quam mihi fabricavit dominus, iubens oculo,
ut non audiat, et auri, ut non videat, sed illi, per
quem videam, huic, per quam audiam, et propria
singillatim ceteris sensibus sedibus et officiis suis:
quae diversa per eos ago unus ego animus. transibo
et istam vim meam; nam et hanc habet equus et
mulus: sentiunt etiam ipsi per corpus.

VIII

CAP.
VIII
Transibo ergo et istam naturae meae, gradibus ascendens ad eum, qui fecit me, et venio in campos et
lata praetoria memoriae, ubi sunt thesauri innumera-

VII

God is not to be found by any Ability in our Bodies

WHAT is it therefore which I love whenas I love my God? Who is he that is above the top of my soul? By this very soul will I ascend up unto him; · I will soar beyond that faculty of mine, by which I am united unto my body, and by which I fill the whole frame of it with life. I cannot by that faculty find my God; for so the horse and mule that have no understanding might as well find him; seeing they have the same faculty by which their bodies live also. But another faculty there is, not that only by which I give life, but that too by which I give sense unto my flesh, which the Lord hath framed for me: commanding the eye not to hear, and the ear not to see, but the eye for me to see by, and this for me to hear withal; assigning what is proper to the other senses severally, in their own seats and offices; which being divers through every sense, yet I the soul being but one, do actuate and govern. I will, I say, mount beyond this faculty of mine; for even the horse and mule have this, seeing they also are sensible in their bodies.

CHAP. VII

Ps. xxxii. 9

VIII

The Force of the Memory

I WILL soar therefore beyond this faculty of my nature, still rising by degrees unto him who hath made both me and that nature. And I come into these fields and spacious palaces of my memory, where the

CHAP. VIII

93

CAP.
VIII

bilium imaginum de cuiuscemodi rebus sensis invec-
tarum. ibi reconditum est, quidquid etiam cogitamus,
vel augendo vel minuendo vel utcumque variando ea
quae sensus attigerit, et si quid aliud commendatum
et repositum est, quod nondum absorbuit et sepelivit
oblivio. ibi quando sum, posco, ut proferatur quidquid volo, et quaedam statim prodeunt, quaedam
requiruntur diutius et tamquam de abstrusioribus
quibusdam receptaculis eruuntur, quaedam catervatim
se proruunt et, dum aliud petitur et quaeritur, pro-
siliunt in medium quasi dicentia: "ne forte nos
sumus?" et abigo ea manu cordis a facie recordationis meae, donec enubiletur quod volo atque in
conspectum prodeat ex abditis. alia faciliter atque
inperturbata serie sicut poscuntur suggeruntur, et
cedunt praecedentia consequentibus, et cedendo
conduntur, iterum cum voluero processura. quod
totum fit, cum aliquid narro memoriter.

Vbi sunt omnia distincte generatimque servata,
quae suo quaeque aditu ingesta sunt, sicut lux atque
omnes colores formaeque corporum per oculos, per
aures autem omnia genera sonorum omnesque odores
per aditum narium, omnes sapores per oris aditum,
a sensu autem totius corporis, quid durum, quid molle,
quid calidum frigidumve, lene aut asperum, grave
seu leve sive extrinsecus sive intrinsecus corpori.

treasures of innumerable forms brought into it from CHAP.
these things that have been perceived by the senses VIII
be hoarded up. There is laid up whatsoever besides
we think, either by way of enlarging or diminishing,
or any other ways varying of those things which the
sense hath come at : yea, and if there be anything
recommended to it and there laid up, which forgetfulness hath not swallowed up and buried. To this
treasury whenever I have recourse, I demand to have
anything brought forth whatsoever I will : whereupon some things come out presently, and others
must be longer enquired after, which are fetched, as
it were, out of some more secret receptacles : other
things rush out in troops ; and while a quite contrary
thing is desired and required, they start forth, as
who should say : Lest peradventure it should be we that
are called for. These I drive away with the hand of
my heart from the face of my remembrance ; until
that at last be discovered which I desire, appearing
in sight out of its hidden cells. Other things are
supplied more easily and without disorder, just as they
are desired : former notions giving way to the following, by which giving way are they laid up again, to be
forthcoming whenever I will have them. Which takes
place all together, whenas I repeat anything by heart.

Where are all things distinctly and under general
heads preserved, according to the several gates that
each notion hath been brought in at ? as, (for example)
light and all colours and forms of bodies brought in
by the eyes : and by the ears all sorts of sounds : and
all smells by the nostrils ; all tastes by the gate of
the mouth : and by the sense which belongs to the
whole body, is brought in whatsoever is hard or soft :
whatsoever is hot or cold ; whatsoever is smooth or
rugged, heavy or light, in respect of the body either

CAP.
VIII

haec omnia recipit recolenda, cum opus est, et retractanda grandis memoriae recessus et nescio qui secreti atque ineffabiles sinus eius : quae omnia suis quaeque foribus intrant ad eam et reponuntur in ea. nec ipsa tamen intrant, sed rerum sensarum imagines illic praesto sunt cogitationi reminiscentis eas. quae quomodo fabricatae sint, quis dicit, cum appareat, quibus sensibus raptae sint interiusque reconditae ? nam et in tenebris atque in silentio dum habito, in memoria mea profero, si volo, colores, et discerno inter album et nigrum et inter quos alios volo, nec incurrunt soni atque perturbant quod per oculos haustum considero, cum et ipsi ibi sint et quasi seorsum repositi lateant. nam et ipsos posco, si placet, atque adsunt illico, et quiescente lingua ac silente gutture canto quantum volo, imaginesque illae colorum, quae nihilo minus ibi sunt, non se interponunt neque interrumpunt, cum thesaurus alius retractatur, qui influxit ab auribus. ita cetera, quae per sensus ceteros ingesta atque congesta sunt, recordor prout libet et auram liliorum discerno a violis nihil olfaciens, et mel defrito, lene aspero, nihil tum gustando neque contractando, sed reminiscendo antepono.

Intus haec ago, in aula ingenti memoriae meae.

outwardly or inwardly: all these doth that great CHAP
receipt of the memory receive in her many secret VIII
and inexpressible windings, to be forthcoming, and
to be called for again, whenas need so requireth,
each entering in by his own port, and there
laid up in it. And yet do not the things themselves enter the memory; only the images of the
things perceived by the senses are ready there
at hand, whenever the thoughts will recall them.
Which images who can tell how they came to be
formed, notwithstanding it plainly appears by which
of the senses each hath been fetched in and locked
up? For even whilst I dwell in the darkness and
silence, yet into my memory can I draw colours, if
I please, and can discern betwixt black and white,
and what others I desire; nor yet do sounds break
in and disturb that notion drawn in by mine eyes,
which I am now considering upon: seeing these
sounds be in the memory too, and laid up as it
were apart by themselves. For I can call for them
if I please, and they present themselves to me at
an instant; and though my tongue be quiet, and
my throat silent, yet can I sing as much as I will.
Nor do the images of those colours which notwithstanding be then there, now encroach and interrupt
me, when another piece of treasure is called for which
came in by the ears. And thus all other things
brought in and laid up by other of the senses, do I
call to remembrance at my pleasure. Yea, I discern
the breath of lilies from that of violets, though at
the instant I smell nothing: and I prefer honey
before sweet wine, smooth before rough; though
at that time I neither taste, nor handle, but remember
only.

All this do I within, in that huge court of my

ibi enim mihi caelum et terra et mare praesto sunt
cum omnibus, quae in eis sentire potui, praeter illa,
quae oblitus sum. ibi mihi et ipse occurro, meque
recolo, quid, quando et ubi egerim quoque modo,
cum agerem, affectus fuerim. ibi sunt omnia, quae
sive experta a me sive credita memini. ex eadem
copia etiam similitudines rerum vel expertarum vel
ex eis, quas expertus sum, creditarum alias atque
alias et ipse contexo praeteritis; atque ex his etiam
futuras actiones et eventa et spes, et haec omnia
rursus quasi praesentia meditor. "faciam hoc et
illud" dico apud me in ipso ingenti sinu animi mei
pleno tot et tantarum rerum imaginibus, et hoc aut
illud sequitur. "o si esset hoc aut illud!" "avertat
deus hoc aut illud!": dico apud me ista, et cum
dico, praesto sunt imagines omnium quae dico ex
eodem thesauro memoriae, nec omnino aliquid eorum
dicerem, si defuissent.

Magna ista vis est memoriae, magna nimis, deus,
penetrale amplum et infinitum: quis ad fundum eius
pervenit? et vis est haec animi mei atque ad meam
naturam pertinet, nec ego ipse capio totum, quod
sum. ergo animus ad habendum se ipsum angustus
est: ut ubi sit quod sui non capit? numquid extra
ipsum ac non in ipso? quomodo ergo non capit?
multa mihi super hoc oboritur admiratio, stupor ad-
prehendit me. et eunt homines mirari alta montium,
et ingentes fluctus maris, et latissimos lapsus fluminum,

memory. For there have I in a readiness the heaven, the earth, the sea, and whatever I could perceive in them, besides those which I have forgotten. There also meet I with myself; I recall myself, what, where, or when I have done a thing; and how I was affected when I did it. There be all whatever I remember, either upon mine own experience, or on others' credit. Out of the same store do I myself combine fresh and fresh likelihoods of things, which I have experienced, or believed upon experience: and by these do I infer actions to come, events and hopes: and upon all these again do I meditate, as if they were now present. I will do this or that (say I to myself in that great receipt of my soul, stored with images of things so many and so great), and this or that follows. Oh that this would come to pass, or that! God deliver us from this or that! Thus talk I to myself: which when I speak of, the images of all the things that I do speak of are present, all out of the same treasury of my memory; nor could I talk of any of these things, were the images wanting.

Great is this force of memory, excessive great, O my God; a large and an infinite roomthiness: who can plummet the bottom of it? Yet is this a faculty of mine, and belongs unto my nature: nor can I myself comprehend all that I am. Therefore is the mind too strait to contain itself: so where could that be which cannot contain itself? Is it without itself and not within? How then doth it not contain itself? A wonderful admiration surprises me, and an astonishment seizes me upon this. And men go abroad to wonder at the heights of mountains, the lofty billows of the sea, the long courses of rivers, the vast compass of the ocean, and the circular

et Oceani ambitum, et gyros siderum, et relinquunt se
ipsos, nec mirantur, quod haec omnia cum dicerem,
non ea videbam oculis, nec tamen dicerem, nisi
montes et fluctus et flumina et sidera, quae vidi, et
Oceanum, quem credidi, intus in memoria mea viderem spatiis tam ingentibus, quasi foris viderem.   nec
ea tamen videndo absorbui, quando vidi oculis; nec
ipsa sunt apud me, sed imagines eorum, et novi : quid
ex quo sensu corporis impressum sit mihi.

IX

SED non ea sola gestat immensa ista capacitas memoriae meae.   hic sunt et illa omnia quae de doctrinis
liberalibus percepta nondum exciderunt, quasi remota interiore loco, non loco ; nec eorum imagines,
sed res ipsas gero.   nam quid sit litteratura, quid
peritia disputandi, quot genera quaestionum, quidquid horum scio, sic est in memoria mea, ut non
retenta imagine rem foris reliquerim, aut sonuerit aut
praeterierit, sicut vox inpressa per aures vestigio,
quo recoleretur, quasi sonaret, cum iam non sonaret ;
aut sicut odor dum transit et vanescit in ventos

motions of the stars, and yet pass themselves by, nor CHAP.
wonder that while I spake of all these things I did not VIII
then see them with mine eyes ; yet could I not have
spoken of them, unless those mountains, and billows,
and rivers, and stars which I have seen, and that
ocean which I believed to be, I saw inwardly in my
memory, yea, with such vast spaces between, as if I
verily saw them abroad. Yet did I not swallow them
into me by seeing, whenas with mine eyes I beheld
them. Nor are the things themselves now within
me, but the images of them only. And I distinctly
know by what sense of the body each of these took
impression in me.

IX

The Memory of divers Sciences

AND yet is not this all, that this unmeasurable CHAP.
capacity of my memory bears in mind. Here also IX
be all these precepts of those liberal sciences as yet
unforgotten ; couched as it were further off in a more
inward place, though properly no place : nor is it the
images of the precepts which I bear, but the sciences
themselves. For what grammar or logic is, how
many kinds of questions there be, whatsoever of all
these I know, 'tis in such manner in my memory, as
that I have not merely taken in the image, and left
out the thing, as though the noise of it having
sounded is again vanished, like a voice left in the ear
by the air of it, whereby it was to be called into
memory again, as if now presently sounded, whenas
indeed it doth not sound ; or like an odour, even

CAP. IX olfactum afficit, unde traicit in memoriam imaginem sui, quam reminiscendo repetamus; aut sicut cibus, qui certe in ventre iam non sapit et tamen in memoria quasi sapit; aut sicut aliquid, quod corpore tangendo sentitur, quod etiam separatum a nobis imaginatur memoria. istae quippe res non intromittuntur ad eam, sed eorum solae imagines mira celeritate capiuntur, et miris tamquam cellis reponuntur, et mirabiliter recordando proferuntur.

X

CAP. X AT vero, cum audio tria genera esse quaestionum, an sit, quid sit, quale sit, sonorum quidem, quibus haec verba confecta sunt, imagines teneo, et eos per auras cum strepitu transisse, ac iam non esse scio. res vero ipsas, quae illis significantur sonis, neque ullo sensu corporis attigi neque uspiam vidi praeter animum meum, et in memoria recondidi non imagines earum, sed ipsas: quae unde ad me intraverint dicant, si possunt. nam percurro ianuas omnes carnis meae nec invenio, qua earum ingressae sint. quippe oculi dicunt: "si coloratae sunt, nos eas nuntiavimus"; aures dicunt: "si sonuerunt, a nobis indicatae sunt";

while it passes away and is fanned into wind, does CHAP.
affect the smelling; whence it conveys the image of IX
itself into the memory, which remembering, we smell
over again: or like meat, which verily in the belly
having now no taste, hath a kind of relish in the
memory still: or like anything that is by touching
sensibly felt by the body, which also being taken
away, is notwithstanding in our memory imagined
by us still. For surely the things themselves are not
let into the memory, but the images of them only
are with an admirable swirtness catched in, and in
most wonderful cabinets stored up; whence they
are as wonderfully fetched out again by the act of
remembering.

X

Our Senses convey things into our Memory

BUT now when I hear that there be three kinds of CHAP.
questions: Whether the thing be? What it is? X
And of what nature it is? I do indeed hold fast the
images of the sounds of which those words be composed, and I know that they passed through the air
with a noise, and now are not. As for the things
themselves which are signified by those sounds, I
never so much as reached them with any sense of my
body, nor ever discerned them otherwise than by my
very mind; yet have I laid up not their images only,
but their very selves. Which how they gat into me,
let them tell if they can: I for mine own part have
run over all the Cinque-ports of my flesh, but cannot
find by which they gat in. For mine eyes say, If
those images were coloured, 'twas we then that
brought tidings of them. The ears say; If they

nares dicunt: "si oluerunt, per nos transierunt";
dicit etiam sensus gustandi: "si sapor non est, nihil
me interroges": tactus dicit: "si corpulentum non
est, non contrectavi, si non contrectavi, non indicavi."
unde et qua haec intraverunt in memoriam meam?
nescio quomodo; nam cum ea didici, non credidi
alieno cordi, sed in meo recognovi, et vera esse
approbavi et commendavi ei tamquam reponens, unde
proferrem, cum vellem. ibi ergo erant et antequam
ea didicissem, sed in memoria non erant. ubi ergo,
aut quare, cum dicerentur, agnovi et dixi: "ita est,
verum est," nisi quia iam erant in memoria, sed tam
remota et retrusa quasi in cavis abditioribus, ut, nisi
admonente aliquo eruerentur, ea fortasse cogitare
non possem?

XI

QUOCIRCA invenimus nihil esse aliud discere ista,
quorum non per sensus haurimus imagines, sed sine
imaginibus, sicuti sunt, per se ipsa intus cernimus,
nisi ea, quae passim atque indisposite memoria
continebat, cogitando quasi colligere atque animad-

gave any sound, then 'twas we gave notice of them. CHAP.
The nostrils say; If they had any smell, then they X
passed in by us. The sense of taste also says;
Unless they had a savour with them, never ask me
for them. The touch says; Were it not a body,
I handled it not; and if I never handled it, then I
gave no notice of it. Look now, whence and which
way gat these things into my memory? I, for my
part, know not how. For when I first learned them
I gave not credit to another man's heart, but I took
knowledge of them in mine; and approving them
for true, I recommended them over unto my heart,
there laying them up as it were, whence I might fetch
them again whenever I desired. In my heart therefore they were even before I learned them, but
in my memory they were not. Where were they
then? Or wherefore, whenas they were spoken
of, did I acknowledge them, and affirmed, So is it;
It is true; unless because they were already in my
memory; though so far off yet, and crowded so far Plato's doc-
back as it were into certain secret caves, that had trine of re-
they not been drawn out by the device of some other miniscence
person, I had never perchance been able so much as
to have thought of them?

XI

The Forms of things are in the Soul

WHEREFORE we find that to learn these things of which CHAP.
we suck not in any images by our senses, but perceive XI
them within by themselves, without images, as they
are; is nothing else but by meditating to gather
together those same things which the memory did
before contain more scatteringly and confusedly;

CAP.
XI
vertendo curare, ut tamquam ad manum posita in
ipsa memoria, ubi sparsa prius et neglecta latitabant,
iam familiari intentioni facile occurrant. et quam
multa huius modi gestat memoria mea, quae iam
inventa sunt, et sicut dixi, quasi ad manum posita,
quae didicisse et nosse dicimur: quae si modestis
temporum intervallis recolere desivero, ita rursus de-
merguntur et quasi in remotiora penetralia dilabuntur,
ut denuo velut nova excogitanda sint indidem iterum
—neque enim est alia regio eorum—et cogenda
rursus, ut sciri possint, id est velut ex quadam dispersione colligenda, unde dictum est cogitare. nam
cogo et cogito sic est, ut ago et agito, facio et factito.
verum tamen sibi animus hoc verbum proprie vindi-
cavit, ut non quod alibi, sed quod in animo colligitur,
id est cogitur, cogitari proprie iam dicatur.

XII

CAP.
XII
ITEM continet memoria numerorum dimensionumque
rationes et leges innumerabiles, quarum nullam corporis sensus inpressit, quia nec ipsae coloratae sunt

and by diligent marking to provide, that being orderly CHAP.
and at hand as it were laid up in the memory, (where XI
before they lurked uncollected and neglected) they
may more easily make proffer of themselves unto our
attention, now made familiar unto them.   And how
many of this kind does my memory still bear in mind
which are found out already, and as I said, ready
at hand as it were; which we are said to have
learned and to know: which yet if I should give
over to call to mind but for some short space of time,
they become so drowned again, and so give us the
slip, as it were, back into such remote and privy
lodgings, that I must be put again unto new pains of
meditation for the recovery of them from the same
places—for other quarter to retire unto they have
not—and they must be rallied and drawn together
again, that they may be known; that is to say, they
must as it were be collected and gathered together
from their dispersions: whence the word cogitation
is derived.   For cogo and cogito are of the same
relation as ago and agito, facio and factito.   Notwithstanding hath the mind of man so properly laid claim
unto this word (cogitation) as that now, not that
which is gathered together in any other place, but
in the mind only, (that is drawn together) is by
custom of speech properly now said to be cogitated
or thought upon.

XII

The Memory of Mathematicians

THE memory containeth also the reasons and innu- CHAP.
merable laws of numbers and dimensions; none of XII
which hath been by any sense of the body imprinted
in it: seeing they have neither colour, nor sound,

CAP.
XII aut sonant aut olent aut gustatae aut contrectatae sunt. audivi sonos verborum, quibus significantur, cum de his disseritur, sed illi alii, istae autem aliae sunt. nam illi aliter graece, aliter latine sonant, istae vero nec graecae nec latinae sunt nec aliud eloquiorum genus. vidi lineas fabrorum vel etiam tenuissimas, sicut filum araneae; sed illae aliae sunt, non sunt imagines earum, quas mihi nuntiavit carnis oculus: novit eas quisquis sine ulla cogitatione qualiscumque corporis intus agnovit eas. sensi etiam numeros omnibus corporis sensibus, quos numeramus; sed illi alii sunt, quibus numeramus, nec imagines istorum sunt et ideo valde sunt. rideat me ista dicentem, qui non eos videt, et ego doleam ridentem me.

XIII

CAP.
XIII Haec omnia memoria teneo et quomodo ea didicerim memoria teneo. multa etiam, quae adversus haec falsissime disputantur, audivi et memoria teneo; quae tamenetsi falsa sunt, tamen ea meminisse me non est falsum; et discrevisse me inter illa vera et haec falsa, quae contra dicuntur, et hoc memini, aliterque nunc video discernere me ista, aliter autem

nor taste, nor smell, nor feeling. I have heard the sounds of those words by which these things are signified, whenas they have been argued upon: but the sounds are of another nature from the things. For the sounds are one way in Greek, and another in Latin: but the things themselves are neither Greek, nor Latin, nor any other language. I have likewise seen the lines drawn by architects, even as small as the thread of a spider's web; but these are of another kind; they are not the images of those dimensions which mine eye of flesh shewed unto me. He knoweth them, whosoever without any conception whatsoever of a body recognizes them within himself. I have also perceived with all the senses of my body those numbers which we name in counting; but those numbers by which we count, are far different; nor are they the images of these, and therefore they have a real existence. Let him now laugh at me for all that, who sees not these; and I will pity him, whilst he derides me.

Quos nume-ramus—i.e., their names, figures, &c. *Quibus:* the "ideal" numbers, the innate sense of proportion

XIII

The Memory of Memory

ALL these things I well remember, and how I first learnt them do I well remember. Many things most falsely objected against these things have I both heard, and do yet remember: which though they be false, yet it is not false that I have remembered them; and that I have discerned withal betwixt these truths and these falsehoods, which are objected against them. And this I remember too; and I perceive myself to discern these things one

109

CAP. memini saepe me discrevisse, cum ea saepe cogi-
XIII
tarem. ergo et intellexisse me saepius ista memini, et
quod nunc discerno et intellego, recondo in memoria,
ut postea me nunc intellexisse meminerim. et meminisse me memini, sicut postea, quod haec reminisci
nunc potui, si recordabor, utique per vim memoriae
recordabor.

XIV

CAP. AFFECTIONES quoque animi mei eadem memoria con-
XIV
tinet non eo modo, quo eas habet ipse animus, cum
patitur eas, sed alio multum diverso, sicut sese habet
vis memoriae. nam et laetatum me fuisse reminiscor
non laetus, et tristitiam meam praeteritam recordor
non tristis, et me aliquando timuisse recolo sine timore,
et pristinae cupiditatis sine cupiditate sum memor.
aliquando et e contrario tristitiam meam transactam
laetus reminiscor, et tristis laetitiam. quod miran-
dum non est de corpore : aliud enim animus, aliud
corpus itaque si praeteritum dolorem corporis gaudens memini, non ita mirum est. hic vero, cum
animus sit etiam ipsa memoria—nam et cum man-
110

way now, and I remember myself to have sometimes discerned them otherways, whenas I often thought upon them. That I have therefore understood these things heretofore, do I remember often; and what I now discern and understand do I lay up in my memory, that hereafter I may remember that I have understood it now. And I remember myself to have remembered; like as if hereafter I shall call to remembrance that I have been able to remember these things now; it shall be by the force of my memory, that I shall be able to call it to remembrance.

XIV

*How, when we are not glad, we call to mind things
that have made us glad*

My memory contains also the affections of my mind, not in the same manner that my mind itself contains them, whenas it suffers them: but far another way, like as the force of the memory is. For even then when I am not merry, yet do I remember myself to have been merry heretofore; and when I am not sad, yet do I call to mind my forepassed sadness. And that I have been afraid heretofore, I now remember without fear; and I sometimes call to mind a forepassed desire, without any desire at all now. Sometimes on the contrary, in joy do I remember my forepassed sorrow, and in sadness my joy. Which is not to be wondered at, if meant of the body; for the mind is one thing, and the body another. If I therefore with joy remember some past pain of the body, 'tis not so strange a thing. But now seeing this mind is the very same with the memory, (for that when we

CAP. damus aliquid, ut memoriter habeatur, dicimus:
XIV "vide, ut illud in animo habeas," et cum obliviscimur, dicimus : "non fuit in animo" et "elapsum
est animo," ipsam memoriam vocantes animum—cum
ergo ita sit, quid est hoc, quod cum tristitiam meam
praeteritam laetus memini, animus habet laetitiam et
memoria tristitiam, laetusque est animus ex eo, quod
inest ei laetitia, memoria vero ex eo, quod inest ei
tristitia, tristis non est ? num forte non pertinet ad
animum ? quis hoc dixerit ? nimirum ergo memoria
quasi venter est animi, laetitia vero atque tristitia
quasi cibus dulcis et amarus : cum memoriae commen-
dantur, quasi traiecta in ventrem recondi illic possunt, sapere non possunt. ridiculum est haec illis
similia putare, nec tamen sunt omni modo dissimilia.

Sed ecce de memoria profero, cum dico quattuor
esse perturbationes animi, cupiditatem, laetitiam, me-
tum, tristitiam, et quidquid de his disputare potuero
dividendo singula per species sui cuiusque generis et
definiendo, ibi invenio quid dicam atque inde profero,
nec tamen ulla earum perturbatione perturbor, cum
eas reminiscendo commemoro ; et antequam recole-
rentur a me et retractarentur, ibi erant ; propterea
inde per recordationem potuere depromi. forte ergo
sicut de ventre cibus ruminando, sic ista de memoria
recordando proferuntur. cur igitur in ore cogitationis

give command to have a thing kept in memory, CHAP. we say, Look to it, that you bear this well in XIV mind: and so, when we forget a thing, we say; It did not come into my mind, and, 'Tis quite slipped out of my mind; calling the memory mind:) seeing therefore so it is, how comes this to pass, that when in cheerful vein I remember a sad passage, my mind hath joy, and my memory sadness: my mind is glad because joy is in it, and yet my memory is not sad because sadness is in it? Does not the memory perchance belong unto the mind? Who will say so? Doubtless therefore memory is as it were the belly of the mind, and joy and sadness like sweet and sour meat; which when they are committed unto the memory, be as it were passed away into the belly; where stowage they may have, but taste none at all. Ridiculous it is to imagine these to be like those; and yet are they not utterly unlike.

But behold, this also bring I out of my memory, whenas I say there be four perturbations of the mind, desire, joy, fear, and sorrow: and how far soever I am able to dispute upon these heads, both by dividing all up, each into his parts, and by defining, in my memory find I what to say, and out of my memory do I bring it: yet am I not moved for all this, with any of these perturbations, whenas by calling them to mind I do remember them: yea, and before I recalled and meditated them over, in my memory they were, and therefore by calling to mind could they be fetched from thence. Perchance, therefore, even as meat is by chewing of the cud brought up again out of the belly, so by recalling are these brought up again out of the memory. Why therefore does not the disputer perceive the

CAP.
XIV

non sentitur a disputante, hoc est a reminiscente,
laetitiae dulcedo vel amaritudo maestitiae? an in
hoc dissimile est, quod non undique simile est? quis
enim talia volens loqueretur, si quotiens tristitiam
metumve nominamus, totiens maerere vel timere
cogeremur? et tamen non ea loqueremur, nisi in
memoria nostra non tantum sonos nominum secundum imagines inpressas a sensibus corporis, sed etiam
rerum ipsarum notiones inveniremus, quas nulla ianua
carnis accepimus, sed eas ipse animus per experientiam passionum suarum sentiens, memoriae commen-
davit, aut ipsa sibi haec etiam non commendata
retinuit.

XV

CAP.
XV

SED utrum per imagines an non, quis facile dixerit?
nomino quippe lapidem, nomino solem, cum res ipsae
non adsunt sensibus meis; in memoria sane mea
praesto sunt imagines earum. nomino dolorem corporis, nec mihi adest, dum nihil dolet; nisi tamen
adesset imago eius in memoria mea, nescirem, quid
dicerem nec eum in disputando a voluptate discerne-
rem. nomino salutem corporis, cum salvus sum corpore; adest mihi res ipsa; verum tamen nisi et imago
eius esset in memoria mea, nullo modo recordarer,

114

taste of it in the mouth of his musing? Why does CHAP. not the rememberer feel (I mean) the sweetness of XIV joy, or the bitterness of sorrow? Is the comparison unlike in this, that it is not every way alike? Who then would willingly discourse of these subjects, if so oft as we name grief or fear, so oft we should be compelled to be sad or fearful? And yet could we never speak of them, did we not find in our memory, not the sounds of the names alone according to their images imprinted in it by the senses of the body, but even the very notions of the things themselves, which we never received in by any of the cinque-ports of our body, but which the very mind itself, perceiving by the experience of its own passions, hath committed unto the memory; or else which the memory hath of itself retained, being never committed unto it.

XV

We remember absent Things also

BUT whether all this be done by images or no, CHAP. who can easily affirm? When, for example, I name XV a stone, when I name the sun, at such time as the things themselves are not before my senses; yet present in my memory are images of them. I name some bodily pain, yet I do not feel it whenas nothing aches about me: yet for all this, unless the image were in my memory, I should never know what to say, nor should in discoursing discern pain from pleasure. I name bodily health, whenas I am sound in body; the thing itself is present with me; and yet for all this, unless the image of health also were fixed in my memory, I could by no means recall

CAP.
XV
quid huius nominis significaret sonus; nec aegrotantes
agnoscerent salute nominata, quid esset dictum, nisi
eadem imago vi memoriae teneretur, quamvis ipsa res
abesset a corpore. nomino numeros, quibus numeramus; en assunt in memoria mea non imagines eorum,
sed ipsi. nomino imaginem solis, et haec adest in
memoria mea; neque enim imaginem imaginis eius,
sed ipsam recolo : ipsa mihi reminiscenti praesto est.
nomino memoriam et agnosco quod nomino. et ubi
agnosco nisi in ipsa memoria? num et ipsa per
imaginem suam sibi adest ac non per se ipsam?

XVI

CAP
XVI
Quid, cum oblivionem nomino atque itidem agnosco
quod nomino, unde agnosco rem, nisi meminissem?
non eundem sonum nominis dico, sed rem, quam
significat; quam si oblitus essem, quid ille valeret
sonus, agnoscere utique non valerem. cum memoriam memini, per se ipsam sibi praesto est ipsa
memoria; cum vero memini oblivionem, et memoria
praesto est et oblivio, memoria, ex qua meminerim, oblivio, quam meminerim. sed quid est oblivio
nisi privatio memoriae? quomodo ergo adest, ut
eam meminerim, quando cum adest meminisse non

into my remembrance what the sound of this name CHAP.
should signify: nor would sick people know when XV
health were named, what were spoken, unless the
same image were preserved by the force of the
memory, although the thing itself were far enough
from the body. I name numbers by which we
number: see, they are in my memory; not their images
but themselves. I name the image of the sun, and
that image is also in my memory. Nor do I call to
mind the image of that image, but the image itself;
that is it which is present with me whenas I remember it. I name memory, and I acknowledge
what I name. But where do I acknowledge it, but
in my memory itself? May the memory itself be
present unto itself by its own image, or not by itself
rather?

XVI

There is a Memory of Forgetfulness also

WHAT when I name forgetfulness, and recognize CHAP.
withal what I name; whence do I recognize a thing, XVI
did I not remember it? I speak not now of the
sound of the name, but of the thing which it
signifies: which if I had forgotten, I could never
recognize what that sound signified. When I
remember memory, then is the memory itself
present with me by itself: but when I remember
forgetfulness, then is present both memory and
forgetfulness: memory is present, by which I have
remembered; forgetfulness is present which I have
remembered. But what is forgetfulness but a
privation of memory? How then is that present
for me to remember, which when it is so, I cannot
remember? Now if what we remember, we hold

117

possum? at si quod meminimus memoria retinemus, oblivionem autem nisi meminissemus, nequaquam possemus audito isto nomine rem, quae illo significatur, agnoscere, memoria retinetur oblivio. adest ergo, ne obliviscamur, quae cum adest, obliviscimur. an ex hoc intellegitur non se per ipsam inesse memoriae, cum eam meminimus, sed per imaginem suam, quia, si per se ipsam praesto esset oblivio, non ut meminissemus, sed ut oblivisceremur, efficeret? et hoc quis tandem indagabit? quis comprehendet, quomodo sit?

Ego certe, domine, laboro hic et laboro in me ipso: factus sum mihi terra difficultatis et sudoris nimii. neque enim nunc scrutamur plagas caeli, aut siderum intervalla demetimur, vel terrae libramenta quaerimus: ego sum, qui memini, ego animus. non ita mirum, si a me longe est quidquid ego non sum: quid autem propinquius me ipso mihi? et ecce memoriae meae vis non conprehenditur a me, cum ipsum me non dicam praeter illam. quid enim dicturus sum, quando mihi certum est meminisse me oblivionem? an dicturus sum non esse in memoria mea quod memini? an dicturus sum ad hoc inesse oblivionem in memoria mea, ut non obliviscar? utrumque absurdissimum est. quid illud tertium? quo pacto dicam imaginem oblivionis teneri memoria mea, non ipsam oblivionem, cum eam memini? quo pacto et hoc dicam, quandoquidem cum inprimitur rei cuiusque imago in memoria, prius necesse est, ut adsit res

it in memory, yet unless we did remember forgetfulness, we could never at hearing of the name
recognize the thing that is signified by it, then
forgetfulness is retained in the memory. Present
therefore it is, that we may not forget, which
when it is present, we do forget. Is it to be
understood by this, that the forgetfulness is not
present unto the memory, whenas we remember it,
by itself but by its image, because if it were present
by itself, it would cause us not to remember, but to
forget? Who now shall search out that? Who shall
comprehend how that should be?

For mine own part, Lord, I yet labour upon this,
yea and I labour in myself, and am become a soil that
requires hard labour and very much sweat. For we
are not now quartering out the regions of heaven, or
taking the distances of the stars, or devising where
the hinges of the earth should hang: it is I myself
that remember, I the mind. 'Tis then no such
wonder if the knowledge of that be far from me,
which I myself am not: but what is nearer to me
than myself? Yet lo, I am not able to comprehend
the force of mine own memory; no, though I cannot
so much as call myself myself without it. For what
shall I say, when I see it so certain that I remember
forgetfulness? Shall I say that that is not in my
memory, which I remember? Or shall I say that
forgetfulness is for this purpose in my memory, that
I may not forget? Both these are most absurd.
What is to be thought of this third doubt? How
can I say that the image of forgetfulness is kept in
memory, and not forgetfulness itself, whenas I do
remember it? With what colour may I affirm this
also, seeing that when the image of anything is
imprinted in the memory, 'tis necessary that the

CAP. ipsa, unde illa imago possit imprimi? sic enim Car-
XVI thaginis memini, sic omnium locorum, quibus interfui;
sic facies hominum, quas vidi, et ceterorum sensuum
nuntiata; sic ipsius corporis salutem sive dolorem: cum
praesto essent ista, cepit ab eis imagines memoria,
quas intuerer praesentes et retractarem animo, cum
illa et absentia reminiscerer. si ergo per imaginem
suam, non per se ipsam in memoria tenetur oblivio,
ipsa utique aderat, ut eius imago caperetur. cum
autem adesset, quomodo imaginem suam in memoria
conscribebat, quando id etiam, quod iam notatum invenit, praesentia sua delet oblivio? et tamen quocumque modo, licet sit modus iste incomprehensibilis
et inexplicabilis, ipsam oblivionem meminisse me
certus sum, qua id quod meminerimus obruitur.

XVII

CAP. MAGNA vis est memoriae, nescio quid horrendum,
XVII deus meus, profunda et infinita multiplicitas; et hoc
animus est, et hoc ego ipse sum. quid ergo sum,
deus meus? quae natura sum? varia, multimoda
vita et inmensa vehementer. ecce in memoriae meae
campis et antris et cavernis innumerabilibus atque
120

thing itself be present first, by which that image
may be imprinted? For in this sort do I remember
Carthage, and all other places where I have been:
thus remember I men's faces also, whom I have seen,
and the reports of the other senses: thus do I too
with the health or sickness of the body. For when
these objects were present with me, my memory
received their images from them; which as ever
present, I might look unto and repeat over in my
mind, whenever I desired to remember the objects
themselves even when absent. If therefore this
forgetfulness is held in memory by means of its
image, and not immediately by itself, then plainly,
hath itself been sometime present, that its image
might be then taken. But when it was present,
how did it write that image in the memory, seeing
the property of forgetfulness is, by its presence
to blot out whatever it finds there noted? Well!
which way soever it be, notwithstanding that way be
past conceiving and expressing; yet most certain I
am, that I do well remember this same forgetfulness,
by which whatsoever we remember is defaced.

XVII

A threefold Power of Memory

GREAT is this power of memory; a thing, O my God,
to be amazed at, a very profound and infinite multi-
plicity: and this thing is the mind, and this thing
am I. What am I therefore, O my God? What
kind of nature am I? A life various and full of
changes, yea exceedingly immense. Behold, in
those innumerable fields, and dens, and caves of my
memory, innumerably full of innumerable kinds of

CAP.
XVII

innumerabiliter plenis innumerabilium rerum generibus sive per imagines, sicut omnium corporum, sive
per praesentiam, sicut artium, sive per nescio quas
notiones vel notationes, sicut affectionum animi—
quas et cum animus non patitur, memoria tenet, cum
in animo sit quidquid est in memoria—per haec
omnia discurro et volito hac illac, penetro etiam,
quantum possum, et finis nusquam: tanta vis est
memoriae, tanta vitae vis est in homine vivente
mortaliter! quid igitur agam, tu vera mea vita,
deus meus? transibo et hanc vim meam, quae
memoria vocatur, transibo eam, ut pertendam ad
te, dulce lumen. quid dicis mihi? ego ascendens
per animum meum ad te, qui desuper mihi manes,
transibo et istam vim meam, quae memoria vocatur
volens te attingere, unde attingi potes, et inhaerere
tibi, unde inhaereri tibi potest. habent enim memoriam et pecora et aves, alioquin non cubilia nidosve
repeterent, non alia multa, quibus assuescunt; neque
enim et assuescere valerent ullis rebus nisi per memoriam.   transibo ergo et memoriam, ut attingam
eum, qui separavit me a quadrupedibus et volatilibus
caeli sapientiorem me fecit.   transibo et memoriam,
ut ubi te inveniam, vere bone et secura suavitas, ut
ubi te inveniam? si praeter memoriam meam te
invenio, inmemor tui sum. et quomodo iam invenio
te, si memor non sum tui?

things, brought in, first, either by the images, as CHAP.
all bodies are: secondly, or by the presence of the XVII
things themselves, as the arts are: thirdly, or by
certain notions and impressions, as the affections of
the mind are,—which even then when the mind
doth suffer, yet doth the memory retain, since whatsoever is in the mind, is also in the memory:—through
all these do I run and flit about, on this side, and on
that side, mining into them so far as ever I am able,
but can find no bottom. So great is the force of
memory, so great is the force of life, even in man
living as mortal. What am I now to do, O thou
my true Life, my God? I will pass even beyond this
faculty of mine which is called memory: yea, I will
pass beyond it, that I may approach unto thee, O
sweet Light. What sayest thou to me now? See,
I am now mounting up by the steps of my soul,
towards thee who dwellest above me. Yea, I will
pass beyond this faculty of mine which is called
memory, desirous to touch thee, whence thou
mayest be touched; and to cleave fast unto thee,
whence one may cleave to thee. For even the
beasts and birds have memory; else could they never
find their dens and nests again, nor those many
other things which they are used unto: nor indeed
could they ever enure themselves unto anything, but
by their memory. I will pass beyond my memory,
therefore, that I may arrive at him who hath separated
me from the four-footed beasts and made me wiser
than the fowls of the air: yea, I will soar beyond
mine own memory, that I may find thee—where,
O thou truly Good, and thou secure Sweetness?
where shall I be able to find thee? If I now find
thee not by my memory, then am I unmindful of thee:
and how shall I find thee, if I do not remember thee?

XVIII

CAP.
XVIII
Perdiderat enim mulier drachmam et quaesivit eam
cum lucerna et, nisi memor eius esset, non inveniret
eam. cum enim esset inventa, unde sciret, utrum
ipsa esset, si memor eius non esset? multa meminí
me perdita quaesisse atque invenisse. inde istuc
scio, quia, cum quaererem aliquid eorum et diceretur
mihi: "num forte hoc est?" "num forte illud?"
tamdiu dicebam : "non est," donec id offerretur quod
quaerebam. cuius nisi memor essem, quidquid illud
esset, etiamsi mihi offerretur, non invenirem, quia
non agnoscerem. et semper ita fit, cum aliquid
perditum quaerimus et invenimus. verum tamen si
forte aliquid ab oculis perit, non a memoria, veluti
corpus quodlibet visibile, tenetur intus imago eius et
quaeritur, donec reddatur aspectui. quod cum in-
ventum fuerit, ex imagine, quae intus est, recognoscitur. nec invenisse nos dicimus quod perierat,
si non agnoscimus, nec agnoscere possumus, si
non meminimus : sed hoc perierat quidem oculis,
memoria tenebatur.

XVIII

Of the Remembrance

For the woman had lost her groat, and sought it CHAP. with a light; unless she had remembered it, she XVIII had never found it. For when it was found, whereby Luke xv. 8 should she have known whether it were the same or no, had she not remembered it? I remember many a thing that I have both lost and found again: and this I thereby know, because that when I was seeking for any of them, and some one asked me, Is this it? or, Is that it? so long said I no, until that were offered me that I sought for: which had I not remembered, (whatever it were) though it were offered me, yet should I not find it, because I could not recognize it. And at the same pass still we are, as often as we find what we seek for. Notwithstanding, when anything is by chance lost from the eyes, not from the memory, (as every visible body), yet the image of it is kept still within, and it is sought for until it be again restored unto the sight: which when it is found, is known again by the image which is within. Nor do we say that we have found what we have lost, unless we remember it. This was only lost to the eyes, but surely preserved in the memory.

XIX

CAP.
XIX

Quid? cum ipsa memoria perdit aliquid, sicut fit, cum obliviscimur et quaerimus, ut recordemur, ubi tandem quaerimus nisi in ipsa memoria? et ibi si aliud pro alio forte offeratur, respuimus, donec illud occurrat quod quaerimus. et cum occurrit, dicimus: "hoc est"; quod non diceremus, nisi agnosceremus, nec agnosceremus, nisi meminissemus. certe enim obliti fueramus. an non totum exciderat, sed ex parte, quae tenebatur, pars alia quaerebatur, quia sentiebat se memoria non simul volvere, quod simul solebat, et quasi detruncata consuetudine claudicans reddi quod deerat flagitabat? tamquam si homo notus sive conspiciatur oculis sive cogitetur, et nomen eius obliti requiramus, quidquid aliud occurrerit non conectitur, quia non cum illo cogitari consuevit; ideoque respuitur, donec illud adsit, ubi simul adsuefacta notitia non inaequaliter adquiescat. et unde adest nisi ex ipsa memoria? nam et cum ab alio conmoniti recognoscimus, inde adest. non enim quasi

126

XIX

What Remembrance is

WHEN now the memory itself loses anything, (as it
falls out whenas we forget anything, and seek out
for the recovery of it); where at last do we search,
but in the memory itself? Where, if one thing be
offered instead of another, we so long refuse it, until
we meet that which we seek for: which so soon as
we have met withal, we say, This is it: which we
could never do, did we not know it to be the same;
and that never could we do that, unless we did remember it. Certainly therefore we had forgotten
it. Or had not all of it slipped us; but by that part
whereof we had some hold, was the lost part sought
for? because the memory now feeling that it did not
bear about so much of it together as it had wont to
do, and halting as it were upon the maim received
in the loss of what it had been used unto, it eagerly
demanded to have that made up again, which was
wanting? For instance, if we see or think on some
known man, and having forgotten his name we study
to recover it; whatever name but his comes into our
memory, it will not peize in with it; and all because
that name was never used to be thought upon together with that man: which name therefore is so
long rejected, until that at length presents itself unto
the memory, with which, as having been acquainted
with the knowledge of it, it may evenly jump in
withal. And from whence does that name .present
itself, but out of the memory? For even when being
put in mind by some other man, we know it to be the
same, 'tis by virtue of the memory. Nor do we now

CAP.
XIX
novum credimus, sed recordantes adprobamus hoc
esse, quod dictum est. si autem penitus aboleatur
ex animo, nec admoniti reminiscimur. neque enim
omni modo adhuc obliti sumus, quod vel oblitos nos
esse meminimus. hoc ergo nec amissum quaerere
poterimus, quod omnino obliti fuerimus.

XX

CAP.
XX
Quomodo ergo te quaero, domine? cum enim te,
deum meum, quaero, vitam beatam quaero. quaeram te, ut vivat anima mea. vivit enim corpus meum
de anima mea, et vivit anima mea de te. quomodo
ergo quaero vitam beatam? quia non est mihi,
donec dicam: "sat, est illic," ubi oportet ut dicam.
quomodo eam quaero, utrum per recordationem,
tamquam eam oblitus sim oblitumque me esse adhuc
teneam, an per appetitum discendi incognitam, sive
quam numquam scierim sive quam sic oblitus fuerim,
ut me nec oblitum esse meminerim. nonne ipsa est
beata vita, quam omnes volunt et omnino qui nolit
nemo est? ubi noverunt eam, quod sic volunt eam?
ubi viderunt, ut amarent eam? nimirum habemus
eam nescio quomodo. et est alius quidam modus,
quo quisque cum habet eam, tunc beatus est, et sunt,
qui spe beati sunt. inferiore modo isti habent eam

believe it as any new name, but upon the assurance CHAP.
of our remembrance do we allow it to be the same XIX
that was named to us. But were the name utterly
blotted out of the mind, we should not remember
it, even when we were again put in mind of it. For
we have not yet utterly forgotten that, which we
even remember ourselves to have forgotten. That lost
notion therefore, which we have utterly forgotten,
shall we never be able so much as to seek after.

XX

All Men desire Blessedness

How then do I seek after thee, O Lord? For when CHAP.
I seek thee, my God, I seek an happy life. I will XX
seek thee, that my soul may live. For my body, Is. lv. 3
that liveth by my soul: and my soul by thee.
Which way then am I seeking the happy life? for I
do not possess it so long as I say, It is enough, it is *I.e.,* "It is
there. Whereas I ought to say, How am I seeking there, never
it? whether by way of remembrance, as one that had mind how"
forgotten it, remembering that I had forgotten it? or
by way of appetite to learn it as a thing unknown,
which either I never knew, or at least I have so far
forgotten it, as that I do not so much as remember that
I have forgotten it? Is not an happy life the thing
which all desire, and there is no man at all that desires
it not? But where gat they the knowledge of it, that
they are so desirous of it? Where did they ever see it,
that they are now so enamoured of it? Truly we have
it, but which way I know not: yea, there is a certain
other way, which when any hath, he is even then
blessed; and some there be that be blessed in hope.
These have it in a meaner kind than those who are

quam illi, qui iam re ipsa beati sunt," sed tamen
meliores quam illi, qui nec re nec spe beati sunt:
qui tamen etiam ipsi nisi aliquo modo haberent eam,
non ita vellent beati esse: quod eos velle certissimum
est. nescio quomodo noverunt eam ideoque habent
eam in nescio qua notitia, de qua satago, utrum in
memoria sit, quia, si ibi est, iam beati fuimus aliquando; utrum singillatim omnes, an in illo homine,
qui primus peccavit, in quo et omnes mortui sumus
et de quo omnes cum miseria nati sumus, non quaero
nunc; sed quaero, utrum in memoria sit beata vita.
neque enim amaremus eam, nisi nossemus. audivimus nomen hoc et omnes rem, omnes nos adpetere
fatemur; non enim solo sono delectamur. nam hoc
cum latine audit Graecus, non delectatur, quia ignorat, quid dictum sit; nos autem delectamur, sicut
etiam ille, si graece hoc audierit; quoniam res ipsa
nec graeca nec latina est, cui adipiscendae Graeci
Latinique inhiant ceterarumque linguarum homines.
nota est igitur omnibus, qui una voce si interrogari
possent, utrum beati esse vellent, sine ulla dubitatione velle responderent. quod non fieret, nisi
res ipsa, cuius hoc nomen est, eorum memoria
teneretur.

in possession : who yet are much better than such CHAP.
as are neither blessed in deed, nor in hope : which   XX
very same men for all this, had they it not in some
sort or other, would not so desire to be happy;
which that they do desire, is most certain. Some-
how they come to know it, and therefore have
they it in some sort of knowledge; concerning which,
in much doubt I am, whether it be in the memory
or no : for if it be, then have we sometimes been
blessed heretofore; whether all severally, or as in
that man who first sinned, and in whom we are all
dead, and from whom being descended, we are all
born with misery, I now enquire not : but this I
demand, whether this blessed life be in the memory ?
For, never should we love it, did we not know it.
We have heard the name, and we all confess our
desire unto the thing : for we are not delighted with
the sound only. For when a Grecian hears the name
sounded in Latin, he is in no ways delighted, for that
he knows not what is spoken; but we Latins are
delighted with it, even as he is if he hears it pronounced in Greek : because the thing itself is neither
Greek nor Latin, the attaining whereof both Greeks
and Latins do earnestly look after, like as the men of
other languages do. Known therefore unto all it is,
and could they with one voice be demanded, whether
they would be happy or no ? without doubt they
would all answer, that they would. And this could
not be, unless the thing itself expressed by this name
were still reserved in their memory.

XXI

CAP.
XXI

Numquid ita, ut memini Carthaginem qui vidi? non;
vita enim beata non videtur oculis, quia non est
corpus. numquid sicut meminimus numeros? non;
hos enim qui habet in notitia, non adhuc quaerit
adipisci; vitam vero beatam habemus in notitia, ideoque amamus, et tamen adhuc adipisci eam volumus,
ut beati simus. numquid sicut meminimus eloquen-
tiam? non: quamvis et hoc nomine audito recor-
dentur ipsam rem, qui etiam nondum sunt eloquentes,
multique esse cupiant, unde apparet eam esse in
eorum notitia; tamen per corporis sensus alios eloquentes animadverterunt et delectati sunt et hoc esse
desiderant: quamquam nisi ex interiore notitia, non
delectarentur, neque hoc esse vellent, nisi delectarentur:—beatam vero vitam nullo sensu corporis in
aliis experimur. numquid sicut meminimus gaudium?
fortasse ita. nam gaudium meum etiam tristis
memini sicut vitam beatam miser; neque umquam
corporis sensu gaudium meum vel vidi vel audivi vel
odoratus sum vel gustavi vel tetigi, sed expertus
sum in animo meo, quando laetatus sum, et adhaesit
eius notitia memoriae meae, ut id reminisci valeam
132

XXI

We also remember what we never had

But is it so in memory, as I remember Carthage that CHAP. have seen it? No. For a blessed life is not to be XXI seen with the eye, because it is not a body. Do we then so remember it as we do numbers? No. For these, he that already hath in his knowledge, seeks not further to attain unto; but a happy life we have already in our knowledge, therefore do we love it, and yet desire to attain, that we may be blessed. Do we remember it then as we do eloquence? No. For although some upon hearing of the name, do thereupon call to mind the thing, who yet were never eloquent, and although many desire to be so, whereupon it appears to be already in their knowledge: yet having by their outward senses observed others to be eloquent, they are both delighted at it, and desire to be so themselves: notwithstanding, if by their inward knowledge they had not observed it, they could not have been delighted with it, nor would they wish to be eloquent, but that they were delighted with such as were eloquent. But what this blessed life should be, we can by no sense of our body get the experience of in others. Or is it so in memory as the joy is that we remember? Perchance so indeed. For my joy I remember even whilst I am sad, like as I do a happy life, even whilst I am unhappy: nor did I ever with any bodily sense either see, or hear, or smell, or taste, or touch that joy of mine: but I found it in my mind whenever I rejoiced, and the knowledge of it stuck so fast in my memory, that I am well able to call it to

aliquando cum aspernatione, aliquando cum desiderio, pro earum rerum diversitate, de quibus me gavisum esse memini. nam et de turpibus gaudio quodam perfusus sum, quod nunc recordans detestor atque exsecror, aliquando de bonis et honestis, quod desiderans recolo, tametsi forte non adsunt, et ideo tristis gaudium pristinum recolo.

Vbi ergo et quando expertus sum vitam meam beatam, ut recorder eam et amem et desiderem? nec ego tantum aut cum paucis, sed beati prorsus omnes esse volumus. quod nisi certa notitia nossemus, non tam certa voluntate vellemus. sed quid est hoc? quid? si quaeratur a duobus, utrum militare velint, fieri possit, ut alter eorum velle se, alter nolle respondeat: si autem ab eis quaeratur, utrum esse beati velint, uterque se statim sine dubitatione dicat optare, nec ob aliud ille velit militare, non ob aliud iste nolit, nisi ut beati sint. num forte quoniam alius hinc, alius inde gaudet? ita se omnes beatos esse velle consonant, quemadmodum consonarent, si hoc interrogarentur, se velle gaudere atque ipsum gaudium vitam beatam vocant. quod etsi alius hinc, alius illinc assequitur, unum est tamen, quo pervenire omnes nituntur, ut gaudeant. quae quoniam res est, quam se expertum non esse nemo potest dicere,

remembrance, with contempt sometimes, and with
fresh desire otherwhiles, even according to the diversity of those things for which I remembered myself to have rejoiced. For even at unclean things
was I sometimes overjoyed; which calling to mind
again, I now both detest and curse: and otherwhiles
at good and honest things, which I call to mind with
longing, although they perchance present not themselves; and therefore again sad at it, do I call to
mind my former rejoicing.

Where therefore and when had I any feeling of a
happy life, that I should remember, and love, and
long for it? Nor is it my desire alone, or of some
few besides, but every man verily would be happy;
which, unless by some certain knowledge we had
notice of, we should not with so certain a will desire
it. But what is this? If two men be asked whether
they would go to the wars, one, perchance, would
answer that he would, and the other that he would
not; but if both were asked whether they would be
happy, both of them would without all doubting
affirm that they desire it: nor for any other reason
would this man go to the wars, and the other not,
but to be happy. Is it perchance, because that one
man rejoices upon this occasion, and another upon
that? So do all men agree in their desire of being
happy, even as they would agree, if they were asked,
whether they desired to have occasion of rejoicing:
(this very joy being the thing which they call the
blessed life). And that joy, though one man obtains
it by one means, and another man by another means,
yet is this the thing agreed upon that they all
strive to attain unto, namely, that they may rejoice:
which for that it is a thing which no man can
rightly say, but that he hath had some experience

CAP.
XXI
propterea reperta in memoria recognoscitur, quando beatae vitae nomen auditur.

XXII

CAP.
XXII
ABSIT, domine, absit a corde servi tui, qui confitetur tibi, absit, ut, quocumque gaudio gaudeam, beatum me putem. est enim gaudium, quod non datur inpiis, sed eis, qui te gratis colunt, quorum gaudium tu ipse es. et ipsa est beata vita, gaudere de te, ad te, propter te: ipsa est et non est altera. qui autem aliam putant esse, aliud sectantur gaudium neque ipsum verum. ab aliqua tamen imagine gaudii voluntas eorum non avertitur.

XXIII

CAP.
XXIII
NON ergo certum est, quod omnes esse beati volunt, quoniam qui non de te gaudere volunt, quae sola vita beata est, non utique vitam beatam volunt. an omnes hoc volunt, sed quoniam caro concupiscit adversus spiritum et spiritus adversus carnem, ut non faciant quod volunt, cadunt in id quod valent eoque contenti sunt, quia illud, quod non valent, non tantum volunt, quantum sat est, ut valeant? nam quaero ab omnibus, utrum malint de veritate quam de falsi-

of, being therefore found in the memory, it is CHAP.
recognized, whenever the name of a happy life is XXI
mentioned.

XXII

True Joy, is this blessed Life

FAR be it O Lord, far be it from the heart of thy CHAP.
servant who confesseth unto thee, far be it from me XXII
to imagine, that for every joy that I rejoice withal, I
should think me happy. For there is a joy which is
not granted unto the ungodly; but unto those only
which love thee for thine own sake, whose joy thyself art. And this is the happy life, to rejoice concerning thee unto thee, and for thy sake : this is the
happy life, and there is no other. As for them that
think there is another, they pursue another joy, which
is not the true one. However their mind is not
utterly turned aside from some kind of resemblance
of rejoicing.

XXIII

A blessed life ; what, and where it is

IT is not certain therefore that all men desire to be CHAP.
happy, for that those who have no desire to rejoice XXIII
in thee, (which to do is the one happy life) do not
verily desire the happy life. Or do all men desire
this, but because the flesh lusteth against the spirit, Gal. v. 17
and the spirit against the flesh, that they cannot do
what they would, do they fall upon that which they
are able to do; resting themselves contented therewith, because that they are not able to do, they
do not will so earnestly as were sufficient throughly
to make them able ? For I demand of every man,

CAP.
XXIII
tate gaudere : tam non dubitant dicere de veritate
se malle, quam non dubitant dicere beatos esse se
velle. beata quippe vita est gaudium de veritate.
hoc est enim gaudium de te, qui veritas es, deus, in-
luminatio mea, salus faciei meae, deus meus. hanc
vitam beatam omnes volunt, hanc vitam, quae
sola beata est, omnes volunt, gaudium de veritate
omnes volunt. multos expertus sum, qui vellent fallere, qui autem falli, neminem. ubi ergo noverunt
hanc vitam beatam, nisi ubi noverunt etiam veritatem ? amant enim et ipsam, quia falli nolunt, et
cum amant beatam vitam (quod non est aliud quam
de veritate gaudium), utique amant etiam veritatem
nec amarent, nisi esset aliqua notitia eius in memoria
eorum. cur ergo non de illa gaudent ? cur non beati
sunt ? quia fortius occupantur in aliis, quae potius
eos faciunt miseros quam illud beatos, quod tenuiter
meminerunt. adhuc enim modicum lumen est in
hominibus ; ambulent, ambulent, ne tenebrae con-
prehendant.

Cur autem veritas parit odium, et inimicus eis factus
est homo tuus verum praedicans, cum ametur beata
vita, quae non est nisi gaudium de veritate ? nisi quia
sic amatur veritas, ut, quicumque aliud amant, hoc
quod amant velint esse veritatem, et quia falli nol-
lent, nolunt convinci, quod falsi sint. itaque propter

whether they had rather rejoice in the truth, or in
falsehood? They do as little doubt to say, in the
truth, as they do to say, that they desire to be
happy. For a happy life is a rejoicing in the truth:
for this is a joying in thee, who art the Truth, O God
my Light, the Health of my countenance, and my
God. This is the blessed life that all desire; this
life which is only blessed, do all desire; to joy in
the truth, is all men's desire. I have had experience
of divers that would deceive, but not a man that
would willingly be deceived. Where therefore gained
they the knowledge of this happy life, but even there,
where they learned the truth also? Yea, verily, they
love this truth, for that they would not be deceived:
and whenas they love a happy life (which is nothing
else but a joying in the truth) then also do they love
the truth: which yet they would not love, were there
not some knowledge of it remaining in their memory.
Wherefore then joy they not in it? Why are they
not happy? Even because they are more strongly
taken up with other things which have more power
to make them miserable, than that hath to make
them happy, which they remember so little of.
For there is a dim glimmering of light unput-out in
men: let them walk, let them walk, that the darkness
overtake them not.

Why now doth truth bring forth hatred, and thy
man become enemy unto them, whom he preaches
the truth unto; whenas a happy life is loved, which
is nothing else but a joying in the truth: unless
the reason be, because truth is in that kind loved,
that all which love any other thing, would gladly
have that to be the truth, which they so love:
and because they would not willingly be deceived,
are unwilling to be convinced that they are so?

CAP.
XXIII

eam rem oderunt veritatem, quam pro veritate amant.
amant eam lucentem, oderunt eam redarguentem.
quia enim falli nolunt et fallere volunt, amant eam,
cum se ipsa indicat, et oderunt eam, cum eos ipsos
indicat. inde retribuet eis, ut, qui se ab ea mani-
festari nolunt, et eos nolentes manifestet et eis ipsa
non sit manifesta. sic, sic, etiam sic animus humanus,
etiam sic caecus et languidus, turpis atque indecens
latere vult, se autem ut lateat aliquid non vult.
contra illi redditur, ut ipse non lateat veritatem,
ipsum autem veritas lateat. tamen etiam sic, dum
miser est, veris mavult gaudere quam falsis. beatus
ergo erit, si nulla interpellante molestia, de ipsa, per
quam vera sunt omnia, sola veritate gaudebit.

XXIV

CAP.
XXIV

ECCE quantum spatiatus sum in memoria mea quaerens te, domine, et non te inveni extra eam. neque
enim aliquid de te invenio, quod non meminissem,
ex quo didici te. nam ex quo didici te, non sum
oblitus tui. ubi enim inveni veritatem, ibi inveni
deum meum, ipsam veritatem, quam ex quo didici,

Therefore do they hate the truth, for the sake of CHAP. that thing, which they love instead of truth. They XXIII love truth when it enlightens them, but they hate it when it reprehends them. For because they would not willingly be deceived, and fain would deceive, do they love it when it discovers itself, but they hate it, when it discovers them. But thus shall it pay them in their own coin; so that, those who would not have themselves discovered by it, even those in despite of their teeth shall it uncase, and yet not reveal itself unto them. Thus, thus; yea very thus, yea just thus, desires this purblind, this lazy, this slovenly, and this ill-behaved mind of man to muffle up itself from the view of others; but that anything should be concealed from it, it desires not. But the quite contrary does befall it; for that it cannot lie undiscovered from the truth, but the truth shall be veiled from it. Yet this mind of man notwithstanding, even thus wretched as it is, takes joy rather in truths than in falsehoods. Happy therefore shall it one day be, if no distraction interloping, it shall settle its joy upon that only truth, by which all things else are true.

XXIV

That the Memory containeth God too

SEE now, how great a space I have coursed over in CHAP. my memory seeking thee, O Lord; and I found XXIV thee not outside it. For I find nothing at all concerning thee, but what I have kept in memory, ever since I first learnt thee: for I have never forgotten thee, since the hour I first learnt thee; for where I found truth, there found I my God who is the truth itself; which from the time I first

CAP.
XXIV
non sum oblitus. itaque ex quo te didici, manes in
memoria mea, et illic te invenio, cum reminiscor tui
et delector in te. hae sunt sanctae deliciae meae,
quas donasti mihi misericordia tua, respiciens pauper-
tatem meam.

XXV

CAP.
XXV
Sed ubi manes in memoria mea, domine, ubi illic
manes? quale cubile fabricasti tibi? quale sanc-
tuarium aedificasti tibi? tu dedisti hanc dignationem
memoriae meae, ut maneas in ea, sed in qua eius
parte maneas, hoc considero. transcendi enim partes
eius, quas habent et bestiae, cum te recordarer (quia
non ibi te inveniebam inter imagines rerum corpora-
lium), et veni ad partes eius, ubi commendavi affectiones animi mei, nec illic inveni te. et intravi ad
ipsius animi mei sedem (quae illi est in memoria mea,
quoniam sui quoque meminit animus), nec ibi tu eras,
quia sicut non es imago corporalis nec affectio viven-
tis, qualis est, cum laetamur, contristamur, cupimus,
metuimus, meminimus, obliviscimur, et quidquid huius
modi est, ita nec ipse animus es, quia dominus deus
animi tu es, et commutantur haec omnia, tu autem
inconmutabilis manes super omnia, et dignatus es

142

learnt it, have I not forgotten. Since therefore I CHAP.
learnt to know thee, hast thou still kept in my XXIV
memory; and there do I find thee, whenever I call
thee to remembrance, and delight myself in thee.
These be my holy delights, which thou hast bestowed
upon me through thy mercy, having respect unto my
poverty.

XXV

In what degree of the Memory God is found

But whereabouts in my memory is thy residence, O CHAP.
Lord? Whereabouts there abidest thou? What kind XXV
of lodging hast thou there framed for thyself? What
manner of shrine hast thou builded for thyself?
Thou hast afforded this honour unto my memory, as
to reside in it; but in what quarter of it, that am I
now considering upon. For I have already passed
beyond such parts of it as are common to me with
the beasts, whilst I called thee to mind (for as much
as I found not thee there amongst the images of
corporeal things:) and I proceeded to these parts of
it, whither I had committed the affections of my
mind: nor could I find thee there. Yea, I passed
further into it, even to the very seat of my mind
itself (which is there in my memory, as appears by
the mind's remembering of itself:) neither wert thou
there: for that as thou art not either any corporeal
image, no more art thou any affection of a living
man; like as when we rejoice, condole, desire, fear,
remember, forget, or whatsoever else we do of the
like kind: No, nor yet art thou the mind itself;
because thou art the Lord God of the mind; and
all these are changed, whereas thou remainest unchangeable over all; who yet vouchsafest to dwell

CAP.
XXV
habitare in memoria mea, ex quo te didici. et quid quaero, quo loco eius habites, quasi vero loca ibi sint? habitas certe in ea, quoniam tui memini, ex quo te didici, et in ea invenio, cum recordor te.

XXVI

CAP.
XXVI
Vbi ergo te inveni, ut discerem te? neque enim iam eras in memoria mea, priusquam te discerem. ubi ergo te inveni, ut discerem te, nisi in te supra me? et nusquam locus, et recedimus et accedimus, et nusquam locus. veritas, ubique praesides omnibus consulentibus te simulque respondes omnibus diversa consulentibus. liquide tu respondes, sed non liquide omnes audiunt. omnes unde volunt consulunt, sed non semper quod volunt audiunt. optimus minister tuus est, qui non magis intuetur hoc a te audire quod ipse voluerit, sed potius hoc velle quod a te audierit.

in my memory, ever since that first time that I
learnt to know thee. But why seek I now in what
particular place of my memory thou dwellest, as if
there were any places at all in it? Sure I am, that
in it thou dwellest: even for this reason, that I have
preserved the memory of thee since the time that
I first learnt thee: and for that I find thee in it,
whensoever I call thee to remembrance.

CHAP.
XXV

XXVI

Whereabouts God is to be found

WHERE then did I find thee, that I might learn thee?
For in my memory thou wert not before I learnt
thee. In what place therefore did I find thee, that
so I might learn thee, but even in thine own self, far
above myself? Place there is none; we go back-
ward and forward, but place there is none. Everywhere O Truth, dost thou give audience to those
that ask counsel of thee, and at one dispatch dost
thou answer all, yea though they ask thy counsel
upon divers matters. Clearly dost thou answer them,
though all do not clearly understand thee. All may
advise with thee about what they will, though they
hear not always such answer as they desire. He is
thy best servant that looks not so much to hear that
from thee which himself desired; as to will that
rather, which from thee he heareth.

CHAP.
XXVI

Job xxiii. 8

XXVII

CAP.
XXVII

Sero te amavi, pulchritudo tam antiqua ét tam nova,
sero te amavi! et ecce intus eras et ego foris, et ibi
te quaerebam, et in ista formosa, quae fecisti, deformis
inruebam. mecum eras, et tecum non eram. ea
me tenebant longe a te, quae si in te non essent,
non essent. vocasti et clamasti et rupisti surditatem
meam : coruscasti, splenduisti et fugasti caecitatem
meam : fragrasti, et duxi spiritum, et anhelo tibi,
gustavi et esurio et sitio, tetigisti me, et exarsi in
pacem tuam.

XXVIII

CAP.
XXVIII

Cum inhaesero tibi ex omni me, nusquam erit mihi
dolor et labor, et viva erit vita mea tota plena te.
nunc autem quoniam quem tu imples, sublevas eum,
quoniam tui plenus nondum sum, oneri mihi sum.
contendunt laetitiae meae flendae cum laetandis
maeroribus, et ex qua parte stet victoria nescio. ei
146

XXVII

How God draws us to himself

Too late came I to love thee, O thou Beauty both
so ancient and so fresh, yea too late came I to love
thee.   And behold, thou wert within me, and I out
of myself, where I made search for thee: I ugly
rushed headlong upon those beautiful things thou
hast made.   Thou indeed wert with me ; but I was
not with thee: these beauties kept me far enough
from thee : even those, which unless they were in
thee, should not be at all.   Thou calledst and criedst
unto me, yea thou even breakedst open my deafness :
thou discoveredst thy beams and shinedst unto me,
and didst chase away my blindness : thou didst most
fragrantly blow upon me, and I drew in my breath
and I pant after thee; I tasted thee, and now do
hunger and thirst after thee ; thou didst touch me,
and I even burn again to enjoy thy peace.

XXVIII

The Misery of this Life

WHEN I shall once attain to be united unto thee in
every part of me, then shall I no more feel either
sorrow or labour: yea, then shall my life truly be
alive, every way full of thee.   Whereas now for that
whom thou fillest thou also raisest, am I a burden
unto myself, because I am not yet full of thee.
The joys of this my life which deserve to be lamented,
are at strife with my sorrows which are to be rejoiced
in : and which way the victory will incline, I yet

CAP.
XXVIII

mihi! domine, miserere mei! contendunt maerores mei mali cum gaudiis bonis, et ex qua parte stet victoria nescio. ei mihi! domine, miserere mei! ei mihi! ecce vulnera mea non abscondo: medicus es, aeger sum; misericors es, miser sum. numquid non temptatio est vita humana super terram? quis velit molestias et difficultates? tolerari iubes ea, non amari. nemo quod tolerat amat, etsi tolerare amat. quamvis enim gaudeat se tolerare, mavult tamen non esse quod toleret. prospera in adversis desidero, adversa in prosperis timeo. quis inter haec medius locus, ubi non sit humana vita temptatio? vae prosperitatibus saeculi semel et iterum, a timore adversitatis et a corruptione laetitiae! vae adversitatibus saeculi semel et iterum et tertio, a desiderio prosperitatis, et quia ipsa adversitas dura est, et ne frangat tolerantiam! numquid non temptatio est vita humana super terram sine ullo interstitio?

XXIX

CAP.
XXIX

ET tota spes mea non nisi in magna misericordia tua. da quod iubes et iube quod vis. imperas nobis continentiam. et cum scirem, ait quidam, quia nemo

know not. Woe is me, O Lord, have pity on me: CHAP.
my sorrows that be bad are in contention with my XXVIII
joys that be good : and on which side is the victory
I know not. Alas for me O Lord, have pity on
me. Woe is me; behold I hide not my wounds:
thou art the physician and I the patient : thou
the merciful, and I the miserable. Is not the
life of man upon earth all trial ? Who is he that Job vii. 1
would willingly endure troubles and difficulties? (Old
These thou commandest to be endured, not to be Vulgate)
loved : for no man loveth what he endures,
though he love to endure. For notwithstanding
that he rejoices to endure, yet he would rather that
there were nothing to endure. In adversity I desire
prosperity, and in prosperity am I afraid of adversity :
what middle place now is there betwixt these two,
where this life of man is free from trial ? Woe is
threatened unto the prosperities of this world again
and again ; both for the fear of adversity, and corruption of joy. Woe unto the adversities of this world,
again and again, yea woe the third time unto them ;
and that because of the great desire men have unto
prosperity and because adversity is hard, and lest it
break down endurance. Is not the life of man all
trial upon earth, and that without intermission ?

XXIX

Our Hope is all in God

Now is all my hope nowhere but in thy very great CHAP.
mercy. Give what thou commandest, and command XXIX
what thou wilt. Thou imposest continency upon us ;
and when I perceived, as one saith, that no man can be

CAP.
XXIX
potest esse continens, nisi deus det, et hoc ipsum erat sapientiae, scire cuius esset hoc donum. per continentiam quippe colligimur et redigimur in unum, a quo in multa defluximus. minus enim te amat qui tecum aliquid amat, quod non propter te amat. o amor, qui semper ardes et numquam extingueris, caritas, deus meus, accende me! continentiam iubes: da quod iubes et iube quod vis.

XXX

CAP.
XXX
IVBES certe, ut contineam a concupiscentia carnis et concupiscentia oculorum et ambitione saeculi. iussisti a concubitu, et de ipso coniugio melius aliquid, quam concessisti, monuisti. et quoniam dedisti, factum est, et antequam dispensator sacramenti tui fierem. sed adhuc vivunt in memoria mea, de qua multa locutus sum, talium rerum imagines, quas ibi consuetudo mea fixit; et occursantur mihi vigilanti quidem carentes viribus, in somnis autem non solum usque ad delectationem sed etiam usque ad consensionem factumque simillimum. et tantum valet imaginis illius inlusio in anima mea in carne mea, ut dormienti falsa visa persuadeant quod vigilanti vera non pos-

continent unless thou give it, this also was a point of CHAP.
wisdom, to know whose gift it was. By continency XXIX
verily are we bound up and brought into the one, Wisdom
from which we were scattered abroad into many : viii. 21
for too little doth he love thee, who loves anything
together with thee, which he loves not for thee.
O thou Love which art ever burning, and never
quenched! O Charity, my God! kindle me I
beseech thee. Thou commandest me continency :
give me what thou commandest, and command what
thou wilt.

XXX

The deceitfulness of Dreams

VERILY thou commandest me to contain myself from CHAP.
the lust of the flesh, the lust of the eyes, and the XXX
ambition of this world. Thou hast commanded me 1 John ii.
also to abstain from carnal copulation ; and con- 16
cerning wedlock, thou didst advise me to a better
course than that was which thou leftest me a free
choice in. And because thou gavest it, it was
done, and that before I became a dispenser of
thy Sacrament. But yet there still live in my
memory, (which I have now spoken so much of)
the images of such things as my ill custom had there
fixed ; and they rush into my thoughts (though
wanting in strength) even whilst I am broad waking :
but in sleep they come upon me, not to delight only,
but even so far as consent, and most like to the
deed doing. Yea, so far prevails the illusion of that
image, both in my soul and my flesh, as that these
false visions persuade me unto that when I am asleep,

sunt. numquid tunc ego non sum, domine deus meus? et tamen tantum interest inter me ipsum et me ipsum, intra momentum, quo hinc ad soporem transeo vel huc inde retranseo! ubi est tunc ratio, qua talibus suggestionibus resistit vigilans, et si res ipsae ingerantur, inconcussus manet? numquid clauditur cum oculis? numquid sopitur cum sensibus corporis? et unde saepe etiam in somnis resistimus, nostrique propositi memores atque in eo castissime permanentes nullum talibus inlecebris adhibemus adsensum? et tamen tantum interest, ut, cum aliter accidit, evigilantes ad conscientiae requiem redeamus; ipsaque distantia reperiamus nos non fecisse, quod tamen in nobis quoquo modo factum esse doleamus.

Numquid non potens est manus tua, deus omnipotens, sanare omnes languores animae meae, atque abundantiore gratia tua lascivos motus etiam mei soporis extinguere? augebis, domine, magis magisque in me munera tua, ut anima mea sequatur me ad te, concupiscentiae visco expedita; ut non sit rebellis sibi, atque ut in somnis etiam non solum non perpetret istas corruptelarum turpitudines per imagines animales usque ad carnis fluxum, sed ne consentiat quidem. nam ut nihil tale vel tantulum libeat, quantulum possit nutu cohiberi etiam in casto dormientis affectu non

which true visions cannot do when I am awake. Am
I am not myself at that time, O Lord my God? And
yet there is so much difference betwixt myself and
myself, in that moment wherein I pass from waking
to sleeping, or return from sleeping unto waking!
Where is my reason at that time, by which my mind
when it is awake resisteth such suggestions as these?
At which time, should the things themselves press in
upon me, yet would my resolution remain unshaken.
Is my reason closed up together with mine eyes?
Is it lulled asleep with the senses of my body?
And whence comes it to pass, that we so often
even in our sleep make such resistance; and being
mindful of our purpose, and remaining most chastely in
it, we yield no assent unto such enticements? And
yet so much difference is there, as that when anything hath otherwise happened in our sleep, we upon
our waking return to peace of conscience: by the
distance of time discovering that it was not we that
did it, notwithstanding we be sorry that there is
something some way or other done in us.

Is not thy hand able, O God Almighty, to cure all
the diseases of my soul, and with a more abundant
measure of thy grace, also to quench the lascivious
motions of my sleep? Thou shalt increase, O Lord,
thy graces more and more upon me, that my soul
may follow myself home to thee, wholly freed from
that birdlime of concupiscence; that it may not
rebel against itself, nor may in dreams, not only not
commit these corrupt uncleannesses, by means of
these sensual images, procuring pollution of the
flesh, but that it may not so much as once consent
unto them. For to hinder that no such fancy (no
not so much as should need a nod to restrain it,) do
its pleasure in the chaste affection of those that

CAP.
XXX
tantum in hac vita, sed etiam in hac aetate, non
magnum est omnipotenti, qui vales facere supra quam
petimus et intellegimus. nunc tamen quid adhuc
sim in hoc genere mali mei, dixi bono domino meo ;
exultans cum tremore in eo, quod donasti mihi, et
lugens in eo, quod inconsummatus sum, sperans per-
fecturum te in me misericordias tuas usque ad pacem
plenariam, quam tecum habebunt interiora et exteriora mea, cum absorpta fuerit mors in victoriam.

XXXI

CAP.
XXXI
Est alia malitia diei, quae utinam sufficiat ei. refi-
cimus enim cotidianas ruinas corporis edendo et
bibendo, priusquam escas et ventrem destruas, cum
occideris indigentiam satietate mirifica, et corruptibile
hoc indueris incorruptione sempiterna. nunc autem
suavis est mihi necessitas, et adversus istam suavi-
tatem pugno, ne capiar, et cotidianum bellum gero
in ieiuniis, saepius in servitutem redigens corpus
meum, et dolores mei voluptate pelluntur. nam
fames et sitis quidam dolores sunt : urunt et sicut
febris necant, nisi alimentorum medicina succurrat.
quae quoniam praesto est ex consolatione munerum
tuorum, in quibus nostrae infirmitati terra et aqua et
caelum serviunt, calamitas deliciae vocantur.

154

sleep, (not in this life only, but even in this age of youth) is not hard for the Almighty to do, who art able to do above all that we ask or think. And for this time, in what case I am in this kind of naughtiness have I confessed unto my good Lord; rejoicing with trembling in that grace which thou hast already given me, and bemoaning myself for that wherein I am still unperfect; well hoping that thou wilt one day perfect thy mercies in me, even unto a fulness of peace: which both my outward and inward man shall at that time enjoy with thee, whenas death shall be swallowed up in victory.

CHAP.
XXX
Eph. iii. 20

1 Cor. xv.
54

XXXI

The Temptation of Eating and Drinking

THERE is another evil of the day, which I wish were sufficient unto it. For we are fain by eating and drinking to repair the daily decays of our body, until such time as thou destroyest both belly and meat, whenas thou shalt kill this emptiness of mine with a wonderful fulness, and shalt clothe this corruptible with an eternal incorruption. But now this necessity is sweet unto me; against which sweetness do I fight, lest I should be beguiled by it; yea, a daily war do I make, bringing my body into subjection by my fastings, the pinchings whereof are by the pleasure I take in it expelled. Hunger and thirst verily are painful: they burn up and kill like a fever, unless the physic of nourishments relieve us. Which, for that it is readily to be had, out of the comfort we receive by thy gifts, in which both land and water and air serve our weakness, is our calamity termed our delight.

CHAP.
XXXI
Matt. vi.
34
1 Cor. vi.
13
1 Cor. xv.
54

CAP.
XXXI

Hoc me docuisti, ut quemadmodum medicamenta sic alimenta sumpturus accedam. sed dum ad quietem satietatis ex indigentiae molestia transeo, in ipso transitu mihi insidiatur laqueus concupiscentiae. ipse enim transitus voluptas est, et non est alius, qua transeatur, quo transire cogit necessitas. et cum salus sit causa edendi ac bibendi, adiungit se tamquam pedisequa periculosa iucunditas et plerumque praeire conatur, ut eius causa fiat, quod salutis causa me facere vel dico vel volo. nec idem modus utriusque est : nam quod saluti satis est, delectationi parum est, et saepe incertum fit, utrum adhuc necessaria corporis cura subsidium petat an voluptaria cupiditatis fallacia ministerium suppetat. ad hoc incertum hilarescit infelix anima, et in eo praeparat excusationis patrocinium, gaudens non adparere, quod satis sit moderationi valetudinis, ut obtentu salutis obumbret negotium voluptatis. his temptationibus cotidie conor resistere, et invoco dexteram tuam et ad te refero aestus meos, quia consilium mihi de hac re nondum stat.

Audio vocem iubentis dei mei: Non graventur corda vestra in crapula et ebrietate. ebrietas longe est a me : misereberis, ne adpropinquet mihi. crapula autem nonnumquam subrepsit servo tuo :

156

Thus much hast thou taught me, that I come CHAP.
to take my food as it were physic. But while I XXXI
am passing from the pinching of emptiness unto
the content of replenishing, even in the very passage does that snare of lickerishness lie in ambush
for me: for that passage between is a pleasure, nor
is there any other way to pass by, but that which
necessity constrains us to go by. And whereas
health is the cause of our eating and drinking,
there is a dangerous lickerishness goes along with
health like a handmaid, yea, endeavours ofttimes
so to go before it, as that I eat that for my
tooth's sake, which I either say I do, or desire
to do, for my health's sake. Nor is there the
same moderation in both; for that which is enough
in respect of health, is not near enough in respect of
lickerishness: yea, very uncertain is it oftentimes,
whether the necessary care of my body still requires
sustenance, or whether a voluptuous deceit of greediness offers its services. And for that this case is
uncertain, does my unhappy soul rejoice, and pro-
vides it thereby of a protection of excuse: rejoicing
for that it cannot now appear what may be sufficient for the regimen of health; that so under the
cloak of health, it may disguise the matter of pleasure.
These enticements do I endeavour to resist daily:
yea, I call thy right hand to help me, and to thee do
I refer my perplexities; for that I am resolved of no
counsel as yet in this matter.

I hear the voice of my God commanding, Let Luke xxi.
not your hearts be overcharged with surfeiting and 34
drunkenness. As for drunkenness, I am far enough
from it, and thou wilt have mercy upon me, that it
may never come near me. But full feeding hath
many a time stolen upon thy servant: thou wilt

misereberis, ut longe fiat a me. nemo enim potens
esse continens, nisi tu des. multa nobis orantibus
tribuis, et quidquid boni antequam oraremus accepimus, a te accepimus; et ut hoc postea cognoscere-
mus, a te accepimus. ebriosus numquam fui, sed
ebriosos a te factos sobrios ego novi. ergo a te
factum est, ut hoc non essent qui numquam fuerunt,
a quo factum est, ut hoc non semper essent qui
fuerunt, a quo etiam factum est, ut scirent utrique,
a quo factum est. audivi aliam vocem tuam : Post
concupiscentias tuas non eas et a voluptate tua
vetare. audivi et illam ex munere tuo, quam multum
amavi : Neque si manducaverimus, abundabimus,
neque si non manducaverimus, deerit nobis; hoc est
dicere : nec illa res me copiosum faciet nec illa
aerumnosum. audivi et alteram : Ego enim didici,
in quibus sum, sufficiens esse, et abundare novi et
penuriam pati novi. omnia possum in eo, qui me
confortat. ecce miles castrorum caelestium, non
pulvis, quod sumus. sed memento, domine, quoniam
pulvis sumus, et de pulvere fecisti hominem, et
perierat et inventus est. nec ille in se potuit, quia
idem pulvis fuit, quem talia dicentem adflatu tuae
inspirationis adamavi : Omnia possum, inquit, in eo,
qui me confortat. conforta me, ut possim, da quod

have mercy upon me, that it may be put far from
me: for no man can be temperate, unless thou
give it. Many things thou vouchsafest unto us which
we pray for; and what good thing so ever we have
received before we pray, from thee have we received
it; yea, to this end have we already received it, that we
might acknowledge so much afterwards. Drunkard
was I never: but I have known many a drunkard
made sober by thee. Thy doing therefore it is, that
such should be kept from being drunkards hereafter, who have not been that way faulty heretofore;
as from thee it also was, that those should not
continue faulty for ever, who have been given to
that vice heretofore: yea, from thee it likewise was,
that both these parties should take notice from
whom it was. I heard also another voice of thine:
Go not after thine own lusts, and from thine
own pleasures turn away thy face. Yea, by thy
favour have I heard this saying likewise, which
I have much delighted in: Neither if we eat, shall
we abound; neither if we eat not, shall we lack:
which is to say, that neither shall this make me
rich, nor that miserable. Also another voice have
I heard: For I have learned in whatsoever state I
am, therewith to be content: and I know how to
abound, and how to suffer need. I can do all things
through Christ that strengtheneth me. See here
a soldier indeed of thy celestial armies; not dust,
which we are: but remember, Lord, that we are
dust, and that of dust thou hast made man, who
was lost and is found. Nor yet could he do this
of his own power, because he was of the same
dust; him I mean whom I did so heartily love for
this, saying by thy inspiration: I can do all things
(saith he) through him that strengtheneth me.

CHAP.
XXXI

Ecclesias-
ticus xviii.
30

1 Cor. viii.
8

Phil. iv.
11, 12

Gen. iii. 19
Luke xv.
32

iubes et iube quod vis. iste se accepisse confitetur
et quod gloriatur in domino gloriatur. audivi alium
rogantem, ut accipiat: Aufer, inquit, a me concupiscentias ventris. unde adparet, sancte deus, te dare,
cum fit quod imperas fieri.

Docuisti me, pater bone : Omnia munda mundis,
sed malum esse homini qui per offensionem manducat; et omnem creaturam tuam bonam esse nihilque
abiciendum, quod cum gratiarum actione percipitur;
et quia esca nos non conmendat deo, et ut nemo nos
iudicet in cibo aut potu ; et ut qui manducat non
manducantem non spernat, et qui non manducat,
manducantem non iudicet. didici haec, gratias tibi,
laudes tibi, deo meo, magistro meo, pulsatori aurium
mearum, inlustratori cordis mei : eripe me ab omni
temptatione. non ego inmunditiam obsonii timeo,
sed inmunditiam cupiditatis. scio Noe omne carnis
genus, quod cibo esset usui, manducare permissum,
Elian cibo carnis refectum, Iohannem mirabili absti-
nentia praeditum animalibus, hoc est lucustis in
escam cedentibus, non fuisse pollutum : et scio Esau
lenticulae concupiscentia deceptum, et David propter
aquae desiderium a se ipso reprehensum, et regem
nostrum non carne, sed pane temptatum. ideoque
et populus in heremo non quia carnes desideravit, sed

Strengthen me, that I may be able; give what thou commandest, and command what thou wilt. St. Paul confesses to have received, and when he glorieth, in the Lord he glorieth. Another also have I heard begging of thee: Turn from me (saith he) the greediness of the belly. By which it appeareth, O my holy God, that the power is of thy giving, when anything is done which thou commandest to be done.

CHAP. XXXI

Ecclesiasticus xxiii. 5, 6

Thou hast taught me, good Father, that unto the pure all things are pure; but that it is evil unto the man that eateth with offence. And that every creature of thine is good, and nothing to be refused, which is received with thanksgiving. And that meat commendeth us not unto God: and that no man ought to judge us in meat or drink: and that he which eateth, let him not despise him that eateth not; and let not him that eateth not, judge him that eateth. These things have I learned, thanks and praise be to thee therefore, my God Master; even to thee that knockest at the door of mine ears, the enlightener of my heart: do thou deliver me out of all temptation. It is not any uncleanness in the meat which I fear, but the uncleanness of mine own gormandizing. I know that liberty was granted unto Noah to eat of all kind of flesh that was good for food: that Elijah was fed with flesh: that John Baptist, endued with an admirable abstinence, was not polluted by those living creatures the locusts, which were granted him to feed upon. And on the other side, I know that Esau was deceived by longing after the pottage of lentils: and that David was blamed by himself for so desiring a draught of water: and that our King was tempted, not concerning flesh, but bread. And therefore the people in the

Titus, i. 15

Rom. xiv. 20

1 Tim. iv. 4

1 Cor. viii. 8

Col. ii. 16

Rom. xiv. 13

Gen. ix. 3

1 Kings xvii. 6

Matt. iii. 4

Gen. xxv. 34

2 Sam. xxiii. 15

Matt. iv. 3

quia escae desiderio adversus dominum murmuravit,
meruit inprobari.

In his ergo temptationibus positus, certo cotidie
adversus concupiscentiam manducandi et bibendi:
non enim est quod semel praecidere et ulterius non
attingere decernam, sicut de concubitu potui. itaque
freni gutturis temperata relaxatione et constrictione
tenendi sunt. et quis est, domine, qui non rapiatur
aliquantum extra metas necessitatis? quisquis est,
magnus est, magnificet nomen tuum. ego autem
non sum, quia peccator homo sum. sed et ego
magnifico nomen tuum, et interpellat te pro peccatis
meis, qui vicit saeculum, numerans me inter infirma
membra corporis sui, quia et inperfectum eius viderunt oculi tui, et in libro tuo omnes scribentur.

XXXII

DE inlecebra odorum non satago nimis: cum absunt, non requiro, cum adsunt, non respuo, para-
tus eis etiam semper carere. ita mihi videor;
forsitan fallar. sunt enim et istae plangendae
tenebrae, in quibus me latet facultas mea, quae
in me est, ut animus meus de viribus suis ipse

wilderness deserved to be reproved, not so much for
desiring flesh, but for murmuring against the Lord,
out of a lust to lickerish meats.

Myself therefore, amidst these temptations do
strive daily against mine own appetite of eating and
drinking. For 'tis not of such a nature as that I am
able to resolve to cut myself short of it once for all,
and never to touch it afterward, as I was able to do
concerning carnal copulation. The bridle of the
throat therefore is to be held between a temperate
slackness and a stiffness: and who is he, O Lord, that
is not some whit transported beyond the lists of
necessity? Whatever he is, a great man is he; and
let him magnify thy name for it. But for mine own
part, I am not the man, for I am a sinner. Yet do I
magnify thy name too; yea, and he makes intercession to thee for my sins, who hath overcome the
world; who accounts me among the weak members
of his body; because thine eyes have seen my substance being yet imperfect, and in thy book will all
my members be written.

XXXII

Of our Delight in Smelling

As for the tempting delight of sweet smells, I am
not too much taken with it. When I miss them, I
do not seek them; when I may have them, I
do not refuse them: yet also ready always to be
without them. At least to myself I seem to be,
though perchance deceived I may be. For even that
natural darkness is much to be lamented, wherein
the knowledge of mine own abilities so far lies concealed, as that when my soul makes enquiry into

se interrogans non facile sibi credendum existimet,
quia et quod inest plerumque occultum est, nisi
experientia manifestetur, et nemo securus esse debet
in ista vita, quae tota temptatio nominatur, utrum
qui fieri potuit ex deteriore melior, non fiat etiam
ex meliore deterior. una spes, una fiducia, una
firma promissio misericordia tua.

XXXIII

VOLUPTATES aurium tenacius me inplicaverant et
subiugaverant, sed resolvisti et liberasti me. nunc
in sonis, quos animant eloquia tua, cum suavi et
artificiosa voce cantantur, fateor, aliquantulum ad-
quiesco, non quidem ut haeream, sed ut surgam, cum
volo. attamen cum ipsis sententiis quibus vivunt ut
admittantur ad me, quaerunt in corde meo nonnullius
dignitatis locum, et vix eis praebeo congruentem.
aliquando enim plus mihi videor honoris eis tribuere,
quam decet, dum ipsis sanctis dictis religiosius et
ardentius sentio moveri animos nostros in flammam
pietatis, cum ita cantantur, quam si non ita can-
tarentur, et omnes affectus spiritus nostri pro sui

herself concerning her own powers, it conceives it not safe, too lightly to give credit unto itself; because that what is already in it, lies many times so closely muffled up, as nothing but experience can reveal it : nor ought any man to be secure in this life, (which may well be called one continued trial) whether that he whom it hath been possible of worse to make better, may not likewise of better be made worse again. Our only hope, our only confidence, the only assured promise that we have is thy mercy.

XXXIII

The Pleasures taken in Hearing

THE delights of mine ears, verily, have heretofore more strongly inveigled and engaged me; but thou hast brought me off and freed me. Yet still at hearing of those airs which thy words breathe soul into, whenas they are sung with a well tuned and well governed voice, I do, I confess, receive a little contentment; not so great though as that I am enchanted by it, but that I can go away when I please. But yet for all this, that those airs may together with these words (by virtue of which they receive life) gain full admission with me, do they aspire to be entertained into a place of no mean honour in this heart of mine, nor can I scarce afford them a room befitting for them. For sometimes forsooth, do I seem to myself to attribute more respect unto them than is seemly; yea, even whilst together with those sacred ditties I perceive our minds to be far more religiously and zealously blown up into a flame of devotion, whenas these ditties are thus sung, than they would have been, had they not been so sung:

diversitate habere proprios modos in voce atque cantu, quorum nescio qua occulta familiaritate excitentur. sed delectatio carnis meae, cui mentem enervandam non oportet dari, saepe me fallit, dum rationi sensus non ita comitatur, ut patienter sit posterior, sed tantum, quia propter illam meruit admitti, etiam praecurrere ac ducere conatur. ita in his pecco non sentiens et postea sentio.

Aliquando autem hanc ipsam fallaciam inmoderatius cavens erro nimia severitate, sed valde interdum, ut melos omnes cantilenarum suavium, quibus Daviticum psalterium frequentatur, ab auribus meis removeri velim atque ipsius ecclesiae, tutiusque mihi videtur, quod de Alexandrino episcopo Athanasio saepe dictum mihi commemini, qui tam modico flexu vocis faciebat sonare lectorem psalmi, ut pronuntianti vicinior esset quam canenti. verum tamen cum reminiscor lacrimas meas, quas fudi ad cantus ecclesiae in primordiis recuperatae fidei meae, et nunc ipsum quod moveor non cantu, sed rebus quae cantantur, cum liquida voce et convenientissima modulatione cantantur, magnam instituti huius utilitatem rursus agnosco. ita fluctuo inter periculum voluptatis et

yea, and I perceive withal, how that the several affections of our spirit, have their proper moods answerable
to their variety in the voice and singing, and by
some secret association therewith they be stirred up.
But this contentment of my flesh, (unto which it is
not fit to give over the mind to be enervated) doth
very often beguile me: the sense going not so
along with the reason, as patiently to come behind
it; but having for reason's sake gained admission,
it strives even to run before and be her leader.
Thus in these things I sometimes sin at unawares,
but afterwards am aware of it.

Again at another time, through an indiscreet
weariness of being inveigled, do I err out of too pre-
cise a severity: yea, very fierce am I sometimes, in
the desire of having the melody of all pleasant music,
to which David's Psalter is so often sung, banished
both from mine own ears, and out of the whole
church too: and the safer way it seems unto me,
which I remember to have been often told me
of Athanasius Bishop of Alexandria, who caused the
reader of the psalm to sound it forth with so little
warbling of the voice, as that it was nearer to
speaking, than to singing. Notwithstanding, so often
as I call to mind the tears I shed at the hearing of
thy church songs, in the beginning of my recovered
faith, yea, and at this very time, whenas I am
moved not with the singing, but with the thing
sung (when namely they are set off with a clear
voice and suitable modulation), I then acknowledge
the great good use of this institution. Thus float I
between peril of pleasure, and an approved profitable
custom: inclined the more (though herein I pronounce no irrevocable opinion) to allow of the old
usage of singing in the Church; that so by the

CAP.
XXXIII
experimentum salubritatis magisque, adducor; non quidem inretractabilem sententiam proferens, cantandi consuetudinem approbare in ecclesia, ut per oblectamenta aurium infirmior animus in affectum pietatis adsurgat. tamen cum mihi accidit, ut me amplius cantus quam res, quae canitur, moveat, poenaliter me peccare confiteor, et tunc mallem non audire cantantem. ecce ubi sum ! flete mecum et pro me flete qui aliquid boni vobiscum intus agitis, unde facta procedunt. nam qui non agitis, non vos haec movent. tu autem, domine deus meus, exaudi et respice et vide et miserere et sana me, in cuius oculis mihi quaestio factus sum, et ipse est languor meus.

XXXIV

CAP.
XXXIV
RESTAT voluptas oculorum istorum carnis meae, de qua loquor confessiones, quas audiant aures templi tui, aures fraternae ac piae, ut concludamus temptationes concupiscentiae carnis, quae me adhuc pulsant ingemescentem, et habitaculum meum, quod de caelo est, superindui cupientem. pulchras formas et varias, nitidos et amoenos colores amant oculi. non teneant haec animam meam; teneat eam deus, qui fecit haec bona quidem valde, sed ipse est bonum meum, non haec. tangunt me vigilantem totis diebus, nec

168

delight taken in at the ears, the weaker minds be CHAP.
roused up into some feeling of devotion. And yet XXXIII
again, so oft as it befalls me to be more moved with
the voice than with the ditty, I confess myself to
have grievously offended: at which time I wish
rather not to have heard the music. See now in
what a state I am! Weep with me, and weep
for me, O all you, who inwardly feel any thoughts,
whence good actions do proceed. As for you that
feel none such, these things move you not. But
thou, O Lord my God, look upon me, hearken, and
behold, and pity, and heal me, thou in whose eyes I
am now become a problem to myself; and that is my
infirmity.

XXXIV

The Enticements coming in by the Eyes

THERE remains the pleasure of these eyes of my CHAP.
flesh, concerning which I am now to make this con- XXXIV
fession unto thee; which let the ears of thy temple,
those brotherly and devout ears, well hearken unto:
that with it we may conclude our discourse concerning the temptations of the lusts of the flesh, which as
yet solicit me, groaning earnestly, and desiring to be 2 Cor. v. 2
clothed upon with my house from heaven. Mine
eyes take delight in fair forms, and vanities of them:
in beautiful and pleasant colours. Suffer not these
to hold possession of my soul; let my God rather be
Lord of it, who made all these: very good they be
indeed, yet is he my good, and not they. Verily,

CAP.
XXXIV requies ab eis datur mihi, sicut datur a vocibus
canoris, aliquando ab omnibus, in silentio. ipsa enim
regina colorum lux, ista perfundens cuncta, quae
cernimus, ubiubi per diem fuero, multimodo adlapsu
blanditur mihi, aliud agenti et ad eam non advertenti.
insinuat autem se ita vehementer, ut, si repente sub-
trahatur, cum desiderio requiratur; et si diu absit,
contristat animum.

O lux, quam videbat Tobis, cum clausis istis oculis
filium docebat vitae viam, et ei praeibat pede caritatis
nusquam errans; aut quam videbat Isaac praegravatis
et opertis senectute carneis luminibus, cum filios non
agnoscendo benedicere, sed benedicendo agnoscere
meruit; aut quam videbat Iacob, cum et ipse prae
grandi aetate captus oculis in filiis praesignata futuri
populi genera luminoso corde radiavit, et nepotibus
suis ex Ioseph divexas mystice manus, non sicut
pater eorum foris corrigebat, sed sicut ipse intus
discernebat, imposuit. ipsa est lux, una est et unum
omnes, qui vident et amant eam. at ista corporalis,
de qua loquebar, inlecebrosa ac periculosa dulcedine condit vitam saeculi caecis amatoribus. cum
autem et de ipsa laudare te norunt, deus creator
omnium, assumunt eam in hymno tuo, non assu-
muntur ab ea in somno suo: sic esse cupio. resisto

these entice me broad waking every day, nor find I CHAP.
any rest from these sights, as I find when silence is XXXIV
kept after sweet voices. For this queen of colours,
the light, shedding itself in all whatsoever we
behold, so oft as I enjoy the daylight, gliding by
mine eye in its varied forms, doth most sweetly in-
veigle me, wholly busy about another matter, and
taking no notice of it. For it so forcibly insinuates
itself, that if at any time it suddenly be withdrawn,
it is with much longing looked after again; and if
missing too long, it besaddeth the mind.

O thou light, which Tobias beheld, when with these Tob. iv.
eyes closed up, he directed his son the way to life, and
himself went before with the feet of charity, never
misleading him. Or that light which Isaac beheld, Gen. xxvii.
whenas his fleshly eyes being dim, so that he could ¹
not see, he blessed his sons, not able to discern which
was which; though in blessing of them, he deserved
to have discerned them. Or that light which Jacob
beheld, when taken blind in his old age, he, with an
illuminated heart, in the persons of his own sons, Gen. xlviii.
gave light unto the fortunes of the several families ¹⁴
of people foresignified to be derived from them : and
as when he laid his hands upon his grandchildren by
Joseph, mystically laid across, not as their father by
his outward eye corrected them, but as himself by a
beam of light from within, wittingly discerned them.
This is the light indeed; it is one, and one are all
those who see and love that light. As for this
corporeal light which I now spake of; it besauces
this present life for her blind lovers, with a tempting
and dangerous sweetness : whereas those that know
how to praise thee for that light, take it up, "O An evening
God all-Creator," in singing thy hymn, and are not hymn of St.
taken up from it, in their sleep. Thus desire I to be Ambrose

seductionibus oculorum, ne inplicentur pedes mei,
quibus ingredior viam tuam, et erigo ad te invisibiles
oculos, ut tu evellas de laqueo pedes meos. tu
subinde evelles eos, nam inlaqueantur. tu non cessas
evellere, ego autem crebro haereo in ubique sparsis
insidiis. quoniam non dormies neque dormitabis, qui
custodis Israel.

Quam innumerabilia variis artibus et opificiis in
vestibus, calciamentis, vasis et cuiuscemodi fabricatio-
nibus, picturis etiam diversisque figmentis, atque his
usum necessarium atque moderatum et piam signifi-
cationem longe transgredientibus, addiderunt homines
ad inlecebras oculorum, foras sequentes quod faciunt,
intus relinquentes a quo facti sunt et exterminantes
quod facti sunt. at ego, deus meus et decus meum,
etiam hinc tibi dico hymnum et sacrifico laudem sacri-
ficatori meo, quoniam pulchra traiecta per animas in
manus artificiosas ab illa pulchritudine veniunt, quae
supra animas est, cui suspirat anima mea die ac nocte.
sed pulchritudinum exteriorum operatores et sectato-
res inde trahunt adprobandi modum, non autem inde
trahunt utendi modum. et ibi est et non vident eum,
ut non eant longius, et fortitudinem suam ad te custodiant, nec eam spargant in deliciosas lassitudines.
ego autem haec loquens atque discernens etiam istis
172

employed. These seducements of the eyes do I CHAP. manfully resist, lest my feet wherewith I am to enter XXXIV upon my way, should be ensnared; yea, and I lift up mine invisible eyes unto thee, that thou wouldst be pleased to pluck my feet out of that snare; yea, thou dost ever and anon pluck them out, for they are ensnared. Thou art not slow to pluck them out, though I entangle myself often in the snares everywhere laid: because thou that keepest Israel shalt neither Ps. cxxi. 4 slumber nor sleep.

Oh how innumerable toys made by divers arts and manufactures, both in our apparel, shoes, vessels and all kind of works; in pictures also and divers feigned images, yea, and these far exceeding all necessary and moderate use, and all pious significations, have men added to tempt their own eyes withal: outwardly following after what themselves make, inwardly forsaking him by whom themselves were made; and defacing that which themselves have been made. For mine own part, O my God and my Beauty, I hence also dedicate an hymn unto thee, and do sacrifice praise unto my Sanctifier; because those beautiful patterns which through men's souls are conveyed into their cunning hands, all descend from that beauty which is above our souls, which my soul day and night sighs after. But as for these framers and followers of those outward beauties, they from thence derive the manner of liking them, but fetch not from thence the measure of using them. And yet there he is (though they perceive him not) that they might not wander afar, but might preserve their strength only for thee, and·not wear it out upon tiring delicates. But for mine own part, (who both discourse upon, and well discern these things) I also entangle my steps

CAP.
XXXIV

pulchris gressum innecto, sed tu evelles, domine,
evelles tu, quoniam misericordia tua ante oculos
meos est. nam ego capior miserabiliter, et tu evelles
misericorditer aliquando non sentientem, quia sus-
pensus incideram, aliquando cum dolore, quia iam
inhaeseram.

XXXV

CAP.
XXXV

Huc accedit alia forma temptationis multiplicius periculosa. praeter enim concupiscentiam carnis, quae
inest in delectatione omnium sensuum et voluptatum,
cui servientes depereunt qui longe se faciunt a te,
inest animae per eosdem sensus corporis quaedam
non se oblectandi in carne, sed experiendi per carnem vana et curiosa cupiditas, nomine cognitionis et
scientiae palliata. quae quoniam in appetitu noscendi
est, oculi autem sunt ad noscendum in sensibus prin-
cipes, concupiscentia oculorum eloquio divino adpel-
lata est. ad oculos enim videre proprie pertinet:
utimur autem hoc verbo etiam in ceteris sensibus,
cum eos ad cognoscendum intendimus. neque enim
dicimus: audi quid rutilet, aut: olefac quam niteat,
aut: gusta quam splendeat, aut: palpa quam fulgeat:
videri enim dicuntur haec omnia. dicimus autem non
solum: vide quid lucet, quod soli oculi sentire pos-

in these outward beauties: but thou wilt pluck CHAP.
me back, O Lord, thou wilt pluck me back, because XXXIV
thy mercy is before mine eyes. For I am miserably
taken, and thou as mercifully wilt pluck me back;
sometimes when I perceive it not, when I had
lightly fallen upon them: and otherwhiles grieved
to part with them, because I had already cleaved
to them.

XXXV

Of our Curiosity in knowing

Upon this, another form of temptation assails me; CHAP.
and that many ways more dangerous. For besides XXXV
that concupiscence of the flesh, which lurketh in the
delight of all our senses and pleasures, (wherein
those the slaves of it, who go far from thee, waste
and perish;) there is conveyed into the soul by the
same senses of the body, a certain vain and curious
itch; not of delight taking in the flesh, but of
making experiments by help of the flesh; which
is masked under the title of knowledge and
learning. Which, because it is seated in the
appetite of knowing, and that for the attaining
of knowledge the eyes be the principal of all the
senses, is in Holy Writ called the lust of the eyes. 1 John ii.
For to see, belongeth unto the eyes properly: yet 16
we apply the word of seeing to other senses also,
whenever we employ them towards knowing. For
we do not say, hark how red it is; or smell how
white it is; or taste how shining it is; or feel how
bright it is; because all these are said to be seen.
And yet we say not only, see how it shineth, which
the eye alone can perceive: but we say also, see how

sunt, sed etiam : vide quid sonet, vide quid oleat, vide quid sapiat, vide quam durum sit. ideoque generalis experientia sensuum concupiscentia, sicut dictum est, oculorum vocatur, quia videndi officium, in quo primatum oculi tenent, etiam ceteri sensus sibi de similitudine usurpant, cum aliquid cognitionis explorant.

Ex hoc autem evidentius discernitur, quid voluptatis, quid curiositatis agatur per sensus, quod voluptas pulchra, canora, suavia, sapida, lenia sectatur, curiositas autem etiam his contraria temptandi causa, non ad subeundam molestiam, sed experiendi noscendique libidine. quid autem voluptatis habet videre in laniato cadavere quod exhorreas? et tamen sicubi iaceat, concurrunt, ut contristentur, ut palleant. timent etiam, ne in somnis hoc videant, quasi quisquam eos vigilantes videre coegerit aut pulchritudinis ulla fama persuaserit. ita et in ceteris sensibus, quae persequi longum est. ex hoc morbo cupiditatis in spectaculis exhibentur quaeque miracula. hinc ad perscrutanda naturae, quae praeter nos non est, operata proceditur, quae scire nihil prodest et nihil aliud quam scire homines cupiunt. hinc etiam, si quid eodem perversae scientiae fine per artes magicas quaeritur. hinc etiam in ipsa religione deus temptatur, cum signa et

176

it soundeth; see how it smelleth; see how it tasteth; CHAP.
see how hard it is. The general experience of the XXXV
senses therefore it is, (as was said before) which is
called the lust of the eyes: for that the office of
seeing, wherein the eyes hold the prerogative, do
the other senses by way of similitude usurp unto
themselves, whensoever they make search after any
knowledge.

But by this may the difference more evidently be
discerned betwixt the pleasure and the curiosity that
be acted by the senses; for that pleasure affecteth
objects that be beautiful, clear sounding, sweet
smelling, savoury tasting, soft touching: whereas
curiosity for trial's sake pries into objects clean contrary to the former, not to engage itself in the
trouble they bring, but merely out of an itch of
gaining the knowledge and experience of them.
For what pleasure hath it, to see that in a torn car-
cass, which would strike horror into a man? And
yet, if any such be near lying, they all flock to it,
even of purpose to be made sad and to grow pale at
it: they are afraid also to see it in their sleep; as if
somebody had forced them to go and see it while
they were awake, or any report of beauty had per-
suaded them unto it. And thus is it in the other
senses also, all which it were long to prosecute.
And out of this disease of curiosity are all those
strange sights presented unto us in the theatre.
Hence also men proceed to investigate some concealed powers of that nature which is not beyond our
ken, which it does them no good to know, and yet
men desire to know for the sake of knowing. Hence
proceeds it also, if with that same end of perverted
learning, the magical arts be made use of to enquire
by. Upon this curiosity also even in religion itself, is

prodigia flagitantur, non ad aliquam salutem, sed ad
solam experientiam desiderata.

In hac tam immensa silva plena insidiarum et
periculorum ecce multa praeciderim et a meo corde
dispulerim, sicuti donasti me facere, deus salutis
meae; attamen quando audeo dicere, cum circumqua-
que cotidianam vitam nostram tam multa huius
generis rerum circumstrepant, quando audeo dicere
nulla re tali me intentum fieri ad spectandum et
vana cura capiendum? sane me iam theatra non
rapiunt, nec curo nosse transitus siderum, nec anima
mea umquam responsa quaesivit umbrarum; omnia
sacrilega sacramenta detestor. a te, domine deus
meus, cui humilem famulatum ac simplicem debeo,
quantis mecum suggestionum machinationibus agit
inimicus ut signum aliquod petam! sed obsecro te
per regem nostrum et patriam Hierusalem simplicem,
castam, ut quemadmodum a me longe est ad ista
consensio, ita sit semper longe atque longius. pro
salute autem cuiusquam cum te rogo, alius multum
differens finis est intentionis meae, et te faciente
quod vis das mihi et dabis libenter sequi.

Verum tamen in quam multis minutissimis et con-
temptibilibus rebus curiositas cotidie nostra temptetur
et quam saepe labamur, quis enumerat? quotiens
narrantes inania primo quasi toleramus, ne offendamus
infirmos, deinde paulatim libenter advertimus. canem

178

God tempted; when, namely, certain signs and wonders from heaven are demanded of him: not desired
for any saving end, but merely for our experience.

In this so vast a wilderness, so full of snares and
dangers, behold many of them I have cut off, and
thrust out of my heart, according as thou, O God of
my salvation, hast given me the grace to do. And
yet for all this, when dare I boldly say, (so many of
this kind of things buzz all about this our daily life)
when dare I boldly say, that myself is by no such
like thing provoked to look towards it, or out of
a vain desire to covet it? True it is that the
theatres do not nowadays carry me away; nor do
I much now regard to know the courses of the
stars; nor hath my soul at any time enquired
answers at the ghosts departed: all sacrilegious
compacts I utterly detest. But at thy hands, O
Lord my God, to whom I owe all humble and single-
hearted service, by what fetches of suggestions hath
that spiritual enemy dealt with me to desire some
sign! But by our King I beseech thee, and by our
home of Jerusalem so pure and chaste; that like
as any consenting unto such thoughts hath been
hitherto far enough from me, so ever let it be further and further. But for the health of any when I
entreat thee, the end of my intention is far different from the former: and thyself doing what thou
pleasest in it, givest me the grace, and willingly
ever wilt give me, to obey it.

Notwithstanding, in how many petty and contemptible trifles is this curiosity of ours daily tempted:
and how often we do slip that way, who is able to
recount? How often when people tell vain stories
do we at first bear with them, as it were, for fear of
giving offence to the weak; and yet by degrees, by

currentem post leporem iam non specto, cum in circo fit; at vero in agro, si casu transeam, avertit me fortassis et ab aliqua magna cogitatione atque ad se convertit illa venatio, non deviare cogens corpore iumenti, sed cordis inclinatione, et nisi iam mihi, demonstrata infirmitate mea, cito admoneas, aut ex ipsa visione per aliquam considerationem in te adsurgere, aut totum contemnere atque transire, vanus hebesco. quid cum me domi sedentem stelio muscas captans vel aranea retibus suis inruentes inplicans saepe intentum me facit? num quia parva sunt animalia, ideo non res eadem geritur? pergo inde ad laudandum te, creatorem mirificum atque ordinatorem rerum omnium, sed non inde intentus esse incipio. aliud est cito surgere, aliud est non cadere. et talibus vita mea plena est, et una spes mea magna valde misericordia tua. cum enim huiuscemodi rerum conceptaculum fit cor nostrum et portat copiosae vanitatis catervas, hinc et orationes nostrae saepe interrumpuntur atque turbantur, et ante conspectum tuum, dum ad aures tuas vocem cordis intendimus, nescio unde inruentibus nugatoriis cogitationibus res tanta praeciditur.

and by we willingly give ear to them? I become
not the spectator nowadays of a dog's coursing of a
hare in the public games-place: but if in the field
I by chance ride by, such a sport may, peradventure,
put me off even from some serious thought, and draw
me after it: not to turn out of the road with the
body of my horse, but yet with the inclination of my
heart: yea, and didst not thou, by making me see
my infirmity, quickly admonish me, either through
the sight itself by some contemplation to raise
myself towards thee, or wholly to despise and pass
it by; I dully stand besotted with it. What shall
I say, whenas sitting in mine own house, a lizard
catching flies, or a spider entangling them in her
nets, ofttimes makes me attentive to them? Because these are but small creatures, is it not the
same thing? I proceed hereupon to laud thee the
wonderful Creator and Disposer of all: but that is
not the occasion of my beginning to be attentive
to them. One thing it is to get up quickly, and
another thing not to fall at all. And of such
toys is my life full; and my only hope is in thy
wonderful great mercy. For when this heart of
ours is made the receipt of such things, and over-
charges itself with the throngs of this superabundant
vanity, then are our prayers thereby often inter-
rupted and distracted; and whilst in thy presence
we direct the voice of our heart up unto thy ears,
that so important a business is broken off, by I know
not what idle thoughts rushing in upon us.

XXXVI

Numquid etiam hoc inter contemnenda deputabimus, aut aliquid nos redducet in spem nisi nota misericordia tua, quoniam coepisti mutare nos? et tu scis, quanta ex parte mutaveris, qui me primitus sanas a libidine vindicandi me, ut propitius fias etiam ceteris omnibus iniquitatibus meis, et sanes omnes languores meos, et redimas de corruptione vitam meam, et corones me in miseratione et misericordia, et saties in bonis desiderium meum, qui conpressisti a timore tuo superbiam meam et mansuefecisti iugo tuo cervicem meam. et nunc porto illud, et lene est mihi, quoniam sic promisisti et fecisti; et vere sic erat, et nesciebam, quando id subire metuebam.

Sed numquid, domine, qui solus sine typho dominaris, quia solus verus dominus es, qui non habes dominum, numquid hoc quoque tertium temptationis genus cessavit a me aut cessare in hac tota vita potest, timeri et amari velle ab hominibus non propter aliud, sed ut inde sit gaudium, quod non est gaudium? misera vita est et foeda iactantia. hinc fit vel maxime non amare te nec caste timere te, ideoque tu superbis resistis, humilibus autem das gratiam et

XXXVI

The Sin of Pride

BUT shall I account of this also, amongst such things CHAP. as are to be contemned? Or shall aught bring us XXXVI back to our hope, but thy well-known mercy, sith thou hast begun to change us? And in what degree thou hast already amended me, thyself best knowest; who dost first of all recover me from that burning desire of revenging myself: that so thou mayest the better be favourable unto all my other iniquities, and heal all my infirmities, and redeem Ps. ciii. 3-5 my life from corruption, and crown me with thy pity and mercy, and satisfy my desire with good things: who also hast curbed my pride with thy fear, and tamed my neck to thy yoke. Which now I bear, and it is light unto me; because so hast thou promised, and so hast thou made it: and verily so it was, but I knew it not, because I feared to take it up.

But tell me now, O Lord, thou who only reignest without the ruff of pride; because thou only art the true Lord, who hast no Lord: tell me hath this third kind of temptation given me over, or can it altogether forbear me in this life, this namely, to desire to be feared and loved of men, and that for no other end, but that we may receive a private rejoicing in it; which is indeed no true joy? A miserable life this is, and a dishonourable kind of bragging. For hence especially it comes, that men do neither purely love nor fear thee. And even 1 Pet. v. 5 therefore too dost thou resist the proud, and give James iv. grace unto the humble: yea, thou thunderest down 6

S. AVGVSTINI CONFESSIONVM LIBER X

intonas super ambitiones saeculi, et contremunt fundamenta montium. itaque nobis, quoniam propter quaedam humanae societatis officia necessarium est amari et timeri ab hominibus, instat adversarius verae beatitudinis nostrae, ubique spargens in laqueis Euge, euge, ut, dum avide colligimus, incaute capiamur, et a veritate gaudium nostrum deponamus, atque in hominum fallacia ponamus, libeatque nos amari et timeri non propter te, sed pro te, atque isto modo sui similes factos secum habeat; non ad concordiam caritatis, sed ad consortium supplicii, qui statuit sedem suam ponere in aquilone, ut te perversa et distorta via imitanti tenebrosi frigidique servirent. nos autem, domine, pusillus grex tuus ecce sumus, tu nos posside. praetende alas tuas, et fugiamus sub eas. gloria nostra tu esto; propter te amemur et timeamur in nobis. qui laudari vult ab hominibus vituperante te, non defenditur ab hominibus iudicante te, nec eripietur damnante te. cum autem non peccator laudatur in desideriis animae suae, nec qui iniqua gerit benedicitur, sed laudatur homo propter aliquod donum, quod dedisti ei, at ille plus gaudet sibi laudari se quam ipsum donum habere, unde laudatur, etiam iste te vituperante laudatur, et melior iam ille, qui

184

upon the ambitious designs of this world, and the
foundations of the mountains tremble at it. Because
now certain offices of human society make it necessary both to be loved and feared of men, even
therefore doth the adversary of our true blessedness lay hard at us, everywhere spreading in his
snares Well done, well done; that whilst we too
eagerly gather them up, we may be unawares taken,
and brought to disjoint our rejoicing from thy
truth, and to settle it in the deceiving opinions
of men; pleasing ourselves with being loved and
feared, not for thy sake, but in thy stead; by
which device the adversary may make us his own,
being made like unto him; not joined with him
in any concord of charity, but into the fellow-
ship of punishment: even of him who aspired to
advance his throne in the north, that all darkened
and befrozen, they might serve him, as he imitates
thee in his wry and crooked ways. But we, O Lord,
behold, we are thy little flock; keep thou still the
possession of us: stretch thy wings over us, and let
us fly under them. Be thou our glorying: for the
sake of thee in us let us be beloved and feared.
Whoever is ambitious to be commended of men,
when thou discommendest; he is not defended of
men when thou judgest; nor will he be delivered
when thou condemnest. When—not a sinner is
praised in the desires of his soul, nor he blessed
who doth ungodly, but a man is praised for some
gift which thou hast given him, yet pleases himself better in the hearing of his own praises than
in the gift for which he is praised: this man
also as well as the other, is praised while thou
dispraisest, and better is he that praised than
he that was praised: seeing to the one, the

laudavit, quam iste, qui laudatus est. illi enim placuit in homine donum dei, huic amplius placuit donum hominis quam dei.

XXXVII

TEMPTAMUR his temptationibus cotidie, domine, sine cessatione temptamur. cotidiana fornax nostra est humana lingua. imperas nobis et in hoc genere continentiam : da quod iubes et iube quód vis. tu nosti de hac re ad te gemitum cordis mei et flumina oculorum meorum. neque enim facile colligo, quam sim ab ista peste mundatior, et multum timeo occulta mea, quae norunt oculi tui, mei autem non. est enim qualiscumque in aliis generibus temptationum mihi facultas explorandi me, in hoc paene nulla est. nam et a voluptatibus carnis et a curiositate supervacuanea cognoscendi video quantum assecutus sim posse refrenare animum meum, cum eis rebus careo vel voluntate vel cum absunt. tunc enim me interrogo, quam magis minusve mihi molestum sit non habere. divitiae vero, quae ob hoc expetuntur, ut alicui trium istarum cupiditatum vel duabus earum vel omnibus serviant, si persentiscere non potest animus, utrum eas habens contemnat, possunt et dimitti,
186

gift of God in man was pleasing; but the other CHAP.
was better pleased with the gift of man than of XXXVI
God.

XXXVII

Praise and Dispraise, how they move us

ASSAILED daily we are by these temptations, O Lord; CHAP.
yea, we are assailed incessantly. The furnace we XXXVII
be daily tried in, is the tongue of men. And in this
kind also thou commandest us to be continent. Give
what thou commandest, and command what thou wilt.
Thou knowest what groans my heart, and floods mine
eyes, send up to thee for this. For easily can I not
discern how cleansed I am, more or less, from this
pollution, yea, and do I much fear my secret sins,
which thine eyes perceive well enough, though mine
cannot. For in other kinds of temptations I have
the ability, (such as it is) of examining myself; but
in this, scarce any at all. For, from the pleasures
of the flesh, and from the superfluous curiosity of
knowing, I well perceive how much I have gained
upon myself, in the refraining of my mind : whenas,
namely, I do without those things, forgoing them
or not having them. For then I ask myself how
troublesome it is unto me more or less, not to
have them. But as for riches, which are for this
end desired, that they may serve a man in some
one of those three concupiscences, or in any two, or 1 John ii.
all of them; if the soul be not able to discern, 16
whether, when it hath them it can contemn them;
they may even be cast aside, that it may make

ut se probet. laude vero ut careamus atque in eo
experiamur, quid possumus, numquid male vivendum
est et tam perdite atque immaniter, ut nemo nos
noverit, qui non detestetur? quae maior dementia
dici aut cogitari potest? at si bonae vĭtae bonorumque
operum comes et solet et debet esse laudatio, tam
comitatum eius quam ipsam bonam vitam deseri non
oportet. non autem sentio, sine quo esse aut aequo
animo aut aegre possim, nisi cum afuerit.

Quid igitur tibi in hoc genere temptationis, domine, confiteor? quid, nisi delectari me laudibus?
sed amplius ipsa veritate quam laudibus. nam si
mihi proponatur, utrum malim furens aut in omnibus rebus errans ab omnibus hominibus laudari, an
constans et in veritate certissimus ab omnibus vitu-
perari, video quid eligam. verum tamen nollem, ut
vel augeret mihi gaudium cuiuslibet boni mei suffra-
gatio oris alieni; sed auget, fateor, non solum, sed et
vituperatio minuit. et cum ista miseria mea perturbor subintrat mihi excusatio, quae qualis ṣit, tu scis,
deus; nam me incertum facit. quia enim nobis
imperasti non tantum continentiam, id est a quibus
rebus amorem cohibeamus, verum etiam iustitiam,
id est quo eum conferamus, nec te tantum voluisti a
nobis verum etiam proximum diligi, saepe mihi
videor de provectu aut spe proximi delectari, cum

experience of itself that way. But to enable of ourselves to do without praise, and for making trial what we can do in that kind, is our course to live ill, so desperately and out of all compass, that every body that knows us may detest us? What madder trick can either be said or thought of? But now if praise both useth and ought to be the companion of a good life and of good works; we ought as little to forgo that company, as good life itself. But I neither know whether I can well or ill be without anything, unless when it be absent.

What shall I therefore confess unto thee in this kind of temptation, O Lord? What, but that I am very much delighted with praises: but yet with the truth more than with the praises. For were I put to my choice, whether I would play the madman, or the fool in everything, and be generally praised for it; or be well settled and most assured of being in the right, and be generally discommended for it; I see straight what I would choose. Yet unwilling I should be that the praise given me by another man's mouth, should increase my joy for any good I have; and yet doth praise not only increase it, but dispraise doth diminish it. And when much troubled I am at this hard case of mine, I presently bethink myself of an excuse; which how sufficient it is, God thou knowest, for it leaves me uncertain. And for because thou hast not commanded us continency alone, that is, from what things we should refrain our love: but justice also, that is, which way we should bestow that love: and, that it is not thy will to have us love thee only, but our neighbour also: do I sometimes seem unto myself to be delighted with the proficiency or towardliness of my neighbour, when I am delighted

bene intellegentis laude delector, et rursus eius
malo contristari, cum eum audio vituperare quod aut
ignorat aut bonum est. nam et contristor aliquando
laudibus meis, cum vel ea laudantur in me, in quibus
mihi ipse displiceo, vel etiam bona minora et levia
pluris aestimantur, quam aestimanda sunt. sed
rursus unde scio, an propterea sic afficior, quia nolo
de me ipso a me dissentire laudatorem meum, non
quia illius utilitate moveor, sed quia eadem bona,
quae mihi in me placent, iucundiora mihi sunt, cum
et alteri placent? quodam modo enim non ego
laudor, cum de me sententia mea non laudatur,
quandoquidem aut illa laudantur, quae mihi displicent, aut illa amplius, quae mihi minus placent.
ergone de hoc incertus sum mei?

Ecce in te, veritas, video non me laudibus meis
propter me, sed propter proximi utilitatem moveri
oportere. et utrum ita sim, nescio. minus mihi de
hac re notus sum ipse quam tu. obsecro te, deus
meus, et me ipsum mihi indica, ut confitear oraturis
pro me fratribus meis, quod in me saucium con-
perero. iterum me diligentius interrogem. si
utilitate proximi moveor in laudibus meis, cur minus
moveor, si quisquam alius iniuste vituperetur quam
si ego? cur ea contumelia magis mordeor, quae in
me quam quae in alium eadem iniquitate coram me

with the praise of me, that understands; and I am CHAP.
sorry again for this want in him, when I hear him XXXVII
dispraise either that which he understands not, or
what is good. For I am sometimes very sorry at mine
own praises, when, namely, those things be praised in
me, in which I mislike myself, or that lesser and
lighter good things in me are more esteemed than in
reason they ought to be. But how again come I to
know whether I am thus affected, because I would
not have my commender dissent from me in things
that concern myself, not for that I am moved with the
care of his good, but for that the same good things in
me which very well please me, are the more pleasing
to me when they are so also to another? For in
some sort I am not then praised, when mine own
judgment of myself is not praised : forasmuch as
either those things are praised which please me not
at all; or those are more praised, which please me
less. Am I therefore uncertain of myself in this
matter?

Behold, O Truth, in thee I see, that I ought not
so much for mine own sake to be moved at mine
own praises as for the good of my neighbour. And
whether so I be, I know not. For I know less of
myself in this, than of thee. I beseech now, O my
God, discover me unto myself, that I may confess
unto my brethren who are to pray for me, what I
now find myself defective in. Once again let me
more diligently ask myself; if so I be moved with
the good of my brethren in mine own praises, why
then am I less moved if another man be unjustly
discommended, than if I be? Why am I more nettled
with that reproach which is cast upon myself, than
at that which is cast upon another in my presence,
for the same fault? Am I ignorant of this also?

CAP.
XXXVII

iacitur? an et hoc nescio? etiamne id restat, ut ipse me seducam et verum non faciam coram te in corde et lingua mea? insaniam istam, domine, longe fac a me, ne oleum peccatoris mihi sit os meum ad inpinguandum caput meum.

XXXVIII

CAP.
XXXVIII

EGENUS et pauper ego sum, et melior in occulto gemitu displicens mihi et quaerens misericordiam tuam, donec reficiatur defectus meus et perficiatur usque in pacem, quam nescit arrogantis oculus. sermo autem ore procedens et facta, quae innotescunt hominibus, habent temptationem periculosissimam ab amore laudis, qui ad privatam quandam excellentiam contrahit emendicata suffragia: temptat, et cum a me in me arguitur, eo ipso, quo arguitur, et saepe de ipso vanae gloriae contemptu vanius gloriatur, ideoque non iam de ipso contemptu gloriae gloriatur: non enim eam contemnit, cum gloriatur.

XXXIX

CAP.
XXXIX

INTUS etiam, intus est aliud in eodem genere temptationis malum, quo inanescunt qui placent sibi de se,

Or is this it at last, that I should now seduce myself, CHAP.
and neither think nor speak what is truth before XXXVII
thee? This madness put far from me, O Lord, lest
mine own mouth prove the oil of sinners unto me, to Ps. cxli. 5
make fat my head.

XXXVIII

Virtue is endangered by Vain-glory

I AM poor and needy: yet in better case, whilst in my CHAP.
private groanings I displease myself, and seek for thy XXXVIII
mercy; until my wants be supplied, and perfectly
made up into such an estate of peace, which the eye
of the proud is not acquainted withal. The report
of the people's mouths, and deeds known to men,
carry along with them a most dangerous temptation
from the love of praise: which, for the advancing of
a certain private excellency of our own, collects men's
votes as a beggar craves alms. It tempts, even when
it is reproved by myself in myself: yea, even in that
very particular, that it is reproved. And with a
greater vanity does a man glory oftentimes of his
contemning of vain-glory; for which reason he cannot
now be said to glory in his contempt of vain-glory:
for he does not truly contemn it, who glories at it.

XXXIX

Of Self-love

WITHIN us again, within us is yet another evil in the CHAP.
same kind of temptation, wherewith such people puff XXXIX
themselves up, as please themselves in themselves,

193

CAP.
XXXIX

quamvis aliis vel non placeant vel displiceant nec placere affectent ceteris. sed sibi placentes multum tibi displicent, non tantum de non bonis quasi bonis verum etiam de bonis tuis quasi suis, aut etiam sicut de tuis, sed tamquam de meritis suis, aut etiam sicut ex tua gratia, non tamen socialiter gaudentes, sed aliis invidentes eam. in his omnibus atque in huius modi periculis et laboribus vides tremorem cordis mei, et vulnera mea magis subinde a te sanari quam mihi non infligi sentio.

XL

CAP.
XL

Vbi non mecum ambulasti, veritas, docens, quid caveam et quid appetam, cum ad te referrem inferiora visa mea, quae potui, teque consulerem? lustravi mundum foris sensu, quo potui, et adtendi vitam corporis mei de me sensusque ipsos meos. inde ingressus sum in recessus memoriae meae, multiplices amplitudines plenas miris modis copiarum innumerabilium, et consideravi et expavi, et nihil eorum discernere potui sine te, et nihil eorum te esse inveni. nec ego ipse inventor, qui peragravi omnia et distinguere et pro suis quaeque dignitatibus aestimare conatus sum, excipiens alia nutantibus sensibus

194

however they please not or displease others or care CHAP.
not to please. These may please themselves, but XXXIX
thee do they displease highly: not only for pleasing
themselves in things not good, as if they were good,
but also for so doing in thy good things as if they
were their own: or as if thine, yet as given them for
their own merits: or, if also as proceeding from thy
mere grace, yet not in a neighbourly spirit, but as
grudging it to others. In all these perils and travails,
and others of the like kind, thou seest a trembling of
my heart: yea, and I well feel my wounds to be often
rather cured by thee, than not inflicted upon me.

XL

His Striving against Sin

WHERE hast thou not gone along with me, O thou CHAP.
Truth, teaching me both what to beware, and what XL
to desire; when I made report unto thee of what
I had seen here below, (so well as I could) and asked
thy advice upon them? With my outward senses so
well as I might I took a muster of this world; observ-
ing the life that the body hath of me, and these
senses of mine own. Thence turned I inwardly into
the withdrawing chambers of my memory, those
manifold large rooms, so wonderfully well furnished
of innumerable stores, and I considered, and stood
amazed; being able to discern nothing without thy
help, yet finding none of all these to be thyself.
Nor was I the finder of these things, I, who went
over them all, and who now laboured to distinguish
and to value everything according to its proper
worth: receiving some things with my faltering

et interrogans, alia mecum conmixta sentiens, ipsosque nuntios dinoscens atque dinumerans, iamque in memoriae latis opibus alia pertractans, alia recondens, alia eruens : nec ego ipse, cum haec agerem, id est vis mea, qua id agebam, nec ipsa eras tu, quia lux es tu permanens, quam de omnibus consulebam, an essent, quid essent, quanti pendenda essent : et audiebam docentem ac iubentem. et saepe istuc facio ; hoc me delectat, et ab actionibus necessitatis, quantum relaxari possum, ad istam voluptatem refugio. neque in his omnibus, quae percurro consulens te, invenio tutum locum animae meae nisi in te, quo colligantur sparsa mea nec a te quicquam recedat ex me. et aliquando intromittis me in affectum multum inusitatum introrsus ad nescio quam dulcedinem, quae si perficiatur in me, nescio quid erit, quod vita ista non erit. sed reccido in haec aerumnosis ponderibus et resorbeor solitis, et teneor et multum fleo, sed multum teneor. tantum consuetudinis sarcina digna est ! hic esse valeo nec volo, illic volo nec valeo, miser utrubique.

senses and inquiring, feeling other things that were
mixed with mine own self; yea, and taking particular
notice and tale of the reporters themselves; and anon
thoroughly canvassing over some things laid up in
the large treasury of my memory, storing up some of
them there again, and for my use drawing out some.
Neither was I myself when I did all this (that is, that
ability of mine own by which I did it, neither was it
thou, for thou art that never failing light, which
concerning all these I still advised withal, whether
they were, what they were, and how to be valued
they were:) and I overheard thee directing and
commanding me. And this I do very often: this
it is delights me; yea, and so fast as I get loose
from what necessity lays upon me, unto this pleasure
have I recourse. Nor in all these which I thus run
over consulting thee, can I find any one safe place
to settle my soul in, but in thyself only; into
whom let all my scattered pieces be gathered
together, nor let anything of mine be turned back
from thee. At some times thou inwardly admittest
me into an affection that I am not usually acquainted
with, rising to a strange sweetness, which, could it be
once perfected in me, it should be I know not what,
which this life shall never be. But by my cumber-
some weights am I tumbled down again, yea, quite
swallowed up by mine old wont, and fast holden by
it: much do I weep, yet fast am I still held down.
Such power hath the burden of custom to overload
a man. In this estate I am able to stay, but unwilling: in the other I would willingly be, but am
not able, miserable in both conditions.

XLI

CAP·
XLI
IDEOQUE consideravi languores peccatorum meorum in cupiditate triplici, et dexteram tuam invocavi ad salutem meam. vidi enim splendorem tuum corde saucio et repercussus dixi: quis illuc potest? proiectus sum a facie oculorum tuorum. tu es veritas super omnia praesidens. at ego per avaritiam meam non amittere te volui, sed volui tecum possidere mendacium, sicut nemo vult ita falsum dicere, ut nesciat ipse, quid verum sit. itaque amisi te, quia non dignaris cum mendacio possideri.

XLII

CAP.
XLII
QUEM invenirem, qui me reconciliaret tibi? ambiendum mihi fuit ad angelos? qua prece? quibus sacramentis? multi conantes ad te redire neque per se ipsos valentes, sicut audio, temptaverunt haec, et inciderunt in desiderium curiosarum visionum, et digni habiti sunt inlúsionibus. elati enim te quaerebant doctrinae fastu, exserentes potius quam tundentes pectora, et adduxerunt sibi per similitudinem cordis sui conspirantes et socias superbiae suae

198

XLI

God and a Lie cannot stand together

I HAVE thus considered the infirmities of my sins, in CHAP.
that threefold concupiscence : and I have called thy XLI
right hand to my help.   For with a wounded heart 1 John ii.
have I beheld thy brightness, and being beaten back, 16
I said : Who can attain thither ?   I am cast away from Ps. xxxi. 22
the sight of thine eyes : thou art the Truth which
sittest president over all.   But loth I was through
my covetousness to forgo thee ; but gladly would I
together with thee have possessed a lie : like as no
man there is so desirous to speak falsely, as that
himself may be hindered by it from knowing the
truth.   Verily therefore have I lost thee, because thou
vouchsafest not to be possest together with a lie.

XLII

Angels cannot be our Mediators

WHOM could I find to reconcile myself unto thee by ? CHAP.
Was I to sue the angels ? By what prayer ? By XLII
what sacraments ?   Many a man endeavouring to
return unto thee, and being not able of himself,
hath, as I hear, made trial of this way, and hath
fallen into the desire of curious visions, and hath been
thought worthy to be deluded.   For they being
high-minded, have sought thee out in the pride of
their learning ; swelling out rather than knocking
upon their breasts : and so by an affinity of heart,
have they drawn unto themselves the princes of the Eph. ii. 2
air, their fellow conspirators in pride ; to be deceived

CAP.
XLII

potestates aeris huius, a quibus per potentias magicas deciperentur, quaerentes mediatorem, per quem purgarentur, et non erat. diabolus enim erat ✝ ·ansfigurans se in angelum lucis. et multum inlexit superbam carnem, quod carneo corpore ipse non esset. erant enim illi mortales et peccatores, tu autem, domine, cui reconciliari volebant, immortalis et sine peccato. mediator autem inter deum et homines oportebat ut haberet aliquid simile deo, aliquid simile hominibus, ne in utroque hominibus similis longe esset a deo, aut in utroque deo similis longe esset ab hominibus, atque ita mediator non esset. fallax itaque ille mediator, quo per secreta iudicia tua superbia meretur inludi, unum cum hominibus habet, id est peccatum, aliud videri vult habere cum deo, ut, quia carnis mortalitate non tegitur, pro inmortali se ostentet. sed quia stipendium peccati mors est, hoc habet commune cum hominibus, unde simul damnetur in mortem.

XLIII

CAP.
XLIII

VERAX autem mediator, quem secreta tua misericordia demonstrasti hominibus, et misisti, et eius exemplo etiam ipsam discerent humilitatem, mediator ille dei et hominum, homo Christus Iesus, inter mortales

by them through the force of magic, even while they sought for a mediator by whom they might be purged: but there was none. For the devil it was, transfiguring now himself to an angel of light. And 2 Cor. xi. 14 it much enticed proud flesh, that himself was not of any fleshly body. For they were mortal and sinful; but thou, Lord, to whom they sought to be reconciled, art immortal and without sin. A mediator, now, betwixt God and man, must have something like unto God, and something like unto men; lest, that being like unto man in both natures, he should be too far unlike God: or if like unto God in both natures, he should be too far unlike to men: and so be a mediator neither way. That deceitful mediator, therefore, by whom in thy secret judgment pride deserves to be deluded, hath one thing indeed common with himself to men, and that sin: and desires to seem to share in another thing with God; that because he is not clothed with any mortality of flesh, he might thereby vaunt himself to be immortal. But, for that the wages of sin is death, this hath he Rom. vi. 20 common to himself with men, that together with them he should be condemned unto death.

XLIII

Christ only is the all-sufficient Intercessor

But the true mediator, whom out of thy secret mercy thou hast shewed forth unto men, and whom thou sentest, that by his example they might learn the true humility: that Mediator therefore between 1 Tim. ii. God and man, the man Christ Jesus, appeared betwixt 5

CAP.
XLIII

peccatores et inmortalem iustum apparuit, mortalis cum hominibus, iustus cum deo, ut, quoniam stipendium iustitiae vita et pax est, per iustitiam coniunctam deo evacuaret mortem iustificatorum inpiorum, quam cum illis voluit habere conmunem. hic demonstratus est antiquis sanctis, ut ita ipsi per fidem futurae passionis eius, sicut nos per fidem praeteritae, salvi fierent. in quantum enim homo, in tantum mediator, in quantum autem verbum, non medius, quia aequalis deo et deus apud deum et simul unus deus.

In quantum nos amasti, pater bone, qui filio tuo unico non pepercisti, sed pro nobis inpiis tradidisti eum! quomodo nos amasti, pro quibus ille non rapinam arbitratus esse aequalis tibi factus est subditus usque ad mortem crucis: unus ille in mortuis liber, potestatem habens ponendi animam suam et potestatem habens iterum sumendi eam, pro nobis tibi victor et victima, et ideo victor, quia victima, pro nobis tibi sacerdos et sacrificium, et ideo sacerdos, quia sacrificium, faciens tibi nos de servis filios de te nascendo, tibi serviendo. merito mihi spes valida in illo est, quod sanabis omnes languores meos per eum, qui sedet ad dexteram tuam et te interpellat pro nobis: alioquin desperarem. multi enim et magni sunt idem languores, multi sunt et magni; sed amplior est medicina tua. potuimus putare verbum tuum remotum esse a coniunctione

mortal sinners and the immortal Just One : being CHAP.
mortal with men, and just with God : that because the XLIII
wages of righteousness is life and peace, he might
by his righteousness which was joined to God, make
void the death of as many of the wicked, as were
by him justified, which death his will was to have
common both to them and him. He was shewed
forth unto holy men of old ; to the intent that they
might be saved through faith in his passion to come,
like as we are through faith of it already passed.
For how far forth he was a man, so far forth was he
mediator : but so far forth as he is the Word, he is
not mid-way to God, because he is equal to God,
and God with God, and together one God.

How hast thou loved us, O good Father, that hast
not spared thine only son, but hast delivered him Rom. viii.
unto death for us wicked men ? How hast thou 32
loved us, for whom he that thought it no robbery to Phil. ii.
be equal with God, was made subject unto death, 6, 8
even the death of the cross ? He that was alone free Ps.
among the dead, that had power to lay down his life, lxxxviii. 5
and power to take it up again : for us was he unto John x. 18
thee both the Victor and the Victim, and therefore
Victor, because the Victim : for us was he unto thee
both the Priest and the Sacrifice, and therefore the
Priest, because the Sacrifice : of slaves making us thy
children, by being born of thee, and by becoming a
servant unto thee. Deservedly therefore is my hope
strongly settled upon him, that thou wilt by him cure
all my infirmities ; even by him that sits at thy right
hand, and maketh intercession for us ; whereas otherwise I should despair utterly. For many and great
are those infirmities, yea many they are and great ;
but thy medicine is more sovereign. Imagine we
might that thy word was far enough from being

CAP.
XLIII
hominis et desperare de nobis, nisi caro fieret et
habitaret in nobis.

Conterritus peccatis meis et mole miseriae meae,
agitaveram corde meditatusque fueram fugam in soli-
tudinem, sed prohibuisti me et confortasti me dicens:
Ideo Christus pro omnibus mortuus est, ut et qui
vivunt iam non sibi vivant, sed ei qui pro omnibus mortuus est. ecce, domine, iacto in te curam
meam, ut vivam, et considerabo mirabilia de lege
tua. tu scis inperitiam meam et infirmitatem meam:
doce me et sana me. ille tuus unicus, in quo sunt
omnes thesauri sapientiae et scientiae absconditi,
redemit me sanguine suo. non calumnientur mihi
superbi, quoniam cogito pretium meum, et
manduco et bibo, et erogo et pauper cupio
saturari ex eo inter illos, qui edunt
et saturantur: et laudabunt dominum qui requirunt eum.

united with man, and so despair of ourselves ; unless CHAP.
it had been made flesh and dwelt among us. XLIII

Affrighted thus with mine own sins and the burden
of mine own misery, I cast these thoughts in my
heart, bethinking myself of fleeing into the wilderness : but thou forbadest me, and strengthenedst me,
saying : Therefore Christ died for all, that they which 2 Cor. v. 15
live, may now no longer live unto themselves, but
unto him that died for all. See, Lord, I henceforth
cast all my care upon thee, that I may live, and I will Ps. lv. 22,
consider wonderful things out of thy law. Thou cxix. 18
knowest both my unskilfulness and my infirmity ;
oh, teach me, and heal me. That only Son of thine,
in whom are hid all the treasures of wisdom and Col. ii. 3
knowledge, hath redeemed me with his blood. Let
not the proud speak evil of me now ; for that I medi- Ps. cxix.122
tate upon the price of my redemption, and do
eat and drink, and give unto the poor ;
and being poor myself, desire to be
filled by him, amongst those
that eat, and are satisfied ;
and they shall praise Ps. xxxii.
the Lord who 16
seek him.

BOOK XI

LIBER VNDECIMVS

I

NUMQUID, domine, cum tua sit aeternitas, ignoras, quae tibi dico, aut ad tempus vides quod fit in tempore? cur ergo tibi tot rerum narrationes digero? non utique per me noveris ea, sed affectum meum excito in te et eorum, qui haec legunt, ut dicamus omnes: Magnus dominus et laudabilis valde. iam dixi et dicam: amore amoris tui facio istuc. nam et oramus, et tamen veritas ait: Novit pater vester quid vobis opus sit, priusquam petatis ab eo. affectum ergo nostrum patefacimus in te, confitendo tibi miserias nostras et misericordias tuas super nos, ut liberes nos omnino, quoniam coepisti, ut desinamus esse miseri in nobis et beatificemur in te, quoniam vocasti nos, ut simus pauperes spiritu et mites et lugentes, et esurientes ac sitientes iustitiam, et misericordes et mundicordes et pacifici. ecce narravi tibi multa, quae potui et quae volui, quoniam tu prior voluisti, ut confiterer tibi, domino deo meo, quoniam bonus es, quoniam in saeculum misericordia tua.

THE ELEVENTH BOOK

I

Why we confess unto God who knows all

CANST thou that art the Lord of all eternity, be CHAP.
1 ignorant of what I say unto thee? Or dost thou see in relation to time, that which passeth in time? Why then do I lay in order before thee so many narrations? Not to this end I do it, that thou mayest come to know them upon my relation; but thereby I stir up mine own and my readers' devotions towards thee, that we may say all together: Great is the Lord, and greatly to be praised. Now Ps. xcvi. 4 have I said, and again say it I will; for the love of thy love make I this confession. For we use to pray also, and yet Truth itself hath said: Your Father Matt. vi. 8 knoweth what you have need of, before you ask. 'Tis our affection therefore which we hereby lay open unto thee, while we confess our own miseries, and thy mercies upon us, that thou mayest thoroughly set us free, seeing already thou hast begun, that we may leave to be wretched in ourselves, and may be happy in thee: since thou hast called us, that we may become poor in spirit, and meek, and mournful, and Matt. v. 3–9 hungry and thirsty after righteousness, and merciful, and pure in heart, and peace-makers. See, I have told thee many things, as I could, and as I would; because thou wouldest first that I should confess unto thee my Lord God, for thou art good, for thy Ps. cxviii.
2 mercy endureth for ever.

II

CAP.
II
Quando autem sufficio lingua calami enuntiare omnia
hortamenta tua, et omnes terrores tuos et consolationes et gubernationes, quibus me perduxisti prae-
dicare verbum et sacramentum tuum dispensare
populo tuo? et si sufficio haec enuntiare ex ordine,
caro mihi valent stillae temporum. et olim inardesco
meditari in lege tua, et in ea tibi confiteri scientiam
et inperitiam meam, primordia inluminationis tuae et
reliquias tenebrarum mearum, quousque devoretur a
fortitudine infirmitas. et nolo in aliud horae diffluant,
quas invenio liberas a necessitatibus reficiendi corporis et intentionis animi, et servitutis, quam debemus
hominibus, et quam non debemus et tamen reddimus.

Domine deus meus, intende orationi meae, et
misericordia tua exaudiat desiderium meum, quoniam
non mihi soli aestuat, sed usui vult esse fraternae
caritati: et vides in corde meo quia sic est. sacri-
ficem tibi famulatum cogitationis et linguae meae, et
da quod offeram tibi. inops enim et pauper sum, tu
dives in omnes invocantes te, qui securus curam
nostri geris. circumcide ab omni temeritate omnique
mendacio interiora et exteriora mea, labia mea. sint

II

He sueth to be delivered from his Sins and Errors,
and to be guided unto the true Knowledge

BUT when shall I be able with the tongue of my
pen to set forth all thy exhortations, and all thy
terrors and comforts, and directions, by which thou
hast brought me up to be a preacher of thy word,
and a dispenser of thy Sacrament unto thy people ?
If I now be able to declare these things to thee in
order, the drops of time are very precious with me ;
and I have long since had a burning desire to meditate in thy law ; and therein to confess both my skill
and unskilfulness unto thee, the morning light of thy
enlightening me, and the relics of darkness in me so
long remaining, till infirmity be swallowed up by
strength. Nor would I have my hours to be squan-
dered away upon any other thing, which I find free
from the necessities of refreshing of my body, and
the recreating of my mind, and the complying in
those offices of service which we owe unto men ; yea,
also which we owe not, and yet pay them.

Give ear unto my prayer, O Lord my God, and let
thy mercy hearken unto my petition : because it
striveth not to entreat for myself alone, but to be
useful also to brotherly love. Thou seest in my
heart, that so it is. I would sacrifice unto thee the
service of my thoughts and tongue : now give me,
what I am to offer unto thee. For I am poor
and needy, but thou art rich to all those that
call upon thee ; who not distracted with cares
thyself, takest care of us all. From all rashness
and lying do thou circumcise both my inward and my

CHAP.
II

The hour-
glass then
measured
by water-
drops

Ps. viii. 16
Rom. x. 12

211

CAP. castae deliciae meae scripturae tuae, nec fallar in eis
II nec fallam ex eis. domine, adtende et miserere,
domine deus meus, lux caecorum et virtus infirmorum,
statimque lux videntium et virtus fortium, adtende
animam meam et audi clamantem de profundo. nam
nisi adsint et in profundo aures tuae, quo ibimus?
quo clamabimus? tuus est dies et tua est nox: ad
nutum tuum momenta transvolant. largire inde
spatium meditationibus nostris in abdita legis tuae,
neque adversus pulsantes claudas eam. neque enim
frustra scribi voluisti tot paginarum opaca secreta, aut
non habent illae silvae cervos suos recipientes se in
eas et resumentes, ambulantes et pascentes, recumbentes et ruminantes. o domine, perfice me et revela
mihi eas. ecce vox tua gaudium meum, vox tua
super afluentiam voluptatum. da quod amo: amo
enim. et hoc tu dedisti. ne dona tua deseras nec
herbam tuam spernas sitientem. confitear tibi quidquid invenero in libris tuis, et audiam vocem laudis,
et te bibam, et considerem mirabilia de lege tua
ab usque principio, in quo fecisti caelum et terram,
usque ad regnum tecum perpetuum sanctae civitatis
tuae.

Domine, miserere mei et exaudi desiderium
meum. puto enim, quod non sit de terra, non de
auro et argento et lapidibus aut decoris vestibus aut

outward parts, my lips. Let my chaste delights be
thy Scriptures : let me neither be deceived in them,
nor deceive out of them. Hearken Lord, and have
mercy upon me, O Lord my God, O thou Light of the
blind, and the Strength of the weak ; yea, the Light
of those that see, and the Strength of the strong ;
hearken thou unto my soul, and hear me crying unto
thee out of the deep. For if thine ears be not with
us also in the deep, whither then shall we go ? To
whom shall we cry ? The day is thine, and the
night is thine : at thy beck the moments fly past.
Afford out of it some spare time for my meditation upon the hidden things of the Law; which I
beseech thee shut not up against them that knock.
For in vain it was not, that thou wouldst have so
many leaves full of darksome secrets committed
unto writing : nor are those forests without their
harts which retire themselves into them, making
their range and walks in them ; feeding, lodging,
and chewing the cud in them. Perfect me, O Lord,
and reveal them unto me. Behold thy voice is my
joy ; yea, thy voice exceedeth the abundance of all
pleasures. Give me what I love : for verily I do
love it ; and this love is of thy giving. Forsake not
therefore thine own gifts, nor despise thou him that
thirsteth after thy herbage. Let me confess unto
thee whatsoever I shall find in thy books; and let
me hear the voice of praise ; and let me drink thee
up ; and let me consider of the wonderful things of
thy Law : even from the very beginning wherein
thou madest the heaven and the earth, unto that
everlasting reign of thy holy city with thee.

Have mercy, Lord, upon me, and hear my petition :
for it is not I suppose of the earth ; not for gold and
silver, or precious stones, or gorgeous apparel, or

CAP. honoribus et potestatibus aut voluptatibus carnis
II neque de necessariis corpori et huic vitae peregrina-
tionis nostrae, quae omnia nobis adponuntur quaerentibus regnum et iustitiam tuam. vide, deus
meus, unde sit desiderium meum. narraverunt mihi
iniusti delectationes, sed non sicut lex tua, domine.
ecce unde est desiderium meum. vide, pater, aspice
et vide et adproba, et placeat in conspectu misericordiae tuae invenire me gratiam ante te, ut aperi-
antur pulsanti mihi interiora sermonum tuorum.
obsecro per dominum nostrum Iesum Christum
filium tuum, virum dexterae tuae, filium hominis,
quem confirmasti tibi mediatorem tuum et nostrum,
per quem nos quaesisti non quaerentes te, quaesisti
autem, ut quaereremus te, verbum tuum, per quod
fecisti omnia, in quibus et me, unicum tuum, per
quem vocasti in adoptionem populum credentium,
in quo et me : per eum te obsecro, qui sedet ad
dexteram tuam et te interpellat pro nobis, in quo
sunt omnes thesauri sapientiae et scientiae absconditi. ipsos quaero in libris tuis. Moyses de illo
scripsit : hoc ipse ait, hoc veritas ait.

III

CAP. AUDIAM et intellegam, quomodo in principio fecisti
III caelum et terram. scripsit hoc Moyses, scripsit et
abiit, transiit hinc a te ad te neque nunc ante me

214

honours and offices, or the pleasures of the flesh : or CHAP.
necessaries of the body, or for this life of our earthly II
pilgrimage ; all which shall be added to those that Matt. vi. 33
seek thy kingdom and thy righteousness. Behold
O Lord my God, whence my desire proceeds. The
ungodly have sometimes told me what themselves
delight in : but they are not like the delights of thy Ps. cxix.
Law. See now whence my desire proceeds. See, 85
Father, behold, see and approve; and let it be pleasing
in the sight of thy mercy, that I shall find so much
grace with thee, as that the secrets of thy Word may
be opened unto me when I knock. By our Lord
Jesus Christ thy Son I beseech thee, that Man on
thy right hand, that Son of Man, whom thou hast
appointed a Mediator betwixt thyself and us, by
whom thou soughtest us, who sought not for thee :
yet didst thou seek us, that we might seek thee,
and thy Word by whom thou madest all things, and
me amongst them ; thy only Son by whom thou
hast called the believing people unto thee, and me
amongst them : by him I beseech thee, who sitteth
at thy right hand, and maketh intercession for us, in
whom are hid all the treasures of wisdom and know- Col. ii. 3
ledge. These same do I seek in thy books. Of him
Moses wrote ; this saith himself, this Truth says. John v. 46

III

He desires to understand the Holy Scriptures

LET me hear and understand how thou in the begin- CHAP.
ning hast made heaven and earth. This Moses wrote III
of ; he wrote and passed away, he passed hence from
thee unto thee, and he is not at this present before

CAP.
III

est. nam si esset, tenerem eum et rogarem eum et per te obsecrarem, ut mihi ista panderet, et praeberem aures corporis mei sonis erumpentibus ex ore eius, et si hebraea voce loqueretur, frustra pulsaret sensum meum nec inde mentem meam quicquam tangeret; si autem latine, scirem quid diceret. sed unde scirem, an verum diceret? quod si et hoc scirem, num ab illo scirem? intus utique mihi, intus in domicilio cogitationis nec hebraea nec graeca nec latina nec barbara veritas sine oris et linguae organis, sine strepitu syllabarum diceret: "verum dicit," et ego statim certus confidenter illi homini tuo dicerem: "verum dicis." quum ergo illum interrogare non possim, te, quo plenus vera dixit, veritas, rogo, te, deus meus, rogo, parce peccatis meis, et qui illi servo tuo dedisti haec dicere, da et mihi haec intellegere.

IV

CAP.
IV

ECCE sunt caelum et terra, clamant, quod facta sint; mutantur enim atque variantur. quidquid autem factum non est et tamen est, non est in eo quicquam, quod ante non erat: quod est mutari atque variari. clamant etiam, quod se ipsa non fecerint: "ideo

mine eyes. For if he were, then would I lay hold CHAP.
III of him, and entreat him, and for thy sake would I beseech him to open these things unto me: yea, I would lay the ears of my body unto the sound bursting out of his mouth. And should he speak in the Hebrew tongue, in vain should he beat mine ears, and never should he come near my understanding: whereas if he spake Latin, I should know what he said. But how should I know whether he said truth or no? And if I could learn this too, should I know it from him? Yea, for certainly within me, in that inward house of my thoughts, Truth, neither Hebrew, nor Greek, nor Latin, nor of any other language, without helps of the mouth and tongue, without any sound of syllables, should tell me he says true; and myself thereupon assured of it, would confidently say unto that servant of thine: Thou speakest truth. Seeing, therefore, I have not now the means to confer with Moses, I beg of thee, Truth (inspired by whom he uttered these truths) of thee, my God, pardon of my sins: and thou that enabledst that servant of thine to deliver these truths, enable me also to understand them.

IV

The Creatures proclaim God to be their Creator

BEHOLD, the heavens and the earth are already, they CHAP.
IV proclaim themselves to have been created: for they are changed and altered from what they were. See Book
VII. xi. Whereas whatsoever is not made, and yet hath a being, hath nothing in it now, which it had not before: which is to be changed and altered. They proclaim also, that they made not themselves; but

CAP.
IV

sumus, quia facta sumus; non ergo eramus, antequam essemus, ut fieri possemus a nobis.". et vox dicentium est ipsa evidentia. tu ergo, domine, fecisti ea, qui pulcher es: pulchra sunt enim; qui bonus es: bona sunt enim; qui es: sunt enim. nec ita pulchra sunt nec ita bona sunt nec ita sunt, sicut tu conditor eorum, quo comparato nec pulchra sunt nec bona sunt nec sunt. scimus haec, gratias tibi, et scientia nostra scientiae tuae comparata ignorantia est.

V

CAP.
V

QVOMODO autem fecisti caelum et terram et quae machina tam grandis operationis tuae? non enim sicut homo artifex, formans corpus de corpore arbitratu animae, valentis imponere utcumque speciem, quam cernit in semet ipsa interno oculo—et unde hoc valeret, nisi quia tu fecisti eam?—et imponit speciem iam exsistenti et habenti, ut esset, veluti terrae aut lapidi aut ligno aut auro aut id genus rerum cuilibet. et unde ista essent, nisi tu instituisses ea? tu fabro corpus, tu animam membris imperitantem fecisti, tu materiam, unde facit aliquid, tu ingenium, quo artem capiat et videat intus quid faciat foris, tu sensum corporis, quo interprete traiciat

say: Therefore we are, because we are made; and CHAP.
therefore were we not, before our time was to be, IV
so as to make ourselves. And this utterance of
thine is itself demonstration. 'Tis thou therefore,
O Lord, that madest them: thou who art full of
beauty, for they are beautiful: thou who art good,
for they also are good: even thou who hast being,
seeing these have their beings: yet are they neither
so beautiful, so good, nor are so, as thou their Creator
art; compared with whom, they are neither beautiful,
nor good, nor are at all. Thus much we know, thanks
be to thee for it: yet is our knowledge in comparison
of thine, but mere ignorance.

V

How the World was made of Nothing

BUT how didst thou make heaven and earth? And CHAP.
what engine hadst thou to work all this vast fabric of V
thine? For thou wentest not about it like a human
artificer, who shaping one body by another, purposes
according to the discretion of his mind, which can in
some way cast it into such a figure, as in itself it seeth
by the inward eye. And whence should it be able
to do all this, unless thou hadst made that mind?
And he puts a figure upon that which had being and
existence before; suppose clay, or stone, or wood,
or gold, or other thing. And whence should these
materials have their being, hadst not thou appointed
it them? 'Tis thou that madest the artificer his
body, thou gavest a soul to direct his limbs; thou
madest the stuff of which he makes anything; thou
madest that apprehension whereby he may take his
art, and may see within what he hath to do without:

CAP.
V
ab animo ad materiam id quod facit, et renuntiet animo quid factum sit, ut ille intus consulat praesidentem sibi veritatem, an bene factum sit. te laudant haec omnia creatorem omnium. sed tu .quomodo facis ea? quomodo fecisti, deus, caelum et terram? non utique in caelo neque in terra fecisti caelum et terram neque in aere aut in aquis, quoniam et haec pertinent ad caelum et terram, neque in universo mundo fecisti universum mundum, quia non erat, ubi fieret, antequam fieret, ut esset. nec manu tenebas aliquid, unde faceres caelum et terram: nam unde tibi hoc, quod tu non feceras, unde aliquid faceres? quid enim est, nisi quia tu es? ergo dixisti et facta sunt, atque in verbo tuo fecisti ea.

VI

CAP.
VI
SED quomodo dixisti? numquid illo modo, quo facta est vox de nube dicens: Hic est filius meus dilectus? illa enim vox acta atque transacta est, coepta et finita. sonuerunt syllabae atque transierunt, secunda post primam, tertia post secundam atque inde ex ordine, donec ultima post ceteras silentiumque post

thou gavest him the senses of his body ; which being CHAP.
his interpreters, he may from his mind into the stuff, V
convey that figure which he is now a-working ; which
is to signify unto his mind again, what is done already ;
that he within upon it may consult the truth which
rules him, whether it be well done. All these things
praise thee, the Creator of these things. But yet
which way dost thou make them ? How, O God,
didst thou make heaven and earth ? Verily, neither
in the heaven, nor on the earth didst thou make the
heaven and earth : no, nor yet in the air, or waters,
seeing these also belong unto the heaven and the
earth. Nor yet in the whole world didst thou make
that whole world ; because there was no place where
to make it, before it was made, that it might have a
being. Nor didst thou hold anything in thy hand
whereof to make this heaven and earth : for how
couldst thou come by that which thyself hadst not
made, to make anything ? For what hath any being,
but only because thou art ? Therefore thou spakest,
and they were made, and in thy Word thou madest
them.

VI

*He disputes curiously what manner of Word the
World was created by*

BUT how didst thou speak ? Was it in the same way CHAP.
that the voice came out of a cloud, saying : This is VI
my beloved Son ? As for that voice, it was uttered, Matt. iii. 17
and passed away, had a beginning and ending ; the
syllables made a sound, and so passed over, the second
after the first, the third after the second, and so forth
in order, until the last came after the rest, and
silence after the last. By which most clear and plain

CAP. ultimam. unde claret atque eminet, quod creaturae
VI motus expressit eam, serviens aeternae voluntati tuae,
ipse temporalis. et haec ad tempus facta verba tua
nuntiavit auris exterior menti prudenti, cuius auris
interior posita est ad aeternum verbum tuum. at
illa comparavit haec verba temporaliter sonantia cum
aeterno in silentio verbo tuo et dixit: "aliud est
longe, longe aliud est. haec longe infra me sunt nec
sunt, quia fugiunt et praetereunt: verbum autem dei
mei supra me manet in aeternum." si ergo verbis
sonantibus et praetereuntibus dixisti, ut fieret caelum
et terra, atque ita fecisti caelum et terram, erat iam
creatura corporalis ante caelum et terram, cuius motibus temporalibus temporaliter vox illa percurreret.
nullum autem corpus ante caelum et terram, aut si
erat, id certe sine transitoria voce feceras, unde trans-
itoriam vocem faceres, qua diceres ut fieret caelum
et terra. quidquid enim illud esset, unde talis vox
fieret, nisi abs te factum esset, omnino non esset. ut
ergo fieret corpus, unde ista verba fierent, quo verbo
a te dictum est?

it is, that the motion of a creature expressed it, serving thy eternal will in it, itself being but temporal. And these words of thine thus made to serve for the time, did the outward ear give notice of unto the intelligent soul, whose inward ear lay listening to thy eternal Word. But this latter compared these words thus sounding within a proportion of time, with that eternal Word of thine, which is in the silence, and it said: This Word is far another from that, a very different Word; these words are far beneath me, nay, they are not at all, because they flee and pass away; but the Word of God is far above me, and abides for ever. If therefore in sounding and passing words, thou spakest that heaven and earth should be made, and that way didst create heaven and earth: then was there a corporeal creature even before heaven and earth, by whose motions measured by time that voice took his course in time. But there was not any creature before heaven and earth; or if there were, verily then thou hadst, without such a passing voice created that, whereof thou mightest make this passing voice, by which thou wert to say the word: Let the heaven and earth be made. For whatsoever that were, of which such a voice were to be made, unless by thyself it were made, it should not at all have any being. That a body therefore might be made, by which these words might be made; by what word of thine was it commanded?

VII

CAP.
VII

Vocas itaque nos ad intellegendum verbum, deum
apud te deum, quod sempiterne dicitur et eo sempiterne dicuntur omnia. neque enim finitur, quod
dicebatur, et dicitur aliud, ut possint dici omnia, sed
simul ac sempiterne omnia : alioquin iam tempus et
mutatio, et non vera aeternitas nec vera inmortalitas.
hoc novi, deus meus, et gratias ago. novi, confiteor
tibi, domine deus, mecumque novit et benedicit te
quisquis ingratus non est certae veritati. novimus
enim, domine, novimus, quoniam in quantum quidque
non est quod erat et est quod non erat, in tantum
moritur et oritur. non ergo quicquam verbi tui cedit
atque succedit, quoniam vere inmortale atque aeternum est. et ideo verbo tibi coaeterno simul et
sempiterne dicis omnia, quae dicis, et fit, quidquid
dicis ut fiat; nec aliter quam dicendo facis : nec
tamen simul et sempiterna fiunt omnia, quae dicendo
facis.

VIII

CAP.
VIII

Cur, quaeso, domine deus meus? utcumque video,
sed quomodo id eloquar nescio, nisi quia omne,

VII

The Son of God is the Word co-eternal with the Father

THOU callest us therefore to understand the Word, CHAP. VII
who is God, with thee God : which Word is spoken
unto everlasting, and in it are all things spoken
unto everlasting. For that which was spoken was
not spoken successively, one thing spoken ended
that the next might be spoken : but all at once,
and unto everlasting. Otherwise there should be
time and alteration ; and no true eternity, no true
immortality. Thus much I know, O my God, thanks
to thee therefore. This I know, as I confess, to
thee, O Lord ; yea, he knows and blesses thee as I
do, whoever is not unthankful to thy assured verity.
We know O Lord, we know ; since in as much as
anything is not now which was, or is now which was
not, so far forth it dies and arises. Nothing therefore of thy word doth give place and replace ; because
it is truly immortal and eternal. And therefore by
thy Word co-eternal with thyself, thou dost once
and forever say all thou sayest ; and it is made, whatsoever thou sayest shall be made. Nor dost thou
make it otherwise than by saying : and yet are not
all things made together, or everlasting, which so
thou makest by saying.

VIII

The Word of God is our Teacher in all

WHY, I beseech thee, O Lord my God, is this so ? CHAP. VIII
Verily I see it after a sort ; but how to express it I know

CAP.
VIII
quod esse incipit et esse desinit, tunc esse incipit et tunc desinit, quando debuisse incipere vel desinere in aeterna ratione cognoscitur, ubi nec incipit aliquid nec desinit. ipsum est verbum tuum, quod et principium est, quia et loquitur nobis. sic in evangelio per carnem ait, et hoc insonuit foris auribus hominum, ut crederetur et intus quaereretur, et inveniretur in aeterna veritate, ubi omnes discipulos bonus et solus magister docet. ibi audio vocem tuam, domine, dicentis mihi, quoniam ille loquitur nobis, qui docet nos, qui autem non docet nos, etiam si loquitur, non nobis loquitur. quis porro nos docet nisi stabilis veritas? quia et per creaturam mutabilem cum admonemur, ad veritatem stabilem ducimur, ubi vere discimus, cum stamus et audimus eum, et gaudio gaudemus propter vocem sponsi, reddentes nos, unde sumus. et ideo principium, quia, nisi maneret, cum erraremus, non esset quo rediremus. cum autem redimus ab errore, cognoscendo utique redimus; ut autem cognoscamus, docet nos, quia principium est et loquitur nobis.

IX

CAP.
IX
In hoc principio fecisti, deus, caelum et terram, in verbo tuo, in filio tuo, in virtute tua, in sapientia tua, in veritate tua, miro modo dicens et miro modo faciens.

not, unless thus it be : namely, that whatsoever begins CHAP.
to be, and leaves off to be, begins then, and leaves off VIII
then, when in thy eternal reason it is known that it
ought to have begun or left off: in which reason
nothing does either begin or leave off. This is thy
Word, which is also the beginning, because also it John viii.
speaks unto us. Thus in the Gospel he speaketh 25
through the flesh : and so much sounded outwardly
in the ears of men, to the intent it might be believed
and sought for inwardly, and found in the eternal
verity; where that good and only Master teaches all
his disciples. There Lord, hear I thy voice speaking unto me ; because he there speaks unto us, who
teaches us ; but he that doth not teach us, though he
does speak, yet to us he speaketh not. And who now
teaches us but the unalterable Truth ? seeing that
when we receive any admonishment through a mutable creature, we are but led along unto that unalterable Truth, where we learn truly, while we stand and
hear him, rejoicing greatly because of the bride- John iii. 29
groom's voice ; and return ourselves back to that
from whence we are derived. Which is therefore
the Beginning, because unless it should remain firm,
there should not be, when we erred, whither to
return. Now when we return from error, it is by
knowing, verily, that we do return : and that we may
know, he teaches us; because he is the Beginning
and speaketh unto us.

IX

How the Word of God speaketh unto the Heart

IN this Beginning, O God, hast thou made heaven CHAP.
and earth, namely, in thy Word, in thy Son, in IX
thy Power, in thy Wisdom, in thy Truth; after a

CAP.
IX
quis conprehendet? quis enarrabit? quid est illud,
quod interlucet mihi et percutit cor meum sine
laesione? et inhorresco et inardesco: inhorresco, in
quantum dissimilis ei sum, inardesco, in quantum
similis ei sum. sapientia, sapientia ipsa est, quae
interlucet mihi, discindens nubilum meum, quod me
rursus cooperit deficientem ab ea, caligine atque
aggere poenarum mearum, quoniam sic infirmatus
est in egestate vigor meus, ut non sufferam bonum
meum; donec tu, domine, qui propitius factus es omnibus iniquitatibus meis, etiam sanes omnes languores
meos; quia et redimes de corruptione vitam meam et
coronabis me in miseratione et misericordia; et satiabis
in bonis desiderium meum, quoniam renovabitur iu-
ventus mea sicut aquilae. spe enim salvi facti sumus,
et promissa tua per patientiam expectamus. audiat
te intus sermocinantem qui potest; ego fidenter ex
oraculo tuo clamabo: quam magnificata sunt opera
tua, domine, omnia in sapientia fecisti! et illa principium, et in eo principio fecisti caelum et terram.

X

CAP.
X
NONNE ecce pleni sunt vetustatis suae qui nobis dicunt:
Quid faciebat deus, antequam faceret caelum et ter-
ram? si enim vacabat, inquiunt, et non operabatur

wonderful manner speaking, and after a wonderful CHAP.
manner making. Who is able to comprehend it? IX
Who can declare it? What is that which shines
through me, and strikes upon my heart without
hurting it? And I shudder and kindle: shudder,
in as much as I am unlike it; kindle, in as much
as I am like it. 'Tis Wisdom, Wisdom's self which
thus shines into me; even breaking through my
cloudiness: which yet again overshadows me fainting
from it, under the gross fog and heavy load of mine
own punishment. For my strength is pulled so Ps. xxxi. 10
low in this poor case of mine, as that I am not able
to endure that which should be for my good; till
thou, Lord, becoming favourable to all mine iniquities, Ps. ciii. 3-5
pleasest to heal my diseases. For thou also shalt
redeem my life from corruption, and shalt crown me
with loving kindness and tender mercies; yea, thou
shalt satisfy my desire with good things, because my
youth shall be restored like an eagle's. For by hope Rom. viii.
we are saved: wherefore we through patience await 24
for thy promises. Let him that is able, hear thee
inwardly discoursing to him. For my part, in the
words of thine oracle will I boldly cry out: How
wonderful are thy works, O Lord, in wisdom hast Ps. civ. 24
thou made them all; and this Wisdom is that
Beginning; and in that Beginning hast thou made
heaven and earth.

X

God's Will knows no Beginning

Lo, are they not full of their old leaven which demand CHAP.
of us: How did God employ himself before he made X
heaven and earth? For if he were unemployed, say

CAP.
X

aliquid, cur non sic semper et deinceps, quemadmodum retro semper cessavit ab opere? si enim ullus
motus in deo novus extitit et voluntas nova, ut
creaturam conderet, quam numquam ante condiderat,
quomodo iam vera aeternitas, ubi oritur voluntas,
quae non erat? neque enim voluntas dei creatura
est, sed ante creaturam, quia non crearetur aliquid,
nisi creatoris voluntas praecederet. ad ipsam ergo
dei substantiam pertinet voluntas eius. quod si exor-
tum est aliquid in dei substantia, quod prius non erat,
non veraciter dicitur aeterna illa substantia; si autem
dei voluntas sempiterna erat, ut esset creatura, cur
non sempiterna et creatura?

XI

CAP.
XI

Qui haec dicunt, nondum te intellegunt, o sapientia
dei, lux mentium, nondum intellegunt, quomodo
fiant, quae per te atque in te fiunt, et conantur aeterna
sapere, sed adhuc in praeteritis et futuris rerum
motibus cor eorum volitat et adhuc vanum est. quis
tenebit illud et figet illud, ut paululum stet, et paululum rapiat splendorem semper stantis aeternitatis,
et comparet cum temporibus numquam stantibus, et
videat esse incomparabilem: et videat longum tempus

they, and did no work, why then does he not now CHAP.
from henceforth and for ever abstain from working, X
like as heretofore he did? For if any new motion did
rise up in God, and any new will to make a creation,
which he had never made before, how can there
be a true eternity, where there rises up a new will,
which was not there before? For the will of God is
not a creature, but before every creature; seeing that
nothing could have been created, unless the will of
the Creator had been before it. The will of God
therefore belongeth unto his very substance. But if
aught be newly risen up in God's substance, which
was not there before, then cannot that substance be
truly said to be eternal. Again, if the will of God
had meant from eternity that there should be a
creation, why was not that creation also from all
eternity?

XI

God's Eternity not to be measured by the parts of Time

THEY that prate thus do not yet understand thee, CHAP.
O thou Wisdom of God, thou Light of our minds, XI
they understand not yet how these things be made,
which by thee, and in thee are made: yea, they
strive to relish eternal things, though their heart
be flickering hitherto between the motions of things
past and to come, and be very unstable hitherto.
Who will hold that, and so fix it, that it may
stand a while, and a little catch at a beam of
light from that ever-fixed eternity, to compare it
with the times which are never fixed, that he may
thereby perceive how there is no comparison between

CAP.
XI
nisi ex multis praetereuntibus motibus, qui simul extendi non possunt, longum non fieri; non autem praeterire quicquam in aeterno, sed totum esse praesens; nullum vero tempus totum esse praesens: et videat omne praeteritum propelli ex futuro, et omne futurum ex praeterito consequi, et omne praeteritum ac futurum ab eo, quod semper est praesens, creari et excurrere? quis tenebit cor hominis, ut stet et videat, quomodo stans dictet futura et praeterita tempora nec futura nec praeterita aeternitas? numquid manus mea valet hoc aut manus oris mei per loquellas agit tam grandem rem?

XII

CAP.
XII
Ecce respondeo dicenti: "quid faciebat deus, antequam faceret caelum et terram?" respondeo non illud, quod quidam respondisse perhibetur ioculariter eludens quaestionis violentiam: "alta," inquit, "scrutantibus gehennas parabat." aliud est videre, aliud ridere. haec non respondeo. libentius enim responderim: "nescio, quod nescio" quam illud, unde irridetur qui álta interrogavit et laudatur qui falsa respondit. sed dico te, deus noster, omnis creaturae creatorem, et si caeli et terrae nomine omnis creatura intellegitur, audenter dico: antequam faceret

them : and how that a long time cannot be made long, CHAP.
but out of a many motions still passing onwards, XI
which cannot at the same instant be drawn out
together : but that all this while in the eternal
nothing is flitting, but all is at once present, whereas
no time is all at once present : and that he may perceive all time past to be driven away by time to come ;
and all time to come, to follow upon the past ; and
that all both past and to come, is made up, and flows
out of that which is always present ? Who now shall
so hold fast this heart of man, that it may stand, and
see, how that eternity ever still standing, gives the
word of command to the times past or to come, itself
being neither past nor to come ? Can my hand do
this, or can the hand of my mouth by speech, bring
about so important a business ?

XII

What God did before the Creation of the World

SEE, I now return answer to the demand ; What did CHAP.
God do before he made heaven and earth ? But I XII
will not answer so as one was said to have done
merrily, to break the violence of the question : God
was a preparing hell, saith he, for those that should
pry into such profound mysteries. 'Tis one thing to
look what God did, and another thing to make sport.
This is none of my answer ; rather had I answer that
I know not, what indeed I do not know, than answer
so, as may make him laughed at, that asked such high
questions ; and the other commended, that returned
so false an answer. But I say that thou, O our God,
art Creator of every creature : and if under the name
of heaven and earth, every creature be understood,

CAP.
XII
deus caelum et terram, non faciebat aliquid. si enim faciebat, quid nisi creaturam faciebat? et utinam sic sciam, quidquid utiliter scire cupio, quemadmodum scio, quod nulla fiebat creatura, antequam fieret ulla creatura.

XIII

CAP.
XIII
At si cuiusquam volatilis sensus vagatur per imagines retro temporum, et te, deum omnipotentem et omnicreantem et omnitenentem, caeli et terrae artificem, ab opere tanto, antequam id faceres, per innumerabilia saecula cessasse miratur, evigilet atque adtendat, quia falsa miratur. nam unde poterant innumerabilia saecula praeterire, quae ipse non feceras, cum sis omnium saeculorum auctor et conditor? aut quae tempora fuissent, quae abs te condita non essent? aut quomodo praeterirent, si numquam fuissent? cum ergo sis operator omnium temporum, si fuit aliquod tempus, antequam faceres caelum et terram, cur dicitur, quod ab opere cessabas? id ipsum enim tempus tu feceras, nec praeterire potuerunt tempora, antequam faceres tempora. si autem ante caelum et terram nullum erat tempus, cur quaeritur, quid tunc faciebas? non enim erat tunc, ubi non erat tempus.

Nec tu tempore tempora praecedis: alioquin non

234

then I will boldly say, that before God made heaven CHAP.
XII and earth, he did not make anything. For if he did, what did he make but a creature? And would to God I knew whatsoever I desired to know, to mine own profit, as well as I know this, that no creature was made before there was made any creature.

XIII

That before those Times which God created, there was no Time

IF any giddy brain now wildly roves over the images CHAP.
XIII of fore-past times, and wonders with himself, that thou the God Omnipotent, All-creator and All-supporting, Maker of heaven and earth, didst for innumerable ages forbear to set upon such a work, before thou wouldst make it: let him wake himself and consider well; since he wonders at mere false conceits. For how could innumerable ages pass over, which thyself hadst not made; thou being the author and creator of all ages? Or what times should these have been, which were not made by thee? Or, how should they pass over, if so be they never were? Seeing therefore thou art the Creator of all times; if any time had passed before thou madest heaven and earth, why then is it said, that thou didst forbear to work? For that very time hadst thou made: nor could there any times pass over, before thou hadst made times. But if before heaven and earth there were no time, why is it then demanded, what thou didst? For there was no THEN, whenas there was no time.

Nor dost thou in time precede times: else thou shouldest not precede all times. But thou precedest

CAP.
XIII
omnia tempora praecederes. sed praecedis omnia praeterita celsitudine semper praesentis aeternitatis et superas omnia futura, quia illa futura sunt, et cum venerint, praeterita erunt; tu autem idem ipse es et anni tui non deficient. anni tui nec eunt nec veniunt: isti autem nostri eunt et veniunt, ut omnes veniant. anni tui omnes simul stant, quoniam stant nec euntes a venientibus excluduntur, quia non trans eunt: isti autem nostri omnes erunt, cum omnes non erunt. anni tui dies unus, et dies tuus non cotidie sed hodie, quia hodiernus tuus non cedit crastino neque enim succedit hesterno. hodiernus tuus aeter nitas: ideo coaeternum genuisti, cui dixisti: ego hodie genui te. omnia tempora tu fecisti et ante omnia tempora tu es, nec aliquo tempore non erat tempus.

XIV

CAP.
XIV
Nullo ergo tempore non feceras aliquid, quia ipsum tempus tu feceras. et nulla tempora tibi coaeterna sunt, quia tu permanes; at illa si permanerent, non essent tempora. quid est enim tempus? quis hoc facile breviterque explicaverit? quis hoc ad verbum de illo proferendum vel cogitatione comprehenderit? quid autem familiarius et notius in loquendo con memoramus quam tempus? et intellegimus utique,

236

all times past, by high advantage of an ever present CHAP.
eternity: and thou goest beyond all times to come, XIII
even because they are to come, and when they
shall come, they shall be past: whereas thou art still Ps. cii. 27
the same, and thy years shall not fail. Thy years
neither go nor come; whereas these years of ours
do both go and come, that in their order they may
all come. Thy years stand all at once, because they
stand: nor are those that go thrust out by those
that come, for they pass not away; but these years
of thine shall all be ours, when all time shall cease
to be. Thy years are one day; and thy day is not
every day, but to-day: seeing, thy to-day gives not
place unto to-morrow, for neither comes it in place
of yesterday. Thy to-day is eternity: therefore
didst thou beget him co-eternal to thyself, unto
whom thou saidst: This day have I begotten thee. Ps. ii. 7
Thou hast made all times; and before all times thou
art: nor in any time was time not.

XIV

Of the Nature and three Differences of Time

IN no time therefore, hadst thou "not made" any- CHAP.
thing: because very time itself was of thy making: and XIV
there be no times co-eternal with thee, for that thou
still remainest the same; but should they still remain,
verily they should not be times. For what is time?
Who is able easily and briefly to explain that? Who
is able so much as in thought to comprehend it,
so as to express himself concerning it? And yet
what in our usual discourse do we more familiarly
and knowingly make mention of than time? And

CAP.
XIV
cum id loquimur, intellegimus etiam, cum alio lo-
quente id audimus. quid est ergo tempus ? si nemo
ex me quaerat, scio ; si quaerenti explicare velim,
nescio : fidenter tamen dico scire me, quod, si nihil
praeteriret, non esset praeteritum tempus, et si nihil
adveniret, non esset futurum tempus, et si nihil esset,
non esset praesens tempus. duo ergo illa tempora,
praeteritum et futurum, quomodo sunt, quando et
praeteritum iam non est et futurum nondum est ?
praesens autem si semper esset praesens nec in praeteritum transiret, non iam esset tempus, sed aeternitas.
si ergo praesens, ut tempus sit, ideo fit, quia in praeteritum transit, quomodo et hoc esse dicimus, cui
causa, ut sit, illa est, quia non erit, ut scilicet nòn
vere dicamus tempus esse, nisi quia tendit non
esse ?

XV

CAP.
XV
Et tamen dicimus longum tempus et breve tempus,
neque hoc nisi de praeterito aut futuro dicimus.
praeteritum tempus longum, verbi gratia, vocamus
ante centum annos, futurum itidem longum post
centum annos, breve autem praeteritum sic, ut puta
dicamus ante decem dies, et breve futurum post decem
dies. sed quo pacto longum est aut breve, quod non
est ? praeteritum enim iam non est, et futurum non-

238

surely, we understand it well enough, when we
speak of it: we understand it also, when in speaking with another we hear it named. What is time
then? If nobody asks me, I know: but if I were
desirous to explain it to one that should ask me,
plainly I know not. Boldly for all this dare I
affirm myself to know thus much; that if nothing
were passing, there would be no past time: and
if nothing were coming, there should be no time
to come: and if nothing were, there should now
be no present time. Those two times therefore, past
and to come, in what sort are they, seeing the past
is now no longer, and that to come is not yet? As
for the present, should it always be present and
never pass into times past, verily it should not be
time but eternity. If then time present, to be time,
only comes into existence because it passeth into
time past; how can we say that also to be, whose
cause of being is, that it shall not be: that we cannot, forsooth, affirm that time is, but only because it
is tending not to be?

XV

No Time can be said to be long

AND yet we say long time, and short time: though
neither do we speak this, but of the time past or
to come. A long time past, for example, we call
an hundred years since: and a long time to come,
an hundred years hence. But a short time past,
we call (say) ten days since; and a short time to
come, ten days hence. But in what sense is that
either long or short, which at all is not? For the
past is not now, and the future is not yet. Let us

CAP.
XV

dum est.   non itaque dicamus : longum est, sed dicamus de praeterito : longum fuit, et de futuro : longum erit.   domine meus, lux mea, nonne et hic veritas tua deridebit hominem ?   quod enim longum fuit praeteritum tempus, cum iam esset praeteritum, longum fuit, an ante, cum adhuc praesens esset ? tunc enim poterat esse longum, quando erat, quod esset longum : praeteritum vero iam non erat ; unde nec longum esse poterat, quod omnino non erat.   non ergo dicamus : longum fuit praeteritum tempus ; neque enim inveniemus, quid fuerit longum, quando, ex quo praeteritum est, non est, sed dicamus : "longum fuit illud praesens tempus," quia cum praesens esset, longum erat.   nondum enim praeterierat, ut non esset, et ideo erat, quod longum esse posset ; postea vero quam praeteriit, simul et longum esse destitit, quod esse destitit.

Videamus ergo, anima humana, utrum praesens tempus possit esse longum : datum enim tibi est sentire moras atque metiri.   quid respondebis mihi ? an centum anni praesentes longum tempus est ? vide prius, utrum possint praesentes esse centum anni.   si enim primus eorum annus agitur, ipse praesens est, nonaginta vero et novem futuri sunt, et ideo nondum sunt : si autem secundus annus agitur, iam unus est praeteritus, alter praesens, ceteri futuri.   atque ita mediorum quemlibet centenarii

240

not therefore say it is long; but of the past time let CHAP. us say, it hath been long: and of the time to come, XV it will be long. O my Lord, my Light, shall not here also thy truth mock at a man? For that past time that was long, was it long when it was already past, or when it was yet present? For then might it be long, when there was what could be long; but when past, it was no longer; wherefore that could not either be long, which was not at all. Let us not therefore say, time past hath been long: for we shall never find what hath been long, seeing that ever since it was past, it is no more. But let us say, That time when present was long: because when it was present, then was it long. For it had not hitherto passed away, so as not to be, and therefore there was what could be long: whereas after it was once past, that ceased also to be long, which ceased to be.

Let us see therefore, O thou soul of man, whether the present time may be long. For to thee it is given to be sensible of the distances of time, and to measure them. What now wilt thou answer me? Are an hundred years in present a long time? See first, whether an hundred years can be present. For if the first of these years be now a running, that one is present indeed, but the other ninety and nine be to come, and therefore are not yet: but if the second year be now current, then is one past already, another in present being, and all the rest to come. And if we suppose any middle year of this

241

CAP.
XV

huius numeri annum praesentem posuerimus: ante illum praeteriti erunt, post illum futuri. quocirca centum anni praesentes esse non poterunt. vide saltem, utrum qui agitur unus ipse sit praesens. et eius enim si primus agitur mensis, futuri sunt ceteri, si secundus, iam et primus praeteriit et reliqui nondum sunt. ergo nec annus, qui agitur, totus est praesens, et si non totus est praesens, non annus est praesens. duodecim enim menses annus est, quorum quilibet unus mensis, qui agitur, ipse praesens est, ceteri aut praeteriti aut futuri. quamquam neque mensis, qui agitur, praesens est, sed unus dies: si primus, futuris ceteris, si novissimus, praeteritis ceteris, si mediorum quilibet, inter praeteritos et futuros.

Ecce praesens tempus, quod solum inveniebamus longum appellandum, vix ad unius diei spatium contractum est. sed discutiamus etiam ipsum, quia nec unus dies totus est praesens. nocturnis enim et diurnis horis omnibus viginti quattuor expletur, quarum prima ceteras futuras habet, novissima praeteritas, aliqua vero interiectarum ante se praeteritas, post se futuras. et ipsa una hora fugitivis particulis agitur: quidquid eius avolavit, praeteritum est, quidquid ei restat, futurum. si quid intellegitur temporis, quod in nullas iam vel minutissimas momentorum partes dividi possit, id solum est, quod praesens dicatur; quod tamen ita raptim a futuro in praeteritum transvolat, ut nulla morula extendatur. nam si extenditur, dividitur in praeteritum et futu-

hundred to be now present; all before it will be past, all after it to come. Wherefore an hundred years cannot be present. See again whether that one which is now a running be now present. For even of that, if the first month be now a running, then are all the rest to come : if the second, then is the first past, and the rest not yet come on. Therefore, neither is the year now a spending all present together : and if it be not all present, then is not the year present. For twelve months are a year; of which that one now a running is present, all the rest either past, or to come. Yet neither is that month now a running, present; but one day of it only : if the first, the rest are to come; if the last, the rest are past ; if any of the middle, that is that between the past and the future.

See how the present time, (which only we found meet to be called long) is now abridged to the length scarce of one day. But let us examine that also ; because not so much as one day is wholly present. For four and twenty hours of day and night do fully make it up : of which, the first hath the rest to come ; the last hath them past; and any of the middle ones hath those before it already past, those behind it yet to come ; yea, that one hour is wasted out in still vanishing minutes. How much so ever is flown away, is past; whatsoever remains, is to come. If any instant of time be conceived, which cannot be divided either into none, or at most into the smallest particles of moments ; that is the only it, which may be called present; which little yet flies with such full speed from the future to the past, as that it is not lengthened out with the very least stay. For lengthened out if it be, then is it divided into the past and the future. As for the

CAP. XV rum: praesens autem nullum habet spatium. ubi est ergo tempus, quod longum dicamus? an futurum? non quidem dicimus: longum est, quia nondum est quod longum sit, sed dicimus: longum erit. quando igitur erit? si enim et tunc adhuc futurum erit, non erit longum, quia quid sit longum nondum erit: si autem tunc erit longum, cum ex futuro quod nondum est esse iam coeperit et praesens factum erit, ut possit esse quod longum sit, iam superioribus vocibus clamat praesens tempus longum se esse non posse.

XVI

CAP. XVI Et tamen, domine, sentimus intervalla temporum, et comparamus sibimet, et dicimus alia longiora et alia breviora. metimur etiam, quanto sit longius aut brevius illud tempus quam illud, et respondemus duplum esse hoc vel triplum, illud autem simplum, aut tantum hoc esse quantum illud. sed praetereuntia metimur tempora, cum sentiendo metimur; praeterita vero, quae iam non sunt, aut futura, quae nondum sunt, quis metiri potest, nisi forte audebit quis dicere metiri posse quod non est? cum ergo praeterit tempus, sentiri et metiri potest, cum autem praeterierit, quoniam non est, non potest.

present, it takes not up any space. Where then is CHAP. the time which we may call long? Is it to come? XV Surely we do not say, that that is long: because that of it is not yet come which may be long: but we say, it will be long. When therefore will it be? For if even then it is yet to come, it shall not be long, because there will be not yet that which may be long: but if it shall then be long, when from the future (which it is not yet) it shall begin now to be, and shall be made present, that so there may now be that which may be long, then does the present time cry out in the words above rehearsed, that it cannot be long.

XVI

Of our measuring of Times

AND yet, Lord, are we sensible of the intervals of CHAP. times; yea, we can compare them one with another, XVI and say, that some are shorter, and others are longer. We measure also, how much this time is longer or shorter than that, and we answer, This is double, or thrice as long; and that but once; or this just so much as that. But as the times are passing, we measure them, when by casting them over in our minds we observe them. As for the past times, which now are not; or the future, which yet are not; who is able to measure them? Unless perchance some one man be so bold to affirm me, that that may be measured, which is not. Therefore while time is a passing, it may be observed and measured: but when it is once past, it cannot, because it is not.

XVII

CAP.
XVII

Quaero, pater, non adfirmo : deus meus, praeside mihi et rege me. quisnam est, qui dicat mihi non esse tria tempora, sicut pueri didicimus puerosque docuimus, praeteritum, praesens et futurum, sed tantum praesens, quoniam illa duo non sunt ? an et ipsa sunt, sed ex aliquo procedit occulto, cum ex futuro fit praesens, et in aliquod recedit occultum, cum ex praesenti fit praeteritum ? nam ubi ea viderunt qui futura cecinerunt, si nondum sunt ? neque enim potest videri id quod non est. et qui narrant praeterita, non utique vera narrarent, si animo illa non cernerent : quae si nulla essent, cerni omnino non possent. sunt ergo et futura et praeterita.

XVIII

CAP.
XVIII

Sine me, domine, amplius quaerere, spes mea ; non conturbetur intentio mea. si enim sunt futura et praeterita, volo scire, ubi sint. quod si nondum valeo, scio tamen, ubicumque sunt, non ibi ea futura esse aut praeterita, sed praesentia. nam si et ibi futura sunt, nondum ibi sunt, si et ibi praeterita sunt,

XVII

Where Time past, and to come, now are

I ASK, Father, I affirm not: rule me, O my God, CHAP.
and direct me. Who is he that will tell me how XVII
there are not three times, as we learned when we
were boys, and as we taught other boys, the past,
present, and future; but the present only, because
the other two are not at all? Or have they a being
also; but such as proceeds out of some unknown
secret, when out of the future, the present is made;
and returns it into some secret again, when the past
is made out of the present? For where have they,
who have foretold things to come before, seen them,
if as yet they be not? For that which is not, cannot
be seen. And so for those that relate the things
past, verily they could not relate true stories, if in
their mind they did not discern them: which if they
were none, could no way be discerned. There are
therefore both things past and to come.

XVIII

How Times past, and to come, are now present

YET give me leave, Lord, to look further, O thou CHAP.
my Hope. Suffer not my attention to be disturbed. XVIII
For if there be times past, and times to come; fain
would I know where they be: which yet if I be not
able to conceive, yet thus much I know, that wheresoever they now be, they are not there future or
past, but present. For if there also, future they
be, then are they not there yet: if there also

247

CAP.
XVIII

iam non ibi sunt. ubicumque ergo sunt, quaecumque
sunt, non sunt nisi praesentia. quamquam praeterita
cum vera narrantur, ex memoria proferuntur non res
ipsae, quae praeterierunt, sed verba concepta ex
imaginibus earum, quae in animo velut vestigia per
sensus praetereundo fixerunt. pueritia quippe mea,
quae iam non est, in tempore praeterito est, quod iam
non est; imaginem vero eius, cum eam recolo et
narro, in praesenti tempore intueor, quia est adhuc
in memoria mea. utrum similis sit causa etiam prae-
dicendorum futurorum, ut rerum, quae nondum sunt,
iam exsistentes praesentiantur imagines, confiteor,
deus meus, nescio. illud sane scio, nos plerumque
praemeditari futuras actiones nostras eamque prae-
meditationem esse praesentem, actionem autem,
quam praemeditamur, nondum esse, quia futura est;
quam cum aggressi fuerimus et quod praemeditaba-
mur agere coeperimus, tunc erit illa actio, quia tunc
non futura, sed praesens erit.

Quoquo modo se itaque habeat arcana praesensio
futurorum, videri nisi quod est non potest. quod
autem iam est, non futurum sed praesens est. cum
ergo videri dicuntur futura, non ipsa, quae nondum
sunt, id est quae futura sunt, sed eorum causae vel
signa forsitan videntur, quae iam sunt: ideo non
futura, sed praesentia sunt iam videntibus, ex quibus

they be past, then are they not there still. Wheresoever therefore and whatsoever they be, they are not but as present. Although as for things past, whenever true stories are related, out of the memory are drawn not the things themselves which are past, but such words as being conceived by the images of those things, they, in their passing through our senses, have, as their footsteps, left imprinted in our minds. For example, mine own childhood, which at this instant is not, yet in the time past is, which time at this instant is not: but as for the image of it, when I call that to mind, and tell of it, I do even in the present behold it, because it is still in my memory. Whether or no there be a like cause of foretelling things to come, that, namely, of those things which as yet are not, the images may in the present be fore-conceived, as if already extant, I confess unto thee, O God, that I know not. This one thing surely I know; that we use very often to premeditate upon our future actions, and that that forethinking is present: but as for the action which we forethink ourselves of, that is not yet in being, because it is yet to come. Which, so soon as we have set upon, and are beginning once to do what we premeditated, then shall that action come into being: because then it will be no longer future, but present.

Which way soever then this secret fore-conceiving of things to come may be seen, nothing surely can be, but that which now is. As for that which now is, it is not future, but present. Whenever therefore things to come are said to be seen, 'tis not the things themselves, which as yet are not; that is, which are to come hereafter; but the causes perchance, or the signs of them, that are seen, which now are: therefore they are not future, but present unto the

CAP.
XVIII
futura praedicantur animo concepta. quae rursus conceptiones iam sunt, et eas praesentes apud se intuentur qui illa praedicunt. loquatur mihi aliquod exemplum tanta rerum numerositas. intueor auroram: oriturum solem praenuntio. quod intueor, praesens est, quod praenuntio, futurum: non sol futurus, qui iam est, sed ortus eius, qui nondum est: tamen etiam ortum ipsum nisi animo imaginarer, sicut modo cum id loquor, non eum possem praedicere. sed nec illa aurora, quam in caelo video, solis ortus est, quamvis eum praecedat, nec illa imaginatio in animo meo: quae duo praesentia cernuntur, ut futurus ille ante dicatur. futura ergo nondum sunt, et si nondum sunt, non sunt, et si non sunt, videri omnino non possunt; sed praedici possunt ex praesentibus, quae iam sunt et videntur.

XIX

CAP.
XIX
Tu itaque, regnator creaturae tuae, quis est modus, quo doces animas ea quae futura sunt? docuisti enim prophetas tuos. quisnam ille modus est, quo doces futura, cui futurum quicquam non est? vel potius de futuris doces praesentia? nam quod non

seers : out of which future things conceived in the CHAP.
mind, are foretold. Which conceptions again, are XVIII
now present : and those who foretell the things, do
behold the conceptions already present before them.
Let now the numerous variety of things produce me
some example. I look upon the day breaking ; and
I foreshew upon it, that the sun is about to rise.
That which I look upon is present, that which I
fore-signify is to come : not the sun, I mean, which
already is ; but the sunrising, which is not yet.
And yet if I did not in my mind imagine the sunrising itself, (as I now do whilst I speak of it)
never could I foretell it. But neither is that break
of day which I discern in the sky, the sunrising,
notwithstanding it goes before it ; no, nor that
imagination in my mind neither : which two are
seen now in present, that the other may be foretold
to be a coming hereafter. Future things therefore
are not yet : and if they be not yet, they are not :
and if so they be not, possible to be seen they are
not : yet foretold they may be by some things present, which both are already and are seen.

XIX

He demands of God, how future Things be foreknown

TELL, therefore, O thou Reigner over thy creation, CHAP.
what is the manner by which thou teachest souls XIX
these things that are to come ? For thou hast
already taught thy Prophets. Which is the way that
thou unto whom nothing is to come, dost teach
things to come ? or rather, out of future, dost

CAP.
XIX
est, nec doceri utique potest. nimis longe est modus iste ab acie mea; invaluit : ex me non potero ad illum ; potero autem ex te, cum dederis tu, dulce lumen occultorum oculorum meorum.

XX

CAP.
XX
Quod autem nunc liquet et claret, nec futura sunt nec praeterita, nec proprie dicitur : tempora sunt tria, praeteritum, praesens et futurum, sed fortasse proprie diceretur : tempora sunt tria, praesens de praeteritis, praesens de praesentibus, praesens de futuris. sunt enim haec in anima tria quaedam, et alibi ea non video : praesens de praeteritis memoria, praesens de praesentibus contuitus, praesens de futuris expectatio. si haec permittimur dicere, tria tempora video fateorque, tria sunt. dicatur etiam : tempora sunt tria, praeteritum, praesens, et futurum, sicut abutitur consuetudo; dicatur. ecce non curo nec resisto nec reprehendo, dum tamen intellegatur quod dicitur, neque id, quod futurum est, esse iam, neque id, quod praeteritum est. pauca sunt enim, quae proprie loquimur, plura non proprie, sed agnoscitur quid velimus.

teach of things present? For, that which is not, CHAP.
neither can it be taught at all. Too too far is this XIX
way out of my kenning; it is too mighty for me, I Ps. cxxxix.
cannot from myself attain to it; but from thee I can : 6
even when thou shalt vouchsafe it, O sweet light of
the inward eyes of my soul.

XX

These three differences of Times, how they are to be called

CLEAR now it is and plain, that neither things to CHAP.
come, nor things past, are. Nor do we properly say, XX
there be three times, past, present, and to come; but
perchance it might be properly said, there be three
times : a present time of past things; a present time
of present things; and a present time of future things.
For indeed three such as these in our souls there be ;
and otherwhere do I not see them. The present time
of past things is our memory ; the present time
of present things is our sight; the present time
of future things our expectation. If thus we be
permitted to speak, then see I three times ; yea,
and I confess there are three. Let this also be
said : there be three times, past, present, and to
come, according to our misapplied custom ; let it be
said : see, I shall not much be troubled at it, neither
gainsay, nor find fault with it ; provided that be
understood which is said, namely, that neither that
which is to come, have any being now ; no, nor that
which is already past. For but a very few things
there are, which we speak properly ; but very many
that we speak improperly, though we understand
one another's meaning.

XXI

CAP.
XXI
Dixi ergo paulo ante, quod praetereuntia tempora metimur, ut possimus dicere duplum esse hoc temporis ad illud simplum, aut tantum hoc quantum illud, et si quid aliud de partibus temporum possumus renuntiare metiendo. quocirca, ut dicebam, praetereuntia metimur tempora; et si quis mihi dicat : " unde scis ? " respondeam: scio, quia metimur, nec metiri quae non sunt possumus, et non sunt praeterita vel futura. praesens vero tempus quomodo metimur, quando non habet spatium ? metitur ergo, cum praeterit, cum autem praeterierit, non metitur; quid enim metiatur, non erit. sed unde et qua et quo praeterit, cum metitur ? unde nisi ex futuro ? qua nisi per praesens ? quo nisi in praeteritum ? ex illo ergo, quod nondum est, per illud, quod spatio caret, in illud, quod iam non est. quid autem metimur nisi tempus in aliquo spatio ? neque enim dicimus simpla et dupla et tripla et aequalia et si quid hoc modo in tempore dicimus nisi spatia temporum. in quo ergo spatio metimur tempus praeteriens ? utrum in futuro, unde praeterit ? sed quod nondum est, non metimur. an in praesenti, qua praeterit ? sed nullum spatium non metimur. an in praeterito, quo praeterit ? sed quod iam non est, non metimur.

XXI

How Time may be measured

As therefore I was even now a saying; we take such CHAP.
measure of the times in their passing by, as we may XXI
be able to say, this time is twice so much as that
one; or, this is just so much as that: and so of any
other parts of time, which be measurable. We do
therefore, as I said, take measure of the times as
they are passing by. And if any man should now
ask me: How knowest thou? I might answer, I do
know, because we do measure them: for we cannot
measure things that are not; and verily, things past
and to come are not. But for the present time
now, how do we measure that, seeing it hath no
space? We measure it therefore, even whilst it
passeth, but when it is past, then we measure it
not: for there will be nothing to be measured. But
from what place, and by which way, and whitherto
passes this time while it is a measuring? Whence,
but from the future? Which way, but through the
present? Whither, but into the past? From that
therefore, which is not yet: by that, which hath no
space: into that, which is not still. Yet what is it we
measure, if not time in some space? For we use not
to say, single, and double, and triple, and equal, or
any other way that we speak of time, but with
reference still to the spaces of times. In what space
therefore do we measure the time present? Whether
in the future space, whence it is passing? But that
which is not yet, we cannot measure. Or in the
present, by which it is passing? But no-space we do
not measure. Or in the past, to which it passeth?
But neither do we measure that which is not still.

XXII

CAP.
XXII
EXARSIT animus meus nosse istuc inplicatissimum
aenigma. noli claudere, domine deus meus, bone
pater, per Christum obsecro, noli claudere desiderio
meo ista et usitata et abdita, quominus in ea penetret;
et dilucescant, allucente misericordia tua, domine.
quem percontabor de his? et cui fructuosius confitebor inperitiam meam nisi tibi, cui non sunt molesta
studia mea flammantia vehementer in scripturas tuas?
da quod amo: amo enim, et hoc tu dedisti. da,
pater, qui vere nosti data bona dare filiis tuis, da,
quoniam suscepi cognoscere; et labor est ante me,
donec aperias. per Christum obsecro, in nomine
eius sancti sanctorum, nemo mihi obstrepat. et ego
credidi, propter quod et loquor. haec est spes mea;
ad hanc vivo, ut contempler delectationem domini.
ecce veteres posuisti dies meos, et transeunt, et quomodo, nescio. et dicimus tempus et tempus, tempora et tempora: "quamdiu dixit hoc ille," "quamdiu
fecit hoc ille" et: "quam longo tempore illud non
vidi" et: "duplum temporis habet haec syllaba ad
illam simplam brevem." dicimus haec et audivimus
haec et intellegimur et intellegimus. manifestissima

XXII

He begs of God the Resolution of a Difficulty

MY soul is all on fire to be resolved of this most CHAP. intricate difficulty. Shut it not up, O Lord God, O XXII my good Father; in the name of Christ I beseech thee, do not so shut up these usual, but yet hidden things, from this desire of mine, that it be hindered from piercing into them: and let them shine out unto me, thy mercy, O Lord, enlightening me. Whom shall I make my demands unto concerning these points? And to whom shall I more fruitfully confess my ignorance, than unto thee, to whom these studies of mine (so vehemently burning to understand thy Scriptures) are no ways troublesome? Give me what I love: for love I do, and this love hast thou given me. Give it me, Father, who truly knowest to give good gifts unto thy children. Give Matt. vii. me, because I have taken upon me to know: and 11 it is painful unto me until thou openest it. Even Ps. lxxiii. by Christ I beseech thee, in the name of that 16 Holy of Holies, let no man disturb me. For I believed, and therefore do I speak. This is my hope, Ps. cxvi. 10 this do I pant after, that I may contemplate the Ps. xxvii. 4 delights of the Lord. Behold thou hast made my Ps. xxxix. days old, and they pass away, and I know not how. 5, with And we talk of time and time, and times and times. reading of How long time is it since he said this; How long the LXX. time since he did this; and How long time since I "old" for saw that: and This syllable hath double time to that "short" single short syllable. These words we say, and these we have heard, and understand, and are understood. Most manifest and ordinary they are, and yet the

CAP.
XXII
et usitatissima sunt, et eadem rursus nimis latent, et nova est inventio eorum.

XXIII

CAP.
XXIII
AUDIVI a quodam homine docto, quod solis et lunae ac siderum motus ipsa sint tempora, et non adnui. cur enim non potius omnium corporum motus sint tempora? an vero, si cessarent caeli lumina et moveretur rota figuli, non esset tempus, quo metiremur eos gyros, et diceremus aut aequalibus morulis agi, aut si alias tardius, alias velocius moveretur, alios magis diuturnos esse, alios minus? aut cum haec diceremus, non et nos in tempore loqueremur, aut essent in verbis nostris aliae longae syllabae, aliae breves, nisi quia illae longiore tempore sonuissent, istae breviore? deus, dona hominibus videre in parvo communes notitias rerum parvarum atque magnarum. sunt sidera et luminaria caeli in signis et in temporibus et in diebus et in annis. sunt vero; sed nec ego dixerim circuitum illius ligneolae rotae diem esse, nec tamen ideo tempus non esse ille dixerit.

Ego scire cupio vim naturamque temporis, quo metimur corporum motus, et dicimus illum motum verbi gratia tempore duplo esse diuturniorem quam istum. nam quaero, quoniam dies dicitur non tantum

258

selfsame things are too deeply hidden: yea, the CHAP. finding out of them is new. XXII

XXIII

He clears this Question, what Time is

I HEARD a learned man once deliver it, that the CHAP. motions of the sun, moon, and stars, were the XXIII very true times; and I did not agree. For why should not the motions of all bodies in general rather be times? Or if the lights of heaven should cease, and the potter's wheel run round; should there be no time by which we might measure those whirlings about, and might pronounce of it, that either it moved with equal pauses: or, if it turned sometimes slower, and other whiles quicker, that some rounds took up longer time, and others shorter? Or even whilst we were a saying this should we not also speak in time? Or should there in our words be any syllables short, and others long, but for this reason only, that those took up a shorter time in sounding, and these a longer? Grant unto us men the skill, O God, in a little thing to descry those notions as be common to things both great and small. The stars and lights of heaven, 'tis true, be appointed Gen. i. 14 for signs, and for seasons, and for years, and for days. They be indeed: yet should I never, (on the one side) affirm, the whirling about of that little wooden wheel to be the day; nor should he affirm, (on the other side) that therefore there were no time at all.

I for my part, desire to understand the force and nature of time, by which we measure the motions of bodies; and say, (for example) this motion to be twice longer than that. For I demand: seeing this

S. AVGVSTINI CONFESSIONVM LIBER XI

mora solis super terram, secundum quod aliud est
dies, aliud nox, sed etiam totius eius circuitus ab
oriente usque orientem, secundum quod dicimus:
"tot dies transierunt"—cum suis enim noctibus
dicuntur tot dies, nec extra reputantur spatia noctium
—quoniam ergo dies expletur motu solis atque cir-
cuitu ab oriente usque ad orientem, quaero, utrum
motus ipse sit dies, an mora ipsa, quanta peragitur,
an utrumque. si enim primum dies esset, dies ergo
esset, etiamsi tanto spatio temporis sol cursum illum
peregisset, quantum est horae unius. si secundum,
non ergo esset dies, si ab ortu solis usque in ortum
alterum tam brevis mora esset, quam est horae unius,
sed viciens et quater circuiret sol, ut expleret diem.
si utrumque, nec ille appellaretur dies, si horae
spatio sol totum suum gyrum circumiret, nec ille, si
sole cessante tantum temporis praeteriret, quanto
peragere sol totum ambitum de mane in mane
adsolet. non itaque nunc quaeram, quid sit illud,
quod vocatur dies, sed quid sit tempus, quo metientes
solis circuitum diceremus eum dimidio spatio temporis peractum minus quam solet, si tanto spatio
temporis peractus esset, quanto peraguntur horae
duodecim, et utrumque tempus conparantes diceremus illud simplum, hoc duplum, etiamsi aliquando
illo simplo, aliquando isto duplo sol ab oriente usque

is it which is called the day, not the stay only of the CHAP.
sun upon the earth, (according to which account XXIII
the day is one thing, and the night another;) but
its whole circuit that it runs from east to east
again; (according to which account we say, There
are so many days past):—for the days being
reckoned with their nights, are usually called so
many days, and the nights are not out of the
reckoning:—seeing therefore that a day is made
complete by the motion of the sun, and by his circuit
from east to east again, I thereupon demand, whether
the motion itself makes the day; or the stay in
which that motion is finished; or both? For if the
first be the day; then should we have a day of it,
although the sun should finish that course of his
in so small a space of time as one hour comes to.
If the second, then should not that make a day, if
between one sunrise and another, there were but so
short a stay as one hour comes to, but the sun must
go four and twenty times about for the making of one
day. If both, then could not this neither be called
a day, if the sun should run his whole round in the
space of one hour; no, nor that, if while the sun stood
still, so much time should overpass, as the sun usually
makes his whole course in, from morning to morning.
I will not therefore demand now what that should be
which is called day: but, what time should be, by
which we measuring the circuit of the sun, should
say, that he had then finished it in half the time he
was wont to do, if so be he had gone it over in so
small a space as twelve hours come to: and when
upon comparing of both times together, we should
say, that this is but a single time, and that a double
time, notwithstanding that the sun should run his
round from east to east sometimes in that single

CAP.
XXIII
orientem circuiret. nemo ergo mihi dicat caelestium corporum motus esse tempora, quia et cuiusdam voto cum sol stetisset, ut victoriosum proelium perageret, sol stabat, sed tempus ibat : per suum quippe spatium temporis, quod ei sufficeret, illa pugna gesta atque finita est. video igitur quandam esse distentionem. sed video ? an videre mihi videor ? tu demonstrabis, lux, veritas.

XXIV

CAP.
XXIV
IVBES ut adprobem, si quis dicat tempus esse motum corporis ? non iubes. nam corpus nullum nisi in tempore moveri audio : tu dicis. ipsum autem corporis motum tempus esse non audio : non tu dicis. cum enim movetur corpus, tempore metior, quamdiu moveatur, ex quo moveri incipit, donec desinat. et si non vidi, ex quo coepit, et perseverat moveri, ut non videam, cum desinit, non valeo metiri, nisi forte ex quo videre incipio, donec desinam. quod si diu video, tantummodo longum tempus esse renuntio, non autem, quantum sit, quia et quantum cum dicimus, conlatione dicimus, velut : "tantum hoc, quantum illud" aut : "duplum hoc ad illud" et si quid aliud isto modo. si autem notare potuerimus locorum

time, and sometimes in that double time. Let no CHAP.
man therefore say unto me hereafter, that the motions XXIII
of the celestial bodies be the times; because that Jos. xii.
when at the prayer of a certain man, the sun had
stood still, till he could achieve his victorious battle,
the sun stood indeed, but the time went on: for in a
certain space of time of his own, (enough to serve his
turn) was that battle strucken and gotten. I perceive
time therefore to be a certain stretching. But do I
perceive it, or do I seem to perceive it? Thou,
O Light and Truth, shalt show it.

XXIV

Time it is, by which we measure the Motion of Bodies

DOST thou command me to allow of it, if any man CHAP.
should define time to be the motion of a body? No, XXIV
thou dost not bid me. For there is no body that I
hear of, moved, but in time; this thou sayest: but
that the motion of a body should be time, I never did
hear: nor dost thou say it. For when a body is
moved, I by time then measure how long it may have
moved, from the instant it first began to move, until
it left moving. And if so be I did not see the
instant it began; and if it continues to move so
long as I cannot see when it ends; I am not then
able to measure it, but only perchance from that
instant I first saw it begin, until I myself leave
measuring. And if I look long upon it, I can only
signify it to be a long time, but not how long:
because when we pronounce how long, we must do
it by comparison: as for example: This is as long as
that; or This twice so long as that, or the like. But

CAP.
XXIV spatia, unde et quo veniat corpus, quod movetur, vel partes eius, si tamquam in torno movetur, possumus dicere, quantum sit temporis, ex quo ab illo loco usque ad illum locum motus corporis vel partis eius effectus est. cum itaque aliud sit motus corporis, aliud, quo metimur quamdiu sit, quis non sentiat, quid horum potius tempus dicendum sit? nam si et varie corpus aliquando movetur, aliquando stat, non solum motum eius, sed etiam statum tempore metimur et dicimus: "tantum stetit, quantum motum est" aut: "duplo vel triplo stetit ad id quod motum est" et si quid aliud nostra dimensio sive conprehenderit sive existimaverit, ut dici solet plus minus. non ergo tempus corporis motus.

XXV

CAP.
XXV Et confiteor tibi, domine, ignorare me adhuc, quid sit tempus, et rursus confiteor tibi, domine, scire me in tempore ista dicere, et diu me iam loqui de tempore, atque ipsum diu non esse diu nisi mora temporis. quomodo igitur hoc scio, quando quid sit tempus nescio? an forte nescio, quemadmodum dicam quod scio? ei mihi, qui nescio saltem quid nesciam! ecce, deus meus, coram te, quia non mentior: sicut loquor, ita est cor meum. tu inluminabis lucernam meam, domine, deus meus, inluminabis tenebras meas.

were we able to make observation of the distances CHAP.
of those places, whence and whither a body or his XXIV
parts go, which moveth; (as if, suppose it were
moved in a lathe) then can we say, how much
time the motion of that body or his part, from
this place unto that, was finished in. Seeing therefore the motion of a body is one thing, and that by
which we measure how long it is, another thing; who
cannot now judge which of the two is rather to be
called time? For and if a body be sometimes moved
uncertainly, and stands still other sometimes; then
do we measure, not his motions only, but his standing still too: and we say, It stood still as much as it
moved; or It stood still twice or thrice so long as it
moved; or any other space which our measuring hath
either perfectly taken, or guessed at, more or less,
as we use to say. Time therefore is not the motion
of a body.

XXV

He prayeth again

AND I confess to thee, O Lord, that I yet know not CHAP.
what time is; yea, I confess again unto thee, O Lord, XXV
that I know well enough, how that I speak this in
time, and that having long spoken of time, that very
long is not long but by a stay of time. How then
come I to know this, seeing I know not what time
is? Or is my not knowing, only perchance a not
hitting upon the way of expressing what I know?
Woe is me, that do not so much as know, what that
is which I know not. Behold, O my God, I protest
before thee that I lie not; as my mouth speaketh, Ps. xviii. 28
so my heart thinketh. Thou shalt light my candle,
O Lord my God, thou shalt enlighten my darkness.

S. AVGVSTINI CONFESSIONVM LIBER XI

XXVI

Nonne tibi confitetur anima mea confessione veridica
metiri me tempora? ita, domine deus meus, metior
et quid metiar nescio. metior motum corporis tempore. item ipsum tempus nonne metior? an vero
corporis motum metirer, quamdiu sit et quamdiu hinc
illuc perveniat, nisi tempus, in quo movetur, metirer?
ipsum ergo tempus unde metior? an tempore breviore metimur longius, sicut spatio cubiti spatium
transtri? sic enim videmus spatio brevis syllabae metiri
spatium longae syllabae atque id duplum dicere. ita
metimur spatia carminum spatiis versuum, et spatia
versuum spatiis pedum, et spatia pedum spatiis syllabarum, et spatia longarum spatiis brevium: non in
paginis—nam eo modo loca metimur, non tempora—
sed cum voces pronuntiando transeunt, et dicimus:
"longum carmen est, nam tot versibus contexitur;
longi versus, nam tot pedibus constant; longi pedes,
nam tot syllabis tenduntur; longa syllaba est, nam
dupla est ad brevem." sed neque ita compre-
henditur certa mensura temporis, quandoquidem
fieri potest, ut ampliore spatio temporis personet

266

XXVI

The Measuring of the Feet and Syllables of a Verse

Does not my soul most truly confess unto thee that
I do measure times? Yea I do indeed measure them,
O my God, and yet know not what I measure.
I measure the motion of a body in time; and the
time itself do I not measure? Or could I indeed
measure the motion of a body, how long it were,
and in how long space it could come from this
place to that; unless I could withal measure the
time in which it is moved? This same very time
therefore, which way do I measure it? Do we by
a shorter time measure a longer, as by the space
of a cubit we do the space of a rood? for so
indeed we seem by the space of a short syllable,
to measure the space of a long syllable, and to
say that this is double. Thus measure we the
spaces of the staves of a poem, by the spaces of
the verses; and the spaces of the verses, by the
spaces of the feet; and the spaces of the feet,
by the spaces of the syllables; and the spaces of
long syllables, by the spaces of short syllables.
I do not mean measuring by the pages; for that
way we should measure places, not times: but when
in our pronouncing words pass away, and we say, It
is a long stanza, because it is composed of so many
verses: they be long verses, because they consist of
so many feet; long feet, for that they are stretched
out into so many syllables; it is a long syllable,
because double to a short one. But neither can we
this way comprehend the certain measure of time:
because it may so fall out, that a shorter verse if it

267

CAP.
XXVI

versus brevior, si productius pronuntietur, quam longior, si correptius. ita carmen, ita pes, ita syllaba. inde mihi visum est nihil esse aliud tempus quam distentionem : sed cuius rei, nescio, et mirum, si non ipsius animi. quid enim metior, obsecro, deus meus, et dico aut indefinite : "longius est hoc tempus quam illud" aut etiam definite : "duplum est hoc ad illud?" tempus metior, scio ; sed non metior futurum, quia nondum est, non metior praesens, quia nullo spatio tenditur, non metior praeteritum, quia iam non est. quid ergo metior? an praetereuntia tempora, non praeterita? sic enim dixeram.

XXVII

CAP.
XXVII

INSISTE, anime meus, et adtende fortiter: deus adiutor noster ; ipse fecit nos, et non nos. adtende, ubi albescet veritas. ecce puta vox corporis incipit sonare et sonat et adhuc sonat et ecce desinit, iamque silentium est, et vox illa praeterita est et non est iam vox. futura erat, antequam sonaret, et non poterat metiri, quia nondum erat, et nunc non potest, quia iam non est. tunc ergo poterat, cum sonabat, quia tunc erat, quae metiri posset. sed et tunc non

be pronounced leisurely, may take up more time than CHAP.
a longer verse pronounced roundly. And so for a XXVI
poem, a foot, and a syllable. Upon which ground
it seems unto me, that time is nothing else but a
stretching out in length; but of what, I know not,
and I marvel, if it be not of the very mind. For
what is it, I beseech thee, O my God, that I now
measure, whereas I say, either at large, that this is
a longer time than that: or, more particularly, that
this is double to that? I know it to be time that I
measure: and yet do I neither measure the time to
come, for that it is not yet: nor time present, because
that is not stretched out in any space: nor time past,
because that is not still. What then do I measure?
Is it the times as they are passing, not as they are
past? For so was I a saying.

XXVII

*He begins to resolve the former question, how we
measure time*

COURAGE, my mind, and press on strongly. God CHAP.
is our helper: he made us, and not we ourselves. XXVII
Press on, where truth begins to dawn. Come on, Ps. c. 3
let us put the case. The voice of a body begins
to sound, and it does now sound, yea, it sounds
still; but list, now it leaves sounding: 'tis silence
therefore now, and that voice is quite over, and
is now no more. This voice, before it sounded,
was to come, and so could not then be measured,
because as yet it was not; neither just now can
it, because it is no longer. Then therefore, whilst
it sounded, it might; because there was something
that might be measured. But even then made it

CAP.
XXVII

stabat; ibat enim et praeteriebat. an ideo magis poterat? praeteriens enim tendebatur in aliquod spatium temporis, quo metiri posset, quoniam praesens nullum habet spatium. si ergo tunc poterat, ecce puta altera coepit sonare et adhuc sonat continuato tenore sine ulla distinctione: metiamur eam, dum sonat; cum enim sonare cessaverit, iam praeterita erit et non erit, quae possit metiri. metiamur plane et dicamus, quanta sit. sed adhuc sonat, nec metiri potest nisi ab initio sui, quo sonare coepit, usque ad finem, quo desinit. ipsum quippe intervallum metimur ab aliquo initio usque ad aliquem finem. quapropter vox, quae numquam finita est, metiri non potest, ut dicatur, quam longa vel brevis sit, nec dici aut aequalis alicui, aut ad aliquam simpla vel dupla, vel quid aliud. cum autem finita fuerit, iam non erit. quo pacto igitur metiri poterit? et metimur tamen tempora, nec ea, quae nondum sunt, nec ea, quae iam non sunt, nec ea, quae nulla mora extenduntur, nec ea, quae terminos non habent. nec futura ergo nec praeterita nec praesentia nec praetereuntia tempora metimur, et metimur tamen tempora.

Deus creator omnium: versus iste octo syllabarum brevibus et longis alternat syllabis: quattuor itaque breves, prima, tertia, quinta, septima, simplae sunt ad quattuor longas, secundam, quartam, sextam, octavam. hae singulae ad illas singulas duplum habent temporis;

no stay; for it was passing and passing away. CHAP.
Might it then be measured the rather for that? XXVII
For whilst passing it was being stretched out
into some space of time, by which it might be
measured, since the present hath no space. If
therefore then, it might; then lo, let us put the
case that another voice hath begun to sound, and
still does, with the same continued tenor without
any interruption : let us now while it sounds measure
it : seeing when it hath left sounding, it will then
be past, and nothing left to be measured. Let us
measure it verily, and tell how much it is. But
it sounds still; nor can it be measured but from
the instant it began in, unto the end it left in.
For the very space between is the thing we measure,
namely, from some beginning unto some end. For
which reason, a voice that is not yet ended cannot
be measured, as that it may be said how long, or
how short it is; nor can it be called equal to
another, or single or double to another, or the like :
and so soon, again, as it is ended, it shall be no more.
How may it then be measured? We measure times,
for all this; and yet neither those which are not yet
come; nor those which are now no longer; nor yet
those which are not lengthened out by some pause;
nor yet those which have no bounds. So that we
neither measure the times to come, nor the past, nor
the present, nor the passing times; and yet we do
measure times.

"O God, creator thou of all!" that very verse of See Book
eight syllables interchangeably varies itself between IX. xxxii.
short and long syllables. Four therefore be short,
namely, the first, third, fifth, and seventh : which be
but single in respect of the four long, namely, the
second, fourth, sixth, and eighth. Every one of these,

CAP.
XXVII

pronuntio et renuntio, et ita est, quantum sentitur sensu manifesto. quantum sensus manifestus est, brevi syllaba longam metior eamque sentio habere bis tantum. sed cum altera post alteram sonat, si prior brevis, longa posterior, quomodo tenebo brevem, et quomodo eam longae metiens applicabo, ut inveniam, quod bis tantum habeat, quandoquidem longa sonare non incipit, nisi brevis sonare destiterit? ipsamque longam num praesentem metior, quando nisi finitam non metior? eius enim finitio praeteritio est. quid ergo est, quod metior? ubi est qua metior brevis? ubi est longa, quam metior? ambae sonuerunt, avolaverunt, praeterierunt, iam non sunt: et ego metior, fidenterque respondeo, quantum exercitato sensu fiditur, illam simplam esse, illam duplam, in spatio scilicet temporis. neque hoc possum, nisi quia praeterierunt et finitae sunt. non ergo ipsas, quae iam non sunt, sed aliquid in memoria mea metior, quod infixum manet.

In te, anime meus, tempora mea metior. noli mihi obstrepere; quod est, noli tibi obstrepere turbis affectionum tuarum. in te, inquam, tempora metior. affectionem, quam res praetereuntes in te faciunt, et cum illae praeterierint, manet, ipsam metior praesentem, non ea quae praeterierunt, ut fieret; ipsam

tò every one of those, hath a double time : I pronounce
them over and over ; and even so I find it, as plainly
as sense can shew it. So far as sense can manifest it,
I measure a long syllable by a short, and I sensibly
find it to have twice so much : but now when one
sounds after another, if the former be short, and the
latter long, how shall I then hold fast the short one ;
and how in measuring the long, shall I so lay them
together, as that I may find this to have twice so
much as that ; seeing the long cannot begin to sound,
unless the short leaves sounding ? Yea, that long
one itself do I measure as not present, seeing I
measure it not till it be ended. For his ending
is his passing away. What is it therefore that I
measure ? Where is that short syllable by which I
measure ? Where is that long one which I measure ?
Both have sounded, have flown and gone, they are
now no more : and yet I measure them, and confidently do I answer (so far as a man may trust a well-
experienced sense) that this syllable is but single,
and that double ; in respect of space of time, I
mean : and yet can I not do thus much, unless
these syllables were already past and ended. 'Tis
not therefore these voices (which now are not) that
I measure : but something it is even in mine own
memory, which there remains fastened.

'Tis in thee, O my mind, that I measure my
times. Do not thou interrupt me now, that is,
do not interrupt thine own self with the tumults
of thine own impressions. In thee, I say, it is,
that I measure the times. The impression, which
things passing by cause in thee, and remains even
when the things are gone, that is it which being
still present, I do measure : not the things which
have passed by that this impression might be

metior, cum tempora metior. ergo aut ipsa sunt tempora, aut non tempora metior. quid cum metimur silentia, et dicimus illud silentium tantum tenuisse temporis, quantum illa vox tenuit, nonne cogitationem tendimus ad mensuram vocis, quasi sonaret, ut aliquid de intervallis silentiorum in spatio temporis renuntiare possimus ? nam et voce atque ore cessante, peragimus cogitando carmina et versus, et quemque sermonem motionumque dimensiones quaslibet, et de spatiis temporum, quantum illud ad illud sit, renuntiamus non aliter, ac si ea sonando diceremus. si voluerit aliquis edere longiusculam vocem, et constituerit praemeditando, quam longa futura sit, egit utique iste spatium temporis in silentio, memoriaeque commendans coepit edere illam vocem, quae sonat, donec ad propositum terminum perducatur : immo sonuit et sonabit ; nam quod eius iam peractum est, utique sonuit, quod autem restat, sonabit, atque ita peragitur, dum praesens intentio futurum in praeteritum traicit, deminutione futuri crescente praeterito, donec consumptione futuri sit totum praeteritum.

made. This do I measure, whenas I measure times.
Either therefore times do exist, or I do not measure
times. But what when we measure silence: and
say that this silence hath held as long time as that
voice did; do we not then lengthen out our thoughts
to the measure of a voice, even as if it now sounded,
that so we may be able to say something of the vacant
intervals of silence in a space of time? For when
the voice and tongue give over, yet then in our
meditations go we over poems, and verses, and any
other discourse, or any dimensions of motions; yea,
and as to spaces of times, how much this is respect of
that, do we, in our thoughts, repeat over, no other
wise than if vocally we did pronounce them. Suppose
a man were about to utter a somewhat long sound of
the voice, and in his thoughts should resolve how long
it should be; this man hath even in silence already
spent a space of time, and committing it to his
memory, begins to utter that sound, which continues
sounding until it be brought unto the end proposed.
Yea, it hath sounded, and will sound; for so much of
it as is finished, hath sounded already, and the rest
will sound, and thus passeth it on, until the present
attention conveys over the future into the past:
by the diminution of the future, the past gaining
increase; even until by the wasting away of the
future, all grows into the past.

XXVIII

CAP
XXVII

SED quomodo minuitur aut consumitur futurum, quod nondum est, aut quomodo crescit praeteritum, quod iam non est, nisi quia in animo, qui illud agit, tria sunt? nam et expectat et adtendit et meminit, ut id quod expectat per id quod adtendit transeat in id quod meminerit. quis igitur negat futura nondum esse? sed tamen iam est in animo expectatio futurorum. et quis negat praeterita iam non esse? sed tamen est adhuc in animo memoria praeteritorum. et quis negat praesens tempus carere spatio, quia in puncto praeterit? sed tamen perdurat attentio, per quam pergat abesse quod aderit. non igitur longum tempus futurum, quod non est, sed longum futurum longa expectatio futuri est, neque longum praeteritum tempus, quod non est, sed longum praeteritum longa memoria praeteriti est.

Dicturus sum canticum, quod novi: antequam incipiam, in totum expectatio mea tenditur, cum autem coepero, quantum ex illa in praeteritum decerpsero, tenditur et memoria mea, atque distenditur vita huius actionis meae, in memoriam propter quod dixi, et in expectationem propter

XXVIII

We measure Times in our Mind

But how comes that future, which as yet is not, to be diminished or wasted away? Or how comes that past, which now is no longer, to be increased? Unless in the mind which acteth all this, there be three things done. For it expects, it marks attentively, it remembers; that so the thing which it expecteth, through that which attentively it marketh, passes into that which it remembereth. Who therefore can deny, that things to come are not as yet? Yet already there is in the mind an expectation of things to come. And who can deny past things to be now no longer? But yet is there still in the mind a memory of things past. And who can deny that the present time hath no space, because it passeth away in a moment? But yet our attentive marking of it continues so that that which shall be present proceedeth to become absent. The future therefore is not a long time, for it is not: but the long future time is merely a long expectation of the future. Nor is the time past a long time, for it is not; but a long past time is merely a long memory of the past time.

I am about to repeat a psalm that I know. Before I begin, my expectation alone reaches itself over the whole: but so soon as I shall have once begun, how much so ever of it I shall take off into the past, over so much my memory also reaches: thus the life of this action of mine is extended both ways: into my memory, so far as concerns that part which I have repeated already, and into my expectation too, in respect of what I am about to repeat now; but

Attendit, very nearly the same as "experience"

CAP.
XXVIII
quod dicturus sum : praesens tamen adest attentio mea, per quam traicitur quod erat futurum, ut fiat praeteritum. quod quanto magis agitur et agitur, tanto breviata expectatione prolongatur memoria, donec tota expectatio consumatur, quum tota illa actio finita transierit in memoriam. et quod in toto cantico, hoc in singulis particulis eius, fit atque in singulis syllabis eius, hoc in actione longiore, cuius forte particula est illud canticum, hoc in tota vita hominis, cuius partes sunt omnes actiones hominis, hoc in toto saeculo filiorum hominum, cuius partes sunt omnes vitae hominum.

XXIX

CAP.
XXIX
SED quoniam melior est misericordia tua super vitas, ecce distentio est vita mea, et me suscepit dextera tua in domino meo, mediatore filio hominis inter te unum et nos multos, in multis per multa, ut per eum adprehendam, in quo et adprehensus sum, et a veteribus diebus colligar sequens unum, praeterita oblitus, non in ea quae futura et transitura sunt, sed in ea quae ante sunt non distentus, sed extentus, non secundum distentionem, sed secundum inten-tionem sequor ad palmam supernae vocationis, ubi

all this while is my marking faculty present at CHAP.
hand, through which, that which was future, is XXVIII
conveyed over, that it may become past: which
how much the more diligently it is done over and
over again, so much more the expectation being
shortened, is the memory enlarged; till the whole
expectation be at length vanished quite away, when
namely, that whole action being ended, shall be
absolutely passed into the memory. What is now
done in this whole psalm, the same is done also in
every part of it, yea and in every syllable of it; the
same order holds in a longer action too, whereof
perchance this psalm is but a part; this holds too
throughout the whole course of man's life, the parts
whereof be all the actions of the man; it holds also
throughout the whole age of the sons of men, the
parts whereof be the whole lives of men.

XXIX

How the Mind lengthens out itself

But because thy loving kindness is better than life CHAP.
itself, behold my life is a distraction, and thy right XXIX
hand hath taken hold of me, even in my Lord the Son Ps. lxiii. 3
of Man, the Mediator betwixt thee that art but one, and
us that are many, drawn many ways by many things;
that by him I may apprehend him in whom I am also
apprehended, and that I may be gathered up from my
old conversation, to follow that one, and to forget what
is behind: not distracted but attracted, stretching forth Phil. iii.
not to what shall be and shall pass away, but to those 12-14
things which are before: not, I say, distractedly but
intently, follow I hard on, for the garland of my
heavenly calling, where I may hear the voice of thy Ps. xxvi. 7

CAP.
XXIX
audiam vocem laudis et contempler delectationem tuam nec venientem nec praetereuntem. nunc vero anni mei in gemitibus, et tu solacium meum, domine, pater meus aeternus es ; at ego in tempora dissilui, quorum ordinem nescio, et tumultuosis varietatibus dilaniantur cogitationes meae, intima viscera animae meae, donec in te confluam purgatus et liquidus igne amoris tui.

XXX

CAP.
XXX
Et stabo atque solidabor in te, in forma mea, veritate tua, nec patiar quaestiones hominum, qui poenali morbo plus sitiunt, quam capiunt, et dicunt : "quid faciebat deus, antequam faceret caelum et terram ?" aut "quid ei venit in mentem, ut aliquid faceret, cum antea numquam aliquid fecerit ?" da illis, domine, bene cogitare, quid dicant, et invenire, quia non dicitur numquam, ubi non est tempus. qui ergo dicitur numquam fecisse, quid aliud dicitur nisi nullo tempore fecisse ? videant itaque nullum tempus esse posse sine creatura, et desinant istam vanitatem loqui. extendantur etiam in ea, quae ante sunt, et intellegant te ante omnia tempora aeternum creatorem omnium temporum, neque ulla tempora tibi

praise, and contemplate these delights of thine, which CHAP.
are neither to come, nor to pass away. But now are XXIX
my years spent in mourning, and thou, my Comfort, Ps. xxxi. 11
O Lord, my Father, art Everlasting; but I fall into
dissolution amid the changing times, whose order I
am yet ignorant of: yea, my thoughts are torn asunder
with tumultuous vicissitudes, even the inmost bowels
of my soul; until I may be run into thee, purified and
molten by the fire of thy love.

XXX

He goes on in the same Discourse

AND after that will I stand, and grow hard in thee, CHAP.
in my mould, thy truth: nor will I endure the XXX
questions of such people, who in a penal disease
thirst for more than their bellies will hold; such as
say: What did God make before he made heaven
and earth? Or, Why came it in his mind to
make anything then, having never made anything
before? Give them grace, O Lord, well to bethink
themselves what they say; and to find that they
cannot say Never, when there is no time. That he
is said therefore never to have made, what is it
else to say, than in no time to have made? Let
them see therefore, that there cannot possibly be any
time without some or other of thy creatures: and let
them forbear this so vain talking. Let them stretch Phil. iii. 13
forth rather towards those things which are before;
and understand thee the eternal Creator of all times,
to have been before all times; and that no times be

CAP.
XXX
esse coaeterna, nec ullam creaturam, etiamsi est
aliqua supra tempora.

XXXI

CAP.
XXXI
DOMINE deus meus, quis ille sinus est alti secreti tui
et quam longe inde me proiecerunt consequentia
delictorum meorum? sana oculos meos, et con-
gaudeam luci tuae. certe si est tam grandi scientia
et praescientia pollens animus, cui cuncta praeterita
et futura ita nota sint, sicut mihi unum canticum
notissimum, nimium mirabilis est animus iste atque
ad horrorem stupendus, quippe quem ita non lateat
quidquid peractum et quidquid relicum saeculorum
est, quemadmodum me non latet cantantem illud
canticum, quid et quantum eius abierit ab exordio,
quid et quantum restet ad finem. sed absit, ut tu,
conditor universitatis, conditor animarum et corporum, absit, ut ita noveris omnia futura et praeterita.
longe tu, longe mirabilius longeque secretius. neque
enim sicut nota cantantis notumve canticum audi-
entis expectatione vocum futurarum et memoria
praeteritarum variatur affectus sensusque distenditur,
ita tibi aliquid accidit inconmutabiliter aeterno, hoc

co-eternal with thee : no, nor any other creature, CHAP.
even if there be any creature before all times. XXX

XXXI

How God is known, and how the creature

O LORD my God, what bosom of thy deep secrets CHAP.
is that, and how far from it have the consequences XXXI
of my transgressions cast me ? O cure mine eyes,
that I may share the joy of thy light. Certainly if
there be any mind excelling with such eminent
knowledge and foreknowledge, as to know all
things past and to come, so well as I knew that
one psalm ; truly that is a most admirable mind,
able with horror to amaze : in that nothing done in
the former, or to be done in the after ages of the
world, is hid from him any more than that psalm was
to me whenas I sang it ; namely, what and how much
of it I had sung from the beginning, what and how
much there was yet unto the ending ? But far be
it from us to think, that thou the Creator of this
universe, the Creator of both souls and bodies ; far be
it from us to think, that thou shouldest no better know
what were past, and what were to come. Far, yea,
far more wonderfully, and far more secretly dost thou
know them. For 'tis not as when one sings what he
knows, or hears a well known song, through expectation of the words to come, and the remembering of
those that are past, his feelings are varied and his
senses distracted : not so can anything chance unto
thee that art unchangeably eternal ; that is, the
eternal Creator of minds. Like as therefore thou
in the beginning knewest the heaven and the earth,

CAP.
XXXI

est vere aeterno creatori mentium. sicut ergo nosti
in principio caelum et terram sine varietate notitiae
tuae, ita fecisti in principio caelum et terram sine distinctione actionis tuae. qui intellegit, confiteatur
tibi, et qui non intellegit, confiteatur tibi.
o quam excelsus es, et humiles
corde sunt domus tua! tu enim
erigis elisos, et non cadunt,
quorum celsitudo tu es.

without any variety of thy knowledge; even so didst CHAP.
thou in the beginning create heaven and earth, XXXI
without any change in thy action. Let him that
understandeth confess unto thee; and let him that
understandeth not confess unto thee also. Oh,
how high art thou, and yet the humble in
heart are the house that thou dwellest
in. For thou raisest up those that   Ps. cxlvi.
are bowed down; and never   8
can they fall, whose
uplifting thou art.

BOOK XII

LIBER DVODECIMVS

I

CAP.
I

MULTA satagit cor meum, domine, in hac inopia vitae meae pulsatum verbis sanctae scripturae tuae, et ideo plerumque in sermone copiosa est egestas humanae intellegentiae, quia plus loquitur inquisitio quam inventio et longior est petitio quam inpetratio et operosior est manus pulsans quam sumens. tenemus promissum: quis corrumpet illud? si deus pro nobis, quis contra nos? petite, et accipietis; quaerite, et invenietis; pulsate, et aperietur vobis. omnis enim, qui petit, accipit et quaerens inveniet et pulsanti aperietur. promissa tua sunt, et quis falli timeat, cum promittit veritas?

II

CAP.
II

CONFITETUR altitudini tuae humilitas linguae meae, quoniam tu fecisti caelum et terram, hoc caelum, quod video, terramque, quam calco, unde est haec terra, quam porto. tu fecisti. sed ubi est caelum caeli,

288

THE TWELFTH BOOK

I

'Tis very difficult to find out the Truth

CHAP. I

My heart, O Lord, touched with the words of
Holy Scripture, is busily employed in this poverty
of my life. And therefore in eloquent discourse
oftentimes appears the plentiful poverty of human
understanding: because that enquiring has more
to say than finding out does; and we are longer
about demanding, than about obtaining; and our
hand that knocks, hath more work to do, than our
other hand that receives. A promise have we laid
hold of: who shall defeat us of it? If God be on our
side, who can be against us? Ask, and ye shall have;
seek, and ye shall find; knock, and it shall be opened
unto you. For every one that asks, receives; and he
that seeks, finds: and to him that knocketh, shall
it be opened. There be thine own promises: and
who needs fear to be deceived, whenas the Truth
promises?

Rom. viii. 31

Matt. vii. 7

II

That the Heaven we see is but Earth, in respect of the Heaven of Heavens, which we see not

CHAP. II

Unto thy Highness the lowliness of my tongue
now confesseth, that thou hast made heaven and
earth; this heaven, I mean, which I see, and this
earth that I tread upon, whence is this earthly body
that I wear. Thou madest it. But where is that

CAP.
II domine, de quo audivimus in voce psalmi : caelum
caeli domino ; terram autem dedit filiis hominum ?
ubi es, caelum, quod non cernimus, cui terra est hoc
omne, quod cernimus ? hoc enim totum corporeum
non ubique totum ita cepit speciem pulchram in no-
vissimis, cuius fundus est terra nostra, sed ad illud
caelum caeli etiam terrae nostrae caelum terra est.
et hoc utrumque magnum corpus non absurde terra
est ad illud nescio quale caelum, quod domino est,
non filiis hominum.

III

CAP.
III Et nimirum haec terra erat invisibilis et incomposita
et nescio qua profunditas abyssi, super quam non erat
lux, quia nulla species erat illi : unde iussisti, ut
scriberetur, quod tenebrae erant super abyssum ;
quid aliud quam lucis absentia ? ubi enim lux esset,
si esset, nisi super esset eminendo et inlustrando ?
ubi ergo lux nondum erat, quid erat adesse tenebras
nisi abesse lucem ? super itaque erant tenebrae, quia
super lux aberat, sicut sonus ubi non est, silentium
est. et quid est esse ibi silentium nisi sonum ibi non
esse ? nonne tu, domine, docuisti hanc animam, quae
290

Heaven of Heavens, O Lord, which we hear of in the words of the psalmist: The heaven of heavens is the Lord's; but the earth hath he given to the children of men. Where art thou, O heaven which we see not? in comparison whereof, all this heaven which we see, is but mere earth. For this heaven is wholly corporeal, which is not wholly everywhere, hath in such wise received its portion of beauty in these lower parts, the bottom whereof is this earth of ours: but in comparison of that Heaven of Heavens, even the heaven of this our earth, is but earth: yea, both these great bodies may not absurdly be called earth, in comparison of that I know not what manner of heaven, which is the Lord's, and not given to the sons of men.

CHAP.
II
Ps. cxv.
16

III

Of the Darkness upon the Face of the Deep

AND now was this earth invisible and without form, and there was, I know not what profoundness of the deep, upon which there was no light, because as yet it had no shape. Therefore didst thou command it to be written, that darkness was upon the face of the deep: which what other thing was it, than the absence of light? For if there had been light, where should it have been bestowed, but in being over all, by rising aloft and giving light? Where therefore light was not yet, what was it that darkness was present, but that light was absent? Darkness therefore was all over hitherto, because light was not upon it: like as where there is no sound, there is silence. And what is it to have silence there, but to have no sound there? Hast not thou, O Lord, taught these things

CHAP.
III
Gen. i. 2

^{CAP.} tibi confitetur? nonne tu, domine, docuisti me, quod,
^{III}
priusquam istam informem materiam formares atque
distingueres, non erat aliquid, non color, non figura,
non corpus, non spiritus? non tamen omnino nihil :
erat quaedam informitas sine ulla specie.

IV

^{CAP.} Quid ergo vocaretur, quo etiam sensu tardioribus
^{IV}
utcumque insinuaretur, nisi usitato aliquo vocabulo ?
quid autem in omnibus mundi partibus reperiri potest
propinquius informitati omnimodae quam terra et
abyssus? minus enim speciosa sunt pro suo gradu
infimo, quam cetera superiora perlucida et luculenta
omnia. cur ergo non accipiam informitatem materiae,
quam sine specie feceras, unde speciosum mundum
faceres, ita commode hominibus intimatam, ut appellaretur terra invisibilis et incomposita.

V

^{CAP.} Ut, cum in ea quaerit cogitatio, quid sensus attingat,
^V
et dicit sibi : " non est intellegibilis forma sicut vita,
sicut iustitia, quia materies est corporum, neque sensibilis, quoniam quid videatur et quid sentiatur in

unto the soul which thus confesses unto thee? Hast CHAP.
III thou not taught me, Lord, that before thou shapedst and diversifiedst this unshapen matter, there was nothing, neither colour, nor figure, nor body, nor spirit? And yet was there not altogether an absolute nothing; for there was a certain unshapedness, without any form in it.

IV

Of the Chaos, and what Moses called it

AND how should that be called; and by what sense CHAP.
IV could it be insinuated to people of slow apprehensions, but by some ordinary word? And what, among all the parts of the world, can be found to come nearer to an absolute unshapedness, than the earth and the deep? For surely they be less beautiful in respect of their low situation, than those other higher parts are, which are all transparent and shining. Wherefore then may I not conceive the unshapedness of the first matter which thou createdst without form (of which thou wert to make this goodly world) to be significantly intimated unto men by the name of earth invisible and without form.

V

That this Chaos is hard to conceive

So that, when the thought of man is seeking for CHAP.
V somewhat which the sense may fasten upon; and returns answer to itself: It is no intellectual form as life is, or as justice is, because it is the matter of bodies: nor is it anything sensible, for that in this earth, invisible as yet, and without form, there is

CAP.
V
invisibili et incomposita non est," dum sibi haec dicit
humana cogitatio, conetur eam vel nosse ignorando
vel ignorare noscendo?

VI

CAP.
VI
Ego vero, domine, si totum confitear tibi ore meo et
calamo meo, quidquid de ista materia docuisti me,
cuius antea nomen audiens et non intellegens nar-
rantibus mihi eis, qui non intellegerent, eam cum
speciebus innumeris et variis cogitabam, et ideo non
eam cogitabam; foedas et horribiles formas pertur-
batis ordinibus volvebat animus, sed formas tamen,
et informe appellabam; non quod careret forma, sed
quod talem haberet, ut, si appareret, insolitum et in-
congruum aversaretur sensus meus et conturbaretur
infirmitas hominis; verum autem illud quod cogitabam non privatione omnis formae, sed conparatione
formosiorum erat informe, et suadebat vera ratio, ut
omnis formae qualescumque reliquias omnino detra-
herem, si vellem prorsus informe cogitare, et non
poteram; citius enim non esse censebam, quod omni
forma privaretur, quam cogitabam quiddam inter
formam et nihil, nec formatum nec nihil, informe prope
nihil; et cessavit mens mea interrogare hinc spiritum

nothing to be seen or perceived :—when I say, CHAP.
man's thoughts thus discourse unto himself, he may V
endeavour either to know it, by being ignorant of Compare
it ; or to be ignorant, by knowing it. Book XI.
ch. xiv.

Plotinus,
Enn. ii. 4, 10

VI

What himself sometimes thought of it

For mine own part, O Lord, if I may confess all unto CHAP.
thee, both by tongue and pen, whatever thyself hast VI
taught me of that substance, (the name whereof
having heard before, but without understanding, because they told me of it, who themselves understood
it not, I conceived of it as having innumerable forms
and diverse, and therefore indeed did I not at all conceive of it in my mind): my mind tossed up and down
certain ugly and hideous forms, all out of order, but
yet forms they were notwithstanding ; and this I
called without form ; not that it wanted all form, but
because it had such an one, that if it presented itself
unto me, my sense would straightways turn from it as
a thing unexpected or absurd, and human frailness
would be troubled. But yet that which my conceit ran
upon, was, methought, formless, not for that it was deprived of all form, but in comparison of more beautiful
forms : and true reason did persuade me, that I must
utterly uncase it of all remnants of forms whatsoever,
if so be I meant to conceive a matter absolute without form : and I could not. For sooner could I
imagine that not to be at all, which should be deprived of all form, than once conceive there was
likely to be anything betwixt form and nothing ; a
matter neither formed nor nothing ; formless, almost
nothing. My mind gave over thereupon to question

CAP.
VI

meum, plenum imaginibus formatorum corporum et
eas pro arbitrio mutantem atque variantem, et intendi
in ipsa corpora eorumque mutabilitatem altius inspexi,
qua desinunt esse quod fuerant et incipiunt esse quod
non erant, eundemque transitum de forma in formam
per informe quiddam fieri suspicatus sum, non per
omnino nihil : sed nosse cupiebam, non suspicari :—
et si totum tibi confiteatur vox et stilus meus, quidquid de ista quaestione enodasti mihi, quis legentium
capere durabit ? nec ideo tamen cessabit cor meum
tibi dare honorem et canticum laudis de his, quae
dictare non sufficit. mutabilitas enim rerum muta-
bilium ipsa capax est formarum omnium, in quas
mutantur res mutabiles. et haec quid est ? numquid
animus ? numquid corpus ? numquid species animi
vel corporis ? si dici posset " nihil aliquid " et " est
non est " hoc eam dicerem ; et tamen iam utcumque
erat, ut species caperet istas visibiles et compositas.

VII

CAP.
VII

ET unde utcumque erat, ut species caperet istas
visibiles et compositas, et unde utcumque erat, nisi
esset abs te, a quo sunt omnia, in quantumcumque
sunt ? sed tanto a te longius, quanto dissimilius :

any more about it with my spirit, which was wholly CHAP.
VI taken up already with the images of formed bodies, which I changed and varied as me listed: and I bent my enquiry upon the bodies themselves, and more deeply looked into their mutability, by which they both cease to be what they have been, and begin to be what they never have been. And this shifting out of one form into another, I suspected to be through a certain formless state, not nothing at all: yet this I was desirous to know, not to suspect only.—Then if my voice and pen should here confess all unto thee, whatsoever knots thou didst unknit for me in this question, what reader would have so much patience to be made conceive it? Nor shall my heart, for all this, be slack at any time to give thee honour, and a song of praise, for all those things which it is not able to express. For the changeable condition of changeable things, is of itself capable of all those forms into which these changeable things are changed. And this changeableness, what is it? Is it a soul, or is it a body? Or is it any figure of a soul or a body? If it could be said A something nothing, and An is is-not, I would say, this were it: and yet it was even then in some way, to be capable of these visible and compounded figures.

VII

Heaven is greater than Earth

But whence came it, howsoever it came, that it CHAP.
VII should be capable of these visible and compounded figures? and whence came it, howsoever it came, but from thee, from whom are all things, so far forth as they have being? But so much the further

CAP.
VII
neque enim locis. itaque tu, domine, qui non es
alias aliud et alias aliter, sed id ipsum et id ipsum et
id ipsum, sanctus, sanctus, sanctus, dominus deus
omnipotens, in principio, quod est de te, in sapientia
tua, quae nata est de substantia tua, fecisti aliquid
et de nihilo.   fecisti enim caelum et terram ; non de
te, nam esset aequale unigenito tuo, ac per hoc ac
tibi, et nullo modo iustum esset, ut aequale tibi esset,
quod de te non esset. et aliud praeter te non erat,
unde faceres ea, deus, una trinitas et trina unitas : et
ideo de nihilo fecisti caelum et terram, magnum
quiddam et parvum quiddam, quoniam omnipotens
et bonus es ad facienda omnia bona, magnum caelum
et parvam terram.   tu eras et aliud nihil, unde fecisti
caelum et terram, duo quaedam, unum prope te,
alterum prope nihil, unum, quo superior tu esses,
alterum, quo inferius nihil esset.

VIII

CAP.
VIII
Sed illud caelum caeli tibi, domine ; terra autem,
quam dedisti filiis hominum cernendam atque tan-
gendam, non erat talis, qualem nunc cernimus et
tangimus. invisibilis enim erat et incomposita, et

off from thee, as unliker thee: for it is not farness CHAP.
of places. Thou therefore, O Lord, who art not VII
another in another place, nor otherwise in another See Book
place: but the same, and the very same, and IX. xi.
the very self-same Holy, Holy, Holy, Lord God Is. vi. 3
Almighty, didst in the beginning, which is of thee,
in thy wisdom, which was born of thine own substance, make something, and that out of nothing.
For thou madest heaven and earth; not of thee,
for so should they have been equal to thine only
Begotten Son, and thereby unto thine own self too:
whereas no way just it had been, that anything
should be equal unto thee, which was not of thee.
And there was nothing besides thyself, of which
thou mightest create these things, O God, who art
one in trinity and three in unity. Therefore out of
nothing hast thou created heaven and earth; a great
thing, and a small thing: for thou art omnipotent
and good, to make all things good, even the great
heavens, and the little earth. Thou wert, and
nothing else was there besides, out of which thou
createdst heaven and earth: two certain things;
one near thee, the other near to nothing; one to
which thou alone shouldst be superior: the other,
which nothing should be inferior unto.

VIII

The Chaos was created out of nothing, and out
of that, all things

BUT that Heaven of Heavens was for thyself, CHAP.
Lord; but this earth which thou gavest to the sons VIII
of men to be seen and felt, was not at first such as Ps. cxv. 16
we now both see and feel: for it was invisible, and
without form, and there was a deep, upon which there

CAP.
VIII

abyssus erat, super quam non erat lux, aut tenebrae erant super abyssum, id est magis quam in abysso. ista quippe abyssus aquarum, iam visibilium, etiam in profundis suis habet speciei suae lucem, utcumque sensibilem piscibus et repentibus in suo fundo animantibus : illud autem totum prope nihil erat, quoniam adhuc omnino informe erat; iam tamen erat, quod formari poterat. tu enim, domine, fecisti mundum de materia informi, quam fecisti de nulla re paene nullam rem, unde faceres magna, quae miramur filii hominum. valde hoc mirabile caelum corporeum, quod firmamentum inter aquam et aquam secundo die post conditionem lucis dixisti : fiat, et sic est factum. quod firmamentum vocasti caelum, sed caelum terrae huius et maris, quae fecisti tertio die, dando speciem visibilem informi materiae, quam fecisti ante omnem diem. iam enim feceras et caelum ante omnem diem, sed caelum caeli huius, quia in principio feceras caelum et terram. terra autem ipsa, quam feceras, informis materies erat, quia invisibilis erat et incomposita et tenebrae super abyssum : de qua terra invisibili et incomposita, de qua informitate, de quo paene nihilo faceres haec omnia, quibus iste mutabilis mundus constat et non constat, in quo ipsa mutabilitas apparet, in qua sentiri et dinumerari possunt tempora, quia rerum mutationibus fiunt tempora, dum variantur et vertuntur species, quarum materies praedicta est terra invisibilis.

300

was no light: or, darkness was upon the deep, that is, CHAP.
VIII
darker than in the deep. Because this deep of waters,
visible now, hath even in his deeps a light proper for
its nature; perceivable in whatever degree unto the
fishes and creeping things at the bottom of it. But
all this whole was almost nothing, because hitherto it was altogether without form: but yet there
was now something apt to be formed. For thou,
Lord, madest the world of a matter without form;
which being next to nothing, thou madest out of
nothing: out of which thou mightest make those
great works which we sons of men do wonder at.
For very wonderful is this corporeal heaven; because
a firmament between water and water, the second day
after the creation of light, thou commandedst to be
made, and it was made. Which firmament thou
calledst heaven: the heaven, that is, to this earth
and sea, which thou createdst the third day, by
giving a visible figure unto the unshapen matter
which thou didst make before all days. For even
already hadst thou made an heaven before all
days: but that was the Heaven of this Heaven, That which
because in the beginning thou hadst made heaven is to this
heaven
and earth. As for this same earth which thou hadst what
made, it was unshaped matter, because it was invisible heaven
and without form, and darkness was upon the deep: is to earth
that of this invisible earth and without form, of which
unshapeliness, of which almost nothing, thou wert
to make all these, of which this changeable world
consists and doth not consist, but mutability itself
appears in it, in which times can be observed and
numbered: for times are made by the alterations
of things, whilst, namely, their forms are varied
and turned; the matter whereof, is this invisible
earth aforesaid.

IX

CAP. IX IDEOQUE spiritus, doctor famuli tui, cum te comme-
morat fecisse in principio caelum et terram, tacet de
temporibus, silet de diebus. nimirum enim caelum
caeli, quod in principio fecisti, creatura est aliqua
intellectualis, quamquam nequaquam tibi, trinitati,
coaeterna, particeps tamen aeternitatis tuae, valde
mutabilitatem suam prae dulcedine felicissimae contemplationis tuae cohibet, et sine ullo lapsu, ex quo
facta est, inhaerendo tibi, excedit omnem volubilem
vicissitudinem temporum. ista vero informitas, terra
invisibilis et incomposita, nec ipsa in diebus numerata
est. ubi enim nulla species, nullus ordo, nec venit
quicquam et praeterit, et ubi hoc non fit, non sunt
utique dies nec vicissitudo spatiorum temporalium.

X

CAP. X O VERITAS, lumen cordis mei, non tenebrae meae lo-
quantur mihi ! defluxi ad ista et obscuratus sum, sed
hinc, etiam hinc adamavi te. erravi et recordatus
sum tui. audivi vocem tuam post me, ut redirem, et
vix audivi propter tumultus impacatorum. et nunc

IX

What that Heaven of Heavens is

THE Spirit therefore, the teacher of thy servant, CHAP.
whenas it recounts thee to have in the beginning IX
created heaven and earth, speaks nothing of any
times, nor a word of any days. For verily that
Heaven of Heavens which thou createdst in the
beginning, is some intellectual creature; which,
although no ways co-eternal unto thee, the Trinity,
yet being partaker of thy eternity, doth through
the sweetness of that most happy contemplation of
thyself, strongly restrain its own mutability: and
without any fall since its first creation, cleaving
close unto thee, hath set itself beyond all rolling
interchange of times. Yea, neither is this chaos,
the earth invisible and without form, reckoned in
the numbering of the six days. For where no figure
nor order is, there does nothing either come or go:
and where this is not, there plainly are no days, nor
any interchange of temporal spaces.

X

His Desire to understand the Scriptures

O LET truth, the light of my heart, and not mine CHAP.
own darkness, now speak unto me! I fell off into X
those material things, and became all be-darkened:
but yet even thence, even thence came I to love thee.
I went astray, and I remembered thee. I heard thy
voice behind me calling to me to return; but scarcely
could I discern it for the noise of the enemies of
peace. And see here I return now, sweating and

303

CAP.
X

ecce redeo aestuans et anhelans ad fontem tuum. nemo me prohibeat: hunc bibam et hunc vivam. non ego vita mea sim: male vixi ex me, mors mihi fui: in te revivesco. tu me alloquere, tu mihi sermocinare. credidi libris tuis, et verba eorum arcana valde.

XI

CAP.
XI

IAM dixisti mihi, domine, voce forti in aurem interiorem, quia tu aeternus es, solus habens inmortalitatem, quoniam ex nulla specie motuve mutaris, nec temporibus variatur voluntas tua, quia non est immortalis voluntas, quae alia et alia est. hoc in conspectu tuo claret mihi, et magis magisque clarescat, oro te, atque in ea manifestatione persistam sobrius sub alis tuis. item dixisti mihi, domine, voce forti in aurem interiorem, quod omnes naturas atque substantias, quae non sunt quod tu es et tamen sunt, tu fecisti: hoc solum a te non est, quod non est; motusque voluntatis a te, qui es, ad id quod minus est, quia talis motus delictum atque peccatum est, et quod nullius peccatum aut tibi nocet, aut perturbat ordinem imperii tui vel in primo vel in imo. hoc in conspectu tuo claret mihi, et magis magisque clarescat, oro te, atque in ea manifestatione persistam sobrius sub alis tuis.

panting after thy fountain. Let no man forbid me; this will I drink, this will I live. Let me not be mine own life; I have lived ill of myself, death have I been to myself; in thee I revive again. Speak thou unto me, discourse thou with me. I have believed thy books, and their words be most full of mystery.

XI

What he learnt of God

Now hast thou with a strong voice, O Lord, spoken in my inner ear; because thou art eternal, that only possessest immortality, by reason that thou canst not be changed by any figure or motion, nor is thy will altered by times: seeing no will is immortal, which is now one, and then another. This is in thy sight already clear to me, and let it be more and more cleared to me, I beseech thee; and in the manifestation thereof, let me with sobriety continue under thy wings. Thou toldest me also with a strong voice, O Lord, in mine inner ear, how that 'tis thyself who made all those natures and substances which are not what thyself is, and which yet have their being: and how, that only is not from thee, which has no being, nor the will that slides back from thee, that art, unto that which hath an inferior being, because that all such backsliding is transgression and sin; and that no man's sin does either hurt thee, or disturb the order of thy government, first or last. All this is in thy sight now clear unto me, and let it be so more and more, I beseech thee: and in the manifestation thereof, let me soberly continue under thy wings.

Item dixisti mihi voce forti in aurem interiorem,
quod nec illa creatura tibi coaeterna est, cuius
voluptas tu solus es teque perseverantissima castitate hauriens mutabilitatem suam nusquam et
numquam exerit, et te sibi semper praesente, ad
quem toto affectu se tenet, non habens futurum quod
expectet nec in praeteritum traiciens quod meminerit, nulla vice variatur nec in tempora ulla distenditur. o beata, si qua ista est, inhaerendo beatitudini
tuae, beata sempiterno inhabitatore te atque inlus-
tratore suo! nec invenio, quid libentius appellandum existimem caelum caeli domino, quam domum
tuam contemplantem delectationem tuam sine ullo
defectu egrediendi in aliud, mentem puram concor-
dissime unam stabilimento pacis sanctorum spirituum,
civium civitatis tuae in caelestibus super ista caelestia.

Vnde intellegat anima, cuius peregrinatio longin-
qua facta est,—si iam sitit tibi, si iam factae sunt ei
lacrimae suae panis, dum dicitur ei per singulos dies:
ubi est deus tuus? si iam petit a te unam et hanc
requirit, ut inhabitet in domo tua per omnes dies
vitae suae? (et quae vita eius nisi tu? et qui dies tui nisi
aeternitas tua, sicut anni tui, qui non deficiunt, quia
idem ipse es?)—hinc ergo intellegat anima, quae potest,
quam longe super omnia tempora sis aeternus, quando
tua domus, quae peregrinata non est, quamvis non
306

With a strong voice thou toldest me likewise in
mine inner ear; how that neither is that creature
co-eternal unto thyself, whose desire thou only art,
which with a most persevering chastity greedily
drinking thee in, does in no place and at no time,
put off its natural mutability, which also, thyself
being ever present with it, (unto whom with its whole
affection it keeps itself) it having neither anything
in future to expect, nor conveying anything which it
remembereth into the time past, is neither altered by
any change, nor distracted into any times. O blessed
creature, (if any such there be) even cleaving so fast
unto thy blessedness: blessed in thee, the eternal
Inhabitant and Enlightener thereof. Nor do I find
what I am more glad to call the Heaven of Heavens
which is the Lord's, than thine own house, Lord, which
still contemplateth that delight which in thee it finds,
without any forsaking thee to go into other; a most
pure mind, most harmoniously continuing one, by
that settled estate of peace of those holy spirits,
those citizens of thy city in heavenly places; which
are far above those heavenly places that we see.

By this now may the soul, whose pilgrimage is
made so far off, by this may she understand—if
namely she now thirsts after thee; if her own tears
be now become her bread, while men daily say unto Ps. xlii. 3
her, Where is now thy God? if she now seeks of
thee one thing and desires it, that she may dwell in Ps. xxvii. 4
thy house all the days of her life: (and what is her
life, but thou? and what are thy days, but even
thy eternity? like as thy years, which fail not, Ps. cii. 27
because thou art ever the same:)—by this then may
the soul that is able, understand how far thou art
above all times, eternal; seeing that thy very house,
which at no time went into a far country, although

307

CAP.
XI
sit tibi coaeterna, tamen indesinenter et indeficienter tibi cohaerendo nullam patitur vicissitudinem temporum. hoc in conspectu tuo claret mihi, et magis magisque clarescat, oro te, atque in hac manifestatione persistam sobrius sub alis tuis.

Ecce nescio quid informe in istis mutationibus rerum extremarum atque infirmarum, et quis dicet mihi, (nisi quisquis per inania cordis sui cum suis phantasmatis vagatur et volvitur,) quis nisi talis dicet mihi, quod deminuta atque consumpta omni specie, si sola remaneat informitas, per quam de specie in speciem res mutabatur et vertebatur, possit exhibere vices temporum? omnino enim non potest, quia sine varietate motionum non sunt tempora: et nulla varietas, ubi nulla species.

XII

CAP.
XII
QUIBUS consideratis, deus meus, quantum donas, quantum me ad pulsandum excitas, quantumque pulsanti aperis, duo reperio, quae fecisti carentia temporibus, cum tibi neutrum coaeternum sit: unum, quod ita formatum est, ut sine ullo defectu contemplationis, sine ullo intervallo mutationis, quamvis mutabile, tamen non mutatum, aeternitate atque in-

it be not co-eternal unto thee; yet by continually and inseparably cleaving unto thee, suffers not the least changeableness of times. All this is clear unto me in thy sight, and more and more let it be so, I beseech thee, and in the manifestation thereof, let me abide soberly under thy wings.

There is, behold, I know not what unshapedness in the alterations of these last made, and lowest creatures: and who shall tell me (unless such a one as through the emptiness of his own heart, wanders and tosses up and down with his own fancies?)—who now but even such a one shall tell me, that if all figure be wasted and consumed away, if there only remains unshapedness, by which the thing was changed and turned out of one figure into another, that that could shew the changeable courses of the times? For plainly it can never do it; because, without the variety of motions there are no times: and there is no variety, where there is no figure.

XII

Of two Creatures not within Compass of Time

THESE things considered, as much as thou givest, O my God, as much as thou stirrest me up to knock, and as much as thou openest to me when I knock, two things I find that thou hast made, not within the compass of times; notwithstanding, that neither of them be co-eternal with thyself. One, which is so formed as that without any ceasing to contemplate thee, without any interval of change, though in itself it be changeable, yet having been

S. AVGVSTINI CONFESSIONVM LIBER XII

commutabilitate perfruatur; alterum, quod ita informe
erat, ut ex qua forma in quam formam vel motionis
vel stationis mutaretur, quo tempori subderetur, non
haberet. sed hoc ut informe esset, non reliquisti,
quoniam fecisti ante omnem diem in principio caelum
et terram, haec duo quae dicebam. terra autem invisibilis erat et incomposita et tenebrae super abyssum. quibus verbis insinuatur informitas, (ut gradatim excipiantur, qui omnimodam speciei privationem
nec tamen ad nihil perventionem cogitare non possent,) unde fieret alterum caelum, et terra visibilis
atque composita, et aqua speciosa, et quidquid deinceps
in constitutione huius mundi non sine diebus factum
commemoratur, quia talia sunt, ut in eis agantur vicis-
situdines temporum propter ordinatas commutationes
motionum atque formarum.

XIII

Hoc interim sentio, deus meus, cum audio loquentem
scripturam tuam : in principio fecit deus caelum et
terram : terra autem erat invisibilis et incomposita
et tenebrae erant super abyssum, neque conmemo-
rantem, quoto die feceris haec, sic interim sentio
propter illud caelum caeli,—caelum intellectuale, ubi

never changed, it may thoroughly for ever enjoy CHAP.
XII eternity and unchangeableness : the other which was so formless, as that it had not wherewithal to be changed out of one form into another, whether of motion or of rest, so as to become subject unto time. But this thou didst not leave to be thus formless; because before all days, thou in the beginning didst create heaven and earth ; the two things that I spake of. And the earth was invisible and without Gen. i. 2 shape, and darkness was upon the deep. In which words is the unshapedness noted unto us ; (that such capacities may hereby be drawn on by degrees, as are not able to conceive so utter a privation of all the form of it, as should not yet come so low as a mere nothing :) out of which another heaven was to be created, together with a visible earth and a well formed, and the beautiful waters, and whatsoever beside is in the setting forth of the world recorded to have been, not without days, created : and that because they are of such a nature that the successive changes of times may take place in them, by reason of their appointed alterations of motions and of forms.

XIII

The Nature of the Heaven of Heavens described

THIS, O my God, is my private judgment in the CHAP.
XIII mean time, whenas I hear thy Scripture saying, In the beginning God made heaven and earth : and the earth was invisible and unshaped, and darkness was upon the deep : and not once mentioning what day thou createdst them. This I in the mean time judge to be spoken because of the Heaven of

CAP.
XIII
est intellectus nosse simul, non ex parte, non in aenigmate, non per speculum, sed ex toto, in manifestatione, facie ad faciem ; non modo hoc, modo illud, sed, quod dictum est, nosse simul sine ulla vicissitudine temporum,—et propter invisibilem atque incompositam terram sine ulla vicissitudine temporum, quae solet habere modo hoc et modo illud, quia ubi nulla species, nusquam est hoc et illud :—propter duo haec, primitus formatum et penitus informe, illud caelum, sed caelum caeli, hoc vero terram, sed terram invisibilem et incompositam :—propter duo haec interim sentio sine commemoratione dierum dicere scripturam tuam : in principio fecit deus caelum et terram. statim quippe subiecit, quam terram dixerit. et quod secundo die commemoratur factum firmamentum et vocatum caelum, insinuat, de quo caelo prius sine diebus sermo locutus sit.

XIV

CAP.
XIV
Mira profunditas eloquiorum tuorum, quorum ecce ante nos superficies blandiens parvulis : sed mira profunditas, deus meus, mira profunditas ! horror est intendere in eam, horror honoris et tremor amoris. odi hostes eius vehementer : o si occidas eos de gladio bis acuto, et non sint hostes eius ! sic enim amo eos occidi

312

Heavens,—that intellectual heaven, where it is the CHAP.
property of the intelligence to know all at once, XIII
not in part, not darkly, not through a glass, but in 1 Cor. xiii.
whole, clearly, and face to face; not this thing now, 12
and that thing anon; but, as I said, know all at
once, without all succession of times :—and I judge it
spoken also, because of that invisible and void earth
(without any succession of times) which uses to have
this thing now, and anon that; the reason being, that
where there is not any figure, there can be no variety
of this or that :—because of these two, one first
formed, and one utterly formless; the one heaven,
meaning the Heaven of Heavens, and the other
earth, meaning the invisible and shapeless earth :—
because of these two, as I judge in the mean time,
did thy Scripture say without mention of any days, In
the beginning God created heaven and earth. For
at once it added what earth it spake of; and when
also the firmament is recorded to be created the
second day, and called heaven, it gives us to note, of
which heaven he before spake without mention of
any days.

XIV

The Depth of Holy Scripture

WONDERFUL is the depth of thy words, whose sur- CHAP.
face, see, is before us, gently leading on the little XIV
ones: and yet a wonderful deepness, O my God, a
wonderful deepness. It is awe to look into it; even
an awfulness of honour, and a trembling of love.
The enemies of it do I hate vehemently; oh that
thou wouldst slay them with thy two-edged sword,
that they might no longer be enemies unto it: for

CAP. sibi, ut vivant tibi. ecce autem alii non reprehensores,
XIV
sed laudatores libri Geneseos : "non" inquiunt "hoc
voluit in his verbis intellegi spiritus dei, qui per
Moysen famulum eius ista conscripsit, non hoc voluit
intellegi, quod tu dicis, sed aliud, quod nos dicimus."
quibus ego te arbitro, deus omnium nostrum, ita
respondeo.

XV

CAP. NUM dicetis falsa esse, quae mihi veritas voce forti in
XV
aurem interiorem dicit de vera aeternitate creatoris,
quod nequaquam eius substantia per tempora varietur
nec eius voluntas extra eius substantiam sit? unde
non eum modo velle hoc modo velle illud, sed semel
et simul et semper velle omnia quae vult, non iterum
et iterum, neque nunc ista nunc illa, nec velle postea
quod nolebat aut nolle quod volebat prius, quia talis
voluntas mutabilis est et omne mutabile aeternum
non est; deus autem noster aeternus est. item,
quod mihi dicit in aurem interiorem, expectatio rerum
venturarum fit contuitus, cum venerint, idemque contuitus fit memoria, cum praeterierint : omnis porro
intentio, quae ita variatur, mutabilis est, et omne
mutabile aeternum non est : deus autem noster
aeternus est. haec colligo atque coniungo, et invenio
314

thus do I love to have them slain unto themselves, CHAP.
that they may live unto thee. But now behold others XIV
not fault-finders, but extollers of the book of Genesis.
The Spirit of God, say they, which by his servant
Moses wrote these things, would not have those
words thus understood: he would not have it understood as thou sayest, but another thing as we say:
unto whom making thee judge, O thou God of us
all, do I thus answer.

XV

The Difference betwixt the Creator and the creatures.
Some Discourses about the Heaven of Heavens

WILL you affirm it to be false, which with a strong CHAP.
voice Truth tells me in my inner ear, concerning XV
the true eternity of the Creator: namely, that his substance is no ways changed by time, nor his will separated from his substance? Wherefore he willeth
not one thing now, and another thing anon, but that
once, and at once, and always, he willeth all things
that he willeth: not again and again, nor now this,
now that: nor willeth afterwards, what before he
would not: nor be unwilling with that now, which
he was willing with before: because such a will is
mutable, and no mutable thing is eternal: but our
God is eternal. Again, this is told me also in my
inner ears, that the expectation of things to come is See Book
turned to sight, whenas they are once come: and the XI. xxvi.
same sight again is turned to memory, so soon as
they be once past. Now every thought which is
thus varied, is mutable, and no mutable is eternal:
but our God is eternal. These things I infer, and
put together, and find that God, even my eternal

CAP.
XV

deum meum, deum aeternum non aliqua nova voluntate condidisse creaturam, nec scientiam eius transitorium aliquid pati.

Quid ergo dicetis, contradictores? an falsa sunt ista? "non" inquiunt. quid illud? num falsum est omnem naturam formatam materiamve formabilem non esse nisi ab illo, qui summe bonus est, quia summe est? "neque hoc negamus" inquiunt. quid igitur? an illud negatis, sublimem quandam esse creaturam, tam casto amore cohaerentem deo vero et vere aeterno, ut, quamvis ei coaeterna non sit, in nullam tamen temporum varietatem et vicissitudinem ab illo se resolvat et defluat, sed in eius solius veracissima contemplatione requiescat, quoniam tu, deus, diligenti te, quantum praecipis, ostendis ei te et sufficis ei, et ideo non declinat a te nec ad se? haec est domus dei non terrena neque ulla caelesti mole corporea, sed spiritalis et particeps aeternitatis tuae, quia sine labe in aeternum. statuisti enim eam in saeculum et in saeculum saeculi; praeceptum posuisti et non praeteribit. nec tamen tibi coaeterna, quoniam non sine initio: facta est enim.

Nam etsi non invenimus tempus ante illam—prior quippe omnium creata est sapientia; nec utique illa sapientia tibi, deus noster, patri suo, plane coaeterna et coaequalis, et per quam creata sunt omnia, et in quo principio fecisti caelum et terram, sed profecto

God, hath not upon any such new will made any CHAP.
creature; nor that his knowledge admits of any XV
transitory affection.

What will you then say, O ye gainsayers? Are
these things false? No, they say. What is this?
Is this false then, that every nature that is formed,
or every matter capable of form, hath no other
being, but from him who is supremely good, because
supremely he hath his being? Neither, say they,
do we deny this. What then; do you deny this,
that there is a certain sublime creation, with so
chaste a love cleaving unto the true, and truly eternal
God, as that notwithstanding it be not co-eternal to
him, yet that upon occasion of no variety and turn
of times does it let go its hold, or parteth with him,
but rests itself contented in the most true contemplation of him only? because thou, O God, unto
him that loveth thee so much as thou commandest,
dost show thyself, and give him satisfaction: and
even therefore doth he neither decline from thee,
nor toward himself. This is the house of God; not
of earthly mould, no, nor of any celestial bulk corporeal: but a spiritual house, and partaker of thy
eternity, because it remains without blemish for ever.
For thou hast made it fast for ever and ever, thou Ps. cxlviii. 6
hast given it a law which shall not be broken. And
yet is it not co-eternal unto thee, because it is not
without beginning, for it was made.

For notwithstanding we find no time before it—
for wisdom was created before all things: not that
Wisdom, I mean, which is altogether equal and co- Ecclus. i. 4
eternal unto thee his Father, by which all things were
created, and in whom, being the beginning, thou
createdst heaven and earth; but that wisdom verily
which is created; that is to say, the intellectual

317

CAP.
XV

sapientia, quae creata est, intellectualis natura scilicet,
quae contemplatione luminis lumen est ; dicitur enim
et ipsa, quamvis creata, sapientia. sed quantum
interest inter lumen, quod inluminat et quod inlumi-
natur, tantum inter sapientiam, quae creat, et istam,
quae creata est, sicut inter iustitiam iustificantem et
iustitiam, quae iustificatione facta est ; nam et nos
dicti sumus iustitia tua ; ait enim quidam servus
tuus : ut nos simus iustitia dei in ipso. ergo quia
prior omnium creata est quaedam sapientia, quae
creata est, mens rationalis et intellectualis castae
civitatis tuae, matris nostrae, quae sursum est et
libera est et aeterna in caelis—quibus caelis, nisi qui
te laudant caeli caelorum, quia hoc est et caelum
caeli domino ?—etsi non invenimus tempus ante illam,
quia et creaturam temporis antecedit, quae prior
omnium creata est, ante illam tamen est ipsius creatoris aeternitas, a quo facta sumpsit exordium, quamvis non temporis, quia nondum erat tempus, ipsius
tamen conditionis suae.

Vnde ita est abs te, deo nostro, ut aliud sit plane
quam tu et non id ipsum, et non solum ante illam,
sed nec in illa invenimus tempus, quia est idonea
faciem tuam semper videre nec uspiam deflectitur ab
ea ; quo fit, ut nulla mutatione varietur. inest ei
tamen ipsa mutabilitas, unde tenebresceret et frige-
sceret, nisi amore grandi tibi cohaerens tamquam
semper meridies luceret et ferveret ex te. o domus

nature; which by contemplating of the light, is CHAP.
become light: for this, though created, is also XV
called wisdom. But look what difference there is
betwixt that light which enlighteneth, and the light
that is enlightened, so much is there betwixt that
wisdom that creates, and this wisdom which is created:
like as there is betwixt that righteousness which
justifieth, and that righteousness which is made by
justification. For we also are called thy righteousness;
for so saith a certain servant of thine: That we may 2 Cor. v. 21
be made the righteousness of God in him. There-
fore since a certain created wisdom was created before
all things, the rational and intellectual mind of that
chaste city of thine, our mother which is above, and Gal. iv. 26
is free, and eternal in the heavens: (in what heavens,
if not in those that praise thee, even the heaven of
heavens? because this is also the Heaven of Heavens
made for the Lord):—though we find no time before
it, (because that which hath been created before all
things, precedeth also the creature of time) yet is the
eternity of the Creator himself even before it; from
whom that, being created, took beginning: not beginning of its time (for time was not yet in being)
but of its creation.

Hence comes it so to be of thee, our God, as that
it is altogether another from thee, and not the
Self same: and we neither find time before it, nor
in it, (it being most meet ever to behold thy face,
nor is ever drawn away from it, for which cause it
is not changed by any alteration). Yet is there a
mutable condition in it for all this, which would cause
it to wax dark and cold, but for that by so strong
an affection, it cleaveth unto thee, that it receives
both light and heat from thee, as a perpetual noon.
O house most lightsome and delightsome! I have

luminosa et speciosa, dilexi decorem tuum et locum
habitationis gloriae domini mei, fabricatoris et posses-
soris tui! tibi suspiret peregrinatio mea, et dico ei
qui fecit te, ut possideat et me in te, quia fecit et me.
erravi sicut ovis perdita, sed in umeris pastoris mei,
structoris tui, spero me reportari tibi.

Quid dicitis mihi, quos alloquebar contradictores,
qui tamen et Moysen pium famulum dei et libros
eius oracula sancti spiritus creditis? estne ista domus
dei, non quidem deo coaeterna, sed tamen secundum
modum suum aeterna in caelis, ubi vices temporum
frustra quaeritis, quia non invenitis? supergreditur
enim omnem distentionem et omne spatium aetatis
volubile, cui semper inhaerere deo bonum est. "est"
inquiunt. quid igitur ex his, quae clamavit cor
meum ad deum meum, cum audiret interius vocem
laudis eius, quid tandem falsum esse contenditis?
an quia erat informis materies, ubi propter nullam
formam nullus ordo erat? ubi autem nullus ordo
erat, nulla esse vicissitudo temporum poterat; et
tamen hoc paene nihil in quantum non omnino
nihil erat, ab illo utique erat, a quo est quidquid est,
quod utcumque aliquid est. "hoc quoque" aiunt
"non negamus."

loved thy beauty, and the place of the habitation of CHAP.
the glory of my Lord, thy builder and owner. Let XV
my wayfaring sigh after thee; and to him I speak Ps. xxvi. 8
that made thee, that he would take possession
of me also in thee; seeing he hath likewise made
me. I have gone astray like a lost sheep: yet have I Ps. cxix.
a good hope upon the shoulders of my shepherd, thy 176
builder, to be brought back into thee. Luke xv. 5

What say you now unto me, O ye gainsayers that
I was speaking unto? who yet believe Moses to
have been the faithful servant of God, and his books
to be the oracle of the Holy Ghost? Is not this
house of God, though not co-eternal indeed with
God, yet after its measure, eternal in the heavens;
where you seek for the changes of times all in vain,
because there you shall never find them? For it far
overgoes all extension, and all running space of age:
the happiness of it being ever to cleave unto God.
It is so, say they. What part then of all that which
my heart hath so loudly uttered unto God, whenas
inwardly it heard the voice of his praise; what part,
I say, of all this do you at last affirm to be false? Is
it (I said) that the first matter was without form; in
which by reason there was no form, there was no
order? But then, where no order was, there could
be no succession of times; and yet this almost
nothing, inasmuch as it was not altogether nothing,
was from him certainly, from whom is whatsoever is,
which is something, in what manner so ever it is.
This also, say they, we do not deny.

XVI

CAP
XVI
CVM his enim volo coram te aliquid conloqui, deus
meus, qui haec omnia, quae intus in mente mea non
tacet veritas tua, vera esse concedunt. nam qui
haec negant, latrent quantum volunt et obstrepant
sibi: persuadere conabor, ut quiescant, et viam prae-
beant ad se verbo tuo. quod si noluerint et rep-
pulerint me, obsecro, deus meus, ne tu sileas a me.
tu loquere in corde meo veraciter; solus enim sic
loqueris; et dimittam eos foris sufflantes in pulverem
et excitantes terram in oculos suos, et intrem in cubile
meum et cantem tibi amatoria, gemens inenarrabiles
gemitus in peregrinatione mea et recordans Hierusalem extento in eam sursum corde, Hierusalem
patriam meam, Hierusalem matrem meam, teque
super eam regnatorem, inlustratorem, patrem, tu-
torem, maritum, castas et fortes delicias et solidum
gaudium et omnia bona ineffabilia, simul omnia, quia
unum summum et verum bonum: et non avertar,
donec in eius pacem, matris carissimae, ubi sunt primi-
tiae spiritus mei, unde ista mihi certa sunt, colligas
totum quod sum a dispersione et deformitate hac, et
conformes atque confirmes in aeternum, deus meus,
misericordia mea. cum his autem, qui cuncta illa,

XVI

*Against such as contradict divine Truth : and of
his own Delight in it*

WITH these will I now parley a little in thy presence, CHAP.
O my God, who grant all these things to be true, which XVI
thy truth whispers into my soul.   For as for those
praters that deny all, let them bark and bawl unto
themselves as much as they please; my endeavour
shall be to persuade them to quiet, and to give way
for .thy word to enter them.   But if they shall refuse
me, and give the repulse unto me ; do not thou hold
thy peace from me, I beseech thee, O my God.   Speak
thou truly in my heart ; for only thou so speakest : Ps. xxviii.
and may I let them alone blowing upon the dust 1 (Heb.)
without doors, and raising it up into their own eyes :
and may I enter into my chamber, and sing there a
love-song unto thee, mourning with groans that cannot
be expressed, and remembering Jerusalem, with my
heart lifted up towards her ; Jerusalem my country,
aye, Jerusalem my mother ; and thyself that ruleth
over it, the Enlightener, the Father, the Guardian,
the Husband, the chaste and strong Delight, the
solid Joy of it, and all good things that be unspeak-
able ; yea, all at once, because the only sovereign and
true Good of it.   Nor may I give over, until thou
wholly gather all that is of me from this dispersed and
disordered estate I now am in, into the peace of that
our most dear mother ; (where the first-fruits of my
spirit be already, whence I have received assurance of
these things) and shall both conform, and for ever con-
firm me, O my God, my fount of mercy.   But as for
those who no ways affirm all these truths to be false ;

CAP.
XVI

quae vera sunt, falsa esse non dicunt, honorantes et in culmine sequendae auctoritatis nobiscum constituentes illam per sanctum Moysen editam sanctam scripturam tuam, et tamen nobis aliquid contradicunt, ita loquor. tu esto, deus noster, arbiter inter confessiones meas et contradictiones eorum.

XVII

CAP.
XVII

Dicunt enim: "quamvis vera sint haec, non ea tamen duo Moyses intuebatur, cum revelante spiritu diceret: in principio fecit deus caelum et terram. non caeli nomine spiritalem vel intellectualem illam creaturam semper faciem dei contemplantem significavit, nec terrae nomine informem materiam." quid igitur? "quod nos dicimus" inquiunt "hoc ille vir sensit, hoc verbis istis elocutus est." quid illud est? "nomine" aiunt "caeli et terrae totum istum visibilem mundum prius universaliter et breviter significare voluit, ut postea digereret dierum enumeratione quasi articulatim universa, quae sancto spiritui placuit sic enuntiare. tales quippe homines erant rudis ille atque carnalis populus, cui loquebatur, ut eis opera dei non nisi sola visibilia commendanda iudicaret." terram vero invisibilem et incompositam tenebrosamque abyssum, unde consequenter ostenditur per illos

which give all honour unto thy holy Scripture set out CHAP.
by Moses the holy, placing it, as we did, in the top XVI
of that authority which is to be followed, and do yet
contradict me in some thing or other; to these I
answer thus: Be thyself judge, O our God, between
my confessions and these men's gainsayings.

XVII

What the Names of Heaven and Earth signify

FOR they say: Though all this that you say be true, CHAP.
yet did not Moses intend those two, when by revela- XVII
tion of the Spirit he said, In the beginning God
created heaven and earth. He did not under the
name of heaven, signify that spiritual or intellectual
creation which always beholds the face of God: nor
under the name of earth, that unshaped matter.
What then? That man of God, say they, meant what
we say; this was it he declared by those words.
What's that? By the name of heaven and earth
would he signify, say they, all this visible world, in
universal and compendious terms first; that afterwards in his sorting out the works of the several days,
he might joint by joint, as it were, bring everything
into his order, which it pleased the Holy Ghost in
such general terms to express. For (say they) such
gross heads were that rude and carnal people to which
he spake, as that he thought such works of God only
as were visible, fit to be mentioned unto them. They
do agree, however, that this invisible and unshaped
earth, and that darksome deep (out of which subse-
quently is shown, all these visible things generally

325

dies facta atque disposita esse cuncta ista visibilia,
quae nota sunt omnibus, non incongruenter informem
istam materiem intellegendam esse consentiunt.
quid? si dicat alius, eandem informitatem confu-
sionemque materiae, caeli et terrae nomine prius in-
sinuatam, quod ex ea mundus iste visibilis, cum omnibus naturis quae in eo manifestissime apparent, qui
caeli et terrae nomine saepe appellari solet, conditus
atque perfectus est? quid? si dicat et alius caelum et terram quidem invisibilem visibilemque naturam non indecenter appellatam, ac per hoc universam
creaturam, quam fecit in sapientia, id est in principio, deus, huiuscemodi duobus vocabulis esse conpre-
hensam; verum tamen quia non de ipsa substantia
dei, sed ex nihilo cuncta facta sunt (quia non sunt
id ipsum, quod deus, et inest quaedam mutabilitas
omnibus, sive maneant, sicut aeterna domus dei, sive
mutentur, sicut anima hominis et corpus), communem
omnium rerum invisibilium visibiliumque materiem
adhuc informem, sed certe formabilem, unde fieret
caelum et terra (id est invisibilis atque visibilis iam
utraque formata creatura) his nominibus enuntiatam,
quibus appellaretur terra invisibilis et incomposita et
tenebrae super abyssum ; ea distinctione, ut terra
invisibilis et incomposita intellegatur materies corporalis ante qualitatem formae, tenebrae autem
super abyssum spiritalis materies ante cohibitionem

known unto all, to have been made and set in order
in those six days) may not incongruously be understood to be this unshaped first matter. What now
if another should say, that this unshapedness
and confusedness of matter, was for this reason
first conveyed to us under the name of heaven
and earth, because that this visible world, with
all those natures which most manifestly appear
in it, (which we ofttimes use to call by the name
of heaven and earth) was both created and fully
finished out of it? And what if another should say,
that the invisible and visible natures were not
indeed improperly called heaven and earth; and,
consequently, that the universal creation, which God
made in his wisdom, that is in the beginning, were
comprehended under those two words? Yet (he
goes on) since all these be made not of the substance of God, but out of nothing, (because they
are not the selfsame that God is, and that there is
a mutable nature in them all; whether they stand
at a stay, as the eternal house of God does, or be
changed, as the soul and body of man are:) therefore the common matter of all visible and invisible
things, though yet unshaped, but certainly shape-
able, out of which heaven and earth was to be
made, (that is, both the invisible and visible
creation when formed) was expressed by the
same names which the earth as yet invisible
and unshapen and the darkness upon the deep,
were to be called by: but with this distinction,
that by the earth invisible hitherto and unshapen,
the corporeal matter be understood, before the
quality of any form was introduced: and by the
darkness upon the deep, the spiritual matter be
understood, before it suffered any restraint of its

CAP.
XVII
quasi fluentis inmoderationis et ante inluminationem sapientiae?

Est adhuc quod dicat, si quis alius velit, non scilicet iam perfectas atque formatas invisibiles visibilesque naturas caeli et terrae nomine significari, cum legitur, in principio fecit deus caelum et terram: sed ipsam adhuc informem inchoationem rerum formabilem creabilemque materiam his nominibus appellatam, quod in ea iam essent ista confusa, nondum qualitatibus formisque distincta, quae nunc iam digesta suis ordinibus vocantur caelum et terra, illa spiritalis, haec corporalis creatura.

XVIII

CAP.
XVIII
Quibus omnibus auditis et consideratis, nolo verbis contendere; ad nihil enim utile est nisi ad subversionem audientium. ad aedificationem autem bona est lex, si quis ea legitime utatur, quia finis eius est caritas de corde puro et conscientia bona et fide non ficta; et novit magister noster, in quibus duobus praeceptis totam legem prophetasque suspenderit. quae mihi ardenter confitenti, deus meus, lumen oculorum meorum in occulto, quid mihi obest, cum diversa in his verbis intellegi possint, quae tamen vera sint? quid, inquam, mihi obest, si aliud ego

unlimited fluidness, and before it received any light CHAP.
XVII from wisdom.

There is yet something else to say, if some other be so disposed; that, namely, the already perfected and formed natures, (both visible and invisible), were not comprehended under the name of heaven and earth, when we read, In the beginning God created heaven and earth: but that the yet unshaped rough-hewing of things, that stuff apt to receive shape and making, was called by these names, because in it already were confusedly contained, though not distinguished yet by qualities and forms, all those things which being now digested into order, are called heaven and earth; meaning by that, all spiritual creation, and by this, all corporeal.

XVIII

Divers Expositors may understand one Text several Ways

ALL which things being heard and well considered CHAP. of, I will not strive about words: for that is profitable XVIII to nothing, but the subversion of the hearers; but 2 Tim. ii. the law is good to edify, if a man use it lawfully, for 14 that the end of it is charity, out of a pure heart and 1 Tim. good conscience, and faith unfeigned. And well did i. 8, 5 our Master know upon which two commandments Matt. xxii. he hung all the law and the prophets. And what 40 prejudice does it me now confessing this zealously, O my God, thou Light of my inner eyes, since there may be several meanings gathered out of the same words, and yet all true? What hinders it me, I say, if I think otherwise than another man thinketh

S. AVGVSTINI CONFESSIONVM LIBER XII

sensero, quam sensit alius eum sensisse, qui scripsit?
omnes quidem, qui legimus, nitimur hoc indagare
atque conprehendere, quod voluit ille quem legimus,
et cum eum veridicum credimus, nihil, quod falsum
esse vel novimus vel putamus, audemus eum existi-
mare dixisse. dum ergo quisque conatur id sentire
in scripturis sanctis, quod in eis sensit ille qui
scripsit, quid mali est, si hoc sentiat, quod tu, lux
omnium veridicarum mentium, ostendis verum esse,
etiamsi non hoc sensit ille, quem legit, cum et ille
verum nec tamen hoc senserit?

XIX

VERVM est enim, domine, fecisse te caelum et terram.
verum est esse principium sapientiam tuam, in qua
fecisti omnia. item verum est, quod mundus iste
visibilis habet magnas partes suas caelum et terram,
brevi conplexione factarum omnium conditarum-
que naturarum. et verum est, quod omne mutabile
insinuat notitiae nostrae quandam informitatem, qua
formam capit vel qua mutatur et vertitur. verum
est nulla tempora perpeti quod ita cohaeret formae
incommutabili, ut, quamvis sit mutabile, non mu-
tetur. verum est informitatem, quae prope nihil
est, vices temporum habere non posse. verum est,
330

that he thought? All we readers, verily, strive CHAP. both to find out and to understand the author's XVIII meaning whom we read; and when we believe him to speak truly, we dare not once imagine him to have let fall anything, which ourselves either know or think to be false. Whilst every man endeavours, therefore, to collect the same sense from the holy Scriptures, that the penman himself intended; what hurt is it, if a man so judges of it, even as thou, O the Light of all true-speaking minds, dost show him to be true; even if the author whom he reads, perceived not so much, seeing he also collected a truth out of it, though not this truth?

XIX

Of some particular apparent Truths

FOR true it is, O Lord, that thou madest heaven CHAP. and earth. It is true that the beginning is thy XIX wisdom, in which thou createdst all : and true again, Ps. civ. 24 that this visible world hath for his greater parts the heaven and the earth, which in a brief expression comprehend all made and created natures. And true too, that whatsoever is mutable, gives us to understand that there is a want of form in it, by means whereof it is apt to receive a form, or is changed, or turned, by reason of it. It is true, that that is subject to no times, which cleaveth so close unto that unchangeable form, as that though the nature of it be mutable, yet is itself never changed. 'Tis true, that that unshapedness which is almost nothing, cannot be subject to the alteration of times.

CAP. quod, unde fit aliquid, potest quodam genere locu-
XIX tionis habere iam nomen eius rei, quae inde fit:
unde potuit vocari caelum et terra quaelibet informitas, unde factum est caelum et terra. verum
est omnium formatorum nihil esse informi vicinius
quam terram et abyssum. verum est, quod non
solum creatum atque formatum, sed etiam quidquid
creabile atque formabile est, tu fecisti, ex quo sunt
omnia. verum est omne, quod ex informi formatur,
prius esse informe, deinde formatum.

XX

CAP. Ex his omnibus veris, de quibus non dubitant,
XX quorum interiori oculo talia videre donasti, et qui
Moysen, famulum tuum, in spiritu veritatis locutum
esse immobiliter credunt, ex his ergo omnibus aliud
sibi tollit qui dicit, in principio fecit deus caelum
et terram, id est in verbo suo sibi coaeterno fecit
deus intellegibilem atque sensibilem, vel spiritalem
corporalemque creaturam: aliud qui dicit, in principio fecit deus caelum et terram, id est in verbo suo
sibi coaeterno fecit deus universam istam molem
corporei mundi huius, cum omnibus quas continet
manifestis notisque naturis: aliud qui dicit, in principio fecit deus caelum et terram, id est in verbo suo
sibi coaeterno fecit informem materiam creaturae

332

'Tis true, that that whereof a thing is made, may by CHAP.
a figurative kind of speaking, be called by the name XIX
of the thing made of it, whence might heaven and
earth be said to be any unshaped chaos, whereof
heaven and earth were made. 'Tis true, that of
things having form, there is not any nearer to having
no form, than the earth and the deep. 'Tis true,
that not only every created and formed thing, but
whatsoever is apt to be created and formed, is of
thy making, of whom are all things. 'Tis true, that
whatsoever is formed out of that which had no form,
was unformed before it was formed.

XX

He interprets Genesis i. 1 otherwise

OUT of all these truths, of which they doubt not CHAP.
whose internal eye thou hast enabled to see them, and XX
who immoveably believe thy servant Moses to have
spoken in the spirit of truth : out of all these, therefore, I say, he taketh one sense unto himself, who
saith : In the beginning God made the heaven and
the earth, that is to say, in his Word co-eternal unto
himself, God made the intelligible and the sensible,
or the spiritual and the corporeal creature. And he
another, that saith : In the beginning God made
heaven and earth ; that is, in his Word co-eternal
unto himself, did God make the universal bulk of this
corporeal world, together with all those apparent
and known creatures, which it containeth. And he
another, that saith : In the beginning God made
heaven and earth ; that is, in his Word co-eternal
unto himself, did God make the formless matter both

CAP.
XX
spiritalis et corporalis : aliud qui dicit, in principio
fecit deus caelum et terram, id est in verbo suo sibi
coaeterno fecit deus informem materiam creaturae
corporalis, ubi confusum adhuc erat caelum et terra,
quae nunc iam distincta atque formata in istius
mundi mole sentimus : aliud qui dicit, in principio
fecit deus caelum et terram, id est in ipso exordio
faciendi atque operandi fecit deus informem materiam, confuse habentem caelum et terram, unde
formata nunc eminent et apparent, cum omnibus,
quae in eis sunt.

XXI

CAP.
XXI
ITEM quod adtinet ad intellectum verborum sequen-
tium, ex illis omnibus veris aliud sibi tollit, qui dicit,
terra autem erat invisibilis et incomposita, et tenebrae erant super abyssum, id est corporale illud, quod
fecit deus, adhuc materies erat corporearum rerum
informis, sine ordine, sine luce : aliud qui dicit,
terra autem erat invisibilis et incomposita, et tenebrae
erant super abyssum, id est hoc totum, quod caelum
et terra appellatum est, adhuc informis et tenebrosa
materies erat, unde fieret caelum corporeum et terra
corporea cum omnibus quae in eis sunt corporeis
sensibus nota : aliud qui dicit, terra autem erat

of the creature spiritual and corporeal. And he CHAP.
another, that saith: In the beginning God created XX
heaven and earth; that is, in his Word co-eternal
unto himself, did God create the formless matter of
the creature corporeal, wherein heaven and earth lay
as yet confused, which being now distinguished and
formed, we at this day see in the bulk of this world.
And he another, who saith: In the beginning God
made heaven and earth; that is, in the very first of
creating and of working, did God make that formless
matter, confusedly containing in itself both heaven
and earth; out of which, what were afterwards formed,
do at this day eminently appear, with all that is in
them.

XXI

*These Words, the Earth was void &c., diversely
understood*

AND with regard to the understanding of the words CHAP.
following, out of all these truths that interpreter XXI
chooses one to himself, who saith: But the earth
was invisible, and unfashioned, and darkness was
upon the deep: that is, that corporeal thing, that
God made, was as yet a formless matter of corporeal
things, without order, without light. Another, he
who says: The earth was invisible and unfashioned,
and darkness was upon the deep: that is, this all
now called heaven and earth was shapeless and
darksome matter hitherto; of which the corporeal
heaven and the corporeal earth were to be made,
with all things in them, now known unto our corporeal
senses. Another, he who says: The earth was invisible

CAP.
XXI

invisibilis et incomposita, et tenebrae erant super abyssum, id est hoc totum, quod caelum et terra appellatum est, adhuc informis et tenebrosa materies erat, unde fieret caelum intellegibile—quod alibi dicitur caelum caeli—et terra, scilicet omnis natura corporea, sub quo nomine intellegatur etiam hoc caelum corporeum, id est unde fieret omnis invisibilis visibilisque creatura: aliud qui dicit, terra autem erat invisibilis et incomposita, et tenebrae erant super abyssum, non illam informitatem nomine caeli et terrae scriptura appellavit, sed iam erat, inquit, ipsa informitas, quam terram invisibilem et incompositam tenebrosamque abyssum nominavit, de qua caelum et terram deum fecisse praedixerat, spiritalem scilicet corporalemque creaturam; aliud qui dicit, terra autem erat invisibilis et incomposita, et tenebrae erant super abyssum, id est informitas quaedam iam materies erat, unde caelum et terram deum fecisse scriptura praedixit, totam scilicet corpoream mundi molem in duas maximas partes superiorem atque inferiorem distributam, cum omnibus quae in eis sunt usitatis notisque creaturis.

and unfashioned, and darkness was upon the deep :
that is, this, all now called heaven and earth was but
formless and darksome matter hitherto ; out of which
was to be made, both that intelligible heaven, which
is otherwhere called the Heaven of Heavens, and
the earth, that is to say, the whole corporeal nature :
under which name may be understood this corporeal
heaven also ; that, namely, out of which every visible
and invisible creature was to be created. Another, he
who says : The earth was invisible and unfashioned,
and darkness was upon the deep : that is, the Scripture did not call that unshapedness by the name of
heaven and earth ; for that unshapedness, saith he,
was already in bEing, which he called the earth invisible and unfashioned and darkness upon the deep : of
which he had said before, that God had made heaven
and earth, namely, the spiritual and corporeal creature.
Another, he who says : The earth was invisible and
unfashioned, and darkness was upon the deep : that
is, there was already a certain formless matter, of
which the Scripture said before, that God made
heaven and earth : namely, the whole corporeal bulk
of the world divided into two great parts, upper and
lower ; with all the common and known creatures in
them.

XXII

CAP. XXII Cum enim duabus istis extremis sententiis resistere quisquam ita temptaverit: " si non vultis hanc informitatem materiae caeli et terrae nomine appellatam videri, erat ergo aliquid, quod non fecerat deus, unde caelum et terram faceret; neque enim scriptura narravit, quod istam materiem deus fecerit, nisi intellegamus eam caeli et terrae aut solius terrae vocabulo significatam, cum diceretur: in principio fecit deus caelum et terram, ut id, quod sequitur: terra autem erat invisibilis et incomposita, quamvis informem materiam sic placuerit appellare, non tamen intellegamus nisi eam, quam fecit deus in eo, quod perscriptum est: fecit caelum et terram," respondebunt assertores duarum istarum sententiarum, quas extremas posuimus, aut illius aut illius, cum haec audierint, et dicent: " informem quidem istam materiam non negamus a deo factam, deo, a quo sunt omnia bona valde, quia, sicut dicimus amplius bonum esse quod creatum atque formatum est, ita fatemur minus bonum esse quod factum est creabile atque formabile, sed tamen bonum: non autem conmemorasse scripturam, quod hanc informitatem fecerit deus, sicut alia multa non commemoravit, ut Cherubim et

XXII

*That the waters are also contained under the names
of Heaven and Earth*

FOR if any man shall attempt to dispute against these
two last opinions with this argument: If you will not
allow that this unshapedness of matter seemed to be
called by the name of heaven and earth; ergo, there
was something which God never made, out of which
he was to make heaven and earth; for neither hath
the Scripture told us that God made this substance,
unless we should understand the substance to be
signified either by the name of heaven and earth
together, or of the earth alone, whenas it said,
In the beginning God made heaven and earth: that
so in that which follows, And the earth was invisible
and without fashion, (although it pleased him to
call the formless matter by those terms,) yet may we
understand no other matter, but that which God
made, in that text where 'tis written, God made
heaven and earth:—the maintainers of those two
latter opinions (either this or that) will upon the first
hearing return this answer: We do not deny this formless matter to be indeed created by God, of whom are
all things which are very good: for as we affirm that
to be a greater good, which is created and formed,
so we confess likewise that to be a lesser good, which
is made with no more than an aptness in it to receive
creation and form, yet that is good too. We say
however that the Scripture hath not said that God
made this formlessness, even as it hath not set
down many other things that he made; as the
Cherubim and Seraphim, and the rest which the

Seraphim, et quae apostolus distincte ait, sedes, dominationes, principatus, potestates, quae tamen omnia deum fecisse manifestum est. aut si in eo, quod dictum est : fecit caelum et terram, comprehensa sunt omnia, quid de aquis dicimus, super quas ferebatur spiritus dei ? si enim terra nominata simul intelleguntur, quomodo iam terrae nomine materies informis accipitur, quando tam speciosas aquas videmus ? aut si ita accipitur, cur ex eadem informitate scriptum est factum firmamentum et vocatum caelum, neque scriptum est factas esse aquas ? non enim adhuc informes sunt et invisae, quas ita decora specie fluere cernimus. aut si tunc acceperunt istam speciem, cum dixit deus : congregetur aqua, quae est sub firmamento, ut congregatio sit ipsa formatio, quid respondebitur de aquis, quae super firmamentum sunt, quia neque informes tam honorabilem sedem accipere meruissent, nec scriptum est, qua voce formatae sint ? unde si aliquid Genesis tacuit deum fecisse, quod tamen deum fecisse nec sana fides nec certus ambigit intellectus, nec ideo ulla sobria doctrina dicere audebit istas aquas coaeternas deo, quia in libro Geneseos commemoratas quidem audimus, ubi autem factae sint, non invenimus, cur non informem quoque illam materiem, quam scriptura haec terram invisibilem et incompositam tenebrosamque abyssum

apostle distinctly speaks of, Thrones, Dominions,
Principalities, Powers : all which that God made,
is most apparent. Or, if in that which is said,
He made heaven and earth, all things be comprehended ; what shall we then say of the waters upon
which the Spirit of God moved ? For if all things
be understood to be named in this word earth ; how
then can this formless matter be meant in that name
of earth, when we see the waters to be so beautiful ?
Or if it be so taken ; why then is it written, that out
of the same formlessness the firmament was made,
and called heaven ; and yet that the waters were
created, is not written ? For the waters remain not
formless and invisible unto this day, seeing we behold them flowing in so comely a manner. Or if
they at that time received the beauty they now have,
whenas God said : Let the waters under the firmament be gathered together unto one place, that so
the gathering together of the waters may be taken
for the forming of them ; what will they answer for
those waters which be above the firmament ? Seeing
if they had not any form at all, never should they
have been worthy of so honourable a seat ; nor is it
written by what word they were formed. So that if
Genesis hath said nothing of God's making of some
one thing, (which yet no sound faith nor well grounded
understanding once doubteth, but that he did make)
then no sober knowledge will dare to affirm these
waters to be co-eternal with God (for that we finding them to be barely mentioned in the book of
Genesis, do not find withal where they were created) :
why, (seeing truth teaches us) may we not as well
understand that formless matter, (which this Scripture calls the invisible and unfashioned earth and
darksome deep) to have been created by God out of

CAP.
XXII
appellat, docente veritate intellegamus ex deo factam esse de nihilo ideoque illi non esse coaeternam, quamvis ubi facta sit omiserit enuntiare ista narratio ? "

XXIII

CAP.
XXIII
His ergo auditis atque perspectis pro captu infirmitatis meae, (quam tibi confiteor scienti deo meo,) duo video dissensionum genera oboriri posse, cum aliquid a nuntiis veracibus per signa enuntiatur, unum, si de veritate rerum, alterum, si de ipsius qui enuntiat voluntate dissensio est. aliter enim quaerimus de creaturae conditione, quid verum sit, aliter autem quid in his verbis Moyses, egregius domesticus fidei tuae, intellegere lectorem auditoremque voluerit. in illo primo genere discedant a me omnes, qui ea, quae falsa sunt, se scire arbitrantur. in hoc item altero discedant a me omnes, qui ea quae falsa sunt Moysen dixisse arbitrantur. coniungar autem illis, domine, in te et delecter cum eis in te, qui veritate tua pascuntur in latitudine caritatis, et accedamus simul ad verba libri tui, et quaeramus in eis voluntatem tuam per voluntatem famuli tui, cuius calamo dispensasti ea.

nothing, and therefore not to be co-eternal to him; CHAP.
notwithstanding that this story hath omitted to show XXII
where it was created?

XXIII

*In interpreting of Holy Scripture, Truth is to be
sought with a charitable Construction*

THESE things therefore being heard and perceived, CHAP.
according to the weakness of my capacity, (which I do XXIII
confess unto thee, O Lord, that knowest it) two sorts
of disagreements do I perceive likely to arise, when
a thing is through signs related by true reporters:
one, when the disagreement riseth concerning the
truth of the things; the other, when it is concerning
the meaning of the relator. For we enquire one way
about the making of the thing created, what may be
true; and another way, what it is that Moses, (that
notable minister of thy faith) would have his reader
and hearer to understand in those words. For the first
sort, away with all those which once imagine themselves to know that as a truth, which is in itself
false: and for this other sort, away all them too,
which once imagine Moses to have written things
that be false. But let me ever in thee, O Lord,
take part with them, and in thee delight myself in
them that feed on thy truth, in the largeness of
charity: yea, let us have recourse together unto the
words of thy book, and make search for thy meaning
in them, by the meaning of thy servant, by whose
pen thou hast dispensed them.

XXIV

CAP.
XXIV

SED quis nostrum sic invenit eam inter tam multa vera, quae in illis verbis aliter atque aliter intellectis occurrunt quaerentibus, ut tam fidenter dicat hoc sensisse Moysen atque hoc in illa narratione voluisse intellegi, quam fidenter dicit hoc verum esse, sive ille hoc senserit sive aliud? ecce enim, deus meus, ego servus tuus, qui vovi tibi sacrificium confessionis in his litteris, et oro, ut ex misericordia tua reddam tibi vota mea, ecce ego quam fidenter dico in tuo verbo incommutabili omnia te fecisse, invisibilia et visibilia, numquid tam fidenter dico non aliud quam hoc adtendisse Moysen, cum scriberet: in principio fecit deus caelum et terram, quia non, sicut in tua veritate hoc certum video, ita in eius mente video id eum cogitasse, cum haec scriberet? potuit enim cogitare in ipso faciendi exordio, cum diceret: in principio; potuit et caelum et terram hoc loco nullam iam formatam perfectamque naturam sive spiritalem sive corporalem, sed utramque inchoatam et adhuc informem velle intellegi. video quippe vere potuisse dici, quidquid horum diceretur, sed quid horum in his verbis ille cogitaverit, non ita video, quamvis sive

344

XXIV

The Scripture is true, though we understand not the uttermost Scope or Depth of it

BUT which of us all can find out this full meaning, CHAP. among those so many truths which the seekers shall XXIV everywhere meet withal in those words, sometimes understood this way, and sometimes that way, so that he may as confidently affirm, This Moses thought, and this would he have understood in that story, as he says confidently, This is true, whether he thought this or that? For behold, O my God, I thy servant who have in this book vowed a sacrifice of confession unto thee, and do now beseech thee, that by thy mercy I may have leave to pay my vows unto thee, behold how confidently I affirm, that in thy incommutable Word thou hast created all things visible and invisible : but can I so confidently affirm, that Moses had not another meaning than this when he wrote, In the beginning God made heaven and earth? No. Because though I see this to be certain in thy truth, yet can I not so easily see in his mind, that he thought just so in the writing of it. For he might have his thoughts upon God's very entrance into the act of creating, whenas he said, in the beginning : he might intend to have it understood by heaven and earth, in this place, no one nature either spiritual or corporeal, as already formed and perfected ; but both of them newly begun, and as yet unshapen. For I perceive, that which so ever of the two had been said, it might have been truly said : but which of the two he thought of in these words, I do not perceive so truly. Although,

CAP.
XXIV aliquid horum sive quid aliud, quod a me commemoratum non est, tantus vir ille mente conspexerit, cum haec verba promeret, verum eum vidisse apteque id enuntiavisse non dubitem.

XXV

CAP.
XXV NEMO iam mihi molestus sit dicendo mihi : "non hoc sensit Moyses, quod tu dicis, sed hoc sensit, quod ego dico." si enim mihi diceret : "unde scis hoc sensisse Moysen, quod de his verbis eius eloqueris ?" aequo animo ferre deberem, et responderem fortasse, quae superius respondi vel aliquanto uberius, si esset durior. cum vero dicit : "non hoc ille sensit, quod tu dicis, sed quod ego dico" neque tamen negat, quod uterque nostrum dicit, utrumque verum esse, o vita pauperum, deus meus, in cuius sinu non est contradictio, plue mihi mitigationes in cor, ut patienter tales feram ; qui non mihi hoc dicunt, quia divini sunt et in corde famuli tui viderunt quod dicunt, sed quia superbi sunt nec noverunt Moysi sententiam, sed amant suam, non quia vera est, sed quia sua est. alioquin et aliam veram pariter amarent, sicut ego amo quod dicunt, quando verum dicunt, non quia ipsorum, sed quia verum est : et ideo iam nec ipsorum est, quia verum est. si autem ideo ament illud, quia verum est, iam et ipsorum est et meum est, quoniam in commune omnium est veritatis amatorum.

whether it were either of these, or any sense beside, CHAP.
that I have not here mentioned, which so great a XXIV
man saw in his mind, at the uttering of these
words ; I nothing doubt but that he saw it truly, and
expressed it aptly.

XXV

We are not to break Charity about a different Exposition of Scripture

LET no man vex me now by saying : Moses thought CHAP.
not as you say, but as I say. For if he should ask XXV
me : How know you that Moses thought that which
you infer out of his words ? I ought to take it in
good part ; and would answer him perchance as I
have done heretofore ; or something more at large,
if he were unyielding. But when he saith : Moses
meant not what you say, but what I say ; yet
denieth not, that what either of us say, may both
be true : O my God, thou Life of the poor, whose
breast harbours no contradictions, rain thou a soften-
ing dew into my heart, that I may patiently bear
with such, who say not this to me, because they
are divine, and saw in the heart of thy servant
what they speak ; but because they be proud, not
knowing Moses' opinion but loving their own ;
not for that 'tis truth, but because 'tis theirs.
Otherwise, they would as well love other true
opinion, as I love what they say, when 'tis true
that they say : not because 'tis theirs, but because
'tis true ; and is therefore not theirs either, even
because it is true. But if they therefore love it,
because it is true, then becomes it both theirs
and mine : for that all the lovers of truth have a
common interest in it. But whereas they are so

CAP.
XXV
illud autem, quod contendunt non hoc sensisse Moysen, quod ego dico, sed quod ipsi dicunt, nolo, non amo, quia etsi ita est, tamen ista temeritas non scientiae, sed audaciae est, nec visus, sed typhus eam peperit. ideoque, domine, tremenda sunt iudicia tua, quoniam veritas tua nec mea est nec illius aut illius, sed omnium nostrum, quos ad eius communionem publice vocas, terribiliter admonens nos, ut nolimus eam habere privatam, ne privemur ea. nam quisquis id, quod tu omnibus ad fruendum proponis, sibi proprie vindicat, et suum vult esse quod omnium est, a communi propellitur ad sua, hoc est a veritate ad mendacium. qui enim loquitur mendacium, de suo loquitur.

Adtende, iudex optime, deus, ipsa veritas, adtende, quid dicam contradictori huic, adtende; coram te enim dico et coram fratribus meis, qui legitime utuntur lege usque ad finem caritatis; adtende et vide, quid ei dicam, si placet tibi. hanc enim vocem huic refero fraternam et pacificam: si ambo videmus verum esse quod dicis, et ambo videmus verum esse quod dico, ubi, quaeso, id videmus? nec ego utique in te nec tu in me, sed ambo in ipsa quae supra mentes nostras est incommutabili veritate. cum ergo de ipsa domini dei nostri luce non contendamus, cur de proximi cogitatione contendimus, quam sic videre non possumus, ut videtur incommutabilis veritas, quando, si ipse Moyses apparuisset nobis atque dixisset: "hoc

348

earnest, that Moses did not mean what I say, but CHAP.
what they say; this I neither like nor love: for XXV
even if it is so, yet is this rashness of theirs no
sign of knowledge, but of over boldness; nor hath
seeing further, but swelling bigger, begotten it.
And therefore, O Lord, are thy judgments to be
trembled at; seeing that thy truth is neither mine,
nor his, nor a third's; but belonging to us all, whom
thou callest publicly to partake of it: warning us
terribly not to account it private to ourselves, for
fear we be deprived of it. For whosoever challenges
that as proper to himself, which thou propoundest for
all to enjoy, and would make that his own, which
belongs to all; that man shall be driven from what
is common to all, to what is properly his own; that
is, from truth, to a lie. For he that speaketh a lie, John viii.
speaketh it of his own. 44

Hearken, O God, thou best Judge; Hearken,
O thou very Truth: what answer I shall return unto
my gainsayer. Listen, for before thee do I speak
it, and before my brethren, who employ thy law 1 Tim. i. 8
lawfully, that is, to the end of charity: Hearken,
and behold, if it please thee, what I will now say
to him. For this brotherly and peaceful word will
I return unto him: Suppose both of us see that to
be true that thou sayest; and both again see that
to be true that I say: where, I prithee, do we see
it? I verily see it not in thee; nor thou in me:
but both of us in the self-same unchangeable truth,
which is above both our minds. Since therefore
we strive not about the very light of the Lord our
God, why strive we about the thoughts of our neighbour? which it is impossible for us so clearly to see
into, as we may into the unchangeable truth. For
if Moses himself had appeared to us, and said:

CAP.
XXV

cogitavi," nec sic eam videremus, sed crederemus?
non itaque supra quam scriptum est unus pro altero
infletur adversus alterum. diligamus dominum deum
nostrum ex toto corde, ex tota anima, ex tota mente
nostra, et proximum nostrum sicut nosmet ipsos.
propter quae duo praecepta caritatis sensisse Moysen,
quidquid in illis libris sensit, nisi crediderimus, men-
dacem faciemus dominum, cum de animo conservi
aliter quam ille docuit opinamur. iam vide, quam
stultum sit in tanta copia verissimarum sententiarum,
quae de illis verbis erui possunt, temere adfirmare,
quam earum Moyses potissimum senserit, et pernicio-
sis contentionibus ipsam offendere caritatem, propter
quam dixit omnia, cuius dicta conamur exponere.

XXVI

CAP.
XXVI

ET tamen ego, deus meus, celsitudo humilitatis meae
et requies laboris mei, qui audis confessiones meas et
dimittis peccata mea, quoniam tu mihi praecipis, ut
diligam proximum meum sicut me ipsum, non possum
minus credere de Moyse fidelissimo famulo tuo, quam
mihi optarem ac desiderarem abs te dari muneris, si
tempore illo natus essem quo ille, eoque loci me

This I meant: not even so should we see it, but CHAP.
believe it. Let us not therefore be puffed up in XXV
favour of one, against another, above that which 1 Cor. iv. 6
is written. Let us love the Lord our God with all Deut. vi. 5
our heart, with all our soul, and with all our mind: Matt. xxii.
and our neighbour as ourselves. Unless we believe 37
that in regard to these two precepts of charity Moses
meant, whatsoever in those books he meant, we shall
make God a liar, whenas we imagine otherwise of
our fellow servants' mind, than he hath taught us.
Behold now, how foolish a conceit it is, in such
plenty of most true opinions, as may be fetched
out of those same words, rashly to affirm which of
them Moses principally meant: and thereby, with
pernicious contentions to offend charity itself; for
whose sake he spake everything, whose words we
go about to expound.

XXVI

What Style was fit to write the Scriptures in

YET for mine own part, O my God, thou Height of CHAP.
my humility, thou Rest of my labours, thou which XXVI
hearest my confessions, and which forgivest my sins:
seeing thou commandest me to love my neighbour
as myself, I cannot believe that thou gavest a less
gift unto Moses thy faithful servant, than I would
have wished or desired thee to have given myself,
had I been born in the time he was, and hadst
thou set me in that place, that by the service

CAP.
XXVI
constituisses, ut per servitutem cordis ac linguae meae litterae illae dispensarentur, quae tanto post essent omnibus gentibus profuturae, et per universum orbem tanto auctoritatis culmine omnium falsarum super- barumque doctrinarum verba superaturae. vellem quippe, si tunc ego essem Moyses—ex eadem namque massa omnes venimus; et quid est homo, nisi quia memor es eius?—vellem ergo, si tunc ego essem quod ille, et mihi abs te Geneseos liber scribendus adiungeretur, talem mihi eloquendi facultatem dari et eum texendi sermonis modum, ut neque illi, qui nondum queunt intellegere quemadmodum creat deus, tamquam excedentia vires suas dicta recusarent et illi, qui hoc iam possunt, in quamlibet veram sen- tentiam cogitando venissent, eam non praetermissam in paucis verbis tui famuli reperirent, et si alius aliam vidisset in luce veritatis, nec ipsa in eisdem verbis intellegenda deesset.

XXVII

CAP.
XXVII
Sicut enim fons in parvo loco uberior est pluribusque rivis in ampliora spatia fluxum ministrat quam qui- libet eorum rivorum, qui per multa locorum ab eodem fonte deducitur, ita narratio dispensatoris tui sermo- cinaturis pluribus profutura parvo sermonis modulo

of my heart and tongue, those books might be CHAP.
dispensed, which for so long a time after were to XXVI
profit all nations, and throughout the whole world
from such a height of authority were to surmount
all false and proud opinions. I should have desired
verily, had I then been Moses, (for we are all of the Rom. ix. 21
same lump : and what is man, saving that thou art
mindful of him ?) I would, therefore, I say had I
been in his case at the same time, and that the
book of Genesis had been put upon me to write,
have desired such a faculty of expression to have
been given me, and such a manner of composing
too, that they who cannot as yet understand how
God creates, might not reject the sayings as
beyond their capacity; and that they who are
already able to do it, upon what true solution so
ever their meditations had pitched, might find it
not to have been past by in the few words of thy
servant: and if another man had by the light of
truth discovered another, neither should that have
failed to be picked out of the selfsame words.

XXVII

The best Drawing at the fountain

FOR as a fountain though itself pent within a nar- CHAP.
row compass is more plentiful, and with his streams XXVII
serves more rivers, over larger spaces of ground, than
any of those rivers do, which after traversing wide
regions, is derived out of the same fountain : even
so this narration of that dispenser of thine, which
was to benefit many who were to preach upon it,

CAP.
XXVII

scatet fluenta liquidae veritatis, unde sibi quisque verum, quod de his rebus potest, hic illud, ille illud, per longiores loquellarum anfractus trahat. alii enim cum haec verba legunt vel audiunt, cogitant deum quasi hominem, aut quasi aliquam mole inmensa praeditam potestatem, novo quodam et repentino placito extra se ipsam tamquam locis distantibus fecisse caelum et terram, duo magna corpora supra et infra, quibus omnia continerentur; et cum audiunt: dixit deus: fiat illud, et factum est illud, cogitant verba coepta et finita, sonantia temporibus atque transeuntia, post quorum transitum statim existeret quod iussum est ut existeret, et si quid forte aliud hoc modo ex familiaritate carnis opinantur. in quibus adhuc parvulis animalibus, dum isto humillimo genere verborum tamquam materno sinu eorum gestatur infirmitas, salubriter aedificatur fides, qua certum habeant et teneant deum fecisse omnes naturas, quas eorum sensus mirabili varietate circumspicit. quorum si quispiam quasi vilitatem dictorum aspernatus extra nutritorias cunas superba inbecillitate se extenderit, heu, cadet miser, et, domine deus, miserere, ne inplumem pullum conculcent qui transeunt viam, et mitte angelum tuum, qui eum reponat in nido, ut vivat, donec volet.

does out of a narrow scantling of language, overflow CHAP.
into streams of clearest truths, whence every man XXVII
may draw out for himself such truth as he can
upon these subjects, he, one observation, and he,
another, by larger circumlocutions of discourse.
For some, whenas they read, or hear these words,
presently conceive that God like some man, or like
some unlimited power endued with huge bulk, by
some new and sudden resolution, did outside itself,
as it were at some distances, create heaven and earth,
even two great bodies, above and below; wherein
all things were to be contained. And when they
hear God say: Let that thing be made, and it was
made; they think the words to have had beginning
and ending, to have sounded in time, and so to have
passed away; immediately whereupon, the thing
became in being, which was commanded so to do:
and such other like conceits, which their familiarity
with flesh and blood causes them to imagine. In
whom, being yet little ones and carnal, whilst
their weakness is carried along in this humble
manner of speech, (as it were in the bosom of a
mother) their faith is wholesomely built up; so
that they by it are assured and confirmed in the
belief that God made all these natures, which in
admirable variety their eye beholdeth round about
them. But if any one shall despise these words, as if
too simple, and with a proud weakness but once offer
to crawl out of his cradle, he shall, alas, catch a most
miserable fall. But take thou, O Lord God, some
pity upon them, that such as go by the way tread
not upon this unfeathered young bird, and send thine
angel to put it into the nest again, that it may live,
till it be able to fly.

XXVIII

ALII vero, quibus haec verba non iam nidus, sed opaca
frutecta sunt, vident in eis latentes fructus et voli-
tant laetantes, et garriunt scrutantes, et carpunt eos.
vident enim, cum haec verba legunt vel audiunt, tua,
deus, aeterne stabili permansione cuncta praeterita et
futura tempora superari nec tamen quicquam esse
temporalis creaturae, quod tu non feceris; cuius
voluntas quia id est quod tu, nullo modo mutata vel
quae antea non fuisset exorta voluntate fecisti omnia,
non de te similitudinem tuam formam omnium, sed
de nihilo dissimilitudinem informem, quae formaretur
per similitudinem tuam recurrens in te unum pro
captu ordinato, quantum cuique rerum suo genere
datum est, et fierent omnia bona valde, sive maneant
circa te, sive gradatim remotiore distantia per tempora et locos pulchras variationes faciant aut patian-
tur. vident haec et gaudent in luce veritatis tuae,
quantulum hic valent.

Et alius eorum intendit in id, quod dictum est: in
principio fecit deus, et respicit sapientiam principium,
quia et loquitur ipsa nobis. alius itidem intendit in

XXVIII

How diversely this Scripture is understood by others

But others, unto whom these words are now no longer CHAP.
a nest, but shady shrubberies, discover in them the XXVIII
fruits concealed under the leaves, and gladly flock
thither; and with cheerful chirpings seek out and
pluck off these fruits. For at the reading or hearing
of these words, they discern that all times past and
to come, are out-reached by thy eternally stable
continuance at the same stay: and how there is not
for all that, any one of the temporal creatures which
is not of thy making, O God. And because thy
will is the same that thyself is, therefore by a will
in no way changed, not a new will arising which
before was not, thou createdst all things: not out
of thyself, in thine own similitude, (which is the
form of all things) but out of nothing, in a formless unlikeness to thyself; which might after be
formed by thy similitude; (returning unto thee
who art but one, according to the capacity appointed
for it, so far as is given to each thing in his
kind) and might be all made very good: whether
they abide near about thyself; or in being by
degrees removed, by times and by places, they
do either make or suffer many a goodly variation.
These things they see, and they rejoice in the light
of thy truth, in that little degree they may.

Another bends his observation upon that which
is spoken : In the beginning God made heaven and
earth ; and perceiveth that beginning as wisdom, because that also speaketh unto us. Another bends his
mind likewise upon the same words, and by beginning

CAP.
XXVIII

eadem verba et principium intellegit exordium rerum conditarum, et sic accipit: in principio fecit, ac si diceretur: primo fecit. atque in eis, qui intellegunt in principio, quod in sapientia fecit caelum et terram, alius eorum ipsum caelum et terram, creabilem materiam caeli et terrae, sic esse credit cognominatam; alius iam formatas distinctasque naturas, alius unam formatam eandemque spiritalem caeli nomine, aliam informem corporalis materiae terrae nomine. qui autem intellegunt in nominibus caeli et terrae adhuc informem materiam, de qua formaretur caelum et terra, nec ipsi uno more id intellegunt: sed alius, unde consummaretur intellegibilis sensibilisque creatura; alius tantum, unde sensibilis moles ista corporea, sinu grandi continens perspicuas promptasque naturas. nec illi uno modo, qui iam dispositas digestasque creaturas caelum et terram vocari hoc loco credunt; sed alius invisibilem atque visibilem, alius solam visibilem, in qua luminosum caelum suspicimus et terram caliginosam quaeque in eis sunt.

understands the first entrance of the things created: taking them in this sense, in the beginning he made, as if he should have said: he at first made. And among them that understand in the beginning to mean, in wisdom he created heaven and earth: one believes the matter out of which heaven and earth were to be created, to be there called heaven itself and earth: another, the natures already formed and distinguished: another, under the name of heaven, conceives but one formed matter, and that the spiritual one to be meant, and under the name of earth, the other formless nature of the corporeal matter. And as for them that under the names of heaven and earth, understand the matter as yet unformed, out of which heaven and earth were to be formed, neither do they understand it in one way: but one, that matter out of which both the intelligent and sensible creature were to be made up: another, that matter only out of which this sensible corporeal bulk was to be made, which in his mighty bosom contains these natures visible and ready to hand. Neither do even these understand alike, who believe the creatures already ordered and arranged to be in this place called heaven and earth: but one understands both the invisible and visible nature: another, the visible only, in which we behold this lightsome heaven, and darksome earth, with all things in them contained.

XXIX

CAP.
XXIX

AT ille, qui non aliter accipit : in principio fecit,
quam si diceretur : primo fecit, non habet quomodo
veraciter intellegat caelum et terram, nisi materiam
caeli et terrae intellegat, videlicet universae, id est
intellegibilis corporalisque creaturae. si enim iam
formatam velit universam, recte ab eo quaeri poterit,
si hoc primo fecit deus, quid fecerit deinceps, et post
universitatem non inveniet, ac per hoc audiet invitus :
"quomodo illud primo, si postea nihil?"   cum vero
dicit primo informem, deinde formatam, non est
absurdus, si modo est idoneus discernere, quid. praecedat aeternitate, quid tempore, quid electione, quid
origine : aeternitate, sicut deus omnia ; tempore,
sicut flos fructum ; electione, sicut fructus florem ;
origine, sicut sonus cantum.   in his quattuor primum
et ultimum, quae commemoravi, difficillime intelleguntur, duo media facillime.   namque rara visio
est et nimis ardua conspicere, domine, aeternitatem
tuam incommutabiliter mutabilia facientem, ac per
hoc priorem.   quis deinde sic acutum cernat animo, ut
sine labore magno dinoscere valeat, quomodo sit prior
360

XXIX

How many Ways a Thing may be said to be First

But he that no otherwise understands In the beginning
he made, than if it were said, At first he made; hath
no way to understand heaven and earth in the truth
of their nature, unless he shall understand them as
the matter of heaven and earth: that is to say, of
the whole, to wit, both the intelligible and corporeal
creation. For if he would have the universe to be
already formed; it may be rightly demanded of
him: If so be God made this first, what then made
he afterwards? And after reckoning the universe
he will find nothing left over: whereupon must he
against his will be challenged with another question:
How that At first, if after it there be nothing? But
when he says, God made the matter unformed at
first, and formed it afterwards, there is no absurdity
committed: provided that he be able to distinguish
what is reckoned first by eternity, what by time,
what by choice, what as being the original. First
by eternity, so God is before all things: first by
time, so is the flower before the fruit: first by
choice, so is the fruit before the flower: first as
being the original, so is the sound before the
tune. Of these four, the first and last that I have
mentioned are with extreme difficulty obtained to be
understood; but the two middlemost, easily enough.
For a rare and too lofty a vision it is to behold
thy eternity, O Lord, unchangeably making these
changeable things; and so in that respect to be
before them. And who, in the second place, is of so
sharp-sighted an understanding, as that he is able

sonus quam cantus, ideo quia cantus est formatus
sonus, et esse utique aliquid non formatum potest, formari autem quod non est non potest ? sic est prior
materies quam id, quod ex ea fit, non ideo prior, quia
ipsa efficit, cum potius fiat, nec prior intervallo temporis ; neque enim priore tempore sonos edimus
informes sine cantu et eos posteriore tempore in
formam cantici coaptamus aut fingimus, sicut ligna,
quibus arca, vel argentum, quo vasculum fabricatur ;
tales quippe materiae tempore etiam praecedunt formas rerum, quae fiunt ex eis. at in cantu non ita
est. cum enim cantatur, auditur sonus eius, non
prius informiter sonat et deinde formatur in cantum.
quod enim primo utcumque sonuerit, praeterit, nec
ex eo quicquam reperies, quod resumptum arte con-
ponas : et ideo cantus in sono suo vertitur, qui sonus
eius materies eius est. idem quippe formatur, ut
cantus sit. et ideo, sicut dicebam, prior materies
sonandi quam forma cantandi : non per faciendi po-
tentiam prior ; neque enim sonus est cantandi artifex,
sed cantanti animae subiacet ex corpore, de quo cantum faciat ; nec tempore prior : simul enim cum cantu
editur ; nec prior electione : non enim potior sonus
quam cantus, quandoquidem cantus est non tantum
sonus verum etiam speciosus sonus. sed prior est
origine, quia non cantus formatur, ut sonus sit, sed

without great pains to discern, how the sound should
be before the tune? Yet it is so, for this reason;
because a tune is a sound that hath form in it; and
likewise for that a thing not formed may have a
being, whereas that which hath no being, can not be
formed. Thus is the matter before the thing made
of it, not because it makes it, since itself is made
rather: nor is it before it by an interval of time;
for we do not first in time utter formless sounds
without singing, and then tune or fashion the same
sounds into a form of singing afterwards, just as
wood or silver be served, whereof a chest or vessel
is fashioned; such materials indeed, do in time
precede the forms of those things which are made
of them. But in singing it is not so: for when it
is sung, its sound is heard; it is not a formless
sound first, and then formed into a tune afterwards.
For each sound just as it is made, so it passeth; nor
canst thou find aught of it, which thou mayest call
back and set into a tune by any art thou canst use:
therefore the tune has his being in his sound,
which sound of his, is his matter: this indeed
receives a form, that it may become a tune. And
therefore, as I said, is the matter of the sound
before the form of the tune: not before in respect
of any power it hath to make it a tune; for a
sound is no way the workmaster that makes the
tune, but something is furnished out of the body
for the mind of the singer to make a tune out of.
Nor before in time; for it is sent forth together with
the tune. Nor is it before in our choice; seeing a
sound is not better than a tune: a tune being not
only sound, but a graceful sound. But it is first
as being original; because a tune receives not form
to cause it to become a sound, but a sound receives

CAP.
XXIX
sonus formatur, ut cantus sit. hoc exemplo qui potest intellegat materiam rerum primo factam et appellatam caelum et terram, quia inde facta sunt caelum et terra, nec tempore primo factam, quia formae rerum exserunt tempora, illa autem erat informis iamque in temporibus simul animadvertitur, nec tamen de illa narrari aliquid potest, nisi velut tempore prior sit, cum pendatur extremior, quia profecto meliora sunt formata quam informia, et praecedatur aeternitate creatoris, ut esset de nihilo, unde aliquid fieret.

XXX

CAP.
XXX
In hac diversitate sententiarum verarum, concordiam pariat ipsa veritas, et deus noster misereatur nostri, ut legitime lege utamur, praecepti fine, pura caritate. ac per hoc, si quis quaerit ex me, quid horum Moyses, tuus ille famulus, senserit, non sunt hi sermones confessionum mearum, si tibi non confiteor, nescio; et scio tamen illas veras esse sententias exceptis carnalibus, de quibus quantum existimavi locutus sum. quos tamen bonae spei parvulos haec verba libri tui non territant alta humiliter et pauca copiose;

364

form, to cause it to become a tune. By this example, CHAP.
XXIX let him that is able, understand the matter of things to be first made and called heaven and earth, because heaven and earth were made out of it; yet was not this matter first made in respect of time, because forms of things give rise to time; but that was without form, and now in time is only observed in conjunction with time. And yet is there not anything to be said of that Matter, but as though earlier in time, whenas in value it is latter (because doubtless, better are things that have form, than things that have no form); and though it must yield precedence to the eternity of the Creator, that it might have its being out of Nothing, from which it should be born into Something.

XXX

*The Scriptures are to be searched, with honourable
Respect unto the Penman*

IN this diversity of true opinions, let truth itself CHAP. procure reconcilement, and our God have mercy XXX upon us, that we may use the law lawfully, even the 1 Tim. i. 8 end of the commandment, pure charity. And by this if a man now demands of me, which of all those was the meaning of thy servant Moses; this is not the language of my confessions, if I do not confess unto thee, I know not: and yet this I know, that they are all true senses (those carnal ones excepted) of which I have fully spoken mine opinion. Yet even those little ones of good hope, them do not the words of thy book terrify, which deliver high mysteries in humble phrase, and a few things in

CAP.
XXX
sed omnes, quos in eis verbis vera cernere ac dicere
fateor, diligamus nos invicem, pariterque diligamus
te, deum nostrum, fontem veritatis, si non vana, sed
ipsam sitimus, eundemque famulum tuum, scripturae
huius dispensatorem, spiritu tuo plenum, ita honore-
mus, ut hoc eum te revelante, cum haec scriberet,
adtendisse credamus, quod in eis maxime et luce
veritatis et fruge utilitatis excellit.

XXXI

CAP.
XXXI
Ita cum alius dixerit: "hoc sensit, quod ego," et
alius: "immo illud, quod ego," religiosius me arbitror dicere: cur non utrumque potius, si utrumque
verum est, et si quid tertium et si quid quartum et
si quid omnino aliud verum quispiam in his verbis
videt, cur non illa omnia vidisse credatur, per quem
deus unus sacras litteras vera et diversa visuris multo-
rum sensibus temperavit? ego certe, quod intrepidus
de meo corde pronuntio, si ad culmen auctoritatis
aliquid scriberem, sic mallem scribere, ut, quod veri
quisque de his rebus capere posset, mea verba re-
sonarent, quam ut unam veram sententiam ad hoc
366

copious expression. But as for us all whom I CHAP. confess both to see and speak the truth delivered XXX in those words, let us love one another: yea, and jointly together let us love thee our God, the Fountain of truth; if so be our thirst be after truth, and not after vanities: yea, let us in such manner honour that servant of thine, the dispenser of this Scripture, so full of thy spirit, that we may believe him, when by thy revelation he wrote these things, to have bent his intentions unto that sense in them, which principally excels the rest, both for light of truth, and fruitfulness of profit.

XXXI

Truth is so to be received, whoever speaks it

So now, when another shall say; Moses meant as I CHAP. do: and another; Nay, the very same that I do: XXXI I suppose that with more reverence I may say: Why meant he not as you both mean, if you both mean truly? And if there be a third truth, or a fourth, yea, if any other man may discover any other truth in those words, why may he not be believed to have seen all these; he, by whose ministry, God that is but One, hath tempered these holy Scriptures to the meanings of a many, that were to see things true, and yet diverse? For mine own part verily, (and fearlessly I speak it from my heart) that were I to endite anything that should attain the highest top of authority, I would choose to write in such a strain, as that my words might carry the sound of any truth with them, which any man could apprehend of concerning these matters; rather than so clearly to set down

CAP. apertius ponerem, ut excluderem ceteras, quarum fal-
XXXI
sitas me non posset offendere. nolo itaque, deus meus,
tam praeceps esse, ut hoc illum virum de te meruisse
non credam. sensit ille omnino in his verbis atque
cogitavit, cum ea scriberet, quidquid hic veri potuimus invenire, et quidquid nos non potuimus aut nondum potuimus, et tamen in eis inveniri potest.

XXXII

CAP. Postremo, domine, qui deus es et non caro et
XXXII
sanguis, si quid homo minus vidit, numquid et
spiritum tuum bonum, qui deducet me in terra
recta, latere potuit, quidquid eras in eis verbis tu
ipse revelaturus legentibus posteris, etiamsi ille, per
quem dicta sunt, unam fortassis ex multis veris sententiam cogitavit? quod si ita est, sit igitur illa
quam cogitavit ceteris excelsior, nobis autem, domine,
aut ipsam demonstras aut quam placet alteram veram,
ut, sive nobis hoc quod etiam illi homini tuo sive
aliud ex eorundem verborum occasione patefacias, tu
tamen pascas, non error inludat. ecce, domine deus
meus, quam multa de paucis verbis, quam multa, oro
te, scripsimus! quae nostrae vires, quae tempora

one true sense only concerning some one particular, CHAP.
as that I should thereby exclude all such other XXXI
senses, which being not false, could no ways offend
me. I will not therefore, O my God, be so heady
as not to believe that this man obtained thus much
at thy hands. He without doubt both perceived,
and was advised of, in those words whenas he wrote
them, what truth so ever we have been able to find
in them : yea, and whatsoever we have not heretofore been able, no nor yet are, which nevertheless
can be found in them.

XXXII

He prays to obtain right Meaning

LASTLY, O Lord, thou that art God, and not flesh CHAP.
and blood, what though a man should not see all, XXXII
yet could any part of that be concealed from
thy good Spirit, (who shall lead me in the land of
uprightness), which thou thyself wert by those
words to reveal unto the readers of all times to
come, even if he by whom they were said, might
among the many true meanings pitch his thoughts
perchance upon one only? Which if so it be, let
that meaning then be granted to be more excellent
than the rest; but do thou, O Lord, either reveal
that very same unto us, or any other true one which
thou pleasest: that so, whether thou discoverest
the same unto us which thou didst unto that
servant of thine, or else some other by occasion of
the same words, yet mayst thou thyself feed us,
and not error deceive us. Behold now, O Lord my
God, how much we have written upon a few words,
yea, how much I beseech thee! What strength of

S. AVGVSTINI CONFESSIONVM LIBER XII

CAP.
XXXII omnibus libris tuis ad istum modum sufficient ?   sine
me itaque brevius in eis confiteri tibi, et eligere unum
aliquid quod tu inspiraveris verum, certum et bonum,
etiamsi multa occurrerint, ubi multa occurrere poterunt, ea fide confessionis meae, ut, si hoc dixero,
quod sensit minister tuus, recte atque optime
—id enim conari me oportet—quod si assecutus non fuero, id tamen dicam,
quod mihi per eius verba tua
veritas dicere voluerit, quae
illi quoque dixit quod
voluit.

ours, yea, what ages would be sufficient to go over
all thy books in this manner? Give me leave
therefore brieflier now to confess unto thee concerning them; and to make choice of some one
true, certain, and good sense that thou shalt inspire
me withal, even if many such senses shall offer themselves unto me (where many safely may): with such
honesty in my confession, that if I shall say that
which thine own minister intended, that is right
and best: for that is the thing which my
duty is to endeavour: which if I may
not attain unto, yet I should say that,
which by those words thy truth
was pleased to tell me, which
revealed also unto him,
that which it
pleased.

BOOK XIII

LIBER TERTIVS DECIMVS

I

CAP.
I Invoco te, deus meus, misericordia mea, qui fecisti me et oblitum tui non oblitus es. invoco te in animam meam, quam praeparas ad capiendum te ex desiderio, quod inspirasti: nunc invocantem te ne deseras, qui priusquam invocarem praevenisti, et institisti crebrescens multimodis vocibus, ut audirem de longinquo et converterer, et vocantem me invocarem te. etenim, domine, delevisti omnia mala merita mea, ne retribueres manibus meis, in quibus a te defeci, et praevenisti omnia bona merita mea, ut retribueres manibus tuis, quibus me fecisti, quia et priusquam essem tu eras, nec eram, cui praestares ut essem: et tamen ecce sum ex bonitate tua praeveniente totum hoc, quod me fecisti, et unde me fecisti. neque enim eguisti me, aut ego tale bonum sum, quo tu adiuveris, dominus meus et deus meus, non ut tibi sic serviam, quasi ne fatigeris in agendo, aut ne minor sit potestas tua carens obsequio meo,

THE THIRTEENTH BOOK

I

He calleth upon God

I CALL upon thee, O my God, my mercy; upon thee
that createdst me, and who hast not forgotten me, that had forgotten thee. I invite thee into my soul, which thou now preparest to entertain thee by the longing that thyself inspireth into her. Forsake me not now when I call upon thee, thou who preventedst me before I called, having been earnest with me with much variety of repeating calls; that I would hear thee from afar, and suffer myself to be converted, and call at length upon thee, that didst call after me. For thou Lord hast blotted out all my evil deservings, lest thou shouldst take vengeance upon the work of my hands, for that in which I have fallen off from thee: and thou hast prevented all my well deservings too, that thou mightest recompense the work of thy hands with which thou madest me; because that before I was, thou wert, nor was I anything upon which thou mightest bestow the favour to cause me to be: and yet behold, I now am, merely out of thine own goodness, preventing both all this which thou hast made me, and all that too, whereof thou hast made me. For thou neither hadst any need of me, nor yet am I of such good use, as any ways to be helpful unto thee my Lord and God: nor am I made to be so assistant to thee with my service, as to keep thee from tiring in thy working; or for fear thy power might be less if my

CAP.
I
neque ut sic te colam quasi terram, ut sis incultus,
si non te colam: sed ut serviam tibi et colam te,
ut de te mihi bene sit, a quo mihi est, ut sim, cui
bene sit.

II

CAP.
II
Ex plenitudine quippe bonitatis tuae creatura tua
substitit, ut bonum, quod tibi nihil prodesset nec de
te aequale tibi esset, tamen quia ex te fieri potuit,
non deesset. quid enim te promeruit caelum et
terra, quas fecisti in principio? dicant, quid te
promeruerunt spiritalis corporalisque natura, quas
fecisti in sapientia tua; ut inde penderent (etiam
inchoata et informia, quaeque in genere suo vel
spiritali vel corporali, euntia in immoderationem et
in longinquam dissimilitudinem tuam, spiritale ·in-
forme praestantius, quam si formatum corpus esset,
corporale autem informe praestantius, quam si
omnino nihil esset,) atque ita penderent in tuo
verbo informia, nisi per idem verbum revocarentur
ad unitatem tuam et formarentur et essent ab uno
te summo bono universa bona valde. quid te pro-
meruerant, ut essent saltem informia, quae neque
hoc essent nisi ex te?

Quid te promeruit materies corporalis, ut esset
376

service should be wanting : nor so to ply thee with CHAP.
my service, as a man does his land, that unless I tilled I
thee thou must lie fallow : but made I am both to
serve and worship thee, that I might receive a well-
being from thee ; from whom it proceeds that I have
such a being as is capable of well-being.

II

Of the Creatures' dependency upon their Creator

FOR from the fulness of thy goodness, doth thy CHAP.
creature subsist; that the good, which could in II
no ways profit thee, nor could it be made of thy sub- *Ex* denotes
stance equal to thee, yet because it was from thee, origin, *de*
might not be wanting. For what did Heaven and emanation
earth which thou madest in the beginning deserve
of thee ? Let those spiritual and corporeal natures
which thou madest in thy wisdom, say how they
deserved thee, to have still their dependence upon
thee (being as yet inchoate and unformed, every
one in its own kind, spiritual or corporeal, ready to
fall away into an immoderate liberty and far dis-
tant unlikeness unto thee : the spiritual, though
Without form more noble than the corporeal, though
formed, and the corporeal, though without form,
better than if it were nothing at all), and so to
depend upon thy Word, as formless, unless by the
same Word they were brought back unto thy unity,
endued with a form, and made by thee the only
sovereign good to become very good. How did
they deserve of thee, to be even Without form, seeing they could not have been even this, unless from
thee ?

What did that corporeal matter deserve of thee,

CAP.
II
saltem invisibilis et incomposita, quia neque hoc esset,
nisi quia fecisti? ideoque te, quia non erat, promereri
ut esset non poterat. aut quid te promeruit inchoatio
creaturae spiritalis, ut saltem tenebrosa fluitaret
similis abysso, tui dissimilis, nisi per idem verbum
converteretur ad idem, a quo facta est, atque ab eo
inluminata lux fieret, quamvis non aequaliter et tamen
conformis formae aequali tibi? sicut enim corpori
non hoc est esse, quod pulchrum esse—alioquin de-
forme esse non posset—ita etiam creato spiritui non
id est vivere, quod sapienter vivere: alioquin inconmutabiliter saperet. bonum autem illi est adhaerere
tibi semper, ne quod adeptus est conversione, aver-
sione lumen amittat, et relabatur in vitam tenebrosae
abysso similem. nam et nos, qui secundum animam
creatura spiritalis sumus, aversi a te, nostro lumine, in
ea vita fuimus aliquando tenebrae; et in reliquiis
obscuritatis nostrae laboramus, donec simus iustitia
tua in unico tuo sicut montes dei: nam iudicia tua
fuimus sicut multa abyssus.

that it should be made so much as Invisible and CHAP. Without form; seeing it could not be so much as so, II hadst not thou made it so? And therefore because it was not at all, it could not deserve of thee to be made. Or what could the spiritual creature even now begun to be created deserve of thee, that it might at least all darksomely flit up and down, like unto the deep, but unlike thee; unless it had been by the same Word turned unto that, by whom it was made, and by the same also enlightened, that it might be made light; although not in any equality, yet in some conformity unto that form which is equal unto thee? For like as to a body, simply to be, is not all one with being beautiful, for then it could no ways be deformed : so likewise to a created spirit, to live is not all one with living wisely, for then should it ever continue wise unchangeably. But good it is for it to stick close unto thee; lest what light it hath obtained by turning to thee, it may lose again by turning from thee; and relapse into a state of life resembling the darksome deep. For even we ourselves, who as touching our souls are a spiritual creation, when we were turned away from thee our Light, were once dark- Eph. v. 8 ness in that estate of life : yea, and still we labour amidst the relics of our old darkness, until in thy only One we be made thy righteousness, which is Ps. xxxvi. 6 like the mountains of God. For we have been objects of thy judgments, even as the great deep.[1]

1 *Enarr. in Ps.* xxxv. § 10 : "in ecclesia Christi invenis abyssum, invenis et montes: invenis ibi pauciores bonos, quia montes pauci sunt, abyssus lata est, id est multos male viventes " (from Gibb and Montgomery).

S. AVGVSTINI CONFESSIONVM LIBER XIII

III

CAP. III Quod autem in primis conditionibus dixisti: fiat lux, et facta est lux, non incongruenter hoc intellego in creatura spiritali, quia erat iam qualiscumque vita, quam inluminares. sed sicut non te promeruerat, ut esset talis vita, quae inluminari posset, ita nec cum iam esset promeruit te, ut inluminaretur. neque enim eius informitas placeret tibi, si non lux fieret, non existendo, sed intuendo inluminantem lucem eique cohaerendo, ut et quod utcumque vivit et quod beate vivit, non deberet nisi gratiae tuae, conversa per conmutationem meliorem ad id, quod neque in melius neque in deterius mutari potest: quod tu solus es, quia solus simpliciter es, cui non est aliud vivere, aliud beate vivere, quia tua beatitudo es.

IV

CAP. IV Quid ergo tibi deesset ad bonum, quod tu tibi es, etiamsi ista vel omnino nulla essent vel informia remanerent, quae non ex indigentia fecisti, sed ex plenitudine bonitatis tuae cohibens atque convertens

III

All is of the Grace of God

By that which thou saidst in the first creation : Let
there be light, and there was light ; I do, not unfitly,
understand the spiritual creation : because even then
there was a kind of life which thou mightest enlighten. But yet as then it had no claim upon
thee that there might be a life to be enlightened :
even so when already it was come to be, could it not
deserve of thee to be enlightened. For neither could
its formless estate be pleasing unto thee, unless it
might be made light : light, not by existing simply,
but by beholding the light enlightening, and by
cleaving unto it; so that that it lived at all, and
that it lived thus happily, it owed to nothing but
thy grace, being turned by a better change to that
which can never be changed either into worse or
better : Because thou alone hast being, because
thou only in simple being Art, unto thee it being
not one thing to live, and another thing to live
happily : seeing thyself art thine own bliss.

IV

God needs not the Creatures, but they Him

What therefore could have been wanting unto thy
good, which thou thyself art? although all these
creatures should never have been, or have remained
utterly Without form : which thou madest not out of
any want, but out of the fulness of thy goodness,

CAP.
IV
ad formam, non ut tamquam tuum gaudium conpleatur ex eis? perfecto enim tibi displicet eorum inperfectio, ut ex te perficiantur et tibi placeant, non autem inperfecto, tamquam et tu eorum perfectione perficiendus sis. spiritus enim tuus bonus superferebatur super aquas, non ferebatur ab eis, tamquam in eis requiesceret. in quibus enim requiescere dicitur spiritus tuus, hos in se requiescere facit. sed superferebatur incorruptibilis et incommutabilis voluntas tua, ipsa in se sibi sufficiens, super eam quam feceras vitam; cui non hoc est vivere, quod beate vivere, quia vivit etiam fluitans in obscuritate sua; cui restat converti ad eum, a quo facta est, et magis magisque vivere apud fontem vitae, et in lumine eius videre lumen et perfici et inlustrari et beari.

V

CAP.
V
ECCE apparet mihi in aenigmate trinitas, quod es, deus meus, quoniam tu, pater, in principio sapientiae nostrae, quod est tua sapientia de te nata, aequalis tibi et coaeterna, id est in filio tuo, fecisti caelum et terram. et multa diximus de caelo caeli et de terra invisibili et incomposita et de abysso tenebrosa secundum spiritalis informitatis vagabunda

holding them in and converting them to form, not as CHAP.
if thy joy were fulfilled from them. For unto thee IV
who art perfect, is their imperfection displeasing:
that so they be perfected by thee, and thereby
please thee: but not as if thou wert imperfect, or
wert to receive perfection, from their perfecting.
Thy good Spirit indeed Moved upon the waters, yet Gen. i. 2
was not borne up by the waters, as if he found
rest in them: for those in whom thy good Spirit is
said to rest, those doth he cause to be stayed up
in himself. But thy incorruptible and unchangeable will, which is in itself all-sufficient for itself,
Moved over that life which thyself hadst before
created: unto which, living is not all one with
blissful living, seeing it liveth even when flitting
up and down in its own obscurity: for which it yet
remaineth to be turned unto him, by whom it was
made, and to live more and more near by the
fountain of life; yea, and in his light to see light,
and to be perfected at last, and enlightened, and
brought to bliss.

V

His Confession of the Blessed Trinity

Lo, now, the Trinity appears unto me in a riddle; CHAP.
which is thou, my God: because thou, O Father, in V
him who is the Beginning of our wisdom, that is in
thy Wisdom, born of thyself, equal and co-eternal
unto thee, that is to say, in thy Son, hast created
heaven and earth. Much now have we said of the
Heaven of heavens, and of the invisible and unshapen
Earth, and of the Darksome deep, dark in reference
to the unstable flux of its spiritual formlessness,

CAP.
V

deliquia, nisi converteretur ad eum, a quo erat qualiscumque vita, et inluminatione fieret speciosa vita, et
esset caelum caeli eius, quod inter aquam et aquam
postea factum est. et tenebam iam patrem in dei
nomine, qui fecit haec, et filium in principii nomine,
in quo fecit haec, et trinitatem credens deum meum,
sicut credebam, quaerebam in eloquiis sanctis eius,
et ecce spiritus tuus superferebatur super aquas. ecce
trinitas deus meus, pater et filius et spiritus sanctus,
creator universae creaturae.

VI

CAP.
VI

SED quae causa fuerat, o lumen veridicum, tibi ad-
moveo cor meum, ne me vana doceat, discute tenebras
eius, et dic mihi, obsecro te per matrem caritatem, obsecro te, dic mihi, quae causa fuerat, ut post nomi-
natum caelum et terram invisibilem et incompositam
et tenebras super abyssum tum demum scriptura tua
nominaret spiritum tuum? an quia oportebat sic eum
insinuari, ut diceretur superferri? non posset hoc
dici, nisi prius illud commemoraretur, cui superferri
spiritus tuus posset intellegi. nec patri enim nec
filio superferebatur, nec superferri recte diceretur, si
nulli rei superferretur. prius ergo dicendum erat,
cui superferretur, et deinde ille, quem non oportebat
aliter commemorari, nisi ut superferri diceretur. cur

384

unless it had turned unto him, from whom that life CHAP.
which already it had, was received, and by his en- V
lightening became a beauteous life, and was the
heaven of that heaven which was afterwards set
between water and water. And under the name of
God, I now understood the person of the Father who
made all this; and under the name of the Beginning,
the Son, in whom he made this; and thus believing,
as I did, my God as the Trinity, I searched in his
holy words, and lo, thy Spirit Moved over the face
of the waters. Behold the Trinity, my God, the
Father, the Son, and the Holy Ghost, the Creator
of all creation.

VI

Of the Spirit's moving upon the Waters

But what was the cause, O thou true-speaking Light: CHAP.
unto thee I lift up my heart, let it not teach me VI
vanities, dispel thou the darkness of it; and tell me
by our Mother Charity, I beseech thee, tell me why
after the mention of heaven, and of the invisible and
shapeless Earth, and the Darkness upon the deep,
thy Scriptures should then at length make the
first mention of thy Spirit? Was it because it was
meet so to have him introduced, as that he should be
said to Move above; and so much could not truly be
said, unless that were first mentioned upon which
thy Spirit could be understood to have Moved? For
verily, neither over the Father, nor over the Son,
did he Move; nor could he rightly be said to Move
over, if there were nothing yet for him to move
over. First therefore was that to be spoken of
which he was said to Move over; and then he,
whom it was requisite not to have named otherwise,

CAP.
VI
ergo eum aliter insinuari non oportebat, nisi ut superferri diceretur?

VII

CAP.
VII
HINC sequatur qui potest intellectu apostolum tuum dicentem, quia caritas tua diffusa est in cordibus nostris per spiritum sanctum, qui datus est nobis, et de spiritalibus docentem et demonstrantem supereminentem viam caritatis, et flectentem genua pro nobis ad te, ut cognoscamus supereminentem scientiam caritatis Christi. ideoque ab initio superminens superferebatur super aquas. cui dicam, quomodo dicam de pondere cupiditatis in abruptam abyssum et de sublevatione caritatis per spiritum tuum, qui superferebatur super aquas? cui dicam? quomodo dicam? neque enim loca sunt, quibus mergimur et emergimus. quid similius et quid dissimilius? affectus sunt, amores sunt, immunditia spiritus nostri defluens inferius amore curarum, et sanctitas tui attollens nos superius amore securitatis, ut sursum cor habeamus ad te, ubi spiritus tuus superferebatur super aquas, et veniamus ad supereminentem requiem, cum pertransierit anima nostra aquas, quae sunt sine substantia.

than as he was said to Move over. But wherefore CHAP.
yet was it not fitting to have him introduced other- VI
ways, unless he were said to Move over?

VII

Of the Effect or Working of the Holy Ghost

HENCE let him that is able follow with his under- CHAP.
standing thy Apostle, where he thus speaks: Be- VII
cause thy love is shed abroad in our hearts by the Rom. v. 5
Holy Ghost which is given unto us: and where
concerning spiritual gifts, he teacheth and sheweth 1 Cor. xii.
unto us a supereminent way of charity; and where 1, 31
he bows his knee unto thee for us, that we may
come to learn that supereminent knowledge of the Eph. iii. 19
love of Christ. And therefore even from the very
beginning did the Spirit supereminent Move over
the waters. Whom shall I tell it unto, and in what
terms shall I describe how the huge weight of lust-
ful desires presses down into the steep abyss; and
how charity raises us up again by thy Spirit which
Moved over the waters? Unto whom shall I speak
it? And in what language utter it? For they are no
certain places into which we are plunged, and out of
which we are again lifted. What can be liker, and
what unliker? They be affections, they be loves;
they be the uncleanness of our own spirits, that
floweth downwards with the love of worldly cares:
and it is the holiness of thy Spirit that raiseth us up
again by the love of freedom from cares; that we
may lift our hearts up unto thee, where thy Spirit
was Moved over the waters, and so may come at
length to that supereminent repose: when, namely,
our souls shall have passed over these waters where Ps. cxxiv. 5
is no standing ground.

VIII

CAP. DEFLUXIT angelus, defluxit anima hominis, et indi-
VIII
caverunt abyssum universae spiritalis creaturae in
profundo tenebroso, nisi dixisses ab initio : fiat lux,
et facta esset lux, et inhaereret tibi omnis oboediens
intellegentia caelestis civitatis tuae et requiesceret
in spiritu tuo, qui superfertur incommutabiliter super
omne mutabile. alioquin et ipsum caelum caeli tenebrosa abyssus esset in se ; nunc autem lux est in
domino. nam et in ipsa misera inquietudine defluen-
tium spirituum, et indicantium tenebras suas, nudatas
veste luminis tui satis ostendis, quam magnam rationalem creaturam feceris, cui nullo modo sufficit ad
beatam requiem, quidquid te minus est, ac per hoc
nec ipsa sibi. tu enim, deus noster, inluminabis
tenebras nostras : ex te oriuntur vestimenta nostra,
et tenebrae nostrae sicut meridies erunt. da mihi
te, deus meus, et redde mihi te : en amo et, si parum
est, amem validius. non possum metiri, ut sciam,
quantum desit mihi amoris ad id quod sat est, ut
currat vita mea in amplexus tuos, nec avertatur, donec
abscondatur in abscondito vultus tui. hoc tantum scio,

388

VIII

How God's Spirit cherishes feeble Souls

ANGEL flowed downwards, and man's soul flowed
downwards; and they pointed to the Deep of the
whole spiritual creation which had been in that
most darksome bottom, hadst not thou said from
the beginning: Let there be light, and there was
light, and unless every obedient intelligence of thy
Heavenly City had cleaved unto thee, and rested in
thy Spirit, which Moves unchangeably over everything that is changeable.   Otherwise had even the
Heaven of Heavens itself been in itself a darksome
deep; whereas now it is light in the Lord.   For
even in that miserable restlessness of the falling
spirits that discovered their own darkness, bared of
the garment of thy light, dost thou sufficiently reveal
how noble the reasonable creature is which thou
hast made; unto which nothing will suffice to give
a happy rest, that is in any way inferior unto thyself: and therefore she cannot herself give satisfaction unto herself.   For 'tis thou, O Lord, that
shalt lighten our darkness; from thee grow these
our garments; and then shall our darkness be as
the noonday.   Give thyself unto me, O my God,
yea, restore thyself unto me: lo, I love thee; and
if it be too little, let me love thee with more
might.   I am not able to measure my love, that I
may so come to know how much there wants of
enough: that my life may even run into thy embracements, and not turn from them again, until it be
wholly hidden in the hiding-place of thy coun- Ps. xxxi. 20
tenance.   This one thing I know, that woe is me

S. AVGVSTINI CONFESSIONVM LIBER XIII

quia male mihi est praeter te, non solum extra me
sed et in me ipso, et omnis mihi copia, quae deus
meus non est, egestas est.

IX

NUMQUID aut pater aut filius non superferebatur
super aquas? si tamquam loco sicut corpus, nec
spiritus sanctus; si autem incommutabilis divinitatis
eminentia super omne mutabile, et pater et filius
et spiritus sanctus superferebatur super aquas. cur
ergo tantum de spiritu tuo dictum est hoc? cur de
illo tantum dictus est quasi locus, ubi esset, qui non
est locus, de quo solo dictum est, quod sit donum
tuum? in dono tuo requiescimus: ibi te fruimur.
requies nostra locus noster. amor illuc attollit nos
et spiritus tuus bonus exaltat humilitatem nostram
de portis mortis. in bona voluntate tua pax nobis
est. corpus pondere suo nititur ad locum suum.
pondus non ad ima tantum est, sed ad locum suum.
ignis sursum tendit, deorsum lapis. ponderibus suis
aguntur, loca sua petunt. oleam infra aquam fusum
super aquam attollitur, aqua supra oleum fusa infra
oleum demergitur: ponderibus suis aguntur, loca sua
petunt. minus ordinata inquieta sunt: ordinantur
et quiescunt. pondus meum amor meus; eo feror,
quocumque feror. dono tuo accendimur et sursum

except in thee; not only without myself, but within CHAP.
myself: yea, all other plenty besides my God, is VIII
mere beggary unto me.

IX

Why the Spirit only moved upon the Waters

BUT did not the Father also, or the Son, Move over CHAP
the waters? If we understand moving as it were IX
in a place, like a body; then neither did the Spirit
Move. But if the unchangeable supereminence of
the divinity above every changeable thing be understood: then did both Father, Son, and Holy Ghost
Move over the waters. Why therefore is this said
of thy Spirit only? Why in his case only is a sort
of place, where he should be mentioned (which,
however, is not a place), why in his case, of whom
alone it is said that he is thy gift? In thy gift
we rest; then we enjoy thee. Our rest is thy gift,
our life's place. Love lifts us up thither, and thy
good spirit advances our lowliness from the gates of
death. In thy good pleasure lies our peace. Our
body with its lumpishness strives towards its own
place. Weight makes not downward only, but to his
own place also. The fire mounts upward, a stone sinks
downward. All things pressed by their own weight
go towards their proper places. Oil poured in the
bottom of the water, is raised above it: water poured
upon oil, sinks to the bottom of the oil. They are
driven by their own weights, to seek their own places.
Things a little out of their places become unquiet:
put them in their order again, and they are quieted.
My weight is my love: by that am I carried, whithersoever I be carried. We are inflamed by thy gift,

391

CAP.
IX

ferimur; inardescimus et imus. ascendimus ascensiones in corde et cantamus canticum graduum. igne tuo, igne tuo bono inardescimus et imus, quoniam sursum imus ad pacem Hierusalem, quoniam iucundatus sum in his, qui dixerunt mihi: in domum domini ibimus. ibi nos conlocabit voluntas bona, ut nihil velimus aliud quam permanere illic in aeternum.

X

CAP.
X

BEATA creatura, quae non novit aliud, cum esset ipsa aliud, nisi dono tuo, quod superfertur super omne mutabile, mox ut facta est attolleretur nullo intervallo temporis in ea vocatione, qua dixisti: fiat lux, et fieret lux. in nobis enim distinguitur tempore, quod tenebrae fuimus et lux efficiemur: in illa vero dictum est, quid esset, nisi inluminaretur, et ita dictum est, quasi prius fuerit fluxa et tenebrosa, ut appareret causa, qua factum est, ut aliter esset, id est ut ad lumen indeficien conversa lux esset. qui potest, intellegat, a te petat. ut quid mihi molestus est, quasi ego inluminem ullum hominem venientem in hunc mundum?

and are carried upwards: we wax hot within, and we go on. We ascend thy ways that be in our heart, and we sing a song of degrees; we glow inwardly with thy fire, with thy good fire, and we go, because we go upward to the peace of Jerusalem: for glad I was whenas they said unto me, We will go up into the house of the Lord. There will thy good pleasure settle us, that we may desire no other thing, but to dwell there for ever.

CHAP. IX

Ps. lxxxiv. 5

Degrees: *i.e.*, steps. See notes to Ps. cxx.-cxxiii.

X

All is of God's Gift

O HAPPY creation which knows no other thing, though it would have been another thing, had it not been exalted by thy gift which Moveth over every mutable thing, as soon as it was created, without any interval of time, in virtue of that call whereby thou saidest, Let there be light, and so there was light. For in us there is distinction of time in that we were darkness, and shall be made light: but of that creation it is only said, what it would have been, if it had not been enlightened. And this is so spoken, as if it had been darksome and unsettled before: that so the reason might now appear, for which it was made to be otherwise; that is to say, that it being turned unto the luminary that never faileth, should be Light. Let him understand this that is able: let him ask of God. Why should he trouble me with it, as if I enlighten any man that cometh into this world?

CHAP. X

John i. 9

XI

CAP.
XI.

TRINITATEM omnipotentem quis intelleget? et quis
non loquitur eam, si tamen eam? rara anima, quaecumque de illa loquitur, scit quod loquitur. et contendunt et dimicant, et nemo sine pace videt istam
visionem. vellem, ut haec tria cogitarent homines
in se ipsis. longe aliud sunt ista tria quam illa
trinitas, sed dico, ubi se exerceant et probent et
sentiant, quam longe sunt. dico autem haec tria:
esse, nosse, velle. sum enim et scio et volo: sum
sciens et volens, et scio esse me et velle, et volo esse
et scire. in his igitur tribus quam sit inseparabilis
vita, et una vita et una mens et una essentia, quam
denique inseparabilis distinctio et tamen distinctio,
videat qui potest. certe coram se est; adtendat in
se et videat et dicat mihi. sed cum invenerit in his
aliquid, et dixerit, non iam se putet invenisse illud,
quod supra ista est incommutabile, quod est inconmutabiliter et scit inconmutabiliter et vult inconmutabiliter: et utrum propter tria haec et ibi trinitas,
an in singulis haec tria, ut terna singulorum sint, an
utrumque miris modis simpliciter et multipliciter
394

XI

Of some Impressions or Resemblances of the Blessed
Trinity, that be in man

WHICH of us will sufficiently comprehend the knowledge of the almighty Trinity? And yet which of us but talks of it, if indeed of it? A rare soul it is, which whilst it speaks of it, knows what it speaks of. For men contend and strive about it, and no man sees the vision of it without peace. I could wish that men would consider upon these three things, that are in themselves. Which three be far another thing indeed, than the Trinity is: but I do but now tell them where they may exercise themselves, and prove and feel how far they are from it. Now the three I spake of, are to Be, to Know and to Will. For I both am, and know, and will: I am knowing, and willing; and I know myself to be and to will; and I would both be and know. Betwixt these three, let him discern that can, how unseparable a life there is; yea, one life, one mind and one essence: yea, finally, how unseparable a distinction there is, and yet there is a distinction. Surely a man hath it before him; let him look into himself, and see, and then tell me. But when once he finds anything in these three and says it, yet let him not for all this believe himself to have found that unchangeable which is far above all these, and which is unchangeably, and knows unchangeably, and wills unchangeably; and whether because of these three, there is in God also a Trinity, or whether all three be in each person so that each has all three; or whether in marvellous ways, simply and manifoldly,

CAP. XI

infinito in se sibi fine, quo est et sibi notum est et sibi sufficit inconmutabiliter id ipsum copiosa unitatis magnitudine, quis facile cogitaverit? quis ullo modo dixerit? quis quolibet modo temere pronuntiaverit?

XII

CAP. XII

PROCEDE in confessione, fides mea; dic domino tuo: sancte, sancte, sancte, domine deus meus, in nomine tuo baptizati sumus, pater et fili et spiritus sancte, in nomine tuo baptizamus, pater et fili et spiritus sancte, quia et apud nos in Christo suo fecit deus caelum et terram, spiritales et carnales ecclesiae suae, et terra nostra antequam acciperet formam doctrinae, invisibilis erat et incomposita, et ignorantiae tenebris tegebamur, quoniam pro iniquitate erudisti hominem, et iudicia tua multa abyssus. sed quia spiritus tuus superferebatur super aquam, non reliquit miseriam nostram misericordia tua, et dixisti: fiat lux; paenitentiam agite, appropinquavit enim regnum caelorum. paenitentiam agite; fiat lux. et quoniam conturbata erat ad nos ipsos anima nostra, conmemorati sumus tui, domine, de terra Iordanis et de monte aequali tibi, sed parvo propter nos, et displicuerunt nobis tenebrae nostrae, et conversi sumus ad te, et facta est lux. et ecce fuimus aliquando tenebrae, nunc autem lux in domino.

itself a bound unto itself within itself, yet un- CHAP.
XI
bounded, whereby it is, and is known unto itself, and
sufficeth unto itself, unchangeably the selfsame by the
abundant greatness of its unity, what man can readily
conceive ? Who is able in any terms to express it ?
Who shall dare in any measure rashly to deliver his
opinion upon it?

XII

The Water in Baptism is effectual by the Holy Spirit

PROCEED in thy confession O my faith, say to thy Lord, CHAP.
XII
O holy, holy, holy Lord my God, in thy name have
we been baptised, O Father, Son, and Holy Ghost;
in thy name do we baptise, Father, Son, and Holy
Ghost; because among us also, in his Christ did
God make an heaven and earth, namely, the spiritual
and carnal people of his Church. Yea, and our earth,
before it received the form of doctrine, was invisible Rom. vi. 17
and unformed, and we were covered over with the
darkness of ignorance, for thou hast chastised man
for his iniquity, and thy judgments are a great deep. Ps. xxxvi. 6
But because thy spirit moved upon the waters, thy
mercy forsook not our misery, and thou saidst: Let
there be light; repent ye, for the Kingdom of Heaven Matt. iii. 2
is at hand. Repent, Let there be light. And because
our soul was troubled within us, we remembered thee,
O Lord, concerning the land of Jordan, and that Hill Ps. xlii. 8
which being equal unto thyself, was made little for (Prayer
Book)
our sakes: and so we were displeased at our own
darkness, and we turned unto thee, And there was
light. And behold, we having sometimes been dark- Eph. v. 8
ness, are now light in the Lord.

S. AVGVSTINI CONFESSIONVM LIBER XIII

XIII

Et tamen adhuc per fidem, nondum per speciem.
spe enim salvi facti sumus. spes autem, quae
videtur, non est spes. adhuc abyssus abyssum invocat, sed iam in voce cataractarum tuarum. adhuc
et ille qui dicit : non potui vobis loqui quasi spiritalibus, sed quasi carnalibus, etiam ipse nondum se
arbitratur conprehendisse, et quae retro oblitus, in
ea, quae ante sunt, extenditur, et ingemescit grava-
tus, et sitit anima eius ad deum vivum, quemadmodum cervi ad fontes aquarum, et dicit : quando
veniam ? habitaculum suum, quod de caelo est,
superindui cupiens, et vocat inferiorem abyssum
dicens : nolite conformari huic saeculo, sed reformamini in novitate mentis vestrae, et : nolite pueri
effici mentibus, sed malitia parvuli estote, ut mentibus perfecti sitis, et : o stulti Galatae, quis vos
fascinavit ? sed iam non in voce sua ; in tua enim,
qui misisti spiritum tuum de excelsis, per eum, qui
ascendit in altum, et aperuit cataractas donorum
suorum, ut fluminis impetus laetificarent civitatem
tuam. illi enim suspirat sponsi amicus, habens iam
spiritus primitias penes eum, sed adhuc in semet
ipso ingemescens, adoptionem expectans, redemp-
tionem corporis sui. illi suspirat—membrum est
enim sponsae—et illi zelat—amicus est enim sponsi
—illi zelat, non sibi, quia in voce cataractarum

XIII

His devout longing after God

AND hitherto we walk by faith, and not by sight: for
we are saved by hope; but hope that is seen, is not
hope.   Hitherto doth deep call to deep, but now in
the voice of thy water-spouts; hitherto doth he that
saith: I could not speak unto you as unto spiritual, but
as unto carnal, even he as yet thinketh not himself to
have apprehended, and forgetteth those things which
are behind, and reacheth forth to those things which
are before: yea, he groaneth, being burdened, and his
soul thirsteth after the living God, as the hart after
the water brooks, saying: When shall I come? desiring to be clothed upon with his house which is from
heaven: he calleth also upon this lower deep, saying:
Be not conformed to this world, but be ye transformed by the renewing of your mind; and, Be not
children in understanding, but in malice be ye
children, that in understanding ye may be perfect;
and, O foolish Galatians, who hath bewitched you?
But now no longer in his own voice; for it is in thine,
who sentest thy Spirit from above; through him who
ascended up on high, and set open the flood-gates of
his gifts, that the force of his streams might make
glad the City of God.   Her doth this friend of the
bridegroom sigh after; having now the first fruits of
the Spirit in himself, yet hitherto groaneth he within
himself, waiting for the adoption, to wit the redemption of his body.   For her he sighs, as being a member
of the bride; for her he is jealous, as being a friend
of the bridegroom: for her he is jealous, not for
himself; because in the voice of thy water-spouts, and

CHAP.
XIII
2 Cor. v. 7
Rom. viii. 24
Ps. xlii. 7
1 Cor. iii. 1

Phil. iii. 13

Ps. xlii. 1, 2

2 Cor. v. 1

Rom. xii. 2

1 Cor. xiv.
20

Gal. iii. 1

Acts ii.
Eph. iv. 8
Mal. iii. 10
Ps. xlvi. iv.
John iii. 29
Rom. viii.
23

CAP.
XIII
tuarum, non in voce sua invocat alteram abyssum
cui zelans timet, ne sicut serpens Evam decepit
astutia sua, sic et eorum sensus corrumpantur a
castitate, quae est in sponso nostro, unico tuo.   quae
est illa speciei lux, cum videbimus eum, sicuti est, et
transierint lacrimae, quae mihi factae sunt panis die
ac nocte, dum dicitur mihi cotidie: ubi est deus
tuus?

XIV

CAP.
XIV
Et ego dico: deus meus ubi est? ecce ubi es.
respiro in te paululum, cum effundo super me animam
meam in voce exultationis et confessionis, soni festi-
vitatem celebrantis.   et adhuc tristis est, quia
relabitur et fit abyssus, vel potius sentit adhuc se
esse abyssum.   dicit ei fides mea, quam accendisti
in nocte ante pedes meos: quare tristis es, anima, et
quare conturbas me? spera in domino; lucerna
pedibus tuis verbum eius.   spera et persevera, donec
transeat nox, mater iniquorum, donec transeat ira
domini, cuius filii et nos fuimus aliquando tenebrae,
quarum residua trahimus in corpore propter peccatum
mortuo, donec aspiret dies et removeantur umbrae.
spera in domino: mane astabo et contemplabor;
400

not in his own voice, doth he call to that other deep, CHAP.
for whom he is both jealous and fearful, lest as the XIII
serpent beguiled Eve through his subtilty, so their
feelings should be corrupted from the chastity that
is in our bridegroom, our only Son. Oh what a light
of beauty is that, when we shall see him as he is, 1 John iii.
and those tears shall be passed away, which have 2
been my meat day and night, whilst they daily say Ps. xlii. 3
unto me: Where is now thy God?

XIV

Our Misery is comforted by Faith and Hope

AND so I say too: Where is my God? See, where CHAP.
thou art. In thee take I breath a little while, XIV
whenas I pour out my soul by myself in the voice
of joy and praise, which is the sound of him that Ps. xlii. 4 .
keeps holyday. And still is it be-saddened, even
because it relapseth again, and becomes a darksome deep; or perceives itself rather still to be
one. Unto it speaks my faith which thou hast
kindled to enlighten my feet in the night: Why
art thou so sad, O my soul, and why dost thou Apoc. vii.
disquiet me? Hope in the Lord; his Word is a 17
lanthorn unto thy feet: hope and endure, until the Ps. cxix.
night, the mother of wicked, until the wrath of the 105
Lord be overpast: whose children, even we, were Is. xxvi. 20
sometime darkness: the relics of which we still bear Eph. v. 8
about us in our body, dead because of sin; until the Rom. viii.
day break, and the shadows flee away. Hope thou 10
in the Lord; in the morning I shall stand in thy Cant. ii. 17

CAP.
XIV
semper confitebor illi. mane astabo et videbo salu-
tare vultus mei, deum meum, qui vivificabit et mor-
talia corpora nostra propter spiritum, qui habitat in
nobis, quia super interius nostrum tenebrosum et
fluvidum misericorditer superferebatur. unde in hac
peregrinatione pignus accepimus, ut iam simus lux,
dum adhuc spe salvi facti sumus et filii lucis et filii
diei, non filii noctis neque tenebrarum, quod tamen
fuimus. inter quos et nos in isto adhuc incerto
humanae notitiae tu solus dividis, qui probas corda
nostra et vocas lucem diem et tenebras noctem.
quis enim nos discernit nisi tu? quid autem habemus, quod non accepimus a te, ex eadem massa vasa
in honorem, ex qua sunt et alia facta in contumeliam?

XV

CAP.
XV
AUT quis nisi tu, deus noster, fecisti nobis firmamentum auctoritatis super nos in scriptura tua divina?
caelum enim plicabitur ut liber, et nunc sicut pellis
extenditur super nos. sublimioris enim auctoritatis
est tua divina scriptura, cum iam obierunt istam
mortem illi mortales, per quos eam dispensasti nobis.
et tu scis, domine, tu scis, quemadmodum pellibus
indueris homines, cum peccato mortales fierent.

presence, and contemplate him : yea, I shall for CHAP.
ever confess unto him. In the morning I shall XIV
stand in thy presence and shall see the health of my Ps. xlii. 11
countenance, even my God, who shall quicken our Rom. viii.
mortal bodies, by the Spirit that dwelleth in us : 11
because he hath in mercy moved upon our inner
darksome and unquiet deep : from whom in this our
pilgrimage we have received such a pledge, as that
even now we are light : whilst hitherto we are saved
by hope, made the children of light, and the children
of the day, not the children of the night, nor of the
darkness which yet sometimes we were. Betwixt
whom and us, in this hitherto uncertainty of human
knowledge, thou only canst divide ; thou, who provest
the hearts, and callest the light day, and the darkness night. For who can discern us but thou ? And
what have we, that we have not received of thee ?
out of the same lump made for vessels of honour, Rom. ix. 21
whereof others also are made for dishonour.

XV

By the word Firmament, is the Scripture meant

OR who except thou, O our God, made that firma- CHAP.
ment of the authority of thy divine Scripture to be XV
over us ? As 'tis said : For the heaven shall be folded Apoc. vi. 14
up like a book ; and is even now stretched over us
like a skin. For thy holy Scripture is of more eminent authority, since those mortals departed this life,
by whom thou dispensedst it unto us. And thou
knowest, O Lord, thou knowest, how thou With skins Gen. iii. 21
didst once apparel men, so soon as they by sin
were become mortal. Wherefore hast thou like

CAP.
XV

unde sicut pellem extendisti firmamentum libri tui, concordes utique sermones tuos, quos per mortalium ministerium superposuisti nobis. namque ipsa eorum morte solidamentum auctoritatis in eloquiis tuis per eos editis sublimiter extenditur super omnia, quae subter sunt, quod, cum hic viverent, non ita sublimiter extentum erat. nondum sicut pellem caelum extenderas, nondum mortis eorum famam usquequaque dilataveras.

Videamus, domine, caelos, opera digitorum tuorum: disserena oculis nostris nubilum, quo subtexisti eos. ibi est testimonium tuum sapientiam praestans parvulis: perfice, deus meus, laudem tuam ex ore infantium et lactantium. neque enim novimus alios libros ita destruentes superbiam, ita destruentes inimicum et defensorem resistentem reconciliationi tuae defendendo peccata sua. non novi, domine, non novi alia tam casta eloquia, quae sic mihi persuaderent confessionem, et lenirent cervicem meam iugo tuo, et invitarent colere te gratis. intellegam ea, pater bone, da mihi hoc subterposito, quia subterpositis solidasti ea.

Sunt aliae aquae super hoc firmamentum, credo, inmortales et a terrena corruptione secretae. laudent nomen tuum, laudent te supercaelestes populi angelorum tuorum, qui non opus habent suspicere firmamentum hoc et legendo cognoscere verbum tuum.

a Skin stretched out the Firmament of thy book, CHAP.
that is to say those words of thine so well agreeing XV
together; which by the ministry of mortal men
thou spreadedst over us. For by their very death
is that solid Firmament of authority, in thy sayings set forth by them, stretched on high over
all that be now under it; which whilst they lived
on earth, was not then so eminently stretched out
over us. Thou hadst not as yet Spread abroad
that heaven like a skin; thou hadst not as yet
everywhere noised abroad the report of their
deaths.

Let us look, O Lord, upon the heavens the work Ps. viii. 3
of thy fingers; clear our eyes of that mist with which
thou hast overcast them. There is that testimony
of thine, which giveth wisdom to the little ones : Ps. viii. 2
perfect, O my God, thine own praise out of the
mouth of babes and sucklings. For we know no
other books which so destroy pride, which so destroy
the adversary, and the defender that resisteth thy
reconciliation by defending his own sins. I know
not, Lord, I know not of any other such chaste
words, that are so powerful in persuading me to confession, and in bowing my stiff neck unto thy yoke,
and in inviting me to serve thee for nought. Grant
me to understand them, good Father : grant me thus
much that am placed under them : because that for
them who are placed under them, thou hast estab-
lished them.

Other Waters also there be above this Firmament,
immortal they be, as I believe, and separated from
all earthly corruption. Let those super-celestial
peoples, thine angels, praise thee, yea, let them
praise thy name : they, who have no need to gaze up at
this firmament, and by reading to attain the know-

CAP.
XV

vident enim faciem tuam semper, et ibi legunt sine
syllabis temporum, quid velit aeterna voluntas tua.
legunt, eligunt et diligunt; semper legunt et numquam praeterit quod legunt. eligendo enim et dili-
gendo legunt ipsam incommutabilitatem consilii tui.
non clauditur codex eorum nec plicatur liber eorum,
quia tu ipse illis hoc es et es in aeternum, quia
super hoc firmamentum ordinasti eos, quod firmasti
super infirmitatem inferiorum populorum, ubi suspi-
cerent et cognoscerent misericordiam tuam temporaliter enuntiantem te, qui fecisti tempora. in caelo
enim, domine, misericordia tua et veritas tua usque
ad nubes. transeunt nubes, caelum autem manet.
transeunt praedicatores verbi tui ex hac vita in
aliam vitam, scriptura vero tua usque in finem
saeculi super populos extenditur. sed et caelum et
terra transibunt, sermones autem tui non transibunt,
quoniam et pellis plicabitur, et faenum, super quod
extendebatur, cum claritate sua praeteriet, verbum
autem tuum manet in aeternum; quod nunc in aenigmate nubium et per speculum caeli, non sicuti est,
apparet nobis, quia et nos quamvis filio tuo dilecti
simus, nondum apparuit quod erimus. attendit per
retia carnis, et blanditus est, et inflammavit, et
currimus post odorem eius. sed cum apparuerit,
similes ei erimus, quoniam videbimus eum, sicuti
est: sicuti est, domine, videre nostrum, quod nondum est nobis.

ledge of thy word.   For they always behold thy face, CHAP.
and there do they read without any syllables measur- XV
able by times, what the meaning is of thy eternal will.
They read, they choose, they love.   They are ever
reading; and that never passes away which they read:
because by choosing and by loving, they read the
very unchangeableness of thy counsel.   Their book is
never closed, nor is their scroll folded up: seeing
thyself art this unto them, yea, thou art so eternally;
because thou hast arranged them above this Firmament, which thou hast settled over the infirmity of the
lower peoples: where they might gaze up and learn
thy mercy, which declares in time thee that madest
times.   For thy mercy, O Lord, is in the heavens, Ps. xxxvi.
and thy truth reacheth unto the clouds.   The clouds 5
pass away, but the heaven abides: the preachers of
thy word pass out of this life into another, but thy
Scripture is spread abroad over the peoples, even
unto the end of the world.   Yet, both heaven and Matt. xxiv.
earth shall pass, but thy word shall not pass away: 35
because the scroll shall be rolled together, and the
grass over which it was spread out, shall with the
goodliness of it also pass away; but thy word re- Is. xl. 6, 8
maineth for ever, which word now appeareth unto us
in the riddle of the clouds, and through the mirror
of the heavens, not as it is: because that even
we, though the well beloved of thy Son, yet it hath 1 John iii.
not yet appeared what we shall be.   He looked 2
through the lattice of our flesh, and he spake us fair, Cant. ii. 9
yea, he set us on fire, and we hasten on his scent.
But when he shall appear, then shall we be like him, 1 John iii.
for we shall see him as he is: as he is, Lord, will 2
our sight be, though the time be not yet.

XVI

CAP.
XVI

Nam sicut omnino tu es, tu scis solus, quoniam es
incommutabiliter et scis incommutabiliter et vis incommutabiliter : et essentia tua scit et vult incommutabiliter, et scientia tua est et vult incommutabiliter et voluntas tua est et scit incommutabiliter, nec
videtur iustum esse coram te, ut, quemadmodum se
scit lumen incommutabile, ita sciatur ab inluminato
conmutabili. ideoque anima mea tamquam terra
sine aqua tibi, quia sicut se iniuminare de ́se non
potest, ita se satiare de se non potest. sic enim apud
te fons vitae, quomodo in lumine tuo videbimus
lumen.

XVII

CAP.
XVII

Quis congregavit amaricantes in societatem unam ?
idem namque illis finis est temporalis et terrenae
felicitatis, propter quam faciunt omnia, quamvis in-
numerabili varietate curarum fluctuent. quis, domine, nisi tu, qui dixisti, ut congregarentur aquae in
congregationem unam, et appareret arida, sitiens tibi,
quoniam tuum est mare, et tu fecisti illud, et aridam

XVI

God is unchangeable

For fully, as thou art, thou only knowest; since CHAP.
thou art unchangeably, and knowest unchangeably, XVI
and willest unchangeably. And thy essence both
knoweth, and willeth unchangeably; and thy knowledge is, and wills unchangeably; and thy will is, and
knows unchangeably: nor seems it right in thine
eyes, that in the same manner as an unchangeable
light knoweth itself, so it should be known by a
thing changeable, that receives the light. My soul Ps. cxliii.
is therefore to thee like a land where no water is, 6
because that as it cannot of itself enlighten itself, so
it cannot of itself satisfy itself. For so is the foun- Ps. xxxvi.
tain of life with thee, like as in thy light we shall 9
see light.

XVII

What is meant by dry Land, and by the Sea

Who Gathered the embittered together into one CHAP.
society? Because that all of them propound to XVII
themselves the same end of a temporal and earthly
felicity; for attaining whereof they do whatever they
do, though in the doing they waver up and down
with innumerable variety of cares. Who, Lord, but
thyself? who once commandedst, Let the waters Gen. i. 9
be gathered together into one place, and let the
dry land appear, which thirsteth after thee, since Ps. cxliii. 6
the sea is thine, and thou hast made it, and thy Ps. lxiii. 1

CAP. terram manus tuae formaverunt ?   neque enim amari-
XVII
tudo voluntatum, sed congregatio aquarum vocatur
mare.   tu enim coerces etiam malas cupiditates
animarum, et figis limites, quousque progredi sinantur
aquae, ut in se comminuantur fluctus earum, atque
ita facis mare ordine imperii tui super omnia.

At animas sitientes tibi et apparentes tibi (alio fine
distinctas a societate maris) occulto et dulci fonte
irrigas, ut et terra det fructum suum : et dat fructum
suum, et te iubente, domino deo suo, germinat anima
nostra opera misericordiae secundum genus, diligens
proximum in subsidiis necessitatum carnalium ; habens
in se semen secundum similitudinem, quoniam ex
nostra infirmitate compatimur ad subveniendum in-
digentibus, similiter opitulantes, quemadmodum nobis
vellemus opem ferri, si eodem modo indigeremus ; non
tantum in facilibus tamquam in herba seminali, sed
etiam in protectione adiutorii forti robore, sicut
lignum fructiferum, id est beneficum ad eripiendum
eum, qui iniuriam patitur, de manu potentis, et
praebendo protectionis umbraculum valido robore
iusti iudicii.

hands prepared the dry land. Nor is the bitter-spiritedness of men's wills, but the gathering together of the waters, called sea; for thou restrainest also the wicked desires of men's souls, and settest them their bounds, how far the waters may be suffered to pass; that their waves may break one against another: and in this manner makest thou it a sea, by the order of thy dominion over all things.

But as for the souls that thirst after thee, and that appear before thee (being by other bounds divided from the society of the sea) them dost thou water by a secret and sweet spring, that the Earth may bring forth fruit: and she brings forth her fruit, and thou, her Lord God, so commanding, our soul buddeth forth her works of mercy, According to their kind, loving her neighbour in the relief of his bodily necessities: Having seed in herself according to her likeness, since out of the consideration of our own infirmity, we so far compassionate them, as that we are ready to relieve the needy: helping them, even as we would desire to be helped our own selves, if we in like manner were in any necessity; and that not in things easy to us alone, as in the Herb which hath seed in it, but also in affording them the protection of our assistance with our best strength, like the Tree that brings forth fruit: that is to say, some right good turn for the rescuing him that suffers wrong, out of the clutches of him that is too strong for him: and by affording him the shelter of our protection, by the powerful arm of just judgment.

XVIII

CAP.
XVIII

Ita, domine, ita, oro te, oriatur, sicuti facis, sicuti
das hilaritatem et facultatem, oriatur de terra veritas,
et iustitia de caelo respiciat, et fiant in firmamento
luminaria. frangamus esurienti panem nostrum et
egenum sine tecto inducamus in domum nostram,
nudum vestiamus et domesticos seminis nostri non
despiciamus. quibus in terra natis fructibus, vide,
quia bonum est, et erumpat temporana lux nostra, et
de ista inferiore fruge actionis in delicias contemplationis verbum vitae superius obtinentes appareamus
sicut luminaria in mundo, cohaerentes firmamento
scripturae tuae. ibi enim nobiscum disputas, ut
dividamus inter intellegibilia et sensibilia tamquam
inter diem et noctem, vel inter animas alias intelle-
gibilibus, alias sensibilibus deditas, ut iam non tu solus
in abdito diiudicationis tuae, sicut antequam fieret
firmamentum, dividas inter lucem et tenebras, sed
etiam spiritales tui in eodem firmamento positi atque
distincti (manifestata per orbem gratia tua) luceant
super terram et dividant inter diem et noctem et
significent tempora, quia vetera transierunt, ecce facta
sunt nova, et quia propior est nostra salus, quam cum

XVIII

He continues his Allegory, in alluding to the
Works of the Creation

So, Lord, even so I beseech thee, let it spring out, CHAP.
as already thou makest it do, as already thou givest XVIII
cheerfulness and ability: let truth spring out of Ps. lxxxv.
the earth, and righteousness look down from heaven, 11
and Let there be lights in the firmament. Let us
break our bread unto the hungry, and let us bring Is. lviii. 7
the poor that is homeless into our own house. Let us
clothe the naked, and never despise those near ones
of our own flesh. Which fruits being once sprung out
of the earth, see that it is good: and let our temporary
Light break forth; and let ourselves, from this lower
fruitfulness of action, arriving to the delightfulness
of contemplation, holding on high the word of life, Phil. ii. 16
appear at length like luminaries in the world, fast
settled to the Firmament of thy Scriptures. For there
thou dost so discourse unto us, as that we be enabled
to Divide between intelligible things and things of
sense, as Betwixt the day and the night; or between souls given either to intellectual things or unto
things of sense; insomuch as not only thou thyself
in the secret of thine own judgment, like as before
ever the firmament was made, Dividest between the
light and the darkness, but thy spiritual children
also set and ranked in the same Firmament, (thy
grace now clearly shining throughout their orb)
may now Give their light unto the earth, and
divide betwixt the day and the night, and be for
signs of times, because old things are passed with 2 Cor. v. 17
them (lo, they are become new), and because our

413

credidimus, et quia nox praecessit, dies autem adpro-
pinquavit, et quia benedicis coronam anni tui, mittens
operarios in messem tuam, in qua seminanda alii
laboraverunt, mittens etiam in aliam sementem, cuius
messis in fine est. ita das vota optanti et benedicis
annos iusti, tu autem idem ipse es, et in annis tuis, qui
non deficiunt, horreum praeparas annis transeuntibus.
aeterno quippe consilio propriis temporibus bona
caelestia das super terram, quoniam quidem alii datur
per spiritum sermo sapientiae tamquam luminare
maius (propter eos, qui perspicuae veritatis luce delec-
tantur) tamquam in principio diei; alii autem sermo
scientiae secundum eundem spiritum tamquam luminare minus; alii fides, alii donatio curationum, alii
operationes virtutum, alii prophetia, alii diiudicatio
spirituum, alteri genera linguarum, et haec omnia
tamquam stellae. omnia enim haec operatur unus
atque idem spiritus, dividens propria unicuique prout
vult, et faciens apparere sidera in manifestatione ad
utilitatem. sermo autem scientiae, qua continentur
omnia sacramenta, quae variantur temporibus tamquam luna, et ceterae notitiae donorum, quae deinceps
tamquam stellae commemorata sunt, quantum differunt
ab illo candore sapientiae, quo gaudet praedictus dies,
tantum in principio noctis sunt. his enim sunt
necessaria, quibus ille prudentissimus servus tuus non
potuit loqui quasi spiritalibus, sed quasi carnalibus,

salvation is now nearer than when we believed: and that the night is far spent, and the day is at hand: and that thou crownest thy year with thy blessing, sending labourers into thy harvest, in the sowing whereof others have taken pains before; sending also into another field whose harvest is in the end. Thus givest thou life to him that seeketh it, and thou blessest the years of the just; but thou art the same, and in thy years which fail not, thou preparest corn for the years that are a passing. For thou in thy eternal counsel dost in their proper seasons bestow thy heavenly blessings upon the earth. For to one there is given by thy Spirit, the word of wisdom, resembling the Greater light, (for them who are delighted with the brightness of perspicuous truth) rising as it were at the beginning of the day. To another is given the word of knowledge by the same spirit, resembling the Lesser light. To another, faith; to another the gift of healing, to another the working of miracles; to another prophecy; to another the discerning of spirits; to another divers kinds of tongues: and all these resemble the Stars. All these worketh one and the same Spirit, dividing what is fit for every man, even as he will; and causing the stars to appear in manifestation to profit withal. But the word of knowledge, wherein are all the Sacraments contained, which are varied in their seasons like the Moon; and those other notices of gifts, which are afterwards reckoned up, like the Stars, in so much as they come short of the brightness of wisdom, which gladdens the aforementioned day: these are only for the rule of the night. For these are necessary unto such as that wisest servant of thine could not speak unto as unto spiritual, but as unto

CHAP. XVIII

Rom. xiii. 11, 12

Ps. lxv. 11

Matt. ix. 38

Matt. xiii. 39

Gen. i. 16

1 Cor. xii. 7–11

1 Cor. iii. 1

ille, qui sapientiam loquitur inter perfectos. anima-
lis autem homo tamquam parvulus in Christo lactisque
potator, donec roboretur ad solidum cibum et aciem
firmet ad solis aspectum, non habeat desertam noctem
suam, sed luce lunae stellarumque contentus sit.
haec nobiscum disputas sapientissime, deus noster, in
libro tuo, firmamento tuo, ut discernamus omnia contemplatione mirabili, quamvis adhuc in signis et in
temporibus et in diebus et in annis.

XIX

Sed prius lavamini, mundi estote, auferte nequi-
tiam ab animis vestris atque a conspectu oculorum
meorum, ut appareat arida. discite bonum facere,
iudicate pupillo et iustificate viduam, ut germinet
terra herbam pabuli et lignum fructiferum, et venite,
disputemus, dicit dominus, ut fiant luminaria in firmamento caeli, ut luceant super terram. quaerebat
dives ille a magistro bono, quid faceret, ut vitam
aeternam consequeretur : dicat ei magister bonus,
quem putabat hominem et nihil amplius—bonus est
autem, quia deus est—dicat ei, ut, si vult venire ad
vitam, servet mandata, separet a se amaritudinem
malitiae atque nequitiae, non occidat, non moechetur,
416

carnal men; even he, who also speaketh wisdom
among those that are perfect. As for the natural
man, like him who is a babe in Christ, and a sucker
of milk, till such time as he grows big enough for
strong meat, and can look steadily against the sun,
let him not utterly forsake his night, but rest himself
contented with what light the moon and the stars
afford him. These discourses holdest thou with us,
O our most wise God, in thy book, that Firmament
of thine; that we may discern all things, in an
admirable contemplation: though still but in signs,
and in times, and in days, and in years.

XIX

*Our Hearts are to be purged from Vice, that
they may be capable of virtue. He still
continues his Allegory of the Creation*

But wash you first, make you clean, put away evil
from your souls, and from before mine eyes, that the Is. i. 16–17
dry land may appear. Learn to do good, judge the Gen. i. 9
fatherless, plead for the widow, that The earth may Gen. i. 11,
bring forth the green herb for meat, and the tree 30
bearing fruit: and then come, let us reason together, Is. i. 18
saith the Lord, that there may be luminaries in the Gen. i. 15
firmament of the heaven, and that they may shine
upon the earth. That rich young man demanded of Matt. xix.
our good Master, what he should do to attain eter- 16, 17
nal life. Let our good Master tell him, (whom he
thought to be no more than man, but he is good,
because he is God) let him tell him, that if he would
enter into life, he must keep the commandments: let Rom. x. 5
him put away the bitterness of malice and wicked- 1 Cor. v. 8
ness; let him not kill, nor commit adultery, nor steal,

non furetur, non falsum testimonium dicat, ut appareat arida et germinet honorem matris et patris et dilectionem proximi. feci, inquit, haec omnia. unde ergo tantae spinae, si terra fructifera est ? vade, extirpa silvosa dumeta avaritiae, vende quae possides et implere frugibus dando pauperibus, et habebis thesaurum in caelis, et sequere dominum, si vis esse perfectus, eis sociatus, inter quos loquitur sapientiam ille, qui novit, quid distribuat diei et nocti, ut noris et tu, ut fiant et tibi luminaria in firmamento caeli : quod non fiet, nisi fuerit illic cor tuum ; quod item non fiet, nisi fuerit illic thesaurus tuus, sicut audisti a magistro bono. sed contristata est terra sterilis, et spinae suffocaverunt verbum.

Vos autem, genus electum in firmamento mundi, qui dimisistis omnia, ut sequeremini dominum, ite post eum et confundite fortia, ite post eum, speciosi pedes, et lucete in firmamento, ut caeli enarrent gloriam eius, dividentes inter lucem perfectorum, sed nondum sicut angelorum, et tenebras parvulorum, sed non desperatorum : lucete super omnem terram, et dies sole candens eructet diei verbum sapientiae, et nox, luna lucens, annuntiet nocti verbum scientiae. luna et stellae nocti lucent, sed nox non obscurat eas, quoniam ipsae inluminant eam pro modulo eius. ecce enim tamquam deo dicente : fiant luminaria in firmamento caeli, factus est subito de caelo sonus, quasi

nor bear false witness: that the dry land may appear, CHAP.
and bring forth the honouring of father and mother, XIX
and the love of our neighbour. All these, saith he, Matt. xix.
have I kept. Whence then cometh such store of 18-20
thorns, if so be the earth be fruitful? Go, stub up
those thick bushes of covetousness; sell that thou
hast, and gain a full harvest, by giving to the poor,
and thou shalt have treasure in heaven; and follow
the Lord, if thou wilt be perfect: associated to Matt. xix.
them, among whom he speaketh wisdom; he that 21
well knoweth what to distribute to the day, and what
unto the night; that thou also mayest know it, and
that for thee there may be luminaries made in the
firmament of heaven: which never will be, unless
thy heart be there: nor will that either be, unless
thy treasure be also; like as thou hearest of our Matt. vi. 21
good Master. But the barren earth was sorry at that
saying; and the thorns choked the word in him. Matt. xiii. 7

But you, O chosen generation, in the firmament of 1 Pet. ii. 9
the world, who have forsaken all, that ye may follow 1 Cor. i. 27
the Lord; go ye now after him, and confound the Mark x. 28
strong: go after him, O ye beautiful feet, and shine Is. lii. 7
ye in the firmament, that the heavens may declare Dan. xii. 3
his glory: dividing between the light of the perfect Ps. xix. 1
ones, though not so perfect yet as the angels, and
the darkness of the little ones, though not utterly
despised. Shine ye over all the earth; and let the
day enlightened by the sun utter unto day a speech
of wisdom; and night, enlightened by the moon,
show unto night a word of knowledge. The moon
and stars shine in the night, yet doth not the night
obscure them; seeing they give that light unto it,
in its degree. For behold, as if God had given the
word, Let there be lights in the firmament of heaven:
there came suddenly a sound from heaven, as it

CAP.
XIX
ferretur flatus vehemens, et visae sunt linguae di-
visae quasi ignis, qui et insedit super unumquemque
illorum, et facta sunt luminaria in firmamento caeli
verbum vitae habentia. ubique discurrite, ignes
sancti, ignes decori. vos enim estis lumen mundi
nec estis sub modio. exaltatus est, cui adhaesistis,
et exaltavit vos. discurrite et innotescite omnibus
gentibus.

XX

CAP.
XX
CONCIPIAT et mare et pariat opera vestra, et producant aquae reptilia animarum vivarum. separantes
enim pretiosum a vili facti estis os dei, per quod diceret: producant aquae; non animam vivam, quam terra
producet, sed reptilia animarum vivarum et volatilia
volantia super terram. repserunt enim sacramenta
tua, deus, per opera sanctorum tuorum inter medios
fluctus temptationum saeculi, ad imbuendas gentes
nomine tuo in baptismo tuo. et inter haec facta sunt
magnalia mirabilia tamquam coeti grandes; et voces
nuntiorum tuorum volantes super terram iuxta firmamentum libri tui, praeposito illo sibi ad auctoritatem,
sub quo volitarent, quocumque irent. neque enim
sunt loquellae neque sermones, quorum non audian-
tur voces eorum, quando in omnem terram exiit sonus

had been the rushing of a mighty wind, and there CHAP. appeared cloven tongues like as it had been of fire, XIX and it sat upon each of them; and there were made Acts ii. 2 lights in the firmament of heaven, which had the word of life in them. Run ye to and fro, O you holy 1 John i. 1 fires, O you beauteous fires; for you are the light of Matt. v. 14, the world, nor are you put under a bushel: he whom 15 you clave unto is exalted himself, and hath exalted you. Run you to and fro, and make yourselves known unto all nations.

XX

He allegorizes upon the Creation of Spiritual things

LET the sea also conceive, and Bring forth your works; CHAP. and Waters bring forth the moving creature that hath XX life. For you by separating the precious from the vile, Gen. i. 20 are made the mouth of God, by whom he said: Let Jer. xv. 19 the waters bring forth: not a living soul which the earth brings forth, but the moving creatures, having life in them, and the winged fowls that fly over the earth. For thy Sacraments, O God, by the ministry of thy holy ones, have moved in the midst of the waves of temptation of this present world, for the imbuing of the Gentiles in thy name, in thy Baptism. In the doing whereof mighty wonders were wrought, resembling the huge whales; and the voices of thy messengers flying above the earth, in the open firmament of thy book; that being set over them as their authority under which they were to fly, whithersoever they went. For There is no Ps. xix. 3-4 speech nor language where their voice is not heard: seeing Their sound is gone through all the earth, and

CAP.
XX
eorum, et in fines orbis terrae verba eorum, quoniam tu, domine, benedicendo multiplicasti haec.

Numquid mentior, aut mixtione misceo, neque distinguo lucidas cognitiones harum rerum in firmamento caeli et opera corporalia in undoso mari et sub firmamento caeli? quarum enim rerum notitiae sunt solidae et terminatae sine incrementis generationum tamquam lumina sapientiae et scientiae, earundem rerum sunt operationes corporales multae ac variae; et aliud ex alio crescendo multiplicantur in benedictione tua, deus, qui consolatus es fastidia sensuum· mortalium; ut in cognitione animi res una multis modis per corporis motiones figuretur atque dicatur. aquae produxerunt haec, sed in verbo tuo: necessitates alienatorum ab aeternitate veritatis tuae populorum produxerunt haec, sed in evangelio tuo, quoniam ipsae aquae ista eiecerunt, quarum amarus languor fuit causa, ut in tuo verbo ista procederent.

Et pulchra sunt omnia faciente te, et ecce tu inenarrabiliter pulchrior, qui fecisti omnia. a quo si non esset lapsus Adam, non diffunderetur ex utero eius salsugo maris, genus humanum profunde curiosum et procellose tumidum et instabiliter fluvidum, atque ita non opus esset, ut in aquis multis corporaliter et sensibiliter operarentur dispensatores tui mystica facta et dicta. sic enim mihi nunc occurrerunt reptilia et volatilia, quibus imbuti et initiati homines

their words to the end of the world : because, thou,
O Lord, hast Multiplied them by thy blessing.

Say I not true, or do I mingle and confound, and
not distinguish between the knowledge of these
things in the firmament of heaven, and these corporeal works in the wavy sea, and under the firmament of heaven ? For of those things whereof the
understanding is solid, and defined without any
increase by generation, as it were lights of wisdom
and knowledge, yet even of them, the corporeal
operations be many, and divers ; and one thing
growing out of another, they are multiplied in thy
blessing, O God, who hast refreshed our soon
cloyed mortal senses ; that so the thing that is but
one in the understanding of our minds, may, by the
motions of our bodies, be many several ways set
out, and discoursed upon. These Sacraments have
the waters brought forth ; but in thy Word. The
necessities of the people estranged from the eternity
of thy truth, have brought them forth, but in thy
Gospel : because the waters themselves cast them
forth ; the diseased bitterness whereof was the cause
why they were sent forth in thy Word.

And all things are fair that thou hast made ; and
lo, thyself art ineffably fairer, that madest all these :
from whom had not Adam fallen, this brackishness
of the sea had never flowed out of his loins : namely,
this mankind, so profoundly curious, and so tempestu-
ously swelling, and so restlessly tumbling up and
down. And then, had there been no necessity of
thy dispensers to work in Many waters, after a
corporeal and sensible manner, mysterious doings
and sayings. For in this sense do I now understand those creeping and flying creatures, to which
corporeal sacraments the initiated being subjected

CAP.
XX
corporalibus sacramentis subditi non ultra proficerent, nisi spiritaliter vivesceret anima gradu alio et post initii verbum in consummationem respiceret.

XXI

CAP.
XXI
Ac per hoc in verbo tuo non maris profunditas, sed ab aquarum amaritudine terra discreta eicit, non reptilia animarum vivarum et volatilia, sed animam vivam. neque enim iam opus habet baptismo, quo gentibus opus est, sicut opus habebat, cum aquis tegeretur: (non enim intratur aliter in regno caelorum ex illo, quo instituisti, ut sic intretur;) nec magnalia mirabilium quaerit, quibus fiat fides: neque enim nisi signa et prodigia viderit, non credit, cum iam distincta sit terra fidelis ab aquis maris infidelitate amaris, et linguae in signo sunt non fidelibus, sed infidelibus. nec isto igitur genere volatili, quod verbo tuo produxerunt aquae, opus habet terra, quam fundasti super aquas. immitte in eam verbum tuum per

would make no further progress, unless their soul CHAP were spiritually quickened on yet another stage, and XX unless after the word of beginning, it looked to the Heb. vi. 1 completion.

XXI

He allegorizes upon the Creation of Birds and Fishes;
alluding by them unto such as have received the
Lord's Supper, which are perfecter Christians
than the merely baptized

AND hereby, in thy word, not the deepness of the CHAP. sea, but the earth itself once separated from XXI the bitterness of the waters, brings forth; not the Creeping and flying creatures of souls having life Gen. i. 20 in them, but the Living soul. For now hath it no Gen. ii. 7 more need of baptism, as the heathen yet have, and as itself also had, when it was covered heretofore with the waters: (for there is entrance into the kingdom John iii. 5 of heaven no other way, since the time that thou hast instituted this Sacrament for men to enter in by :) nor does it any more seek after mighty miracles to work belief; for it is not such that unless it see John iv. 48 signs and wonders, it will not believe, now that the faithful earth is separated from the waters that were bitter with unbelief; and that tongues are for a 1 Cor. xiv. sign, not to them that believe, but to them that 22 believe not. The earth therefore which thou hast founded upon the waters, hath no more need now Ps. cxxxvi. of that flying kind, which at thy word the waters 6 brought forth. Send thou thy word into it by thy

CAP.
XXI

nuntios tuos. opera enim eorum narramus, sed tu es, qui operaris in eis, ut operentur animam vivam. terra producit eam, quia terra causa est, ut haec agant in ea, sicut mare fuit causa, ut agerent reptilia animarum vivarum et volatilia sub firmamento caeli, quibus iam terra non indiget, quamvis piscem manducet levatum de profundo, in ea mensa, quam parasti in conspectu credentium; ideo enim de profundo levatus est, ut alat aridam. et aves marina progenies, sed tamen super terram multiplicantur.. primarum enim vocum evangelizantium infidelitas hominum causa extitit; sed et fideles exhortantur et benedicuntur eis multipliciter de die in diem. at vero anima viva de terra sumit exordium, quia non prodest nisi iam fidelibus continere se ab amore huius saeculi, ut anima eorum tibi vivat, quae mortua erat in deliciis vivens, deliciis, domine, mortiferis; nam tu puri cordis vitales deliciae.

Operentur ergo iam in terra ministri tui, non sicut in aquis infidelitatis, annuntiando et loquendo per miracula et sacramenta et voces mysticas, ubi intenta fit ignorantia mater admirationis in timore occultorum signorum—talis enim est introitus ad fidem filiis Adam oblitis tui, dum se abscondunt a facie tua et fiunt abyssus—sed operentur etiam sicut in arida

messengers: for we speak of their labours, but yet
thou art he that worketh in them, that they may
work out a living soul.   The earth brings it forth,
because the earth is the cause that they work this
in the soul: like as the sea was the cause that they
wrought upon the moving things that have life in
them, and the fowls that fly under the firmament of
heaven: of whom this earth hath no need; although   Alluding to
it feeds upon that fish which was taken out of the   the acrostic
deep, upon that table which thou hast prepared in   for Jesus
the sight of the faithful.   For therefore was he   Christ,
taken out of the deep, that he might feed the dry   ἰχθύς
land; and the fowl, though bred in the sea, is yet   Ps. xxiii. 5
multiplied upon the earth.   For of the first preach-
ings of the Evangelists, man's infidelity was the
cause; yet are the faithful also exhorted and blessed
many ways from day to day.   But the living soul
takes his beginning from the earth: for it profits
none save the faithful to contain themselves from
the love of this world: that so their soul may live
unto thee, which was dead while it lived in pleasure;
in such pleasures, Lord, as bring death with them.
For 'tis thou, O Lord, that art the vital delight of a
pure heart.

Now therefore let thy ministers work upon this
Earth; not as sometimes they did upon the waters of
infidelity, when they preached, and spake by miracles,
and Sacraments, and mysterious expressions: wherein
ignorance, the mother of admiration, gives good ear
unto them, out of a reverent fear it had towards
those secret wonders (for such is the entrance that
is made unto faith by the sons of Adam forgetful of
thee: while they Hide themselves from thee, and   Gen. iii. 8
are become a darksome deep): but let thy ministers
work now as upon Dry land that is separated from the

CAP.
XXI

discreta a gurgitibus abyssi, et sint forma fidelibus vivendo coram eis et excitando ad imitationem. sic enim non tantum ad audiendum sed etiam ad faciendum audiunt: quaerite deum, et vivet anima vestra, ut producat terra animam viventem. nolite conformari huic saeculo, continete vos ab eo. evitando vivit anima, quae appetendo moritur. continete vos ab immani feritate superbiae, ab inerti voluptate luxuriae, et a fallaci nomine scientiae, ut sint bestiae mansuetae et pecora edomita et innoxii serpentes. motus enim animae sunt isti in allegoria: sed fastus elationis et delectatio libidinis et venenum curiositatis motus sunt animae mortuae, quia non ita moritur, ut omni motu careat, quoniam discedendo a fonte vitae moritur atque ita suscipitur a praetereunte saeculo et conformatur ei.

Verbum autem, deus, fons vitae aeternae est et non praeterit: ideoque in verbo tuo cohibetur ille discessus, dum dicitur nobis: nolite conformari huic saeculo, ut producat terra in fonte vitae animam viventem, in verbo tuo per evangelistas tuos animam continentem imitando imitatores Christi tui. hoc enim secundum genus, quoniam aemulatio viri ab amico est: estote, inquit, sicut ego, quia et ego sicut vos. ita erunt in anima viva bestiae bonae in mansuetudine actionis. mandasti enim dicens: in mansuetudine opera tua perfice et ab omni homine diligeris. et pecora bona neque si manducaverint, abundantia,

gulfs of the great deep: and let them be a pattern CHAP.
unto the faithful, by living before them, and by XXI
stirring them up to imitation. For thus do men
hear, not so as to hear only, but to do also. Seek
the Lord, and your soul shall live: that the earth Ps. lxix. 32
may bring forth the living soul. Be not conformed Rom. xii. 2
to this world; contain yourselves from it: the soul
lives by avoiding what it dies by affecting. Contain
yourselves from the immoderate wild humour of
pride, the litherly voluptuousness of luxury, and
the false name of knowledge: that so the wild 1 Tim vi.
beasts may be tamed; the cattle made tractable; 20
and the serpents harmless. For these be the
motions of our mind under an allegory; but the
haughtiness of pride, the delight of lust, and the
poison of curiosity, these be the motions of a dead
soul. For the soul dies not so as to lose all motion;
because it dies by Departing from the fountain of Jer. ii. 13
life, and thereupon is taken up by this transitory
world, and is Conformed unto it.

But thy word, O God, is the Fountain of eternal
life, and never passeth away: wherefore this de-
parture of the soul is restrained by thy word, when
'tis said unto us: Be not conformed unto this world; Rom. xii. 2
so that the Earth may in the fountain of life bring
forth a living soul: that is, a soul made continent
in thy word, delivered by thy Evangelists, and by
following the followers of Christ. This is indeed 1 Cor. xi. 1
After his kind; because a man is wont to imitate
his friend. Be ye, saith he, as I am, for I am Gal. iv. 12
as you are. Thus in the Living soul shall there
be good beasts, meek in their actions. For thou
hast commanded: Go on with thy business in meek- Ecclesias-
ness, and thou shalt be beloved of all men. And ticus iii. 17
there shall be Good cattle in it too; which neither

CAP.
XXI
neque si non manducaverint, egentia, et serpentes
boni non perniciosi ad nocendum, sed astuti ad caven-
dum, et tantum explorantes temporalem naturam,
quantum sufficit, ut per ea, quae facta sunt, intellecta conspiciatur aeternitas. serviunt enim rationi
haec animalia, cum a progressu mortifero cohibita
vivunt et bona sunt.

XXII

CAP.
XXII
Ecce enim, domine deus noster, creator noster, cum
cohibitae fuerint affectiones ab amore saeculi, quibus
moriebamur male vivendo, et coeperit esse anima
vivens bene vivendo, completumque fuerit verbum
tuum, quo per apostolum tuum dixisti : nolite conformari huic saeculo, consequetur illud, quod ad-
iunxisti statim et dixisti : sed reformamini in novitate
mentis vestrae, non iam secundum genus, tamquam
imitantes praecedentem proximum, nec ex hominis
melioris auctoritate viventes. neque enim dixisti :
fiat homo secundum genus, sed : faciamus hominem
ad imaginem et similitudinem nostram, ut nos pro-
bemus, quae sit voluntas tua. ad hoc enim ille
dispensator tuus, generans per evangelium filios, ne
semper parvulos haberet, quos lacte nutriret et tamquam nutrix foveret : reformamini, inquit, in novitate
430

if they eat much, shall over abound, nor if they eat not, have any lack : and Good serpents, not dangerous to do hurt, but wise to take heed, and only making such a search into this temporal nature, as may be sufficient, that Eternity may be clearly seen, being understood by the things that are made.   For these creatures are then obedient unto reason, when being once restrained from their deadly prevailing upon us, they live, and become good.

XXII

*Of Regeneration by the Spirit.   He allegorizes
upon the Creation of Man*

FOR behold, O Lord our God, our Creator, so soon as ever our affections are restrained from the love of the world, by which we died through our evil living ; and began to be a Living soul through our good living ; and that the word shall be made good in us by which through thy Apostle thou hast said : Be not conformed to this world : that next shall follow which thou presently subjoinest, saying : But be ye transformed by the renewing of your mind : not as living now after your kind, as if you followed your neighbour next before you ; nor yet as living after the example of some better man.   For thou didst not say, Let man be made after his kind ; but, Let us make man after our own image and similitude : that we may prove what thy will is.   For to this purpose said that dispenser of thine, who begets children by the Gospel, that he might not ever have them babes, whom he must be fain to feed with milk, and bring up like a nurse : Be transformed, saith he, by the renewing of your

CHAP.
XXII

Rom. xii. 2

Gen. i. 26

1 Cor. iv. 15

1 Thess. ii. 7
Rom. xii. 2

CAP.
XXII
mentis vestrae ad probandum vos, quae sit voluntas dei, quod bonum et beneplacitum et perfectum. ideoque non dicis: fiat homo, sed: faciamus, nec dicis: secundum genus, sed: ad imaginem et similitudinem nostram. mente quippe renovatus, et conspiciens intellectam veritatem tuam, homine demonstratore non indiget, ut suum genus imitetur, sed te demonstrante probat ipse, quae sit voluntas tua, quod bonum et beneplacitum et perfectum, et doces eum iam capacem videre trinitatem unitatis vel unitatem trinitatis. ideoque pluraliter dicto: faciamus hominem, singulariter tamen infertur: et fecit deus hominem, et pluraliter dicto: ad imaginem nostram, singulariter infertur: ad imaginem dei. ita homo renovatur in agnitione dei secundum imaginem eius, qui creavit eum, et spiritalis effectus iudicat omnia, quae utique iudicanda sunt, ipse autem a nemine iudicatur.

XXIII

CAP.
XXIII
Quod autem iudicat omnia, hoc est, quod habet potestatem piscium maris et volatilium caeli et omnium pecorum et ferarum et omnis terrae et omnium repentium, quae repunt super terram. hoc enim

mind, that ye may prove what is that good, that CHAP. acceptable and perfect will of God. Wherefore thou XXII sayest not, Let man be made : but, Let us make man. Nor saidest thou, According to his kind : but After our own image and likeness. For man being Renewed in his mind, and able to discern and understand thy truth, needs no more any direction of man, to follow Jer. xxxi. after his kind : but by thy direction doth he Prove 34 what is that good, that acceptable, and perfect will of thine : yea, thou teachest him that is now made capable, to discern the Trinity of the Unity, and the Unity of the Trinity. Wherefore to that spoken in the plural number, Let us make man, yet is it pre- Gen. i. 26 sently added in the singular, And God made man : and to that said in the plural number, After our likeness ; it is added in the singular, After the image of God. Thus is man Renewed in the knowledge of Col. iii. 10 God, after the image of him that created him : and being made spiritual, he now judges all things, (those 1 Cor. ii. 15 namely that are to be judged) yet Himself is judged of no man.

XXIII

Of what Things a Christian may judge.
He allegorizes upon Man's Dominion over Creatures

BUT that he Judgeth all things, this is meant by CHAP. having Dominion over the fish of the sea, and over XXIII the fowls of the air, and over all cattle and wild beasts, and over all the earth, and over every creep- ing thing that creepeth upon the earth. For this he

agit per mentis intellectum, per quem percipit quae
sunt spiritus dei. alioquin homo in honore positus
non intellexit; conparatus est iumentis insensatis
et similis factus est eis. ergo in ecclesia tua, deus
noster, secundum gratiam tuam, quam dedisti ei,
quoniam tuum sumus figmentum creati in operibus
bonis, non solum qui spiritaliter praesunt sed etiam
hi qui spiritaliter subduntur eis qui praesunt—
masculum et feminam fecisti hominem hoc modo
in gratia tua spiritali, ubi secundum sexum corporis
non est masculus et femina, quia nec Iudaeus neque
Graecus neque servus neque liber—spiritales ergo,
sive qui praesunt sive qui obtemperant, spiritaliter
iudicant; non de cognitionibus spiritalibus, quae
lucent in firmamento—non enim oportet de tam
sublimi auctoritate iudicare—neque de ipso libro
tuo, etiamsi quid ibi non lucet, quoniam summittimus
ei nostrum intellectum, certumque habemus etiam
quod clausum est aspectibus nostris, recte veraciter-
que dictum esse. sic enim homo, licet iam spiritalis
et renovatus in agnitione dei secundum imaginem
eius, qui creavit eum, factor tamen legis debet esse,
non iudex. neque de illa distinctione iudicat spirita-
lium videlicet atque carnalium hominum, qui tuis,
deus noster, oculis noti sunt, et nullis adhuc nobis
apparuerunt operibus, ut ex fructibus eorum cognoscamus eos, sed tu, domine, iam scis eos et divisisti
et vocasti in occulto, antequam fieret firmamentum.

doth by the understanding of his mind, by the which CHAP. XXIII
he Perceiveth the things of the Spirit of God;
whereas otherwise, Man being in honour, hath no 1 Cor. ii. 14
understanding, and is compared unto the unreason- Ps. xlix. 20
able beasts, and is become like unto them. In thy
Church, therefore, O our God, according to thy grace
which thou hast bestowed unto it (For we are thy Eph. ii. 10
workmanship, created unto good works:) not those
only who are spiritually set over, but they also which
are spiritually set under those that are over them—
(for in this way hast thou Made man male and female,
in thy grace spiritual, in which according to the sex
of body There is neither male nor female, because
Neither Jew nor Greek, neither bond nor free):— Col. iii. 11
Spiritual persons therefore, (whether such as are set
over or such as obey,) do Judge spiritually; not concerning that spiritual knowledge Which shines in the
firmament, (for they ought not to pass their judgment upon so supreme authority:) nor concerning
thy book itself, even if something in it shines not
out clearly: for we submit our understanding unto
that, and hold for certain, that even that which
is shut from our eyes is yet most rightly and truly
spoken. For so a man, though he be Spiritual and
renewed unto the knowledge of God after his image
that created him; yet may he not presume to be A James iv. 11
judge of the law, but A doer only. Neither taketh he
upon him to judge of that distinction, I mean of
spiritual and carnal men; who are known unto thine
eyes, O our God, and have not as yet discovered
themselves unto us by any of their works, that
By their fruits we might be able to know them: Matt. vii. 16
but thou, Lord, dost even now know them, and
hast already Divided and Called them in secret,
or ever the Firmament was created. Nor doth

CAP.
XXIII

neque de turbidis huius saeculi populis quamquam spiritalis homo iudicat. quid enim ei de his, qui foris sunt, iudicare ignoranti, quis inde venturus sit in dulcedinem gratiae tuae et quis in perpetua inpietatis amaritudine remansurus ?

Ideoque homo, quem fecisti ad imaginem tuam, non accepit potestatem luminarium caeli, neque ipsius occulti caeli, neque diei et noctis, quae ante caeli constitutionem vocasti, neque congregationis aquarum, quod est mare : sed accepit potestatem piscium maris et volatilium caeli et omnium pecorum et omnis terrae et omnium repentium, quae repunt super terram. iudicat enim et approbat, quod recte, improbat autem, quod perperam invenerit ; sive in ea sollemnitate sacramentorum, quibus initiantur quos pervestigat in aquis multis misericordia tua ; sive in ea, qua ille piscis exhibetur, quem levatum de profundo terra pia comedit ; sive in verborum signis vocibusque subiectis auctoritati libri tui, tamquam sub firmamento volitantibus, interpretando, exponendo, disserendo, disputando, benedicendo ·atque invocando te, ore erumpentibus atque sonantibus signis, ut respondeat populus : amen. quibus omnibus vocibus corporaliter enuntiandis causa est abyssus saeculi et caecitas carnis, qua cogitata non possunt videri, ut opus sit instrepere in auribus. ita, quamvis multiplicentur volatilia super terram, ex aquis tamen

he though spiritual pass his censure upon the un- CHAP.
quiet people of this present world: for what hath XXIII
ignorant he to do, to judge those that are without, 1 Cor. v. 12
which of them is likely to come hereafter into the
sweetness of thy grace, and which is likely to continue in the perpetual bitterness of ungodliness?

Man therefore whom thou hast Made after thine
own image, hath not received Dominion over the
luminaries of heaven; nor over the secret heaven
itself: nor over the Day and the night, which thou
calledst before the foundation of heaven: nor yet
over the Gathering together of the waters, which is
the sea: but he hath received Dominion over the
fishes of the sea and the fowls of the air, and over
all cattle, and over all the earth, and over all creeping things which creep upon the earth. For he
judgeth and approveth that which is right; and he
disalloweth what he findeth amiss: be it either in
the solemnity of that Sacrament by which such are
admitted into the Church, as thy mercy searches out
in Many waters: or in that other in which that
Fish is received, which taken out of the deep, the
devout earth now feedeth upon: or else in the
expressions and sounds of words, subject to the
authority of thy book (like the fowls as it were
flying under the firmament); namely, by interpreting, expounding, discoursing, disputing, praising and
praying unto thee with the mouth, expressions
breaking forth with a loud sounding, that the people
may answer, Amen. For the vocal pronouncing of 1 Cor. xiv.
all which words, the cause is the abyss of this present 16
world, and the blindness of flesh, which cannot see
thoughts: so that necessary it is to speak loud unto
our ears. Thus, notwithstanding the Flying fowls
be multiplied upon the earth, yet they derive their

CAP.
XXIII
originem ducunt. iudicat etiam spiritalis appro-
bando, quod rectum, inprobando autem, quod perperam invenerit in operibus moribusque fidelium,
elemosynis tamquam terra fructifera, et de anima
viva mansuefactis affectionibus, in castitate, in
ieiuniis, in cogitationibus piis, de his, quae per sensum corporis percipiuntur. de his enim iudicare
nunc dicitur, in quibus et potestatem corrigendi
habet.

XXIV

CAP.
XXIV
SED quid est hoc et quale mysterium est ? ecce benedicis homines, o domine, ut crescant et multiplicentur
et impleant terram. nihilne nobis ex hoc innuis, ut
intellegamus aliquid, cur non ita benedixeris lucem,
quam vocasti diem, nec firmamentum caeli nec
luminaria nec sidera nec terram nec mare ? dicerem
te, deus noster, qui nos ad imaginem tuam creasti,
dicerem te hoc donum benedictionis homini proprie
voluisse largiri, nisi hoc modo benedixisses pisces et
coetos, ut crescerent et multiplicarentur et imple-
rent aquas maris, et volatilia multiplicarentur super
terram. item dicerem ad ea rerum genera pertinere
benedictionem hanc, quae gignendo ex semet ipsis
propagantur, si eam reperirem in arbustis et frutectis

beginning from the waters. The Spiritual man CHAP.
judgeth also by allowing of what is right, and by XXIII
disallowing what he finds amiss in the works and
manners of the faithful, their alms, which resemble
the Earth bringing forth fruit : and of the soul, Living
by taming her own affections in chastity, in fasting,
and in holy meditations : and of all those things too,
which are perceived by the senses of the body. Upon
all these is he now said to Judge ; and over all these
hath he absolute power of correction.

XXIV

He allegorizes upon increase and multiply

But what is this now, and what kind of mystery ? CHAP.
Behold, thou Blessest mankind, O Lord, that they XXIV
may Increase and multiply, and replenish the earth :
dost thou not give us a privy hint to learn by this,
why thou didst not as well bless the light which
thou Calledst day; or the Firmament of heaven, or
the luminaries, or the Stars, or the Earth, or the Sea ?
I might say, O God that Created us after thine own
image : I might say, that it had been thy good
pleasure to have bestowed this blessing peculiarly
upon man, hadst thou not in like manner blessed the
fishes and the whales, that they also should Increase
and multiply, and replenish the waters of the sea,
and that the Fowls should be multiplied upon the
earth. I might say likewise, that this blessing per-
tained properly unto those creatures, which are bred
of their own kind; had I found it given to the
fruit trees, and plants, and beasts of the earth. But

CAP.
XXIV

et in pecoribus terrae. nunc autem nec herbis et
lignis dictum est nec bestiis et serpentibus: crescite et multiplicamini, cum haec quoque omnia
sicut pisces et aves et homines gignendo augeantur
genusque custodiant.

Quid igitur dicam, lumen meum, veritas? quia
vacat hoc, quia inaniter ita dictum est? nequaquam,
pater pietatis, absit, ut hoc dicat servus verbi tui.
et si ego non intellego, quid hoc eloquio significes,
utantur eo melius meliores, id est intellegentiores
quam ego sum, unicuique quantum sapere dedisti.
placeat autem et confessio mea coram oculis tuis,
qua tibi confiteor credere me, domine, non incassum
te ita locutum, neque silebo, quod mihi lectionis
huius occasio suggerit. verum est enim, nec video,
quid impediat ita me sentire dicta figurata librorum
tuorum. novi enim multipliciter significari per
corpus, quod uno modo mente intellegitur, et multipliciter mente intellegi, quod uno modo per corpus
significatur. ecce simplex dilectio dei et proximi,
quam multiplicibus sacramentis et innumerabilibus
linguis et in unaquaque lingua innumerabilibus locu-
tionum modis corporaliter enuntiatur! ita crescunt
et multiplicantur fetus aquarum. adtende iterum
quisquis haec legis: ecce quod uno modo scriptura
offert et vox personat: in principio deus fecit
caelum et terram, nonne multipliciter intellegitur,

neither unto the herbs, nor the trees, nor the beasts, nor the serpents is it said, Increase and multiply: notwithstanding that all these as well as the fishes, fowls or men, do by generation both increase and continue their kind.

What then shall I say to it, O thou Truth my Light? Shall I say that it was idly, that it was vainly said? Not so, O Father of piety, far be it from a minister of thine own Word to say so. And if I fully understand not what that phrase meaneth, let others that are better, that is, more understanding than myself, make a better use of it; according as thou, O my God, hast enabled every man to understand. But let this confession of mine be pleasing in thine eyes; for that I confess unto thee, O Lord, how that I firmly believe thou spakest not that word in vain; nor will I conceal that which the occasion of reading this place hath put into my mind. For most true it is; nor do I see what should hinder me from thus understanding the figurative phrases of thy books. For I know a thing to be manifoldly signified by corporeal expressions, which the mind understands all one way: and another thing again understood many ways in the mind, which is signified but one way by corporeal expression. See, for example, the single love of God and our neighbour, in what a variety of sacraments, and innumerable languages; and in each several language in how innumerable phrases of speaking, it is corporeally expressed: and thus doth this fry of the waters Increase and multiply. Observe again, reader, whoever thou art: behold, I say, that which the Scripture delivers, and the voice pronounces one way only: In the beginning God created heaven and earth; is it not understood many a several way; not

non errorum fallacia, sed verarum intellegentiarum
generibus?   ita crescunt et multiplicantur fetus
hominum.

Itaque si naturas ipsas rerum non allegorice, sed
proprie cogitemus, ad omnia, quae de seminibus
gignuntur, convenit verbum: crescite et multiplicamini; si autem figurate posita ista tractemus—quod
potius arbitror intendisse scripturam, quae utique
non supervacue solis aquatilium et hominum fetibus
istam benedictionem adtribuit—invenimus quidem
multitudines et in creaturis spiritalibus atque corporalibus tamquam in caelo et terra, et in animis
iustis et iniquis tamquam in luce et tenebris, et in
sanctis auctoribus, per quos lex ministrata est, tamquam in firmamento, quod solidatum est inter aquam
et aquam, et in societate amaricantium populorum
tamquam in mari, et in studio piarum animarum
tamquam in arida, et in operibus misericordiae
secundum praesentem vitam tamquam in herbis
seminalibus et lignis fructiferis, et in spiritalibus
donis manifestatis ad utilitatem sicut in luminaribus
caeli, et in affectibus formatis ad temperantiam tamquam in anima viva: in his omnibus nanciscimur
multitudines et ubertates et incrementa; sed quod
ita crescat et multiplicetur, ut una res multis modis
enuntietur et una enuntiatio multis modis intellegatur, non invenimus, nisi in signis corporaliter editis
et rebus intellegibiliter excogitatis.   signa corporaliter edita generationes aquarum propter necessarias

with any deceit of error, but in several kinds of very CHAP. true senses? Thus does man's offspring Increase and XXIV multiply.

If therefore we can conceive of the natures of things, not allegorically, but properly; then may the phrase, Increase and multiply very well agree unto all things whatsoever that come of any kind of seed. But if we intreat of the words as figuratively spoken, (which I rather suppose to be the purpose of the Scripture, which doth not, I believe, superfluously attribute this benediction unto the increase of watery and human creatures only :) then verily do we find multitudes, both amongst creatures spiritual, and creatures corporeal, as in Heaven and earth; and amongst souls both righteous and unrighteous, as in Light and darkness; and amongst holy authors, who have been the ministers of the law unto us, as in the Firmament which is settled betwixt the waters and the waters; and amid the society of people yet in the bitterness of infidelity, as in the Sea; and in the zeal of holy souls, as in the Dry land; and amongst the works of mercy done in this life, as in the Herb bearing seed, and in the fruitful trees; and amongst Spiritual gifts shining forth for our profit, as in the luminaries of heaven; and amongst men's affections reformed unto temperance, as in the Living soul : in all these instances we meet with multitudes, abundance, and increase. But what should Increase and multiply, so that one thing may be understood and expressed many ways, and one of those expressions understood several ways too, we do nowhere find, except in signs corporeally pronounced, and in things intellectually conceived. By corporeally pronounced we understand the generations of the waters: necessarily

CAP.
XXIV
causas carnalis profunditatis, res autem intellegibiliter excogitatas generationes humanas propter rationis fecunditatem intelleximus. et ideo credidimus utrique horum generi dictum esse abs te, domine: crescite et multiplicamini. in hac enim benedictione concessam nobis a te facultatem ac potestatem accipio et multis modis enuntiare, quod uno modo intellectum tenuerimus, et multis modis intellegere, quod obscure uno modo enuntiatum legerimus. sic implentur aquae maris, quae non moventur nisi variis significatibus, sic et fetibus humanis impletur et terra, cuius ariditas apparet in studio, et dominatur ei ratio.

XXV

CAP.
XXV
Volo etiam dicere, domine deus meus, quod me consequens tua scriptura conmonet, et dicam nec verebor. vera enim dicam te mihi inspirante, quod ex eis verbis voluisti ut dicerem. neque enim alio praeter te inspirante credo me verum dicere, cum tu sis veritas, omnis autem homo mendax. et ideo qui loquitur mendacium, de suo loquitur. ergo ut verum loquar de tuo loquor. ecce dedisti nobis in escam omne

occasioned by the depth of the flesh: by things CHAP. XXIV intellectually conceived we understand human generations, on account of the fruitfulness of reason. And for this end we believe thee, Lord, to have said to both these kinds, Increase and multiply. For within the compass of this blessing, I conceive thee to have granted us a power and a faculty, both to express several ways that which we understand but one; and to understand several ways, that which we read to be obscurely delivered but in one. Thus are the Waters of the sea replenished, which are not moved but by several significations: thus with human increase is the Earth also replenished, whose Dryness appears by its desire, over See ch. xvii. which reason ruleth.

XXV

He allegorically compareth the Fruits of the Earth unto the Duties of Piety

I WILL now also say, O Lord my God, that which CHAP. XXV the following Scripture puts me in mind of: yea, I will say it without fear. For I will say the truth, thyself inspiring me with what thy pleasure was to have me say out of those words. For by no other inspiration than thine, can I believe myself to speak truth; seeing Thou art the very truth, and every man Rom. iii. 4 a liar. He therefore that Speaketh a lie, speaketh Ps. cxvi. 11 it of his own: that therefore I may speak truth, I speak it of thine. Behold, thou hast given unto us For food every green herb bearing seeds, which Gen. i. 29

CAP.
XXV

faenum sativum seminans semen, quod est super
omnem terram, et omne lignum, quod habet in
se fructum seminis sativi. nec nobis solis, sed et
omnibus avibus caeli et bestiis terrae atque serpentibus; piscibus autem et coetis magnis non
dedisti haec. dicebamus enim eis terrae fructibus
significari et in allegoria figurari opera misericordiae,
quae huius vitae necessitatibus exhibentur ex terra
fructifera. talis terra erat pius Onesiphorus, cuius
domui dedisti misericordiam, quia frequenter Paulum
tuum refrigeravit et catenam eius non erubuit. hoc
fecerunt et fratres et tali fruge fructificaverunt, qui
quod ei deerat suppleverunt ex Macedonia. quomodo
autem dolet quaedam ligna, quae fructum ei debitum
non dederunt, ubi ait: in prima mea defensione nemo
mihi affuit, sed omnes me dereliquerunt: non illis
inputetur. ista enim debentur eis, qui ministrant
doctrinam rationalem per intellegentias divinorum
mysteriorum, et ita eis debentur tamquam hominibus.
debentur autem eis sicut animae vivae, praebentibus
se ad imitandum in omni continentia. item debentur
eis tamquam volatilibus, propter benedictiones eorum,
quae multiplicantur super terram, quoniam in omnem
terram exiit sonus eorum.

is upon the face of all the earth: and every tree CHAP.
which has in itself fruit yielding seed to sow.   And XXV
that not to us alone, but also To all the fowls Gen. i. 30
of the air, and to the beasts of the earth, and to
all creeping things: but unto the Fishes and to the
great whales, hast thou not given these.   Now by
these Fruits of the earth, we said before that the
works of mercy were signified, and figured out in an
allegory; which for the necessities of this life are
afforded us out of a fruitful earth.   Such an Earth was
the devout Onesiphorus, unto whose house thou gavest
mercy, who often refreshed thy Paul, and was not 1 Tim. i. 16
ashamed of his chain.   Thus did also the brethren,
and such fruit did they bear, Who out of Macedonia 2 Cor. viii. 2
supplied his wants.   But how much grieves he for
such trees, as did not afford him the fruit due unto
him, where he saith: At my first answer no man 2 Tim. iv. 16
stood by me, but all men forsook me: let it not be
laid to their charge.   For these fruits are due unto
such as minister the spiritual doctrine unto us, out
of their understanding of the divine mysteries: and
they are due so to them, as they are men: yea, and
due so unto them also, as to the living soul, in that
they give themselves as patterns of imitation in all
continency.   And so are they due unto them also as
flying fowls; for their blessings which are multiplied
upon the earth; because their sound is gone out into
all lands.

XXVI

CAP.
XXVI

PASCUNTUR autem his escis qui laetantur eis, nec illi laetantur eis, quorum deus venter. neque enim et in illis, qui praebent ista, ea, quae dant, fructus est, sed quo animo dant. itaque ille, qui deo serviebat, non suo ventri, video plane, unde gaudeat, video et congratulor ei valde. acceperat enim a Philippensibus quae per Epaphroditum miserant ; sed tamen unde gaudeat, video. unde autem gaudet, inde pascitur, quia in veritate loquens : Gavisus sum, inquit, magnifice in domino, qui tandem aliquando repullulastis sapere pro me, in quo sapiebatis; taedium autem habuistis. isti ergo diuturno taedio marcuerant et quasi exaruerant ab isto fructu boni operis, et gaudet eis, quia repullularunt, non sibi, quia eius indigentiae subvenerunt. ideo secutus ait : Non quod desit aliquid dico ; ego enim didici, in quibus sum, sufficiens esse. scio et minus habere, scio et abundare ; in omnibus et in omni imbutus sum, et saturari et esurire et abundare et penuriam pati : omnia possum in eo, qui me confortat.

Vnde ergo gaudes, o Paule magne ? unde gaudes,

448

XXVI

The Pleasure and the Profit redounding to us out of a good Turn done unto our Neighbour

THEY now are fed by these fruits, that are delighted with them, nor are they delighted with them, whose belly is their god. Neither yet even in them that yield them, are the things they give the fruit; but the mind, with which they give. He therefore that served God and not his own belly, I plainly see the thing that caused him so to rejoice, and I rejoice with him. For he hath received from the Philippians, what they had sent by Epaphroditus unto him: and yet I still perceive the cause of his rejoicings. For whereat he rejoiced, upon that he fed, because he speaking, as truth was, of it: I rejoiced, saith he, greatly in the Lord, that now at last your care of me hath flourished again, wherein ye were also careful, but it was tedious unto you. These Philippians had therefore now even dried up with a longsome irksomeness, and withered as it were, in respect of the fruit of this good work: and he now rejoiceth for them that they flourished again; not for himself, because they supplied his wants. Therefore saith he afterwards: I speak somewhat, not in respect of want, for I have learned in whatsoever state I am, therewith to be content. I know both how to lack, and I know how to abound: everywhere, and in all things I am instructed, both to be full, and to be hungry; both to abound, and to suffer need. I can do all things through him which strengtheneth me.

Of what art thou so glad O great Paul, of what art

unde pasceris, homo renovate in agnitionem dei
secundum imaginem eius, qui creavit te, et anima viva
tanta continentia et lingua volatilis loquens mysteria?
talibus quippe animantibus ista esca debetur. quid
est, quod te pascit? laetitia. quod sequitur audiam:
verum tamen, inquit, bene fecistis conmunicantes
tribulationi meae. hinc gaudet, hinc pascitur, quia
illi bene fecerunt, non quia eius angustia relaxata est,
qui dicit tibi: In tribulatione dilatasti mihi, quia et
abundare et penuriam pati novit in te, qui confortas
eum. scitis enim, inquit, etiam vos, Filippenses,
quoniam in principio evangelii, cum ex Macedonia
sum profectus, nulla mihi ecclesia conmunicavit in
ratione dati et accepti nisi vos soli, quia et Thessaloni-
cam et semel et iterum usibus meis misistis. ad haec
bona opera eos redisse nunc gaudet, et repullulasse
laetatur tamquam revivescente fertilitate agri.

Numquid propter usus suos, quia dixit: Vsibus
meis misistis, numquid propterea gaudet? non propterea. et hoc unde scimus? quoniam ipse sequitur
dicens: Non quia quaero datum, sed requiro fructum.
didici a te, deus meus, inter datum et fructum discernere. datum est res ipsa, quam dat, qui impertitur
haec necessaria, veluti est nummus, cibus, potus, vesti-
mentum, tectum, adiutorium. fructus autem bona
et recta voluntas datoris est. non enim ait magister
bonus: Qui susceperit prophetam tantum, sed addidit:
In nomine prophetae; neque ait tantum: Qui susceperit iustum, sed addidit: In nomine iusti; ita

thou so glad? What is it thou so feedest upon, O CHAP.
thou man, renewed unto the knowledge of God, XXVI
after the image of him that created thee, thou
living soul, of so much continency, thou tongue of
the flying fowls speaking mysteries? (For to such
creatures, is this food due.) What is it that thus
feeds thee? Joy? I will list then to what follows:
Notwithstanding, ye have well done, that ye did Phil. iv. 14
share with my affliction. For this he rejoiceth,
upon this he fed: even because they had well
done, not because his strait was eased by them:
his, who saith unto thee: Thou hast enlarged me Ps. iv. 1
when I was in distress: for that he knew to abound,
and to suffer want, in thee who strengthenest him.
For ye Philippians know, saith he, that in the
beginning of the Gospel, when I departed from
Macedonia, no Church shared with me as con-
cerning giving and receiving, but ye only. For even Phil. iv. 16
to Thessalonica ye sent once and again unto my
necessity. Unto these good works he now rejoiceth
that they are returned; and he is glad that they
flourished again, as when a fruitful field revives.

Was it for his own necessities, because he said, ye
sent unto my necessities? Rejoiceth he for that?
Verily not for that. But how know we that? Because
himself says immediately: not because I desire a gift,
but I desire fruit. I have learned of thyself, O my
God, to distinguish betwixt a gift and fruit. A gift
is the very thing which he gives, that imparts these
necessaries unto us; as money, meat, drink, clothing,
harbour, help: but the fruit, is the good and the
upright will of the giver. For our good Master says
not barely: He that receiveth a prophet, but adds, Matt. x. 41,
in the name of a prophet. Not only does he say: 42
He that receiveth a righteous man, but adds, in the

CAP.
XXVI
quippe ille mercedem prophetae, iste mercedem iusti
accipiet. nec solum ait: Qui calicem aquae frigidae
potum dederit uni ex minimis meis, sed addidit:
Tantum in nomine discipuli, et sic adiunxit: Amen
dico vobis, non perdet mercedem suam. datum est
suscipere prophetam, suscipere iustum, porrigere
calicem aquae frigidae discipulo; fructus autem in
nomine prophetae, in nomine iusti, in nomine discipuli hoc facere. fructu pascitur Helias a vidua
sciente, quod hominem dei pasceret, et propter hoc
pasceret; per corvum autem dato pascebatur. nec
interior Helias, sed exterior pascebatur, qui posset
etiam talis cibi egestate corrumpi.

XXVII

CAP.
XXVII
IDEOQUE dicam, quod verum est coram te, domine,
cum homines idiotae atque infideles, (quibus initiandis
atque lucrandis necessaria sunt sacramenta initiorum
et magnalia miraculorum, quae nomine piscium et
coetorum significari credimus,) suscipiunt corporaliter
reficiendos aut in aliquo usu praesentis vitae adiuvan-
dos pueros tuos, cum id quare faciendum sit et quo
pertineat ignorent, nec illi istos pascunt nec isti ab
illis pascuntur; quia nec illi haec sancta et recta volun-

name of a righteous man : one verily shall receive
the reward of a prophet ; and the other the reward
of a righteous man. Nor saith he only : He that shall
give to drink a cup of cold water unto one of my
little ones, but he adds in the name of a disciple :
and so concludeth : verily I say unto you, he shall
not lose his reward. The gift here is, to receive a
prophet, to receive a righteous man, to give a cup of
cold water to a disciple : but the fruit is to do it in
the name of a prophet, in the name of a righteous
man, in the name of a disciple. With fruit was
Elijah fed by the widow that knew she fed a man of
God ; and even therefore she did feed him : but with
a gift did the ravens feed him : nor was the inner
man of Elijah so fed, but the outer man only ; who
might also for want of that food have perished.

XXVII

He allegorizes upon the fishes and the whales

I WILL therefore, O Lord, speak what is true in thy
sight : namely, that when ignorant men and infidels
(for the gaining and admitting of whom into the
Church, these initial Sacraments, and the mighty
workings of miracles are necessary, which we
suppose to be signified under the name of Fishes
and Whales) do entertain for bodily refreshment,
or otherwise succour with something useful for this
present life unto thy children ; whenas themselves
be ignorant, why this is to be done, and to what
end, neither do those feed these, nor are these fed
by those : because that neither do the one sort do it

CAP.
XXVII

tate operantur nec isti eorum datis, ubi fructum nondum vident, laetantur.   inde quippe animus pascitur,
unde laetatur.   et ideo pisces et coeti non vescuntur
escis, quas non germinat nisi iam terra ab amaritudine
marinorum fluctuum distincta atque discreta.

XXVIII

CAP.
XXVIII

Et vidisti, deus, omnia quae fecisti, et ecce bona
valde, quia et nos videmus ea, et ecce omnia bona
valde.   in singulis generibus operum tuorum, cum
dixisses, ut fierent, et facta essent, illud atque illud
vidisti quia bonum est.   septiens numeravi scriptum
esse te vidisse, quia bonum est quod fecisti ; et
hoc octavum est, quia vidisti omnia quae fecisti, et
ecce non solum bona sed etiam valde bona, tamquam simul omnia.   nam singula tantum bona erant,
simul autem omnia et bona et valde.   hoc dicunt
etiam quaeque pulchra corpora, quia longe multo
pulchrius est corpus, quod ex membris pulchris omnibus constat, quam ipsa membra singula, quorum ordi-
natissimo conventu conpletur universum, quamvis et
illa etiam singillatim pulchra sint.

out of an holy and upright intent; nor do the other CHAP. sort rejoice at their gifts, where they as yet behold XXVII no fruit. For upon that is the mind fed, of which it is glad. And therefore do not the Fishes and Whales feed upon such meats as the Earth brings not forth, until after it was separated and Divided from the bitterness of the Sea waters.

XXVIII

Very good, why added last of all?

AND Thou, O God, sawest everything that thou hadst CHAP. made, and behold it was very good: because we also XXVIII have seen the same, and lo, everything is Very good. Gen. i. 31 After every several kind of thy works, when thou hadst said the word that they should be made, and they were made, thou then sawest both this and that, That it was good. Seven times have I counted it to be written that thou Sawest that that was good, which thou madest: this is the eighth, that thou Sawest everything that thou hadst made, and behold, it was not only Good, but also Very good, as being now altogether. For severally they were only Good; but all together, both good, and Very good. In this manner is every kind of body said to be fair; by reason that a body is far more beautiful which is made up of members, all beautiful, than the same members are, when by themselves: by whose most orderly conjuncture, the whole groweth to be complete; notwithstanding that the members severally viewed be also beautiful.

455

XXIX

CAP.
XXIX

Et attendi, ut invenirem, utrum septiens vel octiens videris, quia bona sunt opera tua, cum tibi placuerunt, et in tua visione non inveni tempora, per quae intellegerem, quod totiens videris quae fecisti, et dixi : O domine, nonne ista scriptura tua vera est, quoniam tu verax et veritas edidisti eam ? cur ergo tu mihi dicis non esse in tua visione tempora, et ita scriptura tua mihi dicit per singulos dies ea quae fecisti te vidisse, quia bona sunt, et cum ea numerarem, inveni quotiens ? ad haec tu dicis mihi, (quoniam tu es deus meus et dicis voce forti in aure interiore servo tuo perrumpens meam surditatem et clamans :) "o homo, nempe quod scriptura mea dicit, ego dico. et tamen illa temporaliter dicit, verbo autem meo tempus non accedit, quia aequali mecum aeternitate consistit. sic ea, quae vos per spiritum meum videtis, ego video, sicut ea, quae vos per spiritum meum dicitis, ego dico. atque ita cum vos temporaliter ea videatis, non ego temporaliter video, quemadmodum, cum vos temporaliter ea dicatis, non ego temporaliter dico."

XXIX

God's Works are good for ever

AND I looked narrowly to find whether it were CHAP.
seven or eight times that thou sawest that thy works XXIX
were good, whenas they pleased thee : and in that
seeing of thine I found no times by direction of which
I might understand how that thou sawest so often,
that which thou hadst made. And I said : Lord, is
not this thy Scripture true, since thou art true, and
thou who art Truth hast set it forth ? Why then
dost thou say unto me, That in thy seeing there
be no times ? whereas thy Scripture tells me, that
what thou madest every day, thou sawest that it
was good : and when I counted them, I found how
often ? Unto this thou answeredst me, (for thou art
my God, and with a strong voice thou tellest thy
servant in his inner ear, breaking through my deafness, and crying) O man, that which my Scripture
sayeth, that I myself say : and yet doth that speak
in time, whereas mine own word falls not within the
compass of time ; because my word consists in equal
eternity with myself. Even thus the selfsame things
which you men see through my Spirit, do I also see ;
like as what you speak by my Spirit, I myself speak.
And on the other side, whenas you see the very same
things in compass of time, I myself do not see them
in the compass of time ; as when you speak them in
time, I speak them not in time.

XXX

CAP.
XXX
Et audivi, domine deus meus, et elinxi stillam dulce-
dinis ex tua veritate, et intellexi, quoniam sunt
quidam, quibus displicent opera tua, et multa eorum
dicunt te fecisse necessitate conpulsum, sicut fabricas
caelorum et conpositiones siderum, et hoc non de tuo,
sed iam fuisse alibi creata et aliunde, quae tu con-
traheres et conpaginares atque contexeres, cum de
hostibus victis mundana moenia molireris, ut ea
constructione devincti adversus te iterum rebellare
non possent; alia vero nec fecisse te nec omnino con-
pegisse, sicut omnes carnes et minutissima quaeque
animantia et quidquid radicibus terram tenet, sed
hostilem mentem naturamque aliam non abs te con-
ditam tibique contrariam in inferioribus mundi locis
ista gignere atque formare. insani dicunt haec, quoniam non per spiritum tuum vident opera tua nec te
cognoscunt in eis.

XXX

Against those who dislike God's Works

AND I overheard, O Lord my God, and I sucked a drop of sweetness out of thy truth: and I understood that certain men there be who mislike of thy good works: and who say, that thou madest many of them, merely compelled by necessity; instancing the fabric of the heavens, and the ordering of the stars: and that thou never madest them of thyself, but that they were otherwhere and from other sources created; which thou only drewest together, and joinedst one to another, and framedst up, at such time as out of thine enemies now overcome thou raisedst up the walls of the world, that by this building they being utterly bound down, might never again be able to rebel against thee. As for other things, they say, thou never at all madest them, nor ever so much as joinedst them together, instancing all kinds of flesh, and all sorts of these smaller creatures, and whatsoever hath its root in the earth: but that a certain mind in enmity with thee, and another nature which thou createdst not, and which was contrary unto thee, did, in these lower stages of the world beget and frame these things. Mad men are they to affirm thus: because they look not upon thy works by thy Spirit; neither do they recognize thee in them.

XXXI

CAP.
XXXI

Qui autem per spiritum tuum vident ea, tu vides in eis. ergo cum vident, quia bona sunt, tu vides, quia bona sunt, et quaecumque propter te placent, tu in eis places, et quae per spiritum tuum placent nobis, tibi placent in nobis. quis enim scit hominum, quae sunt hominis, nisi spiritus hominis, qui in ipso est? sic et quae dei sunt nemo scit nisi spiritus dei. nos autem, inquit, non spiritum huius mundi accepimus, sed spiritum, qui ex deo est, ut sciamus quae a deo donata sunt nobis. et admoneor, ut dicam : certe nemo scit, quae dei, nisi spiritus dei. quomodo ergo scimus et nos, quae a deo donata sunt nobis ? respondetur mihi, quoniam quae per eius spiritum scimus etiam sic nemo scit nisi spiritus dei. sicut enim recte dictum est: Non enim vos estis, qui loquimini, eis, qui in dei spiritu loquerentur, sic recte dicitur : "non vos estis, qui scitis" eis, qui in dei spiritu sciunt. nihilo minus igitur recte dicitur : "non vos estis, qui videtis" eis, qui in spiritu dei vident: ita quidquid in spiritu dei vident quia bonum est, non ipsi, sed deus videt, quia bonum est. aliud ergo est, ut putet quisque malum esse quod bonum est, quales supra dicti sunt ; aliud, ut quod bonum est videat homo, quia bonum est, (sicut multis tua

460

XXXI

The Godly allow that which is pleasing to God

But as many as by thy Spirit discern these things, CHAP.
in them thou seest. Therefore when they see that XXXI
these things are Good, thou seest that they are
Good; and whatsoever for thy sake gives content,
'tis thou that givest content in it; and what things
by means of the Spirit please us, please thee in
us. For what man knoweth the things of a man, 1 Cor. ii. 11
save the spirit of a man which is in him? Even so
the things of God knoweth no man, but the Spirit of
God. Now we, saith he, have received not the spirit
of this world, but the spirit which is from God, that
we might know the things that are freely given to us
of God. I am here put in mind still to say, truly the
things of God knoweth no man, but the Spirit of God:
how then do we also know what things are given
us of God? Answer is made to me; that those
things which we know by his Spirit, even so no
man knoweth them, but the Spirit of God. For as
it is rightly said, unto those that were to speak
by the Spirit, It is not you that speak; so is it as Matt. x. 20
rightly said to them that know through the Spirit of
God, it is not you that know. And no less then is
it rightly said to those that see through the Spirit of
God, It is not you that see: so whatsoever through
the Spirit of God they see to be good, 'tis not they,
but God that sees that it is Good. 'Tis one thing
therefore for a man to think that to be ill which
indeed is good, as the forenamed Manichees do:
and another thing that what is good, a man should
see to be so, because indeed it is good, (just as

461

CAP.
XXXI

creatura placet, quia bona est, quibus tamen non tu
places in ea; unde frui magis ipsa quam te volunt:)
aliud autem, ut, cum aliquid videt homo quia bonum
est, deus in illo videat, quia bonum est, ut scilicet
ille ametur in eo, quod fecit, qui non amaretur nisi
per spiritum, quem dedit; quoniam caritas dei diffusa est in cordibus nostris per spiritum sanctum, qui
datus est nobis, per quem videmus, quia bonum est,
quidquid aliquo modo est : ab illo enim est, qui non
aliquo modo est, sed est, est.

XXXII

CAP.
XXXII

GRATIAS tibi, domine! videmus caelum et terram,
sive corporalem partem superiorem atque inferiorem,
sive spiritalem corporalemque creaturam, atque in
ornatu harum partium, quibus constat vel universa
mundi moles vel universa omnino creatura, videmus
lucem factam divisamque a tenebris. videmus firmamentum caeli, sive inter spiritales aquas superiores
et corporales inferiores, primarium corpus mundi,
sive hoc spatium aeris, quia et hoc vocatur caelum,
per quod vagantur volatilia caeli, inter aquas, quae
vaporaliter eis superferuntur et serenis etiam noctibus rorant, et has, quae in terris graves fluitant.
videmus congregatarum aquarum speciem per campos

thy creatures be pleasing unto divers, because they CHAP.
be good; whom for all that thou thyself dost not XXXI
please in those creatures; so that rather would they
enjoy them, than thee :) yea, and another thing it is,
that when a man sees anything that is good 'tis God
that sees in him that it is good; and that to this end
plainly, that himself might be loved in that which he
made : for he should never be loved, but by the Holy
Ghost which he hath given.   Because the love of Rom. v. 5
God is shed abroad in our hearts by the Holy Ghost,
which is given unto us : by whom we see that whatsoever in any degree is is good.   For from him it is,
who himself is not in degree, but he is, he is.   Ex. iii. 14

XXXII

He briefly sums up the Works of God

THANKS to thee, O Lord. We behold the Heaven and CHAP.
the Earth, be it either the corporeal part, superior XXXII
or inferior; or the spiritual and corporeal creation :
and in the adorning of these parts, of which the
universal pile of this world, or the whole creation together doth consist, we see Light made, and Divided Gen. i. 4
from the darkness. We see the Firmament of heaven,
either that which is Between the spiritual upper
Waters and the inferior corporeal Waters, the primary
body of the world, or this space of air (since this
is also styled heaven) through which wander the
fowls of heaven; even Betwixt those waters which
are in vapours lifted up above it, and which in clear
nights distil down in dew again, and those heavier
waters which flow along on the earth. We behold
a face of Waters gathered together in those fields of

maris, et aridam terram vel nudatam vel formatam, ut esset visibilis et composita herbarumque
atque arborum mater. videmus luminaria fulgere
desuper, solem sufficere diei, lunam et stellas con-
solari noctem, atque his omnibus notari et significari
tempora. videmus umidam usquequaque naturam
piscibus et beluis et alitibus fecundatam, quod aeris
corpulentia, quae volatus avium portat, aquarum
exhalatione concrescit. videmus terrenis animalibus
faciem terrae decorari, hominemque ad imaginem et
similitudinem tuam, cunctis inrationabilibus animantibus ipsa tua imagine ac similitudine, hoc est rationis
et intellegentiae virtute, praeponi; et quemadmodum
in eius anima aliud est, quod consulendo dominatur,
aliud, quod subditur ut obtemperet, sic viro factam
esse etiam corporaliter feminam, quae haberet quidem
in mente rationabilis intellegentiae parem naturam,
sexu tamen corporis ita masculino sexui subiceretur,
quemadmodum subicitur appetitus actionis ad con-
cipiendam de ratione mentis recte agendi sollertiam
videmus haec et singula bona et omnia bona valde.

the sea; and the Dry land both bared and formed so CHAP. as to be visible and harmonized; and the mother of XXXII trees. We behold the luminaries shining from above, the Sun to serve the day, the Moon and the Stars to cheer the night; and by all these Times to be marked out and signified. We behold on all sides a moist element, teeming with fishes, beasts, and birds: because the grossness of the air which bears up the flights of birds, thickeneth itself by the exhalation of the waters. We behold the face of the earth decked up with earthly creatures, and Man created after thine own image and likeness, even through that very Image and likeness (that is the power of reason and understanding) made superior to all unreasonable creatures. And like as in his soul there is one power which bears rule by directing, and another nature made subject, that it might obey, so was there for man, corporeally also, made a woman, who in the mind of her reasonable understanding should have a parity of nature, but in the sex of her body, should be in like manner subject to the sex of her husband, as the appetite of doing is fain to conceive the skill of right doing from the reason of the mind. These things we behold, and they are all severally Good, and all together Very good.

XXXIII

CAP.
XXXIII

LAUDANT te opera tua, ut amemus te, et amamus te, ut laudent te opera tua. habent initium et finem ex tempore, ortum et occasum, profectum et defectum, speciem et privationem. habent ergo consequentia mane et vesperam, partim latenter partim evidenter. de nihilo enim a te, non de te facta sunt, non de aliqua non tua vel quae antea fuerit, sed de concreata, id est simul a te creata materia, quia eius informitatem sine ulla temporis interpositione formasti. nam cum aliud sit caeli et terrae materies, aliud caeli et terrae species, materiem quidem de omnino nihilo, mundi autem speciem de informi materia, simul tamen utrumque fecisti, ut materiam forma nulla morae intercapedine sequeretur.

XXXIV

CAP.
XXXIV

INSPEXIMUS etiam, propter quorum figurationem ista vel tali ordine fieri vel tali ordine scribi voluisti, et vidimus, quia bona sunt singula et omnia bona valde, in verbo tuo, in unico tuo, caelum et terram, caput et

466

XXXIII

How every Creature ought to praise the Creator

THY works praise thee, that we may love thee, CHAP.
and we love thee, that thy works may praise thee. XXXIII
They have their beginning and their ending from
time, their rising and their falling, their growth and
their decaying, their form and their privation. They
have therefore their succession of morning and evening, part secretly, part apparently: for they were
made of nothing, by thee, not of thee; not of any
matter that is not thine, nor of any that was before,
but of a matter concreated, that is, at the same time
created by thee: because that into its state Without
form, thou didst introduce a form, without any
interval of time between. For seeing the matter
of Heaven and Earth is one thing, and the form of
heaven and earth is another thing; thou madest
the matter of merely nothing, but the form of the
world out of the matter Without form: yet madest
both matter and form so just at one instant, that the
form should follow the matter, without any respite
of delay between.

XXXIV

The Order and various fruit of a Christian Life

WE have also looked into this, what thou willedst to be CHAP.
shadowed forth by making these things in this order, XXXIV
or having them described in this order. And we have
seen that all things are Good singly of themselves, and
one with another Very good, in thy Word, even in thy

corpus ecclesiae, in praedestinatione ante omnia tempora sine mane et vespera. ubi autem coepisti praedestinata temporaliter exequi, ut occulta manifestares et incomposita nostra conponeres—quoniam super nos erant peccata nostra, et in profundum tenebrosum abieramus abs te, et spiritus tuus bonus superferebatur ad subveniendum nobis in tempore opportuno—et iustificasti impios et distinxisti eos ab iniquis, et solidasti auctoritatem libri tui inter superiores, qui tibi dociles essent, et inferiores, qui eis subderentur, et congregasti societatem infidelium in unam conspirationem, ut apparerent studia fidelium, ut tibi opera misericordiae parerent, distribuentes etiam pauperibus terrenas facultates ad adquirenda caelestia. et inde accendisti quaedam luminaria in firmamento, verbum vitae habentes sanctos tuos, et spiritalibus donis praelata sublimi auctoritate fulgentes; et inde ad imbuendas infideles gentes sacramenta et miracula visibilia vocesque verborum secundum firmamentum libri tui, quibus etiam fideles benedicerentur, ex materia corporali produxisti; et deinde fidelium animam vivam per affectus ordinatos continentiae vigore formasti, atque inde tibi soli mentem subditam, et nullius auctoritatis humanae ad imitandum indigentem, renovasti ad imaginem et similitudinem tuam praestantique intellectui rationabilem actionem tamquam viro feminam subdidisti, omnibusque tuis ministeriis ad

468

only begotten, both Heaven and Earth, the head and CHAP. XXXIV
body of the Church, in thy predestination before all
times, without Morning and Evening. But when thou Gen. i. 1, 2
begannest in time to put in execution thy pre-
destinated decrees, to the end thou mightest reveal
hidden things, and rectify disordered things; (for our
sins hung over us, and we had sunk from thee into the
darksome Deep, and thy good Spirit hovered over us,
to help us in due season;) then thou didst justify the Rom. iv. 5
ungodly, and Dividedst them from the wicked; and
thou madest the Firmament of the authority of thy
book between those Above, who were to be docile
to thee, and those Under, who were to be subject
to them: and thou Gatheredst together the society
of unbelievers into one conspiracy, that the zeal of
the faithful might appear, and that they might
bring forth works of mercy to thee, distributing
even to the poor their earthly riches, to obtain
heavenly. And after this didst thou kindle certain
luminaries in the firmament, even thy holy ones,
holding forth the word of life; shining with spiritual
gifts by virtue of heavenly authority: after that
again for the initiation of the unbelieving Gentiles,
didst thou out of corporeal matter produce the
Sacraments, and certain visible miracles, and sounds
of words, according to the firmament of thy book;
by which the faithful should receive a blessing. Next
after that didst thou form the Living Soul of the
faithful, through their affections well ordered by the
vigour of continency: and after that the mind, subjected to thee alone and needing to imitate no human
authority, didst thou renew after thine own Image and
similitude; and didst subject its rational actions to
the excellency of the understanding, as a woman to
a man; and to all offices of thy ministry necessary for

CAP.
XXXIV
perficiendos fideles in hac vita necessariis, ab eisdem fidelibus ad usus temporales fructuosa in futurum opera praeberi voluisti. haec omnia videmus et bona sunt valde, quoniam tu ea vides in nobis, qui spiritum, quo ea videremus et in eis te amaremus, dedisti nobis.

XXXV

CAP.
XXXV
Domine deus, pacem da nobis—omnia enim praestitisti nobis—pacem quietis, pacem sabbati, pacem sine vespera. omnis quippe iste ordo pulcherrimus rerum valde bonarum modis suis peractis transiturus est: et mane quippe in eis factum est et vespera.

XXXVI

CAP.
XXXVI
Dies autem septimus sine vespera est nec habet occasum, quia sanctificasti eum ad permansionem sempiternam, ut id, quod tu post opera tua bona valde, quamvis ea quietus feceris, requievisti septimo die, hoc praeloquatur nobis vox libri tui, quod et nos post opera nostra ideo bona valde, quia tu

the perfecting of the faithful in this life, thou didst CHAP.
XXXIV will, that for their temporal uses such good things be given by the said faithful, as may be profitable to themselves in time to come. All these we See, and they are Very good, because thou seest them in us, who hast given unto us thy Spirit, by which we might see these things, and might love thee in them.

XXXV

He prays for Peace

GRANT, O Lord God, thy peace unto us : for thou CHAP.
XXXV hast given us all things. Give us the peace of quietness, the peace of the Sabbath, peace without any evening. For all this most goodly array of things so very good, having finished its course, is to pass away, for both a Morning and an Evening was made in them.

XXXVI

Why the seventh Day hath no Evening

BUT the seventh day is without any evening, nor CHAP.
XXXVI hath it any setting : even because thou hast sanctified it to an everlasting continuance ; that that which thyself didst after thy works which were Very good, Rest, namely, the Seventh day, (although even those works thou createdst without breaking thy rest) the same may the voice of thy book speak beforehand unto us ; namely, that we also after our works (which are therefore Very good, because thou hast given

CAP.
XXXVI
nobis ea donasti, sabbato vitae aeternae requiescamus in te.

XXXVII

CAP.
XXXVII
ETIAM tunc enim sic requiesces in nobis, quemadmodum nunc operaris in nobis, et ita erit illa requies tua per nos, quemadmodum sunt ista opera tua per nos. tu autem, domine, semper operaris et semper requiescis; nec vides ad tempus, nec moveris ad tempus, nec quiescis ad tempus; et tamen facis et visiones temporales et ipsa tempora et quietem ex tempore.

XXXVIII

CAP.
XXXVIII
Nos itaque ista quae fecisti videmus, quia sunt, tu autem quia vides ea, sunt. et nos foris vidimus, quia sunt, et intus, quia bona sunt: tu autem ibi vidisti facta, ubi vidisti facienda. et nos alio tempore moti sumus ad bene faciendum, posteaquam concepit de spiritu tuo cor nostrum; priore autem tempore ad male faciendum movebamur deserentes te: tu vero, deus une bone, numquam cessasti bene facere. et sunt quaedam bona opera nostra, ex munere quidem tuo, sed non sempiterna: post illa nos requieturos in

them to us) may Rest in thee in the Sabbath of life everlasting.

XXXVII

When God shall rest in us

FOR then also thou shalt so rest in us, as thou now workest in us : and so shall that rest be thine, through us ; even as these works are thine through us. But thou, O Lord, dost work always, and rest always too. Nor dost thou see for a time, nor art thou moved for a time, nor dost rest for a time ; and yet thou makest those things which are seen in time, yea, the very times themselves, and the rest which proceeds from time.

XXXVIII

God beholds created Things one Way, and Man another

WE therefore behold these things which thou hast created, because they are : but they are, because thou seest them. And we see without, that they are, and within, that they are good : but thou sawest them there already made, where thou sawest them, yet to be made. And we at a later time have been moved to do well, after that our heart had conceived the purpose of it by thy spirit : but at an earlier time we were moved to do evil, when we forsook thee : but thou O God, One and Good, didst never cease doing good. And some certain works of ours there be that be good, of thy gift, but not eternal : after them we trust to find repose in thy grand sanctification. But

CAP.
XXXVIII

tua grandi sanctificatione speramus. tu autem bonum
nullo indigens bono semper quietus es, quoniam tua
quies tu ipse es. et hoc intellegere quis
hominum dabit homini? quis angelus
angelo? quis angelus homini? a
te petatur, in te quaeratur, ad
te pulsetur: sic, sic accipie-
tur, sic invenietur, sic
aperietur.

thou being the Good, needing no good, art at rest
always, because thy rest thou art thyself. And what
man is he that can teach another man to understand
this ? Or what angel, another angel ? Or what
angel, man ? Let it be begged of thee,
be sought in thee, knocked for at
thee ; so, so shall it be received,
so shall it be found, and so
shall it be opened.

AMEN

INDEX

INDEX

478

INDEX

THE LOEB CLASSICAL LIBRARY

VOLUMES ALREADY PUBLISHED

Latin Authors

AMMIANUS MARCELLINUS. Translated by J. C. Rolfe. 3 Vols.

APULEIUS: THE GOLDEN ASS (METAMORPHOSES). W. Adlington (1566). Revised by S. Gaselee.

ST. AUGUSTINE: CITY OF GOD. 7 Vols. Vol. I. G. E. McCracken. Vols. II and VII. W. M. Green. Vol. III. D. Wiesen. Vol. IV. P. Levine. Vol. V. E. M. Sanford and W. M. Green. Vol. VI. W. C. Greene.

ST. AUGUSTINE, CONFESSIONS OF. W. Watts (1631). 2 Vols.

ST. AUGUSTINE, SELECT LETTERS. J. H. Baxter.

AUSONIUS. H. G. Evelyn White. 2 Vols.

BEDE. J. E. King. 2 Vols.

BOETHIUS: TRACTS and DE CONSOLATIONE PHILOSOPHIAE. Rev. H. F. Stewart and E. K. Rand. Revised by S. J. Tester.

CAESAR: ALEXANDRIAN, AFRICAN and SPANISH WARS. A. G. Way.

CAESAR: CIVIL WARS. A. G. Peskett.

CAESAR: GALLIC WAR. H. J. Edwards.

CATO: DE RE RUSTICA. VARRO: DE RE RUSTICA. H. B. Ash and W. D. Hooper.

CATULLUS. F. W. Cornish. TIBULLUS. J. B. Postgate. PERVIGILIUM VENERIS. J. W. Mackail.

CELSUS: DE MEDICINA. W. G. Spencer. 3 Vols.

CICERO: BRUTUS and ORATOR. G. L. Hendrickson and H. M. Hubbell.

[CICERO]: AD HERENNIUM. H. Caplan.

CICERO: DE ORATORE, etc. 2 Vols. Vol. I. DE ORATORE, Books I and II. E. W. Sutton and H. Rackham. Vol. II. DE ORATORE, Book III. DE FATO; PARADOXA STOICORUM; DE PARTITIONE ORATORIA. H. Rackham.

CICERO: DE FINIBUS. H. Rackham.

CICERO: DE INVENTIONE, etc. H. M. Hubbell.

CICERO: DE NATURA DEORUM and ACADEMICA. H. Rackham.

CICERO: DE OFFICIIS. Walter Miller.

CICERO: DE REPUBLICA and DE LEGIBUS. Clinton W. Keyes.

CICERO: DE SENECTUTE, DE AMICITIA, DE DIVINATIONE. W. A. Falconer.

CICERO: IN CATILINAM, PRO FLACCO, PRO MURENA, PRO SULLA. New version by C. Macdonald.

CICERO: LETTERS TO ATTICUS. E. O. Winstedt. 3 Vols.

CICERO: LETTERS TO HIS FRIENDS. W. Glynn Williams, M. Cary, M. Henderson. 4 Vols.

CICERO: PHILIPPICS. W. C. A. Ker.

CICERO: PRO ARCHIA, POST REDITUM, DE DOMO, DE HARUSPICUM RESPONSIS, PRO PLANCIO. N. H. Watts.

CICERO: PRO CAECINA, PRO LEGE MANILIA, PRO CLUENTIO, PRO RABIRIO. H. Grose Hodge.

CICERO: PRO CAELIO, DE PROVINCIIS CONSULARIBUS, PRO BALBO. R. Gardner.

CICERO: PRO MILONE, IN PISONEM, PRO SCAURO, PRO FONTEIO, PRO RABIRIO POSTUMO, PRO MARCELLO, PRO LIGARIO, PRO REGE DEIOTARO. N. H. Watts.

CICERO: PRO QUINCTIO, PRO ROSCIO AMERINO, PRO ROSCIO COMOEDO, CONTRA RULLUM. J. H. Freese.

CICERO: PRO SESTIO, IN VATINIUM. R. Gardner.

CICERO: TUSCULAN DISPUTATIONS. J. E. King.

CICERO: VERRINE ORATIONS. L. H. G. Greenwood. 2 Vols.

CLAUDIAN. M. Platnauer. 2 Vols.

COLUMELLA: DE RE RUSTICA. DE ARBORIBUS. H. B. Ash, E. S. Forster and E. Heffner. 3 Vols.

CURTIUS, Q.: HISTORY OF ALEXANDER. J. C. Rolfe. 2 Vols.

FLORUS. E. S. Forster.

FRONTINUS: STRATAGEMS and AQUEDUCTS. C. E. Bennett and M. B. McElwain.

FRONTO: CORRESPONDENCE. C. R. Haines. 2 Vols.

GELLIUS. J. C. Rolfe. 3 Vols.

HORACE: ODES and EPODES. C. E. Bennett.

HORACE: SATIRES, EPISTLES, ARS POETICA. H. R. Fairclough.

JEROME: SELECTED LETTERS. F. A. Wright.

JUVENAL and PERSIUS. G. G. Ramsay.

LIVY. B. O. Foster, F. G. Moore, Evan T. Sage, and A. C. Schlesinger and R. M. Geer (General Index). 14 Vols.

LUCAN. J. D. Duff.

LUCRETIUS. W. H. D. Rouse. Revised by M. F. Smith.

MANILIUS. G. P. Goold.

MARTIAL. W. C. A. Ker. 2 Vols. Revised by E. H. Warmington.

MINOR LATIN POETS: from PUBLILIUS SYRUS to RUTILIUS NAMATIANUS, including GRATTIUS, CALPURNIUS SICULUS, NEMESIANUS, AVIANUS and others, with "Aetna" and the "Phoenix." J. Wight Duff and Arnold M. Duff. 2 Vols.

MINUCIUS FELIX. Cf. TERTULLIAN.

NEPOS CORNELIUS. J. C. Rolfe.

OVID: THE ART OF LOVE and OTHER POEMS. J. H. Mosley. Revised by G. P. Goold.

OVID: FASTI. Sir James G. Frazer

OVID: HEROIDES and AMORES. Grant Showerman. Revised by G. P. Goold

OVID: METAMORPHOSES. F. J. Miller. 2 Vols. Revised by G. P. Goold.

OVID: TRISTIA and EX PONTO. A. L. Wheeler. Revised by G. P. Goold.

PERSIUS. Cf. JUVENAL.

PERVIGILIUM VENERIS. Cf. CATULLUS.

PETRONIUS. M. Heseltine. SENECA: APOCOLOCYNTOSIS. W. H. D. Rouse. Revised by E. H. Warmington.

PHAEDRUS and BABRIUS (Greek). B. E. Perry.

PLAUTUS. Paul Nixon. 5 Vols.

PLINY: LETTERS, PANEGYRICUS. Betty Radice. 2 Vols.

PLINY: NATURAL HISTORY. 10 Vols. Vols. I–V and IX. H. Rackham. VI.–VIII. W. H. S. Jones. X. D. E. Eichholz.

PROPERTIUS. H. E. Butler.

PRUDENTIUS. H. J. Thomson. 2 Vols.

QUINTILIAN. H. E. Butler. 4 Vols.

REMAINS OF OLD LATIN. E. H. Warmington. 4 Vols. Vol. I. (ENNIUS AND CAECILIUS) Vol. II. (LIVIUS, NAEVIUS PACUVIUS, ACCIUS) Vol. III. (LUCILIUS and LAWS OF XII TABLES) Vol. IV. (ARCHAIC INSCRIPTIONS)

RES GESTAE DIVI AUGUSTI. Cf. VELLEIUS PATERCULUS.

SALLUST. J. C. Rolfe.

SCRIPTORES HISTORIAE AUGUSTAE. D. Magie. 3 Vols.

SENECA, THE ELDER: CONTROVERSIAE, SUASORIAE. M. Winterbottom. 2 Vols.

SENECA: APOCOLOCYNTOSIS. Cf. PETRONIUS.

SENECA: EPISTULAE MORALES. R. M. Gummere. 3 Vols.

SENECA: MORAL ESSAYS. J. W. Basore. 3 Vols.

SENECA: TRAGEDIES. F. J. Miller. 2 Vols.

SENECA: NATURALES QUAESTIONES. T. H. Corcoran. 2 Vols.

SIDONIUS: POEMS and LETTERS. W. B. Anderson. 2 Vols.

SILIUS ITALICUS. J. D. Duff. 2 Vols.

STATIUS. J. H. Mozley. 2 Vols.

SUETONIUS. J. C. Rolfe. 2 Vols.

TACITUS: DIALOGUS. Sir Wm. Peterson. AGRICOLA and GERMANIA. Maurice Hutton. Revised by M. Winterbottom, R. M. Ogilvie, E. H. Warmington.

TACITUS: HISTORIES and ANNALS. C. H. Moore and J. Jackson. 4 Vols.

3

TERENCE. John Sargeaunt. 2 Vols.
TERTULLIAN: APOLOGIA and DE SPECTACULIS. T. R. Glover. MINUCIUS FELIX. G. H. Rendall.
TIBULLUS. Cf. CATULLUS.
VALERIUS FLACCUS. J. H. Mozley.
VARRO: DE LINGUA LATINA. R. G. Kent. 2 Vols.
VELLEIUS PATERCULUS and RES GESTAE DIVI AUGUSTI. F. W. Shipley.
VIRGIL. H. R. Fairclough. 2 Vols.
VITRUVIUS: DE ARCHITECTURA. F. Granger. 2 Vols.

Greek Authors

ACHILLES TATIUS. S. Gaselee.
AELIAN: ON THE NATURE OF ANIMALS. A. F. Scholfield. 3 Vols.
AENEAS TACTICUS. ASCLEPIODOTUS and ONASANDER. The Illinois Greek Club.
AESCHINES. C. D. Adams.
AESCHYLUS. H. Weir Smyth. 2 Vols.
ALCIPHRON, AELIAN, PHILOSTRATUS: LETTERS. A. R. Benner and F. H. Fobes.
ANDOCIDES, ANTIPHON. Cf. MINOR ATTIC ORATORS.
APOLLODORUS. Sir James G. Frazer. 2 Vols.
APOLLONIUS RHODIUS. R. C. Seaton.
APOSTOLIC FATHERS. Kirsopp Lake. 2 Vols.
APPIAN: ROMAN HISTORY. Horace White. 4 Vols.
ARATUS. Cf. CALLIMACHUS.
ARISTIDES: ORATIONS. C. A. Behr. Vol. I.
ARISTOPHANES. Benjamin Bickley Rogers. 3 Vols. Verse trans.
ARISTOTLE: ART OF RHETORIC. J. H. Freese.
ARISTOTLE: ATHENIAN CONSTITUTION, EUDEMIAN ETHICS, VICES AND VIRTUES. H. Rackham.
ARISTOTLE: GENERATION OF ANIMALS. A. L. Peck.
ARISTOTLE: HISTORIA ANIMALIUM. A. L. Peck. Vols. I.–II.
ARISTOTLE: METAPHYSICS. H. Tredennick. 2 Vols.
ARISTOTLE: METEOROLOGICA. H. D. P. Lee.
ARISTOTLE: MINOR WORKS. W. S. Hett. On Colours, On Things Heard, On Physiognomies, On Plants, On Marvellous Things Heard, Mechanical Problems, On Indivisible Lines, On Situations and Names of Winds, On Melissus, Xenophanes, and Gorgias.
ARISTOTLE: NICOMACHEAN ETHICS. H. Rackham.

4

ARISTOTLE: OECONOMICA and MAGNA MORALIA. G. C. Armstrong (with METAPHYSICS, Vol. II).

ARISTOTLE: ON THE HEAVENS. W. K. C. Guthrie.

ARISTOTLE: ON THE SOUL, PARVA NATURALIA, ON BREATH. W. S. Hett.

ARISTOTLE: CATEGORIES, ON INTERPRETATION, PRIOR ANALYTICS. H. P. Cooke and H. Tredennick.

ARISTOTLE: POSTERIOR ANALYTICS, TOPICS. H. Tredennick and E. S. Forster.

ARISTOTLE: ON SOPHISTICAL REFUTATIONS.
On Coming to be and Passing Away, On the Cosmos. E. S. Forster and D. J. Furley.

ARISTOTLE: PARTS OF ANIMALS. A. L. Peck; MOTION AND PROGRESSION OF ANIMALS. E. S. Forster.

ARISTOTLE: PHYSICS. Rev. P. Wicksteed and F. M. Cornford. 2 Vols.

ARISTOTLE: POETICS and LONGINUS. W. Hamilton Fyfe; DEMETRIUS ON STYLE. W. Rhys Roberts.

ARISTOTLE: POLITICS. H. Rackham.

ARISTOTLE: PROBLEMS. W. S. Hett. 2 Vols.

ARISTOTLE: RHETORICA AD ALEXANDRUM (with PROBLEMS. Vol. II). H. Rackham.

ARRIAN: HISTORY OF ALEXANDER and INDICA. Rev. E. Iliffe Robson. 2 Vols. New version P. Brunt.

ATHENAEUS: DEIPNOSOPHISTAE. C. B. Gulick. 7 Vols.

BABRIUS AND PHAEDRUS (Latin). B. E. Perry.

ST. BASIL: LETTERS. R. J. Deferrari. 4 Vols.

CALLIMACHUS: FRAGMENTS. C. A. Trypanis. MUSAEUS: HERO AND LEANDER. T. Gelzer and C. Whitman.

CALLIMACHUS, Hymns and Epigrams, and LYCOPHRON. A. W. Mair; ARATUS. G. R. Mair.

CLEMENT OF ALEXANDRIA. Rev. G. W. Butterworth.

COLLUTHUS. Cf. OPPIAN.

DAPHNIS AND CHLOE. Thornley's Translation revised by J. M. Edmonds: and PARTHENIUS. S. Gaselee.

DEMOSTHENES I.: OLYNTHIACS, PHILIPPICS and MINOR ORATIONS I.–XVII. AND XX. J. H. Vince.

DEMOSTHENES II.: DE CORONA and DE FALSA LEGATIONE. C. A. Vince and J. H. Vince.

DEMOSTHENES III.: MEIDIAS, ANDROTION, ARISTOCRATES, TIMOCRATES and ARISTOGEITON I. and II. J. H. Vince.

DEMOSTHENES IV.–VI: PRIVATE ORATIONS and IN NEAERAM. A. T. Murray.

DEMOSTHENES VII: FUNERAL SPEECH, EROTIC ESSAY, EXORDIA and LETTERS. N. W. and N. J. DeWitt.

DIO CASSIUS: ROMAN HISTORY. E. Cary. 9 Vols.

DIO CHRYSOSTOM. J. W. Cohoon and H. Lamar Crosby. 5 Vols.

DIODORUS SICULUS. 12 Vols. Vols. I.–VI. C. H. Oldfather. Vol. VII. C. L. Sherman. Vol. VIII. C. B. Welles. Vols. IX. and X. R. M. Geer. Vol. XI. F. Walton. Vol. XII. F. Walton. General Index. R. M. Geer.

DIOGENES LAERTIUS. R. D. Hicks. 2 Vols. New Introduction by H. S. Long.

DIONYSIUS OF HALICARNASSUS: ROMAN ANTIQUITIES. Spelman's translation revised by E. Cary. 7 Vols.

DIONYSIUS OF HALICARNASSUS: CRITICAL ESSAYS. S. Usher. 2 Vols.

EPICTETUS. W. A. Oldfather. 2 Vols.

EURIPIDES. A. S. Way. 4 Vols. Verse trans.

EUSEBIUS: ECCLESIASTICAL HISTORY. Kirsopp Lake and J. E. L. Oulton. 2 Vols.

GALEN: ON THE NATURAL FACULTIES. A. J. Brock.

GREEK ANTHOLOGY. W. R. Paton. 5 Vols.

GREEK BUCOLIC POETS (THEOCRITUS, BION, MOSCHUS). J. M. Edmonds.

GREEK ELEGY AND IAMBUS with the ANACREONTEA. J. M. Edmonds. 2 Vols.

GREEK LYRIC. D. A. Campbell. 4 Vols. Vols. I and II.

GREEK MATHEMATICAL WORKS. Ivor Thomas. 2 Vols.

HERODES. Cf. THEOPHRASTUS: CHARACTERS.

HERODIAN. C. R. Whittaker. 2 Vols.

HERODOTUS. A. D. Godley. 4 Vols.

HESIOD AND THE HOMERIC HYMNS. H. G. Evelyn White.

HIPPOCRATES and the FRAGMENTS OF HERACLEITUS. W. H. S. Jones and E. T. Withington. 5 Vols. Vols. I.–IV.

HOMER: ILIAD. A. T. Murray. 2 Vols.

HOMER: ODYSSEY. A. T. Murray. 2 Vols.

ISAEUS. E. W. Forster.

ISOCRATES. George Norlin and LaRue Van Hook. 3 Vols.

[ST. JOHN DAMASCENE]: BARLAAM AND IOASAPH. Rev. G. R. Woodward, Harold Mattingly and D. M. Lang.

JOSEPHUS. 10 Vols. Vols. I.–IV. H. Thackeray. Vol. V. H. Thackeray and R. Marcus. Vols. VI.–VII. R. Marcus. Vol. VIII. R. Marcus and Allen Wikgren. Vols. IX.–X. L. H. Feldman.

JULIAN. Wilmer Cave Wright. 3 Vols.

LIBANIUS. A. F. Norman. 3 Vols. Vols. I.–II.

LUCIAN. 8 Vols. Vols. I.–V. A. M. Harmon. Vol. VI. K. Kilburn. Vols. VII.–VIII. M. D. Macleod.

LYCOPHRON. Cf. CALLIMACHUS.

6

LYRA GRAECA, III   J. M. Edmonds.   (Vols. I. and II. have been replaced by GREEK LYRIC I. and II.

LYSIAS.   W. R. M. Lamb.

MANETHO.   W. G. Waddell.

MARCUS AURELIUS.   C. R. Haines.

MENANDER.   W. G. Arnott.   3 Vols.   Vol. I.

MINOR ATTIC ORATORS (ANTIPHON, ANDOCIDES, LYCURGUS, DEMADES, DINARCHUS, HYPERIDES).   K. J. Maidment and J. O. Burtt.   2 Vols.

MUSAEUS: HERO AND LEANDER.   Cf. CALLIMACHUS.

NONNOS: DIONYSIACA.   W. H. D. Rouse.   3 Vols.

OPPIAN, COLLUTHUS, TRYPHIODORUS.   A. W. Mair.

PAPYRI.   NON-LITERARY SELECTIONS.   A. S. Hunt and C. C. Edgar.   2 Vols.   LITERARY SELECTIONS (Poetry).   D. L. Page.

PARTHENIUS.   Cf. DAPHNIS and CHLOE.

PAUSANIAS: DESCRIPTION OF GREECE.   W. H. S. Jones.   4 Vols. and Companion Vol. arranged by R. E. Wycherley.

PHILO.   10 Vols.   Vols. I.–V.   F. H. Colson and Rev. G. H. Whitaker.   Vols. VI.–IX.   F. H. Colson.   Vol. X.   F. H. Colson and the Rev. J. W. Earp.

PHILO: two supplementary Vols. (*Translation only.*)   Ralph Marcus.

PHILOSTRATUS: THE LIFE OF APOLLONIUS OF TYANA.   F. C. Conybeare.   2 Vols.

PHILOSTRATUS: IMAGINES; CALLISTRATUS: DESCRIPTIONS.   A. Fairbanks.

PHILOSTRATUS and EUNAPIUS: LIVES OF THE SOPHISTS.   Wilmer Cave Wright.

PINDAR.   Sir J. E. Sandys.

PLATO: CHARMIDES, ALCIBIADES, HIPPARCHUS, THE LOVERS, THEAGES, MINOS and EPINOMIS.   W. R. M. Lamb.

PLATO: CRATYLUS, PARMENIDES, GREATER HIPPIAS, LESSER HIPPIAS.   H. N. Fowler.

PLATO: EUTHYPHRO, APOLOGY, CRITO, PHAEDO, PHAEDRUS, H. N. Fowler.

PLATO: LACHES, PROTAGORAS, MENO, EUTHYDEMUS.   W. R. M. Lamb.

PLATO: LAWS.   Rev. R. G. Bury.   2 Vols.

PLATO: LYSIS, SYMPOSIUM, GORGIAS.   W. R. M. Lamb.

PLATO: Republic.   Paul Shorey.   2 Vols.

PLATO: STATESMAN, PHILEBUS.   H. N. Fowler; ION.   W. R. M. Lamb.

PLATO: THEAETETUS and SOPHIST.   H. N. Fowler.

PLATO: TIMAEUS, CRITIAS, CLITOPHO, MENEXENUS, EPISTULAE.   Rev. R. G. Bury.

PLOTINUS: A. H. Armstrong. 7 Vols.

PLUTARCH: MORALIA. 16 Vols. Vols I.–V. F. C. Babbitt. Vol. VI. W. C. Helmbold. Vols. VII. and XIV. P. H. De Lacy and B. Einarson. Vol. VIII. P. A. Clement and H. B. Hoffleit. Vol. IX. E. L. Minar, Jr., F. H. Sandbach, W. C. Helmbold. Vol. X. H. N. Fowler. Vol. XI. L. Pearson and F. H. Sandbach. Vol. XII. H. Cherniss and W. C. Helmbold. Vol. XIII 1–2. H. Cherniss. Vol. XV. F. H. Sandbach.

PLUTARCH: THE PARALLEL LIVES. B. Perrin. 11 Vols.

POLYBIUS. W. R. Paton. 6 Vols.

PROCOPIUS. H. B. Dewing. 7 Vols.

PTOLEMY: TETRABIBLOS. F. E. Robbins.

QUINTUS SMYRNAEUS. A. S. Way. Verse trans.

SEXTUS EMPIRICUS. Rev. R. G. Bury. 4 Vols.

SOPHOCLES. F. Storr. 2 Vols. Verse trans.

STRABO: GEOGRAPHY. Horace L. Jones. 8 Vols.

THEOCRITUS. Cf. GREEK BUCOLIC POETS.

THEOPHRASTUS: CHARACTERS. J. M. Edmonds. HERODES, etc. A. D. Knox.

THEOPHRASTUS: ENQUIRY INTO PLANTS. Sir Arthur Hort, Bart. 2 Vols.

THEOPHRASTUS: DE CAUSIS PLANTARUM. G. K. K. Link and B. Einarson. 3 Vols. Vol. I.

THUCYDIDES. C. F. Smith. 4 Vols.

TRYPHIODORUS. Cf. OPPIAN.

XENOPHON: CYROPAEDIA. Walter Miller. 2 Vols.

XENOPHON: HELLENCIA. C. L. Brownson. 2 Vols.

XENOPHON: ANABASIS. C. L. Brownson.

XENOPHON: MEMORABILIA AND OECONOMICUS. E. C. Marchant. SYMPOSIUM AND APOLOGY. O. J. Todd.

XENOPHON: SCRIPTA MINORA. E. C. Marchant. CONSTITUTION OF THE ATHENIANS. G. W. Bowersock.